THE THREE TEMPLES

THE LITTMAN LIBRARY OF
JEWISH CIVILIZATION

Dedicated to the memory of
LOUIS THOMAS SIDNEY LITTMAN
*who founded the Littman Library for the love of God
and as an act of charity in memory of his father*
JOSEPH AARON LITTMAN
and to the memory of
ROBERT JOSEPH LITTMAN
who continued what his father Louis had begun

יהא זכרם ברוך

'*Get wisdom, get understanding:
Forsake her not and she shall preserve thee*'
PROV. 4: 5

*The Littman Library of Jewish Civilization is a registered UK charity
Registered charity no.* 1000784

THE
THREE TEMPLES

◆

On the Emergence of
Jewish Mysticism

◆

RACHEL ELIOR

Translated by
DAVID LOUVISH

London
The Littman Library of Jewish Civilization
in association with Liverpool University Press

The Littman Library of Jewish Civilization
Registered office: 4th floor, 7–10 Chandos Street, London, WIG 9DQ

in association with Liverpool University Press
4 Cambridge Street, Liverpool L69 7ZU, UK
www.liverpooluniversitypress.co.uk/littman

Managing Editor: Connie Webber

Distributed in North America by
Oxford University Press Inc., 198 Madison Avenue
New York, NY 10016, USA

First published in Hebrew 2002
First published in English 2004
English edition first published in paperback 2005

Catalogue records for this book are available from
the British Library and the Library of Congress

ISBN 978-1-904113-33-1

Publishing Co-ordinator: Janet Moth
Copy-editing: George Tulloch
Proof-reading: Philippa Claiden
Index: Meg Davies
Design: Pete Russell, Faringdon, Oxon.
Typeset by Footnote Graphics Limited, Warminster, Wilts.

Printed and bound in Great Britain by
CPI Group (UK) Ltd., Croydon, CR0 4YY

לזכרם של הוריי האהובים

שמואל פאלאג׳י
(תרע״א–תשמ״א)

ולאה קאליקו־פאלאג׳י
(תרע״ב–תשס״ב)

אנשי חסד ואמת, אוהבי חירות וצדק

———

To the memory of my beloved parents

SHMUEL (1911–1981) AND LEAH (1912–2002) PALAGEE

courageous proponents of compassion and freedom

רוחי דעת אמת וצדק בקודש קודשים

צורות אלוהים חיים צורי רוחות מאירים

כל מעשיהם קודשי דבקי פלא...

צורות אלוהים מחוקקי סביב ללבני כבודם...

וצורות בדניהם מלאכי קודש מתחת לדבירי הפלא

קול דממת שקט אלוהים מברכים... המלך...

מהללים תמיד כל אלוהים

שיר עולת השבת השמינית
בשלושה ועשרים לחודש השני

אמר ר' עקיבא

כביכול כמותנו הוא

והוא גדול מכל

וזה הוא כבודו

שנסתר מפנינו...

הוא עצמו...

כעין השמש כעין הירח

כעין הכוכבים כפני אדם...

וסבר קלסתר פניו

כדמות הרוח וכצורת נשמה

שאין כל ברייה יכולה להכיר בה.

היכלות זוטרתי, 6—25

Spirits of the knowledge of truth and righteousness in the Holy of Holies

Forms of living divine beings, images of luminous spirits

All their deeds are of holy things, of wondrous unifications . . .

Figures of the shapes of divine beings, engraved round around the

    glorious images of the sapphire pavement of spendour and majesty

And the images of their figures are holy angels

From underneath the wondrous *devirim* comes the sound of quiet stillness,

The heavenly beings blessing . . . the King . . . praising continually . . . God

Song of the Eighth Sabbath Sacrifice
on the Twenty-third of the Second Month

Said Rabbi Akiva:

He is like us, as it were,

but He is greater than all;

and His very glory is that He is concealed from us . . .

He Himself . . .

is like the sun, like the moon,

like the stars, like a human face . . .

And His face, His visage,

has the semblance of the spirit the image of the soul,

which no creature can apprehend.

Heikhalot zutarti, 25–6

PUBLISHER'S NOTE

*

The author and publisher wish to thank

THE HEBREW UNIVERSITY INTERNAL FUND

*for its generous contribution towards the cost of
preparing and producing this book*

Preface

THE formative stages of Jewish mystical thought in antiquity and the transition from those early stages, in the late Second Temple period, to later developments in the first centuries CE, still await thorough investigation. Scholars concerned with pseudepigraphic, apocalyptic, and Qumran literature have occasionally pointed out verbal affinities between those literatures and Heikhalot and Merkavah literature; while some students of Jewish mysticism have noted the conceptual continuity between the Heikhalot literature of the first centuries CE and apocryphal and Qumran literature, written in the last centuries BCE. However, the actual relationship between the basic features of the diverse mystical literatures of late antiquity has yet to be determined and the meaning of those affinities explained.

This study is based on two underlying assumptions: (1) The early Jewish mystical literature associated with the tradition of the Merkavah, the divine Chariot Throne, was composed in three distinct but clearly interrelated stages, with reference to three destroyed or desecrated temples, and to three priestly classes, which were barred from performing their sacral duties for a variety of reasons—historical, political, social, and religious. (2) An uninterrupted line can be drawn from the mystical and liturgical literature of the last centuries BCE, associated directly and indirectly with the Merkavah tradition, to the mystical works of the first centuries CE known as Heikhalot and Merkavah literature. Many of the literary corpuses that make up this large body of literature were written by members of the above-mentioned priestly classes who, unable to serve in the Temple, replaced the earthly Temple with a heavenly Merkavah and heavenly sanctuaries—Heikhalot, creating a super-temporal liturgical and ritual relationship between the priests performing the sacred service and the ministering angels in the supernal sanctuaries.

The last decades of the twentieth century saw the publication of scrolls and manuscripts that throw new light on Jewish history in late antiquity. The Dead Sea Scrolls (also known as the Judaean Desert or Qumran Scrolls), written in the last centuries BCE, and the Heikhalot and Merkavah traditions, dating from the first centuries CE, have finally seen the light of day thanks to the co-operative work of numerous scholars in all parts of the world. This rich literature, which reveals the complexity of the Jewish spiritual world over a long and stormy period, dictates a re-examination of much conventional wisdom in the field of historiography and Jewish studies in general. In light of the new material, which enables us to examine the relationships among the creators of Merkavah traditions from a new angle, I believe it is possible to explain the crystallization of mystical tradition, and to that end present here a study of its ties with the priestly traditions of the Bible, on the one hand, and rabbinic and Heikhalot traditions, on the other.

Throughout my work on this volume I have benefited from the help and advice of many friends and colleagues. I am indebted in particular to Professor Yosef Dan, Professor Peter Schäfer, Dr Asi Farber-Ginat, Professor Abraham Shapira, Dr Klaus Hermann, and Mr Magen Broshi, who read various chapters of the book and offered useful and illuminating comments. The underlying assumptions and thesis of the study have been presented to many of my colleagues on scholarly platforms in this country and abroad. My listeners' reactions, questions, and comments have helped me to clarify and sharpen my arguments and conclusions. I am grateful to the late Professor Isadore Twersky of Harvard University and to Professors Martin Goodman of Oxford University, Arthur Hyman and Haym Soloveitchik of Yeshiva University, Karl-Erich Grozinger of Potsdam University, Hiroshi Ichikawa of Tokyo University, Arthur Green of Brandeis University, David Biale of the University of California at Berkeley, Laurence Schiffman of New York University, Mark Geller and Ada Rapoport-Albert of University College, London, April de Conick of Wesleyan University, Sanford Margolis and Shimon Brand of Oberlin College, David Ariel of Cleveland College, Roland Goetschel of Sorbonne University, Mark Verman of Wright State University, Ohio, and Dafna Arbel of the University of Vancouver.

It is also my pleasant duty to thank the various academic institutions and foundations that have supported the research on which the book is based: the Institute of Jewish Studies in the Faculty of Humanities of the Hebrew University, Jerusalem, and the Centre for Jewish Studies at Oxford University; the Memorial Foundation for Jewish Culture, the Amos Foundation of the President of Israel, the Charles Wolfson Foundation of the Institute of Jewish Studies, the Research Committee of the Faculty of Humanities of the Hebrew University, Jerusalem, and the Research and Development Authority of the Hebrew University, Jerusalem. I wish to express my deep gratitude to the translator, David Louvish, and to the members of the Littman team: George Tulloch, who copy-edited the volume together with Lindsey Taylor-Guthartz and enhanced accessibility, style, clarity, and usefulness; Janet Moth, who co-ordinated the publishing; Ludo Craddock, who facilitated the publication of the volume; Connie Webber, who proposed the publication of the study in English; and Felix Posen, who most generously helped to bring the whole project to fruition.

Last, but not least, I should like to express my heartfelt gratitude to the people who immensely enrich my life and my work in so many ways: Michael, Abigail, Shahar, Ariel, and Daniel. My love and thanks to all of them go far beyond words.

Jerusalem 2002

RACHEL ELIOR

Contents

Note on Translations of Sources

QUOTATIONS from the Qumran writings are scattered throughout this volume. There are several English translations available for most of the texts, chief among them being the thirty-nine volumes to date of *Discoveries in the Judaean Desert*, Florentino García Martínez and Eibert Tigchelaar's *Dead Sea Scrolls Study Edition*, and Geza Vermes's *The Complete Dead Sea Scrolls in English*, not to mention various editions of individual Qumran works. None of these translations is invariably in accord with our understanding of the texts; we have therefore not made exclusive use of any one of these editions, but rather have taken an eclectic approach, basing ourselves on one edition or another, amended as necessary to reflect our own interpretation. The edition used is generally specified in the footnotes, preceded by 'cf.' if significantly modified.

Translations of Old Testament material generally follow *Tanakh: The Holy Scriptures* (Philadelphia, New York, and Jerusalem, 1988), referred to as the New Jewish Publication Society Translation, again with occasional modifications in accordance with our own interpretations. For the New Testament the Revised Standard Version has been used.

Finally, most of the quotations from apocryphal and pseudepigraphical literature (Enoch, Jubilees, Testament of Levi) are taken from J. H. Charlesworth's *The Old Testament Pseudepigrapha*; a few exceptions are clearly indicated.

D.L.
R.E.

Note on Transliteration

THE transliteration of Hebrew in this book reflects consideration of the type of book it is, in terms of its content, purpose, and readership. The system adopted therefore reflects a broad approach to transcription, rather than the narrower approaches found in the *Encyclopaedia Judaica* or other systems developed for text-based or linguistic studies. The aim has been to reflect the pronunciation prescribed for modern Hebrew, rather than the spelling or Hebrew word structure, and to do so using conventions that are generally familiar to the English-speaking Jewish reader.

In accordance with this approach, no attempt is made to indicate the distinctions between *alef* and *ayin*, *tet* and *taf*, *kaf* and *kuf*, *sin* and *samekh*, since these are not relevant to pronunciation; likewise, the *dagesh* is not indicated except where it affects pronunciation. Following the principle of using conventions familiar to the majority of readers, however, transcriptions that are well established have been retained even when they are not fully consistent with the transliteration system adopted. On similar grounds, the *tsadi* is rendered by 'tz' in such familiar words as bar mitzvah, mitzvot, and so on. Likewise, the distinction between *ḥet* and *khaf* has been retained, using *ḥ* for the former and *kh* for the latter; the associated forms are generally familiar to readers, even if the distinction is not actually borne out in pronunciation, and for the same reason the final *heh* is indicated too. As in Hebrew, no capital letters are used, except that an initial capital has been retained in transliterating titles of published works (for example, *Shulḥan arukh*).

Since no distinction is made between *alef* and *ayin*, they are indicated by an apostrophe only in intervocalic positions where a failure to do so could lead an English-speaking reader to pronounce the vowel-cluster as a diphthong—as, for example, in *ha'ir*—or otherwise mispronounce the word.

The *sheva na* is indicated by an *e*—*perikat ol*, *reshut*—except, again, when established convention dictates otherwise.

The *yod* is represented by *i* when it occurs as a vowel (*bereshit*), by *y* when it occurs as a consonant (*yesodot*), and by *yi* when it occurs as both (*yisra'el*).

Names have generally been left in their familiar forms, even when this is inconsistent with the overall system.

Thanks are due to Jonathan Webber of Birmingham University's Theology Department for his help in elucidating the principles to be adopted.

Introduction

A TEMPLE stood in Jerusalem for almost one thousand years: from the time of the First Temple, built according to biblical tradition in the tenth century BCE, during the reigns of David and Solomon, till the destruction of the Second Temple in the first century CE. Solomon's Temple, founded around 960 BCE, was destroyed at the beginning of the sixth century—in 597–587 BCE, to be precise—by Nebuchadnezzar. The Second Temple, built around 515 BCE after the edict of the Persian king Cyrus in 538 BCE, remained standing until 70 CE, when the Romans razed it to the ground. These are the data that emerge from biblical tradition—which weaves together various sources describing the First Temple and the early days of the Second Temple—from various historiographic traditions dating to the time of the Second Temple, and from rabbinic tradition.

Ministering in the Temple were the Aaronide priests, who held the exclusive privilege of performing the sacred service from the time of Moses and Aaron.[1] The descendants of Aaron, who had been 'consecrated as most holy',[2] and of his sons Eleazar and Itamar, are referred to as 'sanctuary officers and officers of God'[3] and recognized as holding the exclusive, hereditary right to serve in the Temple for all eternity.

According to the tradition recounted in Chronicles, these guardians of the sanctuary were divided during David's reign into twenty-four priestly divisions, or courses, when the Temple was established.[4] Bible scholars dispute the actual date of this division and are inclined to bring it forward to the time of the Second Temple, but priestly traditions associate it with the organization of the sacred service in the First Temple, as we shall see below. The participation of the priestly courses in the Temple service was arranged according to weekly cycles, determined by the sabbaths, periodic cycles depending on the four seasons of the year, and seven-year cycles, as follows from the Calendar of Priestly Courses found at Qumran.

The role of high priest was reserved, from the foundation of the First Temple under David and Solomon to midway through the Second Temple period, for the Zadokite priests, descended from the priest Phinehas, son of Aaron's son Eleazar;[5]

---

[1] Exod. 28–30; 40: 12–16; Lev. 8; 21–2; Num. 17–18; 25; 1 Chr. 6: 34–8; 23: 13, 28–32; 24: 1–5.

[2] 1 Chr. 23: 13.   [3] Lev. 10: 12–13; 1 Chr. 24: 1–6.   [4] 1 Chr. 24: 4–17.

[5] 1 Kgs. 1: 32, 35, 38–9, 45; 2: 35; 1 Chr. 5: 29–41; 9: 11; 24: 3–6; 29: 22; Ezra 7: 2–5; Neh. 11: 11; 12: 10–11.

it was their task to safeguard the sacred place and sacred time, and to supervise the sacred service.

The twenty-four priestly courses, each of which served one week, twice a year, and four of which served three times a year, were responsible for the order of sabbaths and festivals, which were marked in ritual regularity by sacrifices, burnt offerings and meal-offerings, burning of incense, kindling of the seven-branched lampstand, and blowing of trumpets, as well as songs of praise, benedictions, and enunciations of the Ineffable Name of God. The priests were also responsible for safeguarding the sanctity and purity of the Temple, and for observing the Torah and imparting its laws to the people. In addition to their permanent ritual tasks, they had several additional, variable functions, such as judicial activities and instruction, as well as decisions concerning ritual purity and impurity, and treatment of certain skin diseases.

Biblical tradition, woven together from diverse sources, reflects different views as to the origins of the priestly privileges, duties, and functions. Alongside the priests, according to some traditions, certain functions were also assigned to the Levites, that is, the descendants of Levi through his sons Gershon, Merari, and Kohath: singers and players of musical instruments, gatekeepers, and officials in charge of the Temple treasures.[6] The Levites were also divided into twenty-four divisions of singers[7] and twelve divisions of gatekeepers.[8] The genealogical criteria that determined one's function in the sacred service (priests) or auxiliary services in the Temple (Levites) were highly important, as they derived from divine nomination and level of sanctity.

The exact sequence of the weekly cycles of courses and the annual cycles of service was bound up with the priestly conception of time as a cyclic reflection of an eternal divine order. This cyclic time and the ritual order associated with it were determined by permanent, eternal numerical patterns, which were of paramount importance in priestly tradition; thus, the priests were charged with maintaining the regularity of the terrestrial world and the cycles of cosmic order, as we shall see below.

Historical reality during the First and Second Temple periods was undoubtedly more complex than the historiographic and literary picture that has reached us, which is a fusion of history, myth, ritual memory, sacred scriptures, and diverse historiographic traditions. The history of the Temple and its priests in different periods was by no means continuous and uniform, based on a single tradition; it was, rather, a complex sequence, based on different and sometimes contradictory traditions, attesting both implicitly and explicitly to controversies and fluctuating positions at different times. Nevertheless, one compound thread persists throughout that long, chequered history, as represented by biblical tradition, the Dead Sea Scrolls, and various traditions from the Second Temple period, namely, the sanctity and centrality of the Temple, as well as the ideal pattern of the sacred service.

---

[6] 1 Chr. 9: 14–24; 24: 20–30; 15: 2–10, 15–24; 23: 2–28; 24: 20–31.
[7] 1 Chr. 25   [8] 1 Chr. 26.

Basic to the sacred service was the perception of heaven and earth as a unity, so that one could postulate the existence of a mutual relationship between the cosmic cyclicity of the eternal, incorporeal, divine realm and the ritual cyclicity established in the material, terrestrial realm by the sacred service. The Temple was the earthly embodiment of cosmic order and cyclicity; hence the guardians of the sanctuary, the priests, discharging their duties, maintained a macrocosmic and microcosmic order in which the laws of nature were harmonized with sacred time, sacred place, and sacred service. Calculation and iteration, counting and number, played their roles in representing the harmonic cosmic order of the universe, manifested in its regularity and continuity, in numerical proportions and fixed measures, simple and complex, of durations and changes of creative time. These infinite, eternal, sanctified cycles of time, reflecting the eternity of the divine order, were recreated in sacred space, that is, in the sacred abode of the Deity, which was thus perceived as an everlasting source of life. The sanctity of the Temple and its essence as a divine source of life derived from its purity as a place and from the sanctity of its time, from the ritual cycle that established the oneness of sacred time and place.

The precise ceremonial, symbolic language of the cyclic ritual represented the cosmic cycle in terms of number and time, through the cycle of sabbaths and festivals and in the set times for the offering of sacrifices; the material features of the sacred place represented heavenly structures through prescribed numbers and measures, ranging from the measurements of the Holy of Holies and the Merkavah—the Chariot Throne of the cherubim—to the number of lamps in the lampstand; and the sacred liturgical language of the cycles of songs of praise and songs of the sabbath sacrifice represented the angelic song and partitioned ritual time into cycles of hours, days, and periods. All these elements were in the keeping of the guardians of the sanctuary; taken together, they established the links between the hidden, divine reality and the sanctified, material reality as revealed in the cycles of nature and their ritual reproduction by sabbaths and festivals.

The synchronization thus established between the set times of God, grouped in sevens; the set times of nature, grouped in fours; and the set times of the sacred service, which wove them together, created the tradition of the Merkavah, the holy Chariot Throne, as a bridge between the supernal and its sanctified manifestations in the human world, as deciphered in ritual, cycle, number, and song. All these set times were dependent on a sacred calendar, which regulated the course of time—the creator of life; on the divine structure of sacred space—the source of life; and on the sanctity and purity of the priests as they performed the sacred service—the guarantee that life would continue. The synchronization of the sacred service was established and maintained by virtue of a sacred authority of supernatural origin, with a variety of manifestations: the word and commandments of God, 'wondrous secrets' or divine revelation and angelic testimony, heavenly tablets, books dictated from on high, laws observed by angels and priests, divine election, purity and sanctification, and sacred scriptures.

Various historical stages of a lengthy period, spanning several centuries, two Temples, and changing historical, social, and cultural conditions, saw the emergence of numerous priestly traditions concerning the essence and order of the ritual, its divine authorization, its aspects of purity and impurity, its cyclic nature, the angelic source of its liturgy, and its religious and social ideals as advocated by the priests and the Levites. During that time, a highly diversified priestly literature took shape: certain chapters in Genesis; various chapters in the Pentateuch ascribed to a priestly source, such as Exodus 6: 13–25 and chapters 25–9; the book of Leviticus, known as the Priestly Code; Numbers 1: 48–53 and 3: 1–39, which list the priestly genealogy; various psalms associated with the sacred service; the books of Ezekiel and Chronicles;[9] and finally the book of Jubilees, the Enoch literature, the Songs of the Sabbath Sacrifice, the Temple Scroll, *Miktsat ma'asei hatorah* (MMT), the Calendar of Priestly Courses, the Blessings, the Community Rule, the book of Ben Sira, the Testament of Levi, and numerous other works.

This variegated literature, conserving an ancient ritual and liturgical reality, which converted a mysterious cosmic entity and a hidden visionary reality into an accessible actuality and translated the manifestations of abstract sanctity into palpable form through the ritual representations of the sacred service, was not written in one voice or in one period. It reflects a veritable clamour of common traditions, struggles for authority, arguments and controversies, polemics and schisms, relating to the management of the Temple, the sacred service, and its subjects. Different historiographic traditions attest to stormy disputes on various issues: hallowed traditions and patterns of ritual relating to the representation of cosmic order, to the ritual calendar and its set times; and the sources of the authority of those serving in the Temple and of the laws and rules through which they bridged the chasm between the hidden and the revealed.

Generations of priests in the Temple, guardians of the hallowed traditions, composed and copied sacred scriptures, songs of praise and benedictions, laws and rituals, genealogies and calendars. They calculated the sequence of sabbaths and festivals, and alternately revealed and concealed the details of the worship of an invisible God and his overt and secret representations. They read, studied, wrote, and taught the Torah, rendered judgement in accordance with its laws, and observed the sacred rites associated with the cyclic cosmic order and its numerous manifestations: the cycle of sabbaths and festivals, sacrifices and incense, songs and hymns of praise offered by priests in emulation of the angelic service in heaven, calendrical calculations, pilgrimage, the sequence of seasons and the agricultural year, the bringing of first fruits and tithes, as well as many other concerns of man and the land, assuring them of life and blessing as reflected in ongoing fertility, cycles of agricultural growth, and abundance.

But these priests were not content merely to preserve the conceptual world of the Bible and past tradition with all their sung and written ceremonial expressions.

---

[9] For a detailed list of the priestly sources see Driver, *Introduction*, 159.

They continued to create narrative, historical, ritual, and poetic traditions of religion and law, scripture and number, vision and the holy spirit. They wrote copiously—whether in narrative, legal, or poetic style—on heavenly law and earthly precepts, on past covenants, present life, and hopes for the future; they dealt with the overt and covert qualities of sacred place, sacred time, and sacred service. They gave expression to the divine order reflected in the oneness of time, place, and ritual, and in covenants and festivals—in prayers and hymns, in legal writings, in ritual prescriptions relating to the Temple service, and in mythological narratives about angels and human beings which purported to explain the origins of natural and cultural order, of religion and law.

Until recent years, this rich priestly heritage, the fruit of a thousand years of creativity, came down to us through three main channels: (1) biblical tradition, which preserves many priestly documents; (2) chapters in the literature of the Second Temple period that indicate the complexity of the priestly tradition; and (3) rabbinic tradition, which preserved only faint echoes of the priestly tradition, and even those, moreover, reflected an ambivalent attitude which, while perpetuating the memory of the Temple service, strove to terminate biblical tradition and supplant the priestly hegemony and its traditions. The priestly hegemony—based on the sanctification of the descendants of Aaron, or on the hereditary privilege of the Levites, who were assured of an eternal covenant of priesthood—must surely have aroused complaints at times, generating controversy and criticism through the generations of priestly service; there were surely other centres of power, authority, and knowledge at all times, but no social group other than the priests commanded the sacred authority, the eternal, dynastic privilege, rooted in the sacred scriptures and in divine assurance. Rabbinic tradition conveys many priestly traditions, limits the discussion of certain priestly traditions, preserves traces of arguments with various priestly views, and rejects priestly hegemony as a single, exclusive pattern of leadership.

Central to the priestly hegemony was the conception of a cyclic, eternal, permanent divine time, based on testimony and set times, whose preservation and mode of calculation were entrusted to the priesthood by divine authority. This deterministic concept of divine time was opposed by the Sages, who may also have relied on ancient traditions alluded to fragmentarily in the Bible; their concept of time was based on human sovereignty and human partnership in the reckoning of the sacred calendar. The same historical circumstances that brought about the destruction of the Temple presented an opportunity to replace the centralized Temple ritual—till then the exclusive privilege of the Aaronide priests and Levites, keepers of the Temple heritage by virtue of divine nomination and hereditary right—with a decentralized rabbinic tradition, which demanded human participation in determining the fixed times and declared human understanding to be a legitimate source of authority. At the centre of this tradition stood a sacred body of literature which was open to study by all Jewish men, irrespective of lineage or membership in any group enjoying special sanctity and inherited privilege. Alongside this canonical text the Sages created the Oral Law, untrammelled by the limitations of priestly hegemony. They transferred the centre of gravity from a regular, priestly ritual, anchored in holy time and holy place, to an ever-changing, variously interpreted order entrusted to sages from all classes of the population, who took charge of humanly declared time and taught a new perception of holiness.

The tradition as we have received it, edited by the Sages in the first centuries CE, largely shaped the Jews' collective memory, their perception of historical reality, their historiography and consciousness after the destruction of the Second Temple; but it also displaced and suppressed considerable chapters of the priestly opus created during the centuries of the Temple's existence. Rabbinic tradition was the central voice that shaped views of the past, interpreted the meaning of religious worship and its innermost values, and determined the nature of Jewish normalcy and daily life after the destruction of the Temple. The rabbinic endeavour to ensure the continuity of Jewish life, divorced from the site of the Temple or any other cultic centre and from the guardians of an exclusive sacred authority, was based on several factors: the external historical constraints due to destruction and exile; internal social processes set in motion by new forces and alternative centres of knowledge and authority; struggles for power and hegemony between centralization and decentralization of worship; considerations of the public benefit in changing circumstances; and an ability to look beyond the narrow interests of the present. All these factors caused the creation of new priorities which gradually supplanted the old order. The old was characterized by the *ritual* and the *esoteric*: priests and angels, Temple and Temple rite, a fixed, permanent, sacred order of fixed times engraved on heavenly tablets and based on divine authority and sacred (but never finalized) Written Law, entrusted to the priests, who continued to create works of divine and angelic inspiration. The new, in contrast, was typified by the *textual* and the *exoteric*, accessible to all, shaped by rabbis and scholars whose leadership and decision-making were based on variable, human sapience and earthly authority, on patriarchal tradition and an Oral Law, entrusted to the Sages and through them to the entire community of Israel.

The significance of the shift was that it deprived the priesthood of its exclusive right to sanctify time, place, and ritual practice. That is to say, the Sages gradually replaced the Temple ritual, priestly, angelic tradition, with its reliance on heavenly sources and priestly custody over written tradition, by a mode of worship based on (oral) Torah scholarship and observance of the commandments, on changeable human interpretation and understanding of the eternal divine law. In the new tradition, legal discussions and rulings were concerned with the corporeal, the earthly, and the concrete, within the context of changing time and place. Human beings could now be partners in the divine order; the sacred texts were interpreted and the calendar with its fixed times regulated by human deliberation, based on the exoteric knowledge of scholars. Instead of an angelic, priestly, Temple order—

exclusively controlled by a privileged group, who alone taught the law and acted as guardians of the sanctuary, relying on heavenly authority, on visionary traditions and angelic revelation, on sacred writings, 'wondrous secrets' and 'heavenly tablets' upon which the eternal world order was engraved—the Sages declared the supremacy of Torah study, determination of the law based on exegetical and homiletical principles, entrusted, at least theoretically, to the entire Jewish people. Authority was invested in human scholars exercising their intelligence in the interpretation of what was admittedly a sacred text, but within the limits of human apprehension in changing circumstances.

This 'change of the guard' took place in several stages, in the last few centuries BCE and the first few centuries CE, amid internal controversies and external constraints. The result was the gradual quietening, marginalization, and even prohibition of most of the other voices present before the destruction of the Temple, particularly those representing the circles of priestly tradition with their concentration on the Temple and its rite: priests and angels, heavenly shrines, the priestly calendar and fixed times, the priestly courses, esoteric traditions of Merkavah and cherubim, all reflecting cosmic order through ritual order. These hidden voices found their place in various categories of non-canonical ('extraneous', Heb. *hitsoni*, in talmudic terminology) literature such as the apocrypha and pseudepigrapha, and the literature concealed in the Qumran caves at the beginning of the first millennium CE, around the time of the destruction of the Second Temple, to be discovered only in 1947 on the shores of the Dead Sea.

The labelling of this literature as non-canonical, apocryphal, and pseudepigraphic (to be explained below in detail) is inherently anachronistic, as these labels originated in conceptions rooted in the first centuries CE, when the biblical canon received its final form, whereas the literature in question was created primarily before the Common Era and had nothing to do with this classification. As long as our knowledge of this literature was based only on fragmentary traditions and remote descriptions preserved in various sources, and on historiographic evidence and translations preserved in church literature, such adjectives, which reflect the position of the authorities who rejected it but not that of its own authors, who saw themselves as upholding hallowed traditions, were perhaps applicable. However, as we are now in possession of the Judaean Desert Scrolls, dated to the last centuries BCE, which clearly reveal the authors' views and world outlook, the time has come to re-examine this literature and try to relocate it within the literary corpus of its period.

A large proportion of the literary works discovered in the Judaean Desert bears a distinctly priestly stamp; it refers explicitly to the Zadokite priests and deals in detail with questions germane to the Temple, the sacred service, and the ritual calendar of sabbaths and festivals. The relationship of these traditions to biblical and rabbinic tradition is highly complex; there are signs, on the one hand, of affinity and derivation from a common ancient and hallowed heritage, but, on the other, of a tendency to suppress traditions relating to the sacred service and classify them as esoteric. We discern evidence of polemics and controversy concerning different sources of authority and ritual matters, both between rival priestly houses and between priests and Sages. We will be concerned in this volume with the complex nature of the controversy between the *secessionist priesthood* and the *Temple priesthood*—the Zadokite priests and the Hasmonaeans—from the middle of the second century BCE on.

The Zadokite priests ministered in the Temple from the time of the First Temple until the disputes between the two sons of the high priest Simeon II, the 'Just'—Onias III and his brother Joshua-Jason.[10] Onias III was appointed high priest in 187 BCE, under the reign of the Seleucids, when Seleucus IV ascended the throne in Syria. Suspected of supporting the Seleucids' rivals, the Ptolemies, Onias was summoned to Antioch and imprisoned there by the new Seleucid ruler, Antiochus IV Epiphanes, who came to the throne in 175 BCE after his predecessor's assassination. Onias was replaced by his brother Jason, who paid Antiochus a considerable sum of money for the appointment and also undertook to Hellenize Jerusalem. His term of office lasted three years, from 175 to 172 BCE, during which he indeed encouraged the Hellenization of Jerusalem and tried to establish a Hellenistic *polis* within the city. These plans, supported by Antiochus IV, angered various circles and were perceived as a threat to religious life and the sanctity of the Temple.

The situation deteriorated in 172, when Jason was ousted by Menelaus, a member of the Tobiad family, who were avid advocates of Hellenization. Menelaus, a more extreme Hellenizer than Jason, also bought his office from the Seleucid ruler and continued to work for Hellenization. Jason fled to Ammonite territory, while Onias III, remaining in Antioch on Antiochus' instructions, was murdered in 171 BCE by an emissary of Menelaus. In 168 BCE, following an unfounded rumour of Antiochus' death, Jason returned to Jerusalem and tried to regain his office; he massacred Menelaus's allies and revolted against the Seleucid king, but failed and took flight. Antiochus retaliated by marching on Jerusalem, slaughtering many of its inhabitants, looting the Temple, and imposing various oppressive measures, including a prohibition against observing the sabbath and circumcision, on pain of death. The Temple became a temple of Zeus and the Jews were ordered to offer swine as sacrifices and participate in the idolatrous rites.

Following Antiochus' persecution and the desecration of the Temple, a priestly family known as the Hasmonaeans, of the priestly course of Jehoiarib, launched a religious war, leading the rebellion of 167 BCE against the Greek-Syrian rulers and the champions of Hellenization.[11] Mattathias, who died in 165 BCE, and his sons

---

[10] Their direct descent from Levi, Kohath, Amram, and Aaron, up to the destruction of the First Temple, is documented in detail in 1 Chr. 5: 27–41; 6: 34–7; the later genealogy of the Second Temple period may be found in Ezra 7, Neh. 11: 11; 12: 12, and Ben Sira 49: 12; 50: 1, 35; 51: 29.

[11] 1 Macc. 2: 1; Josephus, *Antiquities*, XII. vi. 1.

Johanan, Simeon, Judah, Jonathan, and Eleazar, fought Antiochus and his army until 162 BCE, when the Hellenist high priest Menelaus was executed and the autonomy and freedom of the Jewish religion were restored.

Upon the accession to the throne of Seleucus IV's son Demetrius in that year, Judah Maccabee's Hellenist opponents appealed to the new Syrian king and requested his help against Judah and his allies. The delegation was headed by a Hellenist of priestly descent, Alcimus, who, complaining that the Hellenists were being persecuted, asked for assistance in the struggle against the Hasmonaeans and their followers; he also demanded to be appointed high priest, in return for a promise to remain loyal to Syria and oppose Judah and his supporters. Demetrius agreed, and Alcimus returned to Judaea accompanied by a Syrian garrison under Bacchides; he served as high priest from 162 to 160 BCE. When Bacchides left to return to Syria, however, Judah drove Alcimus out of the city, but he returned to Demetrius, again requesting and receiving military aid. A new army, under Nicanor, was sent from Syria, but Judah defeated it in two battles. In 161 BCE, Demetrius sent Bacchides back to Judaea; this time, Judah was defeated and died in battle.

Judah's brother Jonathan took his place and successfully overpowered his internal and external enemies. Following a civil war in Syria, Alexander Balas seized the Seleucid throne, defeating the previous ruler Demetrius. In 153, Alexander, eager to secure Jonathan's support against Demetrius, appointed him high priest and ruler of the Jews. In the autumn of 153 BCE Jonathan officiated as high priest in the sacred service, which had been suspended for seven years, and was appointed ethnarch of Judaea with the recognition of the Syrian authorities. Jonathan continued his political activities, fortifying Jerusalem and waging war with and against the kings of Syria, continuing to serve as high priest until he was assassinated in 143/2 BCE by Tryphon, regent to the king of Syria, Antiochus VI, son of Alexander Balas.

Jonathan's brother Simeon succeeded him in 142 BCE as ethnarch, military commander, and, from 140 BCE, high priest, until he too was murdered by his son-in-law Ptolemy in 135 BCE. He was succeeded by his son John Hyrcanus, who ruled from 135 to 104. The latter's son, Judah Aristobulus, served as military commander and high priest for one year, 104–103 BCE, having killed his mother and his brother and crowned himself king.[12] Upon his death, his widow Salome Alexandra married his brother Alexander Yannai, who became high priest and king, ruling from 103 to 76 BCE. Yannai inscribed his coins 'king and high priest'; the first phase of his rule was marked by military conquests aimed at expanding the borders of his kingdom. During Yannai's reign, the Pharisee leadership demanded that the roles of king and high priest be separated, and on that basis instigated a revolt against him; he reacted with considerable ferocity, and the ensuing civil war lasted several

---

[12] Josephus, *Antiquities*, XIII. xi. 1–3.

years. Yannai died in 76 BCE and was succeeded by his widow Salome Alexandra, who appointed their firstborn son Hyrcanus II high priest with Pharisee approval. Her younger son, Aristobulus, was opposed to the ascendancy of the Pharisees and the designation of his brother Hyrcanus as heir to the throne. After Salome Alexandra's death in 67 BCE, civil war broke out between her sons Hyrcanus and Aristobulus. Aristobulus prevailed and seized both royal throne and high priesthood, reigning from 67 to 63 BCE.

The struggles between the two brothers continued, each of them appealing for assistance to foreign powers, until the Hasmonaean kingdom ceased to exist as an independent entity in 63 BCE. In that year, Pompey and the Roman legions wrested the more recently conquered areas, including Hellenistic cities along the coast and in Transjordan, from Judaean hands, destroyed the walls of Jerusalem, deposed Aristobulus, and carried him off in chains to Rome. The high priesthood, now devoid of political significance and once again a purely religious function, was given to Hyrcanus, who had sided with Pompey.[13]

Hyrcanus' weakness cleared the way for the rise of his Idumaean adviser Antipater, who was loyal to Rome, and later for the advent of Antipater's son Herod, who supported the Romans and enjoyed their backing. Descendants of the Hasmonaeans continued to rule and officiate as priests, engaging in savage disputes, intrigues, and murders, up to 37 BCE, when Herod and the Roman forces defeated the Hasmonaean king Antigonus II after besieging him in Jerusalem. Antigonus was executed and Herod, who had married the Hasmonaean princess Mariamne, ascended the throne in his place. Thus the reign of the Hasmonaean dynasty came to an end, and it lost both throne and high priesthood.

Throughout this lengthy period of some 120 years, during which the Hasmonaeans ruled as temporal leaders—later kings—and high priests, waged wars that expanded the borders of their state, ultimately causing the occupation of Judaea by foreign armies, and were involved in considerable bloodshed, various circles among both priests and Pharisees contested the Hasmonaeans' right to priesthood and kingship. Some priests considered the Hasmonaeans to have seized the priesthood by force and denied their legitimacy as high priests, in light of the exclusive right of priesthood held by the Zadokite priests, who traced their ancestry back to Aaron's sons Eleazar and Phinehas and could point to their genealogy, as preserved in biblical tradition, from the time of Moses and Aaron, through the reign of David and Solomon, until the time of Ezra and Nehemiah. The legitimacy of the biblical genealogies recorded in Chronicles and Ezra–Nehemiah was engraved in historical memory because, according to biblical tradition, the Zadokites had served in the Temple as high priests from the time of David and Solomon until the destruction of the First Temple, continuing to officiate in the Second Temple until the seventies of the second century BCE. As reported by Josephus, the priests and the

---

[13] Josephus, *Antiquities*, XIV. i–iv; *War*, I. vi–vii.

Pharisees also disapproved of Hasmonaean kingship, as biblical tradition had associated the monarchy with the tribe of Judah and the House of David. As noted, the
Hasmonaeans held the high priesthood and controlled the Temple rites from
the time of Mattathias' son Jonathan, who ruled from 153/2 to 143/2 BCE, till that
of Antigonus II, who was deposed by Herod in 37 BCE. During that entire period,
the Zadokite priests and their supporters, who contested the legitimacy of the
Hasmonaeans as high priests and monarchs, were denied access to the Temple (or
voluntarily avoided it), at the same time preserving the priestly nature of their
heritage and insisting on their claim to the high priesthood and to spiritual leadership.

The literature discovered at Qumran reflects two corpuses, definable as 'preserved' and 'produced'. The first, 'preserved', category represents the ancient,
centuries-old, priestly literature, the exclusive heritage of the Temple priesthood,
preserved by the Zadokite priests and their allies among those priests, Levites and
Israelites, who acknowledged their age-old leadership. The second, 'produced',
category reflects the viewpoint of the displaced Zadokites and their supporters,
who established a holy congregation without a Temple, created alternative patterns of sacred service, and fought for their authority and position, as rooted in the
ancient tradition violated by a rival priestly house and its supporters in the second
century BCE. The authors of this literature zealously guarded their perception of
sacred time, sacred space, and sacred rites in the changing circumstances of the
Hasmonaean period, relying on the 'preserved' corpus in their creation of the 'produced' one. The former includes the books of the Torah in the different formulations found at Qumran, as well as priestly works concerned with a variety of
subjects: the books of Enoch and Jubilees dealt with the calendar of sabbaths and
festivals; the Calendar of Priestly Courses, the Temple Scroll, the Scroll of Blessings, and the Songs of the Sabbath Sacrifice pertained to the various functions performed in the Temple and the sacred service. The 'produced' corpus includes
secessionist and polemical literature, such as the Community Rule, the Damascus
Document (or Damascus Covenant, Heb. *Berit damesek*), the *pesher* literature,[14]
MMT, the War of the Sons of Light against the Sons of Darkness, and more.

In the course of the struggle for the priesthood, new groups of Torah scholars
emerged—the Pharisees, later known as the Sages or Rabbis (Heb. *ḥakhamim*).
The highly complex attitudes of the Sages to the Zadokite and Hasmonaean priests
will be discussed below in connection with issues of redaction, canonization, suppression, and esoteric classification. It was the Sages who ultimately prevailed in
shaping the historical memory of the Jewish people, in leadership, in literary creation, and in finalization of the canon; they did not, however, operate in a vacuum,
but were direct and indirect heirs to the rich priestly tradition, which constituted a

---

[14] Commentaries on the biblical books of the prophets, interpreting their prophecies as applying to
the present situation of the secessionist community.

not inconsiderable proportion of their work: they sanctified parts of that tradition, accepted other parts conditionally, and rejected the rest.

A brief account of the various literary genres in which the priestly opus was preserved may be found at the end of this prologue, but one insufficiently noted bibliographical and historical fact should be mentioned at the outset: some 400 years elapsed from the composition of the latest books of the Bible in the second century BCE (the visions of Daniel were written in 167–164 BCE) to the final redaction of the Mishnah around 200 CE. Those four centuries were far from silent in the literary sense, and they were not exclusively devoted to the Oral Law; neither were they free of struggle. Nevertheless, some bearers of historiographic traditions preferred to forget and even suppress those years. Many works were composed in and before that period, as is clearly evident from the finds from the Qumran library, which testify to some 650 different works, not counting biblical manuscripts, of which some 250 were discovered. All this voluminous material was condemned to oblivion. A similar conclusion follows from the contemporaneous non-canonical literature, which preserves many interesting works and various traditions. However, as already indicated, complex circumstances contributed to the suppression and disappearance of these traditions. The first stage involved internecine strife between different priestly dynasties, the Zadokites and the Hasmonaeans, resulting in the replacement of the traditional priestly hegemony by a new one. In the second stage, this new priestly hegemony itself was ultimately supplanted by rabbinic leadership. Underlying this second stage were new historical and cultural circumstances (Roman rule and later the rise of Christianity) which culminated in the destruction of the Temple, the cessation of its sacrificial rites, and the consequent emergence of new patterns of memorialization and suppression, new sources of validity and authority. It became necessary to find alternatives for the Temple rituals in a new reality, deprived of a cultic centre.

The rabbinic attitude to the rich priestly heritage was by no means monolithic. Among the ranks of the Sages were several priests who could trace their lineage to all the priestly families, and the Mishnah and Talmud include detailed discussions of numerous priestly traditions. At the same time, however, despite this common interest in the hallowed ancient traditions, laws, and customs, rabbinic literature also offers evidence of opposition to those traditions in many areas, ranging from questions of legitimacy, authority, and hegemony, through ritual issues with respect to the basic validity of the priestly perception of time, to priestly works and areas of cultic and mystical activity which were thought to deserve suppression. When rabbinic tradition discusses the Temple and its service, it is always concerned with the *past*, with describing the lost magnificence of the sanctuary and its no longer extant rituals; one finds discussions of laws relating to the discontinued sacred service and of the relevant controversies, mainly between the Pharisees (= Sages) and the Sadducees (= Zadokites), but sometimes also between the Sages and the Hasmonaean priesthood. The Sages were acquainted not only with deviant priestly traditions relating to internal disputes over hegemony and ritual matters, but also with various priestly traditions of varying antiquity relating to the Temple and the Merkavah, *shiur komah* and *ma'aseh bereshit*, Ezekiel and the Song of Songs—all of which mainstream rabbinic tradition preferred to circumscribe if not to suppress completely.

Nevertheless, such suppression of Temple priestly traditions, their sources, and divergent ritual expressions, as well as the tendentious redaction of certain works and withdrawal of others from circulation—mainly those concerned with priestly hegemony over the concept of sacred time—were not complete. Both traditions, crystallized mainly after the destruction of the Temple, preserved the living memory of the Temple service and of priestly tradition in the *present tense*, thus conserving the priestly experience and perpetuating the sacred rites: (1) One such expression is Heikhalot and Merkavah literature, which preserves the sacred service in the supernal, heavenly sanctuary and in the ministration of the angels, relying on ancient priestly traditions which also left their mark in the books of Enoch and in Qumran literature. (2) Another manifestation of these traditions is the synagogue, called a 'small sanctuary',[15] in which Temple ritual traditions were preserved along with traditions relating to the sacred language of hymns, songs of praise, blessings, and holy names, sometimes associated with angels and priests. In the synagogue it was possible to pray for the re-establishment of the Temple and the sacred service.

I have no intention here of discussing the various views of the origins, essence, and function of the synagogue; but it is surely obvious that the memory of the Temple service was preserved in the use of the holy tongue ('Instead of bulls we will pay the offering of our lips'[16]); in prayer, referred to in rabbinic literature by the same Hebrew word *avodah* that previously denoted the Temple service, and thus closely associated with the latter; in the sanctity ascribed to angels and priests; in the ceremonial perpetuation of the weekly and seasonal cycles of ritual; and in iconography preserving traces of a ritual affinity between heaven and earth. There were indeed many traditions practised in the Temple that carried over to the synagogue: recitation of the biblical passage describing the sacred incense; the priestly benediction and the weekly designation of the twenty-four priestly courses; recitation of the Kedushah formula ('Holy, holy, holy . . .') in emulation of the angels; blowing of the ram's horn and prostration.

The curtain hung before the Holy Ark—the latter known in some traditions as *heikhal*, literally meaning 'sanctuary'—in memory of the curtain once hung in the Tent of Meeting in the desert and in the Temple was a tangible remnant of the sacred service, as was the list of twenty-four priestly courses engraved on stone in some synagogues. Similarly, there were graphic representations in various media—painting, engraving, embroidering, mosaic, etc.—of the lampstand, incense shovel

[15] Ezek. 11: 16.   [16] Hos. 14: 3.

and ram's horn, table, altar, and other motifs, such as palms and pomegranates, all mentioned in connection with the Temple and its utensils.[17] Among other synagogue decorations associated with the Temple ceremonies one finds citrons and palm branches, which recall the institution of pilgrimage; and perhaps one can similarly associate the zodiac, with its division of the year into twelve 'signs', with conceptions of the cosmic and ritual cycle represented in the Temple and its service. Josephus, in his description of the Temple, refers to the curtain demarcating the Holy of Holies: 'Worked in the tapestry was the whole vista of the heavens, except for the signs of the zodiac.'[18] Works discovered at Qumran also refer to the zodiac, as does *Sefer yetsirah* (The Book of Creation), an ancient priestly work which discusses the zodiac in detail in connection with the priestly conception of the universe.[19]

The synagogue service, like the Temple service, is based on a weekly calendar of sabbaths, with the week established as the basic unit of the sacred service; as already indicated, the names of the priestly courses were also perpetuated in the synagogue, orally and in writing, long after the destruction of the Temple. Priests still receive special ritual treatment in the synagogue: they are called first to read the Torah, recite the same priestly benediction as in the Temple, and observe various priestly rituals, such as raising their hands to bless the congregation and redeeming firstborn sons.

In the course of centuries, many further traditions were added to the priestly substrate perpetuating the memory of the Temple and the sacred service in the 'small sanctuary', and the synagogue met various other needs that arose as time passed. The rabbinic heritage, which became the dominant voice after the destruction of the Temple, also left its imprint on the synagogue, in a variety of dialectical motifs representing profound social and cultural transformations. Nevertheless, it is perhaps no accident that the institution most explicitly representing the values and criteria of rabbinic tradition, the *beit midrash* (study house), preserves no priestly traditions whatever and does not give priests preferential treatment, while the synagogue clearly bears the stamp of priesthood and Temple, evidence of the desire to perpetuate the memory of the sacred service in various ways.

Heikhalot literature preserves the living continuation of the sacred service by removing it from the realm of time and space: the Temple/*heikhal* is lifted up to the heavens, and the priests serving therein become the ministering angels in the supernal Temples; the sacred service in these heavenly sanctuaries is described explicitly in terms of the rituals in the earthly Temple. This metamorphosis is implemented through the terminology of Merkavah mysticism, combining the hallowed memory of ritual with creative imagination and visionary inspiration,

---

[17] 1 Kgs. 6–7; 2 Chr. 2–4.   [18] *War*, v. v. 4.

[19] *Sefer yetsirah* 5: 8–21. It is interesting to note that both the biblical solar calendar and the zodiac start the annual counting from the month of spring (Exod. 12: 2; 13: 4) known as Nisan in *Sefer yetsirah* 5: 8.

creating a bridge between the 'revealed' and the 'hidden'. The present work will deal with the circumstances under which Merkavah tradition took shape in the First Temple period, its attitudes to the rituals performed in the Temple before and after its destruction, and the place of that tradition in the context of the mystical and liturgical tradition reflected in Qumran and Heikhalot literature, which links together priests and angels, beyond the limits of time and space.

The origins of Merkavah tradition lie in the two winged cherubim shielding the cover of the Ark in the sanctuary in the desert,[20] also described by David in his exhortation to Solomon concerning the building of the First Temple: 'for the pattern of the chariot [Heb. *merkavah*]—the cherubim—those with outspread wings screening the Ark of the Covenant of the Lord'.[21] The Chariot Throne/Merkavah of the cherubim in Solomon's Temple, which stood in the Holy of Holies, is described in various traditions,[22] which differ slightly in details, but all feature its central position and sanctity in the sacred enclosure. Different traditions associate the winged cherubim with the site of divine revelation, with God's hallowed seat on earth, with the structure of the heavens, and with the Chariot Throne. The cherubim appeared in many parts of the Temple as cultic sculptures, as well as being a central ornamental motif; they possessed a mythical, mystical significance, heavenly figures representing the divine in the sanctified earthly realm.

The Merkavah did not remain confined to the earthly ritual space, but underwent a visionary, mystical transformation in its heavenly representation. The Merkavah appears in the vision of Ezekiel son of Buzi the priest, prophesying at the time of the destruction of the First Temple, who transformed the ruined Temple into a heavenly Chariot Throne with cherubim, wheels, and sacred creatures, facing the four corners of the earth,[23] similar to their plastic representations drawn and sculpted in the Temple.[24] The details of this visionary metamorphosis from the end of the First Temple period will be discussed below with regard to the fact that in the Second Temple period, a time of controversy and strife, the Zadokite priests, who play a key role as divinely nominated priests in Ezekiel's vision of the future (chs. 40–8), revived the priestly prophet's Merkavah vision, perpetuating the angelic sacred service in the supernal Heikhalot. They engineered this mystical and ritual revival after being deprived of their right to minister in the sanctuary as high priests, towards the end of the first third of the second century BCE.

The majority of the Judaean Desert Scrolls were written by these deposed priests and the supporters of their claim to legitimacy and authority. The scrolls, as well as other works that preserved many chapters of the priestly myth—such as Enoch and Jubilees, the Testament of Levi, the Temple Scroll, the Songs of the Sabbath Sacrifice, and other non-canonical works—contain numerous traditions

---

[20] Exod. 25: 17–22.   [21] 1 Chr. 28: 18.   [22] 1 Kgs. 6: 23–8; 1 Chr. 28: 18; 2 Chr. 3: 10–14.
[23] Ezek. 1: 4–22.   [24] 1 Kgs. 6–7; 2 Chr. 3: 7, 10–14; 4: 4.

relating to priests, angels, Merkavah and cherubim, the Kedushah formula and the Temple, the sacred liturgy, the calendar, and the festivals, all of which perpetuate an eternal cosmic order based on sevens and sabbaths, on fours and on seasons. The Merkavah tradition was thus preserved in this secessionist priestly literature in a variety of formulations, until the destruction of the Second Temple in 70 CE. After the destruction one finds a partial continuation of this tradition in Heikhalot and Merkavah literature, which preserves cosmic and angelic traditions of the priesthood, the Temple, and the sacred liturgy in connection with the ritual and liturgical cycle, immortalizing the continuity of the sacred service in the supernal sanctuaries after it had been discontinued in the earthly world.

Literary evidence of these developments and of the conceptual world that reflects them, of the struggles between the different priestly houses before the Common Era, and of the later conflict between priests and Sages may be found in a literary progression stretching from the Bible, through Qumran literature, and reaching Heikhalot literature, the Mishnah, and the Talmud. The following quotations are excerpts from this progression, from the Chariot Throne of the cherubim in the desert sanctuary and in the Jerusalem Temple, to its metamorphosis in Ezekiel's vision of the Merkavah; they describe the mystical and liturgical metamorphosis of the Merkavah in Ezekiel and the Songs of the Sabbath Sacrifice, written before the Common Era but found in Qumran. The tradition is continued in Heikhalot literature, which was written after the destruction of the Temple, at the time of the Mishnah and the Talmud; echoes may be found in the Talmud itself, in two mystical traditions concerning the Merkavah and in the prohibition on dealing with such matters:

You shall make a cover of pure gold . . . Make two cherubim of gold—make them of hammered work—at the two ends of the cover . . . The cherubim shall have their wings spread out above, shielding the cover with their wings. They shall confront each other, the faces of the cherubim being turned toward the cover.[25]

In the Shrine [Heb. *devir*] he made two cherubim . . . He placed the cherubim inside the inner chamber. And the wings of the cherubim were extended . . . He overlaid the cherubim with gold.[26]

He made two sculptured(?) cherubim in the Holy of Holies, and they were overlaid with gold . . . The wingspread of these cherubim was thus 20 cubits across, and they were standing up facing the House.[27]

and the gold for the pattern of the *merkavah*—the cherubim—those with outspread wings screening the Ark of the Covenant of the Lord.[28]

I could see that there were four wheels beside the cherubim. The cherubim ascended; those were the creatures that I had seen by the Chebar Canal . . . And I saw the cherubim lift their wings and rise from the earth.[29]

[25] Exod. 25: 17–20.   [26] 1 Kgs. 6: 23–8.
[27] 2 Chr. 3: 10–13.   [28] 1 Chr. 28: 18.   [29] Ezek. 10: 9–19.

Ezekiel saw a vision and he recounted the visions of the *merkavah*.[30]

The vision that Ezekiel saw . . . The brilliance of the *merkavah* and the four creatures.[31]

The cherubim bless the pattern of the *merkavah* above the firmament.[32]

And the chariots of His inner shrine give praise together, and their *cherubim* and thei[r] *ophanim* bless wondrously . . .[33]

If you wish to achieve oneness in the world, to discover for yourself the secrets of the world and hidden things of the *merkavah*.[34]

R. Ishmael said: What are these songs said by whoever wishes to gaze upon the *merkavah*?[35]

R. Ishmael said: When I ascended on high to gaze upon the *merkavah*, I entered six *heikhalot*, one chamber within the other, and when I reached the gate of the seventh *heikhal* . . .[36]

When [the people of] Israel made the pilgrimage, the curtain was pulled aside and they were shown the cherubim intertwined with one another; and they were told: See how beloved you are before God, like the love of male and female.[37]

It is forbidden for three persons to discuss the secrets of sexual union, for two persons to discuss *ma'aseh bereshit*, and for a single person to discuss *ma'aseh merkavah*, unless [that person] is wise and insightful.[38]

(The portion of) the *merkavah* is not read as a *haftarah* . . .[39]

R. Johanan b. Zakkai (was proficient in) . . . great matters and small matters: 'great matters' means *ma'aseh merkavah*, 'small matters'—the discussions of Abaye and Rava.[40]

The significance of this progression, its numinous and cultic beginnings and its culmination in a mystical and liturgical context, the circumstances under which it took shape and the development of its basic concepts, and their close relationship with the Temple service, on the one hand, and the mystical alternative thus created for a no longer extant earthly reality, on the other, will be discussed in detail in the coming chapters. For the moment, I shall present only a brief account of the various literary corpuses that reflect its post-biblical phases and list the works underlying the discussion, as a preliminary to presenting the aim of the whole study, which will be done at the end of this bibliographical survey.

Qumran literature consists of the remains of some 900 scrolls, found in the Judaean Desert near the Dead Sea, written in the Land of Israel between the last two or

---

[30] Ben Sira 49: 8. [31] Second Ezekiel, 4Q385, frg. 4, 5–6 (*DJD* XXX, 44).

[32] Songs of the Sabbath Sacrifice, 4Q405, frg. 20 ii, 22, 8 (*DJD* XI, 347).

[33] Ibid., 4Q403, frg. 1 ii, 15 (*DJD* XI, 282).

[34] *Heikhalot zutarti* 1 (Elior (ed.), *Heikhalot zutarti*, 22; Schäfer (ed.), *Synopse*, §335).

[35] *Heikhalot rabati* 1 (Schäfer (ed.), *Synopse*, §81).

[36] *Sefer heikhalot* 1 (cf. Charlesworth (ed.), *OT Pseudepigrapha*, i. 255; Schäfer (ed.), *Synopse*, §1).

[37] BT *Yoma* 54a. [38] Mishnah *Ḥag.* 2: 1.

[39] Mishnah *Meg.* 4: 10. [40] BT *Suk.* 28a.

three centuries BCE and the year 70 CE, before the final canonization of the books of the Bible. This literature presents an unprecedented textual variety: in addition to about 250 fragments of biblical texts and works of 'extraneous' literature, it includes religious works of the secessionist priesthood, as well as poetical works and other texts with literary characteristics similar to those of biblical literature, alongside works of a previously unknown nature, whose very existence was unknown until fifty years ago. Most of this literature, many of whose definitions are still disputed, has been published in scholarly editions, chief among which are surely the thirty-nine volumes of *Discoveries in the Judaean Desert (DJD)* published from 1955 to 2002, which present authoritative texts of these works in a critical edition. In the context of the present study, the following editions deserve special mention: Y. Yadin, *The Scroll of the War of the Sons of Light against the Sons of Darkness* (Hebrew, 1955; English edn. 1962); N. Avigad and Y. Yadin, *A Genesis Apocryphon* (1956); J. Licht, *Megilat hahodayot* (The Scroll of Thanksgiving Hymns; 1957); id., *Megilat haserakhim mimegilot midbar yehudah* (The Rule Scroll; 1965); E. Qimron and J. H. Charlesworth, *Rule of the Community*, in J. H. Charlesworth with F. M. Cross *et al.* (eds.), *The Dead Sea Scrolls*, i (1994); P. S. Alexander and G. Vermes, *Serekh Ha-Yaḥad and Two Related Texts* (= *DJD* XXVI; 1998); Y. Yadin, *The Temple Scroll* (Hebrew, 1977; English edn. 1983); E. Qimron, *The Temple Scroll* (1996); C. Newsom, *Songs of the Sabbath Sacrifice* (1985; revised and expanded as part of *DJD* XI, 1998); E. Qimron in M. Broshi (ed.), *The Damascus Document Reconsidered* (1992); J. M. Baumgarten, *The Damascus Document* (= *DJD* XVIII; 1996); E. Qimron and J. Strugnell, *Miqṣat Maʿaśe Ha-Torah* (= *DJD* X; 1994); J. A. Sanders, *The Psalms Scroll of Qumrân Cave 11* ((= *DJD* IV; 1965); B. Nitzan, 4QBerakhot 286–290 (in *DJD* XI, 1998); J. C. VanderKam, the Qumran fragments of the book of Jubilees (in *DJD* XIII, 1994); S. Talmon *et al.*, *Calendrical Texts* (= *DJD* XXI; 2001); and the fragments published by various editors in the volumes of *DJD*. A preliminary edition of works from Qumran Cave 4 not published till the early 1990s was prepared by B. Z. Wacholder and M. G. Abegg in 1991–2. Fragments of scrolls currently under investigation, in various stages, may be found in the various scholarly journals devoted to Qumran studies (see Bibliography). A convenient compendium of all the texts, in Hebrew and English, was published in 1997–8 by F. García Martínez and E. J. C. Tigchelaar as *The Dead Sea Scrolls Study Edition*. A comprehensive English edition of the Qumran scrolls in one volume is G. Vermes, *The Complete Dead Sea Scrolls in English* (London, 1997).[41]

[41] As to the dating of Qumran literature, also known as the Dead Sea Scrolls or the Judaean Desert Scrolls, palaeographic, radiocarbon, and other scientific tests of the materials on which the scrolls were written indicate that they were copied sometime between the 3rd century BCE and the first half of the 1st century CE: see Cross, *The Ancient Library of Qumran*, 127–60. For bibliographical details of the various editions of Qumranic works see Fitzmyer, *Dead Sea Scrolls*; García Martínez and Parry, *Bibliography*. For a comprehensive survey of Qumran and its literature see Dimant, 'Qumran Sectarian Literature'; García Martínez and Parry, *Bibliography*.

Non-canonical ('Extraneous') literature, written in the last centuries BCE and in the first century CE, is generally divided into three categories: apocrypha, pseudepigrapha, and apocalyptic literature. Most of this corpus was not known in its original Hebrew or Aramaic until the discoveries in the Judaean Desert, but was preserved by various Christian communities in Greek, Latin, Ethiopic, Church Slavonic, and Armenian translations, as parts of it were included in the Septuagint and in the New Testament canon of those communities.

The designation *apocrypha* (from the Latin, meaning 'hidden scriptures') refers to books included not in their original Hebrew in the Bible but in Greek translation in the Septuagint, and subsequently in the Catholic canon of the Bible (during the Reformation, Martin Luther denied the divinity of these books and included them in a separate group). The term may also denote certain 'secret', esoteric, or hidden literature, destined exclusively for the eyes of an 'elect' few; this meaning, however, is late and does not necessarily represent the position of the authors before the Common Era or of those who rejected these works in the first century. The Sages did not consider this literature to have been divinely inspired, clearly differentiating it from the books of the Bible, which enjoyed that status and were consequently considered to enjoy divine authority. Towards the end of the Second Temple period, the status of many books was still disputed, and there is a significant difference between the Qumran library, which was written before the finalization of the canon, and the traditional canonical library. Today the adjective 'apocryphal' is applied to literature related to the Bible or rewritten with the Bible in mind.

The term *pseudepigrapha* refers to books by Jewish authors, written in the last centuries BCE and the first century CE and hence included neither in the Bible nor in the Septuagint, which was edited in the third century BCE. The adjective 'pseudepigraphic' indicates that the real author of the work is concealed by an assumed identity from the past, the work being ascribed to some illustrious figure so as to enhance its sanctity. Though most pseudepigraphic works were not included in the Catholic and Greek Orthodox canons, some were admitted to the canons of various eastern Christian churches. The many fragments of important pseudepigrapha discovered at Qumran, in Hebrew and Aramaic, have inspired a re-evaluation of the status of this literature.

Finally, the adjective *apocalyptic* refers to works inspired, as the authors claim, by an apocalypse or vision. The entire body of non-canonical literature represented by the above three corpuses, with its variety of editions, includes, *inter alia*, the Ethiopic Book of Enoch, also known as the First Book of Enoch, fragments of eleven different copies of which were found at Qumran; Jubilees, fifteen Hebrew copies of which were found at Qumran; and the Testament of Levi, of which three copies appear in the Qumran material.[42]

---

[42] On these genres see the following: Schürer, *History*; Russell, *Method and Message*, 104–39; Koch, *Rediscovery of Apocalyptic*; Hanson, *Dawn of Apocalyptic*; Stone, *Scriptures, Sects and Visions*;

Until the Judaean Desert discoveries of some fifty years ago, this literature was known only in Ge'ez, Slavonic, and Greek translation; Hebrew translations of these versions were published by Abraham Kahana, *Hasefarim haḥitsonim* (Apocrypha), vols. i–ii (1937), with accompanying introductions describing the history of the works and their dates of composition, of course reflecting the state of scholarship in the first third of the twentieth century; another Hebrew translation was published between 1958 and 1967 by E. S. Artom, including some works not translated by Kahana (for full details of these editions, the reader may consult the Bibliography at the end of this volume). English translations of the various apocryphal, pseudepigraphic, and apocalyptic works, with introductions reviewing their research history up to the beginning of the twentieth century, may be found in R. H. Charles (ed.), *The Apocrypha and Pseudepigrapha of the Old Testament in English*, 2 vols. (1913; repr. 1963–6); a more up-to-date edition, reflecting scholarship up to the early 1980s, is J. H. Charlesworth (ed.), *The Old Testament Pseudepigrapha*, 2 vols. (1983–5).

The various editions differ in the selection of works presented, depending on the editor's discretion and advances in research. For example, the Damascus Document, discovered in the Cairo Genizah at the beginning of the century before being found at Qumran, is included in Charles's 1913 edition, but neither Kahana nor Charlesworth saw fit to include it in their editions. The fact that parts of this literature were found among the Judaean Desert Scrolls, as already mentioned, in their original Hebrew or Aramaic, implies that the classification still routinely accepted in the scholarly world is anachronistic and needs reconsideration. Indeed, the various finds at Qumran have established hitherto unknown links between apocryphal, pseudepigraphic, and apocalyptic literature.

It would seem that the works of the last centuries BCE discovered at Qumran, such as Jubilees and Enoch, enjoyed a status no less hallowed and authoritative than that of the Bible in the circles to which the authors belonged; they were clearly held to be divinely inspired or revealed by angels. Fragments of the apocryphal, pseudepigraphic, and apocalyptic literature found at Qumran (Jubilees, Enoch, Testament of Levi) have been published in critical editions in the thirty-nine volumes of *DJD* (1955–2002); see also J. T. Milik, *The Books of Enoch: Aramaic Fragments of Qumran Cave 4* (1976); also of interest in this connection are the updated critical editions of Enoch and Jubilees published by Black (1985) and VanderKam (1989), as listed in the Bibliography.

The various works of *Heikhalot* and *Merkavah* literature were written in Hebrew and Aramaic, in the Land of Israel and in Babylonia, around the time of the Mishnah and the Talmud. Among these works are *Heikhalot rabati*, *Heikhalot*

Rowland, *Open Heaven*; Charlesworth (ed.), *OT Pseudepigrapha*; Stone (ed.), *Jewish Writings*; Vander-Kam, *Enoch and the Growth of an Apocalyptic Tradition*; J. J. Collins, *Apocalyptic Imagination*; Kvanvig, *Roots of the Apocalyptic*; Hellholm (ed.), *Apocalypticism*; Himmelfarb, *Ascent to Heaven*.

zutarti, Sefer heikhalot (= 3 Enoch), *Shivḥei metatron, Merkavah rabah, Ma'aseh merkavah,* and *Shiur komah*; partial and sometimes corrupted editions were published from manuscripts by A. Jellinek, *Beit hamidrash* (1853–5); S. A. Wertheimer, *Batei midrashot* (1883–94); and S. Musajoff, *Merkavah shelemah* (1921). Parts of this literature were published in critical editions by H. Odeberg, *3 Enoch, or the Hebrew Book of Enoch* (1928); G. Scholem, *Ma'aseh merkavah,* in his *Jewish Gnosticism* (1965); R. Elior, *Heikhalot zutarti* (1982); and M. S. Cohen, *Shi'ur Qomah* (1985).

The bulk of the corpus is available in two synoptic collections by P. Schäfer, in collaboration with M. Schlüter and H. G. von Mutius, offering continuous, unedited texts for comparison, without critical or other annotation: Peter Schäfer (ed.), *Synopse zur Hekhalot-Literatur* (1981); id. (ed.), *Geniza-Fragmente* (1984). The text of the *Synopse,* presented as a continuous sequence of seven manuscripts printed side by side, is divided into 985 consecutively numbered paragraphs, with no regard for headings and internal divisions. The *Geniza-Fragmente* is divided according to a separate numerical system and is compared to the numbered sections of the *Synopse.* Quotations from Heikhalot literature below will refer to these editions. The two anthologies have been provided with a two-volume concordance (Schäfer, *Konkordanz zur Hekhalot-Literatur,* 1986–8) for the corpus of all manuscripts in the two volumes of Heikhalot traditions, referring to the aforementioned paragraph numbers and including all conjunctions in context.[43]

Much of this rich literary corpus has reached us in fragments of scrolls copied in antiquity, which remained hidden for thousands of years; other parts were preserved in medieval manuscripts from the Cairo Genizah and in manuscripts and books by Jews of different generations, scattered all over the world, or in inaccurate printed editions, translations, and the like—all preserving excerpts from this tremendous mosaic, which shaped the world of a variety of Jewish groups in the last centuries of the first millennium BCE and the first centuries of the first millennium CE. Critical editions of this abundant, centuries-old heritage, representing

---

[43] On Heikhalot and Merkavah literature see Scholem, *Major Trends,* 40–79; id., *Jewish Gnosticism;* Urbach, 'Traditions about Mysticism'; Dan, 'Chambers of the Merkavah'; Gruenwald, *Apocalyptic and Merkavah Mysticism;* Schäfer (ed.), *Synopse;* id. (ed.), *Geniza-Fragmente;* Elior, 'Concept of God'; Gruenwald, 'Place of Priestly Traditions'; Dan, 'Hidden Chambers'; Gruenwald, *From Apocalypticism to Mysticism;* Elior, '*Merkabah* Mysticism'; Schäfer, *Hidden and Manifest God;* Dan, *Ancient Jewish Mysticism;* Morray-Jones, 'Paradise Revisited'; Elior, 'Mysticism, Magic and Angelology'; ead., 'From Earthly Temple to Heavenly Shrines'; Dan, 'Revealing the Secret'; Arbel, 'Mythical Elements'; Swartz, *Mystical Prayer;* Lesses, *Ritual Practices.*

On the relationship between Qumran and non-canonical literature, on the one hand, and Heikhalot literature, on the other, see Strugnell, 'Angelic Liturgy'; Maier, *Vom Kultus zur Gnosis;* Scholem, *Jewish Gnosticism,* 128; Scholem, *Major Trends,* 40–79; Gruenwald, *Apocalyptic and Merkavah Mysticism,* 32–6; Schiffman, '*Merkavah* Speculation'; Newsom, 'Merkabah Exegesis'; Schiffman, 'Heikhalot Literature'; Halperin, *Faces of the Chariot,* 49–55; J. M. Baumgarten, 'Qumran Sabbath *Shirot*'. On the relationship between 1 Enoch and 3 Enoch see Odeberg, *3 Enoch;* Gruenwald, *Apocalyptic and Merkavah Mysticism;* Alexander, 'Hebrew Apocalypse of Enoch'.

the work of many scholars, in Israel and elsewhere, have opened up new vistas for our view of the past, from standpoints not available to earlier students of the Second Temple period and the time of the Mishnah and the Talmud. Readers who wish to decipher the relationship between the different parts of this mosaic, which preserve in poetry and prose the memory of the priestly reality of those times, can now avail themselves of textual material immeasurably richer than that which was at their predecessors' disposal. Nevertheless, despite the richness and variety of the mosaic, would-be students of the period must grapple with a host of difficulties; the realia of those far-distant times are discernible only through mists of obscurity and fragmentation, created not only by the teeth of time and accident, but also by struggles for hegemony, dissenting and polemical traditions of writing and redaction, which retained certain sections of the literary heritage in centre stage while suppressing others and pushing them into the wings. Historiographic traditions strove for ascendancy—for remembrance versus oblivion, for canonization versus rejection, and the overarching view was obscured by anachronistic classifications and faulty concepts. It is easy to be discouraged by the preponderance of unknown over known, of doubtful over certain; or to be perplexed by conventional perceptions of central traditions as against peripheral, of accepted as against disputed religious values. Nevertheless, despite such problems and quandaries, the attempt to decipher and reconstruct that explicitly and implicitly recorded, multi-voiced past, to seek, interpret, and conjecture, seems worthwhile, as far as the textual evidence, both written and implied, will allow us.

Literature from the distant past, which weaves together myth and history, patterns of memory, and interpretive and narrative models, to create humanly organized divine voices and holy scriptures, clearly indicates that there was never merely a single voice, a unanimity subject to a single hegemony. Interpreters of these works now have at their disposal a formidable arsenal of tools—critical, historical, philological, historiographic, literary, theological, and philosophical. All these aspects come together to illuminate one another, sometimes even revealing inconsistencies; but it should be remembered that we have to be content with verbally recorded impressions of no longer extant worlds; echoes of different memories and different voices resound through these shifting pictures. The meanings of words and terms composed in a religious, liturgical, mythical, and mystical context by many different people, identifying with different cultural heritages at different times, striving to contribute to the perpetuation of a constantly changing and gradually emerging hallowed tradition—such meanings may shift and change over the generations. Fluctuating spiritual transformations of collective memory leave their mark on the deepest layers of language, creating obscure traces, flickering embers of recollection, linguistic allusions which call for comparative, critical decipherment, with due attention to historical context, in the attempt to understand as accurately as possible what the words meant to those who spoke, heard, and wrote them, in their own time and place. Perhaps one of the best definitions of the dialectics necessarily involved in extracting the past from the language of the present is the profound observation by the Polish Jewish author Bruno Schulz:

As we manipulate everyday words, we forget that they are fragments of lost but eternal stories, that we are building our houses with broken pieces of sculptures and ruined statues of Gods as the barbarians did. Even the soberest of our notions and categories are remote derivatives of myths and ancient oral epics. Not one scrap of an idea of ours does not originate in myth, isn't transformed, mutilated, denatured mythology.[44]

Bruno Schulz's statement about the mythological layers of language, about ancient narratives stored in words inadvertently and routinely used as they are in the language of the present, echoes Thomas Mann's striking description of the essence of the quest for historical truth:

Very deep is the well of the past. Should we not call it bottomless? Bottomless indeed, if—and perhaps only if—the past we mean is the past merely of the life of mankind, that riddling essence of which our own normally unsatisfied and quite abnormally wretched existences form a part; whose mystery, of course, includes our own and is the alpha and omega of all our questions . . .[45]

These surviving works from the past deal not only with that unfathomable 'riddling essence' of human existence, but also with its profound relationship with a hidden divine existence whose infinity, reflected in life itself, becomes manifest when one tries to decipher its secrets, encoded in the sacred service, and to capture its fluctuating meanings in *sefer, mispar, vesipur*—'book, number, and narrative'— to use the phrasing of the Book of Creation.

Any study of the various works discussed in this book is based on the assumption that the written lines afford a glimpse into the well of the past, where entire worlds lie submerged but strive to rise again and shine through the text, to be deciphered through the varying contexts of the words upon which they have left their impressions, sometimes faint, sometimes more pronounced. The lines of which I speak are part of literary corpuses in which the vicissitudes of time have inserted sometimes anachronistic, not previously extant, borderlines, obscuring the tensions and disputes that nourished the works. Links once part of a single chain have been torn asunder and dispersed among different literary genres; sometimes, however, one can identify and locate the separated fragments at points of linguistic and conceptual juncture, which unexpectedly come together and cohere. Some support for the attempt to decipher the past, to read the lines and between the lines with an awareness of the difficulties involved, may be found further on in Thomas Mann's essay: 'For the deeper we sound, the further down into the lower world of the past we probe and press, the more do we find that the earliest

---

[44] 'The Mythologization of Reality', in *The Collected Works of Bruno Schulz*, ed. Jerzy Ficowski (London, 1998), 372 (originally published as 'Mityzacja rzeczywistości', *Studio* (Warsaw), 1936, nos. 3–4).   [45] *Joseph and His Brothers*, trans. H. T. Lowe-Porter (New York, 1934), 3.

foundations of humanity, its history and culture, reveal themselves unfathomable.'[46] The profound relationship between language—the well of the past, preserving the depths of human experience and the abyss of memory—and the duty of the scholar to exercise care in linking revealed and hidden, remembered and forgotten, to listen to the marginal voice through the hegemonic voice, to discern the subversive echo through the dominant sound and rescue these lost voices from oblivion, was enunciated by Walter Benjamin: 'The moral duty facing critical scholarship [is] to redeem the obliterated past, to save it from oblivion by exposing its hidden truth',[47] and by Dov Sadan's echoing sentiments: 'The goal of criticism is not to be content with what it hears, with what reverberates loudly, openly and clearly in the lines; it must also listen to what is percolating, quietly and secretly, glimmering between the lines.'[48]

APPENDIX

'ESSENES' OR 'THE PRIESTS, SONS OF ZADOK'

While the identity of the authors of the Judaean Desert Scrolls is hotly contested, it has become customary in scholarly literature to refer to them as 'Essenes', following Philo's account of a brotherhood called the *Essaioi* in his works *Quod omnis probus liber sit* (75–91) and *Apologia pro Iudaeis*. Pliny the Elder mentions a quasi-monastic sect called the *Esseni* living near Ein Gedi, in his *Secundi Naturalis Historiae*, written around 77 CE; and Josephus also gives an account of them in the last two or three decades of the first century CE.[49]

One should remember that the historians' accounts, written in Greek, of the organizational aspects of the Qumran community's life—communal principles, humility and monasticism, purity and strict observance of the commandments—on the shore of the Dead Sea are not based directly on the writings of the community in question, but on the description of an outside observer. Because of the partial similarity between these accounts and those Qumranic works attesting to a similar lifestyle, the members of the community are referred to as Essenes. However, no such concept is mentioned anywhere in the scrolls or in what I have called non-canonical literature, or, for that matter, in rabbinic literature. The

---

[46] *Joseph and His Brothers*, trans. H. T. Lowe-Porter (New York, 1934), 3.

[47] *Gesammelte Schriften*, i, ed. R. Tiedemann and H. Schweppenhäuser (Frankfurt am Main, 1991), 144.   [48] *Orahot ushvilim*, III, p. 64.

[49] Josephus, *Antiquities*, XIII. v. 9; *War*, II. viii. 2–13. For a concise compilation of the evidence from the classical literature, in the original languages and in translation, see Stern, *Greek and Latin Authors*, i. 472–81, 538, 540. See also A. Baumgarten, *Flourishing of Jewish Sects*, and Vermes and Goodman, *Essenes according to Classical Sources*. For an analysis of the sources see the comprehensive survey by Stegemann, 'Qumran Essenes'. An up-to-date survey of the methodological difficulties, which unfortunately misunderstands the meaning of the schism, is Boccaccini, *Beyond the Essene Hypothesis*, 8–17.

authors of the scrolls repeatedly (dozens of times) call themselves 'sons of Zadok, the priests, keepers of the Covenant', etc.[50]—a designation whose significance will be discussed below. They constantly stress the priestly leadership of the Community: 'there shall never be lacking a Priest learned in the Book of Meditation; they shall all be ruled by him';[51] 'The sons of Levi shall hold office, each in his place, under the authority of the sons of Aaron. They shall cause all the Community to go and come, each man in his rank . . . under the authority of the sons of Zadok, the Priests';[52] 'This refers to those about whom it is written in the book of Ezekiel the Prophet . . . (quoting Ezek. 44: 10). This (refers to) the Sons of Zadok and to the men of their Council';[53] '"And I will lay your foundations with sapphires" (Isa. 54: 11)—Interpreted, this concerns the Priests and the people who laid the foundations of the Council of the Community'.[54] There are numerous further instances in the *pesher* scrolls, in the War of the Sons of Light against the Sons of Darkness, and in numerous other works, as we shall see below.

Further self-designations of the Community members are 'Sons of Righteousness', 'Sons of Light', '*yahad*, those who enter the new Covenant'.[55] Their leader is referred to as 'the chief priest' (Heb. *kohen harosh*) or 'the chief priest of the whole Community of Israel'; 'the priest who is appointed [to head] the Community'.[56] Other self-references also point to their priestly identity: 'The sons of Aaron will have authority in matters of judgment and of goods';[57] and to their seclusive, ascetic lifestyle: 'who depart from the way of the people',[58] or 'we have separated from the mass of the people'.[59]

The priestly identity of the Community and its members' claim to descent from the Zadokite priests are also indicated by the designations of the founder of the Community: 'Teacher of Righteousness' (Heb. *moreh (ha)tsedek*); or '[he] who shall teach righteousness' (Heb. *yoreh hatsedek*).[60] Even angelic protagonists of Qumranic writings are referred to in similar terms or names: 'the angel of righteousness', Melchizedek, and the like.

It was Eliezer Sukenik who, at the very beginning of Qumran studies, proposed the identification with the Essenes on the basis of the aforementioned passages by

---

[50] See e.g. Community Rule V, 2, 9 (Vermes, *Complete Dead Sea Scrolls in English* [hereafter *CDSSIE*], 103–4), and *passim*; Damascus Document III, 21–IV, 1; IV, 3–4 (Vermes, *CDSSIE*, 130).

[51] Damascus Document XIII, 2 (Vermes, *CDSSIE*, 141).

[52] Messianic Rule (1Q28a) I, 23–5 (Vermes, *CDSSIE*, 158).

[53] Florilegium = 4Q174 I, 16–18 (cf. Vermes, *CDSSIE*, 494).

[54] *DJD* V, 27 (Vermes, *CDSSIE*, 469).   [55] Cf. Jer. 31: 30–3.

[56] Messianic Rule (1Q28a) II, 12 (Vermes, *CDSSIE*, 159); War Scroll II, 1 (Vermes, *CDSSIE*, 164); XV, 4 (Vermes, *CDSSIE*, 179); Damascus Document XIV, 6–7 (Vermes, *CDSSIE*, 143).

[57] 1QS IX, 7 (García Martínez and Tigchelaar, *Study Edition*, i. 91).

[58] See Ch. 1, n. 10.   [59] MMT 4Q397, frgs. 14–21: 7–11), *DJD* X, 27, 58.

[60] 'Teacher of Righteousness': Damascus Document I, 11; Commentary on Habakkuk I, 12; II, 2; and *passim*; 'he who shall teach righteousness': Damascus Document VI, 10–11. On the connection in Hebrew between 'righteousness' and 'sons of Zadok' see Ch. 1, n. 24, and p. 127 below.

Philo, Pliny, and Josephus, notwithstanding all this evidence.[61] This identification
has been accepted to the extent that the clearly priestly character of many of the
Community's writings, as well as their fiercely polemical position in relation to
divine authority, the attestation of sanctity, the sacred charge of the Temple priesthood and the meaning of memory of the divine Covenant, the divine tablets, and
divine laws—all of which are quite apparent in the sources from the last centuries
BCE—have been relegated to the periphery of the discussion.

Only relatively recently, following the examination of MMT, have historians of
halakhah (Jewish law) begun to observe the similarity, if not identity, of the
halakhah as taught in Qumran literature with that described in rabbinic literature
as Sadducean halakhah, as indeed already noted by Schechter at the beginning of
the twentieth century.[62] Schechter considered the Damascus Document a 'Zadokite', i.e. Sadducean, work (the Hebrew word for 'Sadducee' is *tseduki* = Zadokite)
and published it as such. Indeed, since then many scholars have directed attention
to the striking similarity of Qumranic religious law to positions attributed in rabbinic literature to the 'Boethusians' and the Sadducees, though the relationship is
by no means straightforward.[63]

A distinction should be made between the 'sons of Zadok' of the scrolls (the
group that seceded from Jerusalem and the Temple service in the second century
BCE, some of whose views are expressed in the strict 'Sadducean–Boethusian'
halakhah alluded to in the Mishnah) and the Hellenizing Sadducean aristocracy
living in Jerusalem in the first century CE. The latter's principles and way of life, as
described by Josephus and the authors of the New Testament, were quite different
from those practised by the former group.[64] Josephus associates the first group
with the Zadokite priests who had officiated in the Temple before the Hasmonaeans; the other group originally consisted of Zadokite priests, who actually dis-
charged at least some priestly duties in Jerusalem in the spirit of the Zadokite
heritage, as follows from the controversies with the Sadduceans/Zadokites regarding the high priest's burning of incense on the Day of Atonement. Josephus writes
that the first group opposed the Hasmonaean priesthood, objecting to Jonathan the
Hasmonaean's appointment as high priest on the grounds that he was not descended from the House of Zadok (Jonathan served as high priest from 153/2 to 143/2
BCE); at this time Onias IV, the last Zadokite high priest, established a rival temple
at Leontopolis in Egypt, protesting his usurpation by Menelaus, Alcimus, and
later by Jonathan.[65] As to the authors of MMT, they were probably priests who

---

[61] Sukenik, *Dead Sea Scrolls*, 29.   [62] Schechter, *Documents of Jewish Sectaries*.

[63] For some scholarly views of the relationship between the religious law of the Qumranites and
Sadducean halakhah, with references, see Ch. 9, n. 10.

[64] See Josephus, *Antiquities*, XII. ix. 5; XIII. iii. 1, x. 6.

[65] On the Zadokite priests who officiated in the Jerusalem Temple until the deposition of Onias III
and Antiochus IV's appointment of Jason and Menelaus, leading to the Hasmonaean seizure of the
high priesthood, see M. Z. Segal's edition of the book of Ben Sira, 51: 29 and the editor's comments
ibid. 356, and in his introduction, pp. 3–5; cf. Liver, 'Sons of Zadok'; and see also below.

had seceded from the Temple after the Hasmonaean takeover of the high priest-
hood and the Pharisees' rise to power under Jonathan the Hasmonaean.[66] The
'Sadducean' halakhah in the text reflects that predating the Hasmonaean revolt.
This dating also explains the similarities with the halakhah of Jubilees, which was
written around the year 168 BCE and is in several respects similar to that of the
Temple Scroll and MMT.

Clearly, the meaningless names, such as 'Essenes', given to the community that
lived near the Dead Sea by Philo, Pliny, and Josephus in the first century CE should
be rejected in favour of the very meaningful designations used by the members of
the Community themselves in their writings, in the last centuries BCE; this is particularly so in view of the fact that these designations, anchored in biblical tradition, conform to the writers' distinctive identity and their self-declared priestly
lineage (sons of Zadok; priests; plantation of righteousness; *yaḥad* = community;
'those who enter the Covenant').[67]

The ideal societal picture that emerges from Qumran literature is one of distinct
class divisions; a society emulating the world of the Bible, giving preference to
members of the priestly leadership, basing their lives on extreme communal principles but social inequality, with the individual fully assimilated in the group. As
we shall see below, the Qumranites themselves considered their society a testimony to divine order and to a covenant between priests and angels.[68]

Talmon objects to the use of the word 'sect' in relation to the group whose writings were discovered at Qumran, and rejects the traditional identification with the
groups described in the classical literature. In his view, the *yaḥad* of Qumran
should be regarded as a distinct group in the mosaic of Second Temple period
Jewish society, alongside *hasidim*, Essenes, Pharisees, and Samaritans; in addition
the Qumranites, he believes, were part of a broader movement, scattered in all
parts of the country.[69] Boccaccini argues that Philo and Josephus (the Jewish
sources) were describing a voluntary Essene group whose members, numbering
more than 4,000 souls, were religious fanatics and elitists who lived in various parts

---

[66] See Schürer, *History*, i. 174–88; Cross, 'Early History', 70; and cf. the studies of MMT cited in
Ch. 1, n. 10.

[67] On the Essene identity as described in Latin and Greek historiography see Vermes, in Schürer,
History, ii. 555–90.

[68] For the diverse scholarly understandings of Qumran see Lauterbach, 'Sadducees and Pharisees';
Flusser, 'Judaean Desert Sect'; Yadin (ed.), *Scroll of the War*; Rabin, *Qumran Studies*; Licht, *Rule
Scroll*; Cross, 'Early History'; Schürer, *History*, ii. 562–74; Stern, *Greek and Latin Authors*; Flusser,
Judaism and the Origins of Christianity; Dimant, 'Qumran Sectarian Literature'; Kister, 'History of the
Essene Sect'; Broshi *et al.* (eds.), *Judaean Desert Scrolls*; Schwartz, 'Law and Truth'; J. M. Baum-
garten, 'Disqualifications of Priests'; Qimron and Strugnell in *DJD* X; Talmon, 'Community of the
Renewed Covenant'; Vermes, *CDSSIE*, 3, 14–15, 46–8; Boccaccini, *Beyond the Essene Hypothesis*. For
a summary of research into the question of the Essenes, based on a comprehensive survey of the literature but nevertheless drawing what I believe to be erroneous conclusions, see Stegemann, 'Qumran
Essenes'; and cf. Talmon's critique in 'Community of the Renewed Covenant'.

[69] Talmon, 'Community of the Renewed Covenant'.

of the country; whereas Pliny and Dio (the non-Jewish sources) were referring to Essene recluses living on the shore of the Dead Sea. While this group was, in Boccaccini's view, part of a broader movement advocating similar ideas, it was generally more extreme in its principles. Thus, if the movement in general, as described by Philo and Josephus, favoured sharing property, the community described by Pliny and Dio renounced all property; if the larger movement was reserved in its attitude to women, the community practised celibacy.[70]

I agree with Talmon's reservations as cited; to my mind, the clearly priestly atmosphere evident in the Qumran writings is of paramount importance, and the identity of the writers should be considered on the basis of the contents of those writings and their own testimony as recorded in the last centuries BCE; such testimony is of far greater weight than external testimony dating from the last third of the first century CE.

[70] Boccaccini, *Beyond the Essene Hypothesis*, 21–49.

ONE

The Merkavah and the
Sevenfold Pattern

It seems that they consider the number as the principle of things, in respect both of matter and of their changes and situations . . . And all these heavens, as it is said, are number.[1]

THE MERKAVAH

THE origins of the Merkavah concept lie in the Chariot Throne of the cherubim, whose divine pattern or prototype was shown to Moses in heaven and whose first representation in a cultic context is as 'two cherubim of gold', with outstretched wings, mounted on the cover of the Ark of the Covenant in the desert sanctuary.[2] In the Holy of Holies (*devir*) of Solomon's Temple, two gold-plated cherubim shielded the cover of the Ark with their wings;[3] their appearance, revealed to David in a vision as a divine pattern, is described in the parallel passage in Chronicles, which explicitly links the cherubim with the heavenly Chariot Throne: 'for the pattern of the chariot—the cherubim—those with outspread wings screening the Ark of the Covenant of the Lord'.[4] The various traditions that pictured the cherubim as screening the Ark differ in their particulars: some place them above the cover of the Ark, others have them standing before it; common to all is the fact that their four wings touched. The divinely patterned chariot of the cherubim in the First Temple's Holy of Holies, the supposed throne of the Deity or site of his revelation in the Temple, did not survive the destruction, but lived on in mystical memory, which linked its cosmic prototype with its ritual meaning, and was perpetuated in prophetic and priestly traditions and in liturgical testimony. In these traditions, the very word *merkavah* became a symbolic concept expressive of the Holy of Holies and the Temple, both as a whole and in detail; it figured both in the divine prototype of the Temple (the supernal Heikhalot and their angelic cult), and in the memory of its earthly archetype (the Temple and its priests); its roots lay in the numinous foundations of an ancient ritual tradition that forged a bond between heaven and earth.

[1] Aristotle, *Metaphysics*, 986ª15.   [2] Exod. 25: 17–22; 37: 6–9.
[3] 1 Kgs. 6: 23–35; 8: 6–7.   [4] 1 Chr. 28: 18.

Biblical tradition explicitly ascribed the origins of the Merkavah to a divine pattern or prototype.[5] The visionary tradition of the Merkavah repeatedly emphasized its four faces,[6] while post-biblical tradition associated this divine prototype, facing all four points of the compass, with the universe and its microcosmic cultic representations: the Merkavah represented the annual cyclic cosmic order of time, based on a chronotopic fourfold axis unifying time and space.[7] This unified space-time concept governed the fourfold cycle of seasons in nature, the 'four winds of the heavens', the 'four foundations of the wondrous firmament', and other multiples and derivatives of four in fixed proportions to the twelve months of the year. Thus, there were twelve diagonal divisions of the universe, twelve signs of the zodiac and forty-eight constellations, twenty-four hours in a day, twenty-four priestly and angelic courses performing their sacral duties, and 'twenty-four myriad thousand miles'. All these divisions derived from the divine chronotopic division melding time and place; they represented unifying links between the cosmic, the chronotopic, and the ritual, or between cycles of nature and cycles of time as reflected in the cultic order.

The Merkavah reflected time as the mystery of the creative process in nature, the eternal, divine order of Creation as embodied in fixed numerical proportions of cycles of time. Its constituent parts formed a multidimensional, concrete representation, in cultic terms, of the great clock of nature with its numerous fourfold subdivisions, whose interrelations were based on a fixed cyclic order that transformed time and place in accordance with the four seasons of the year. Correlated with this cosmic order was a fixed, fourfold order of ritual which observed the solar calendar; the latter was divided into 364 days, fifty-two sabbaths, and four equal quarters of ninety-one days—the annual seasons—each consisting of thirteen sabbaths (see below).

The Merkavah was thus a representation of the ritual order of *cyclic ritual time*, measured in *sabbaths of days*, i.e. weeks. But the four annual seasons in turn subdivided in accordance with a fixed sevenfold cyclic order; similarly, the concept of *sacred cosmic place* was also associated with a fixed sevenfold axis. The cyclic axis of sacred time derived from the seven days of Creation; accordingly, there are seven days in a week, counted in 'sabbaths of days'; seven days of service performed by each priestly course serving in the Temple; seven days of consecration (*miluim*; see Lev. 8: 33); and seven-week intervals between harvesting times (see below). The fixed spatial axis of sacred place, on the other hand, was embodied in seven firmaments, seven *heikhalot*, seven *devirim*, and seven *merkavot*.

The Merkavah tradition, then, established a chronotopic synchronization between the fourfold cycle and the sevenfold cycle, in regard to sacred time and

---

[5] Exod. 25: 9, 18–22; 1 Chr. 28: 18–19.   [6] Ezek. 1: 5–6, 8, 10, 15–18; 10: 9–14, 21.
[7] The term 'chronotope' was coined by Mikhail Bakhtin to denote the inseparability of *topos* and *chronos*, that is, of space and time, in the sense that space and time are fused together in a literary or numerical context; see Bakhtin, *Dialogic Imagination*, 84.

sacred place alike, as a manifestation of the creative process of nature; the eternal, cyclic, cosmic order was preordained in terms of set times and testimonies, a divine pattern maintained by angelic forces. This tradition was preserved by priests and angels, all observing a hallowed solar calendar based on these two cycles, to which ritual and liturgy conformed in both earthly Temple and supernal Heikhalot. Thus, sacred time was reflected on a microcosmic ritual scale by the natural cosmic order and the divine order in the calendar of seasons, weeks, and set times (= festivals), correlated with a cyclic order of liturgy; while sacred place was similarly reflected by various sevenfold, fourfold, and twelvefold ritual representations linking the Earthly Temple with the supernal worlds. All these elements came together in the sacred service as performed on earth by the priests and in the heavens by the angels, all guardians of the sacred heritage.

The origins of the mystical Merkavah tradition lie in the vision of the exiled priest Ezekiel son of Buzi, who prophesied towards the end of the First Temple period.[8] Deported from Jerusalem to Babylonia with Jehoiachin, he saw a vision in which the Chariot Throne and its cultic representations in the ruined Temple assumed a divine dimension, to become the Merkavah, combining various elements from the Holy of Holies and the Temple courts into an eternal, visionary, cosmic entity transcending the limits of time and space. In addition to the heavenly Chariot Throne, Ezekiel also envisioned the future earthly Temple, whose service was entrusted exclusively—as Ezekiel repeatedly stressed—to the priests of the House of Zadok.[9]

The next stage in the Merkavah tradition was the mystical vision of seceding priestly circles,[10] who were barred from serving in the Second Temple in the last

---

[8] Ezek. 1: 1–28; 3: 12–14; 8: 2–4; 10: 1–22. For scholarly positions on the book of Ezekiel see Cassuto, 'Ezekiel', 636–9; Haran, 'Topics in Bible' and bibliography ibid.; Zimmerli, *Ezekiel*; Greenberg, *Ezekiel 1–20*. For an extensive bibliographical survey see Halperin, *Faces of the Chariot*, 547–9. For the Merkavah see Ch. 2 below. On Qumran finds associated with Ezekiel see Lust (ed.), *Ezekiel and his Book*. Among these finds were unknown formulations of Ezekiel, now known as the Ezekiel Apocryphon, Pseudo-Ezekiel, or Second Ezekiel; see Strugnell and Dimant, '4Q Second Ezekiel'; *DJD* XXX, 1–51; Brooke, 'Ezekiel in Some Qumran and NT Texts'. For Ezekiel's place in apocalyptic tradition see Kvanvig, *Roots of the Apocalyptic*, 510–24, 550–1; and see the discussion below.

[9] Ezek. 40–8.

[10] See 4Q 397, frgs. 14–21, in *DJD* X, 27, 58, 59, 57. Compare the parallel expression 'who depart from the way of the people' and similar expressions. The seceding priests' opponents earned a variety of derogatory epithets at Qumran, such as 'men of injustice who walk in the way of wickedness' (Community Rule V, 12–13); and especially in the Damascus Document, such as 'a congregation of traitors who stray from the way'. The faithful are explicitly commanded 'to keep away from the ways of wickedness' (*DJD* XVIII, 31). The work *Miktsat ma'asei hatorah* (MMT), six (fragmentary) copies of which were found at Qumran, is concerned with certain legal controversies relating to the sacred service and ritual affairs; see J. M. Baumgarten, 'Pharisaic-Sadducean Controversies'; Sussmann, 'History of Halakhah'; Qimron and Strugnell in *DJD* X; Qimron and Strugnell, 'Unpublished Halakhic Letter'; Strugnell, 'MMT: Second Thoughts'; Morag, 'Style and Language'; Kampen and Bernstein (eds.), *Reading 4Q MMT*. Qimron and Strugnell have dated MMT to the beginning of the Hasmonaean period (mid 2nd century BCE). The common denominator of the various laws discussed

centuries BCE because of fundamental dissension concerning the sanctity of time and place and polemical disputes about sabbath and festivals, calendar and cult. Having withdrawn, as a consequence, from the earthly Temple, these circles, who called themselves 'sons of Zadok, the priests', ministered in their mind's eye, together with their angelic counterparts, in a divine Chariot Throne which, inspired by Ezekiel's Merkavah vision and the tradition of the Temple service, they recreated in their writings in poetic and visionary terms. The Zadokite priests are referred to by a variety of priestly epithets: in the Community Rule;[11] in the 'Rule for all the congregation of Israel . . ., when they shall join the Community to walk according to the law of the sons of Zadok the priests';[12] in a Qumran scroll known as the Damascus Document, which calls them 'the sons of Zadok, the priests . . ., behold they are the interpretation of the last Law';[13] in the fragments of the Damascus Document found in the Cairo Genizah;[14] in the War Scroll;[15] and in other Qumranic works. They served *together with* their mystical angelic counterparts, referred to in Songs of the Sabbath Sacrifice in typically priestly terms: 'priests of the inner sanctum (*kohanei korev*) who serve before the King of holiest holiness', 'Priests of the inner sanctum in his royal sanctuary, ministers of the Presence in his glorious *devir*', 'priests of the highest of high', 'Angels of Holiness', 'chief priests', 'seven priestly factions for the wondrous Temple', 'Chief Princes', and 'Chiefs of the Princes of Wondrous Priesthoods'.[16] The terrestrial chief

in the work, as revealed by recent research, is the defilement of the sacred service caused by the illicit priests officiating in the Temple, who had violated the sanctity and purity of the ritual.

On the Damascus Document see Schechter, *Documents of Jewish Sectaries*; Rowley, *Zadokite Fragments*; Rabin, *Zadokite Documents*; Wacholder and Abegg, *Preliminary Edition*, fasc. i; Broshi (ed.), *Damascus Document Reconsidered*; *DJD* XVIII. After the first edition of the Damascus Document had been published by Schechter, the work was included in Charles's 1913 edition of the pseudepigrapha. After the discovery of the Qumran version, it is no longer included in modern editions of the pseudepigrapha. The discovery of fragments of Enoch and Jubilees at Qumran, however, did not cause the similar exclusion of those works.

On the identity of the secessionists see Introduction, Appendix. The members of the Qumran community, whose lives were informed by a consciousness of continuity with the biblical world, were governed by a priestly leadership along biblical lines; they considered the priests senior in every respect and saw them as the founders and leaders of the community.

[11] V, 2–3, 9–10.   [12] Messianic Rule I, 2, 25 (Vermes, *CDSSIE*, 157, 158).
[13] 4Q266, frg. 5 i, 16–17 (*DJD* XVIII, 48–9).   [14] III, 21; IV, 1–3; V, 5.
[15] XII, 9–10; XVII, 6, 8.
[16] Ten manuscripts of the Songs of the Sabbath Sacrifice, also known in the scholarly literature as 'Angelic Liturgy', '4Q Shir Shabb', and 'Shire Olat hash-Shabbat', were found at Qumran and Masada: eight in Qumran Cave 4, one in Cave 11, and one at Masada. On these poems and their affinity with Temple priesthood traditions see Strugnell, 'Angelic Liturgy'; Maier, *Vom Kultus zur Gnosis*, 133 ff.; Schiffman, '*Merkavah* Speculation'; Newsom, *Songs*, esp. discussion on pp. 23–72 (this edition includes a very useful, detailed, alphabetical concordance); Qimron, 'Review Article'; Newsom, 'Merkabah Exegesis'; Puech, 'Review of *Songs of the Sabbath Sacrifice*'; J. M. Baumgarten, 'Qumran Sabbath *Shirot*'; Newsom, 'He has Established for Himself Priests'; ead., 'Sectually Explicit Literature from Qumran'; Maier, 'Shire Olat hash-Shabbat'; Nitzan, *Qumran Prayer*; Newsom, *Songs*, in *DJD* XI, 173–400 (also including a detailed concordance on pp. 445–72). For the concepts referred to

priests, who had withdrawn from the Temple, and the heavenly priests of the inner sanctum, who were painted with a clearly priestly brush, sang together, in a permanent cyclic order, the Songs of the Sabbath Sacrifice; in a regular, prescribed daily, weekly, monthly order of set times they recited psalms, songs, hymns, and Kedushahs, shared by angels and men. They did all this in a cyclic, weekly order of liturgy, governed by the ritual solar calendar of weeks (sabbaths) and quarterly seasons, and correlated with the order of priestly courses, also subdivided in conformity with sabbaths and multi-annual cycles, and named after the new months and the festivals.[17]

The last stage of the Merkavah tradition in ancient mystical literature was formulated by certain circles of priestly affiliation, active after the destruction of the Second Temple, who composed the Heikhalot literature in the first centuries CE. The protagonists of this literature—known as 'descenders of [*or* to] the Chariot' and associated with the high priest Rabbi Ishmael[18] and with Rabbi Akiva, who 'entered the Pardes' (an expression symbolizing engagement in esoteric speculation pertaining to the heavenly sanctuaries[19])—aimed to perpetuate the destroyed Temple and its cult through their vision, by 'descending' to the Chariot Throne and 'ascending' to the supernal Heikhalot—that is, heavenly temples or sanctuaries. There they met their mystical counterparts: the ministering angels, the angels of glory and the angels on high, as well as the high priest of the supernal worlds, Enoch son of Jared, also known as Metatron, the mystical angelic protagonist of the priestly literature from Qumran. The angels who serve in those supernal worlds bathe and purify themselves, sing and recite the Kedushah, exalt, bless with holy names, the kindle fiery flames, thus perpetuating the priestly and Temple ceremonies in the seven supernal sanctuaries, the Heikhalot.[20]

Scholars are divided as to the historical identity and social, religious, and cultural venue of the various circles that were associated at different times in antiquity with the Merkavah and Heikhalot traditions, the mystical priesthood and the angels, the Songs of the Sabbath Sacrifice, the heavenly Kedushah, and the songs of the ministering angels.[21] However, sizeable excerpts and fragments from the highly diverse literary opus of these circles are now available and invite discussion and investigation. Though generally incomplete, these excerpts provide sufficient evidence of the cosmic, mystical, and ritual attitudes of these circles; of their affiliation with the priesthood and the Temple; of their connections with worship and

---

in the text cf. Newsom, *Songs*, 26. The expression 'ministers of the *devir*' may be found in other Qumran sources, such as 4Q 392, frg. 1, 9; cf. Wacholder and Abegg, *Preliminary Edition*, ii. 38. The Songs of the Sabbath Sacrifice from Cave 11 were published in 1998 in *DJD* XXIII.

[17] For the traditions relating to the solar calendar see Chs. 3 and 4; for priests and angels see Ch. 8.
[18] BT *Ber.* 7*a*.
[19] See BT *Ḥag.* 14*b*; for a discussion of the specific term 'Pardes' see pp. 245–7.
[20] On Heikhalot and Merkavah literature see Ch. 10.
[21] On the identity of the authors of the Judaean Desert Scrolls see Introduction, Appendix.

the cyclic liturgical ceremonies performed together with the angels; of their myths, mystical lore, and cult, linking heaven and earth; of their stringent rules of purity and impurity; of their calendar and festivals; of the prohibitions that they practised; and of their polemical position and self-perception as earthly correlates of the angels. In what follows I shall discuss the various stages in the formation and development of the mystical priestly tradition in antiquity, with its visionary metamorphoses of Temple and priesthood which, destroyed and desecrated, became objects of controversy; lost in earthly reality, they were perpetuated in an ideal, utopian guise through the divine Chariot Throne—the Merkavah—and the angelic priesthood in the supernal sanctuaries.

THE SEVENFOLD PATTERN

As already stated, the mystical Merkavah tradition evolved from the vision of Ezekiel son of Buzi the priest, in which the cherubim and sacred creatures in the earthly and heavenly Temples were fused together. Ezekiel envisioned a fourfold configuration of sacred, multi-faced, winged creatures, which could not be subsumed under any category clearly distinguishable as either earthly or heavenly; the fourfold nature of these creatures, facing all four points of the compass, is stressed again and again. The Merkavah tradition was taken up again in the literature of the secessionist priesthood discovered at Qumran, which is frequently concerned with deciphering the cosmic order as revealed through harmonies expressed in fourfold numbers and sevenfold cycles, in both earthly Temple and heavenly sanctuaries. Many of the works of this literature, written in the heat of polemics and controversy towards the end of the Second Temple period, ignore the barriers between heaven and earth, angels and human beings, providing descriptions of visions featuring Merkavah, cherubim and angels, priests and their heavenly counterparts blessing, praising, and singing sacred songs in the supernal sanctuaries, according to a fixed, cyclic, cosmic order.[22] The final stage was that of Heikhalot and Merkavah literature, composed in mystical, ornamented language in the first centuries after

---

[22] Traditions relating to the heavenly origins of the priests, to angels, Chariot Throne, and heavenly Temple, appear in the following works of Qumran and other non-canonical literature: the Ethiopic Book of Enoch, Jubilees, Songs of the Sabbath Sacrifice, Community Rule, Blessings Scroll, War of the Sons of Light against the Sons of Darkness, Temple Scroll, Damascus Document, Testament of Levi, Levi Apocryphon, Testaments of the Twelve Tribes, and the Slavonic Book of Enoch. For discussion of such angelic traditions see Bietenhard, *Himmlische Welt*; Yadin (ed.), *Scroll of the War*, 229–42; Strugnell, 'Angelic Liturgy'; Maier, *Vom Kultus zur Gnosis*; Newsom, 'He has Established for Himself Priests'; Dimant, 'Children of Heaven'; Mach, 'Studies in Angelology'; Dimant, 'Men as Angels'. For the relationship between Ezekiel and Qumranic perceptions of cult and Temple see Fujita, 'Temple Theology'; Klinzing, *Umdeutung des Kultus*; Gartner, *The Temple and the Community*; Lichtenberger, 'Atonement and Sacrifice'; Newsom, *Songs*; Himmelfarb, *Ascent to Heaven*; and see also studies of the books of Enoch, Jubilees, the Testament of Levi, the Songs of the Sabbath Sacrifice, and other Qumranic works cited below.

the destruction of the Temple with the aim of mystically perpetuating the tradition. Many works of Merkavah tradition feature such subjects as crossing the borders between the worlds; 'descending to the Merkavah', heavenly sanctuaries, angelic rituals and sacred song; the cyclic liturgies preserved by the angels whose task it was to supervise cosmic order; and the portrayal of that order in the divine Merkavah in the supernal worlds.[23]

In the early, formative stages of Merkavah tradition, the priestly authors, whose writing drew on their own mythical and mystical traditions and displayed a unique affinity for the book of Ezekiel and its peculiar perceptions of priesthood and the Temple (chs. 40–8), were unreservedly opposed to the Temple cult as performed in their times and to the very concept of time that governed it. In their works, written in the last centuries BCE and the first century CE (before the destruction of the Temple), they referred to themselves by various names alluding to the priesthood in general and the House of Zadok in particular, to concepts bound up with adherence to the righteous path and observance of the covenant, with upholding testimony and the sacred set times (festivals), with light, sanctity, and the priestly-angelic community: 'sons of Zadok, the priests, guardians of the Covenant', 'chief priests', 'knowers of righteousness', 'plantation of righteousness', 'root of growth', 'shoot of righteousness', 'congregation of holiness', 'Council of the Community', 'those who enter the Covenant', 'Sons of Light', 'Sons of Dawn', or 'those who enter the new Covenant'.[24] In Heikhalot literature, composed after the destruction of the Temple, they were known by names referring to the divine Merkavah: 'descenders of [*or* to] the Merkavah', 'viewers of the Merkavah', or 'heroes of the company', as against 'band after band of angels from the firmament and company after company from the heavens'.[25]

[23] Traditions relating to the priesthood, angels, Merkavah, and the heavenly Temple in Heikhalot literature may be found in *Heikhalot zutarti*, *Heikhalot rabati* = *Sefer sheva hekheli kodesh*, *Ma'aseh merkavah*, 3 Enoch = *Sefer heikhalot*, *Merkavah rabah*, *Shivhei metatron*, *Re'uyot yehezkel*, and *Sefer harazim*. For discussion of the traditions and of these works see Scholem, *Major Trends*, 40–79; id., *Jewish Gnosticism*; Maier, *Vom Kultus zur Gnosis*, 133–5; M. Margaliot (ed.), *Sefer harazim*; Alexander, 'Historical Setting'; Gruenwald, *Apocalyptic and Merkavah Mysticism*; id., 'Angelic Song'; Elior (ed.), *Heikhalot zutarti*; Alexander, 'Hebrew Apocalypse of Enoch'; Dan, 'Hidden Chambers'; Gruenwald, 'Place of Priestly Traditions'; Elior, 'Concept of God'; Bar-Ilan, *Mysteries of Jewish Prayer*; Dan, *Ancient Jewish Mysticism*; Janowitz, *Poetics of Ascent*; Schäfer, *Hidden and Manifest God*; Swartz, *Mystical Prayer*; Elior, 'From Earthly Temple to Heavenly Shrines'.

[24] On these diverse names see Habermann, *Judaean Desert Scrolls*, concordance; cf. 1 En. 93: 1, 5. For a discussion of the significance of the names see Flusser, 'Judaean Desert Sect'; Yadin (ed.), *Scroll of the War*, index; Liver, 'Sons of Zadok'; Licht, 'Judaean Desert Sect', esp. 99 ff.; id., *Rule Scroll*, index; Newsom, *Songs*, 1–80; Talmon, *World of Qumran from Within*, index; Sussmann, 'History of Halakhah'. It should be noted that many of the names involve the concept of *tsedek*, 'righteousness'— a word derived from the same root as the name 'Zadok' (Heb. *tsadok*), on which see further below.

[25] See Schäfer (ed.), *Synopse*, §7, and compare with the various heavenly camps in §§180, 773, 810, 875. For the diverse names see the concordances in Schäfer, *Konkordanz*, s.vv. For the significance of the names see Scholem, *Jewish Gnosticism*; Gruenwald, *Apocalyptic and Merkavah Mysticism*; Elior (ed.), *Heikhalot zutarti*; Dan, 'Hidden Chambers'; Elior, 'Concept of God'; Dan, *Ancient Jewish Mysticism*; Schäfer, *Hidden and Manifest God*.

The priestly circles whose works were found at Qumran were adamantly opposed to the Temple cult of their times. They rejected the lunar calendar then governing the cult and instead upheld the superiority of a cultic calendar based on the solar year, demanding that the regular succession of sabbaths and festivals be derived from that calendar. Up until the destruction of the Second Temple, they fought for the concept of the Covenant and the Festival of Oaths or Covenants, also known as the Festival of Weeks (Heb. *shavuot/shevuot*), for every dimension of the sacred service that explicitly involved any aspect of cycle, number, date, fixed time, and counting, thus reflecting the regularity of the cosmic order; they stressed observance of the laws of purity and the rules of the Temple service associated with the perception of sacred place; and insisted on the superior right of the Zadokite priests to settle any question relating to Temple rituals and matters of purity and impurity, by virtue of their divine election to serve in the Temple and their eternal, sacred, heaven-granted authority.[26] In much of their struggle over the legitimate performance of the cult, in questions relating to the calendar, the festivals, and the administration of Temple affairs, they relied on traditions of angelic origin found in Enoch, Jubilees, the Rule Scroll, and the Songs of the Sabbath Sacrifice. They saw themselves as a congregation or community revolving, so they believed, around an angelic and priestly 'oneness' or 'togetherness' (Heb. *yahad*), beyond time, from which derived the authority and legitimacy of their traditions, laws, and sacred service; they in fact referred to themselves, the Community, by the same word, *yahad*. The angels were witnesses to the Covenant, guardians of the calendar of sabbaths and festivals, and partners in sacred rites that conformed to the cyclic solar calendar, with its subdivision into quarters (= seasons) and sabbaths (= weeks).

The Heikhalot mystics, active after the destruction of the Temple, relinquished the oppositional aspect of their thought and the cultic controversies characteristic of the mystical priesthood prior to the destruction. Instead, they formulated heavenly, priestly, and mystical perceptions of the Temple and its rites, concentrating on perpetuating the now defunct earthly cult through its angelic counterpart in the world of the Merkavah—the Chariot Throne—and the Heikhalot—the heavenly sanctuaries. To that end, they created mythical, mystical, and liturgical modes of expression that bridged the gap between the sacred service of angels and human beings. These modes of expression were a numinous written record of priestly and angelic traditions concerning (1) *sacred place*—the world of the Merkavah, portrayed as seven sanctuaries or palaces in vertical sequence, facing all four points of the compass, thus preserving a sevenfold liturgical cyclicity synchronized with the four seasons of the year; (2) *sacred time*—the solar calendar, subdivided into four seasons and into sequences of seven-day sabbaths or weeks, associated with the figure of Enoch son of Jared, the seventh patriarch of the world, also known as Metatron, the Angel or Prince of the Countenance; and (3) *sacred ritual*—the tradition of

---

[26] See Yadin (ed.), *Temple Scroll*; J. M. Baumgarten, *Studies in Qumran Law*; Sussmann, 'History of Halakhah'; Schiffman, 'Temple Scroll'. For Shavuot see esp. Ch. 6 below.

oaths and covenants, names, songs of praise and blessings, the Kedushah, thanks-giving, all associated with septuples, shared by angels and priests, rooted in the teachings of Metatron and the angels.[27]

The cultic conceptions and controversial positions espoused by the secessionist priesthood, which took shape in the stormy atmosphere of the last centuries BCE, were excluded from the canon and considered non-canonical or 'extraneous' liter-ature; their traditions were suppressed and almost vanished until rediscovered in the Judaean Desert Scrolls at Qumran. They were opposed, directly and other-wise, to the positions commonly maintained in the second and first centuries BCE, the Hasmonaean period, in regard to the three foundations of the cult: sacred place, sacred time, and sacred ritual.

All over the ancient world, temples were considered as a microcosm of the universe; they embodied sacred place, expressing the oneness of time, space, and ritual as a reflection of cosmic order, the numerical harmony inherent in that order, and the eternal cycles of heaven and earth. This ideal order, seen as an archetypal reproduction of the order of Creation and the underlying secret of creation and life, had a sacred numerical dimension, associated with the laws of nature and the fixed times of cult and ritual; a mythical, narrative dimension, delimiting the group's shared identity with its commandments and prohibitions, of heavenly origin but recorded in an earthly text; and a ritual dimension, creating a bond between secret and manifest and perpetuating these affinities between text, num-ber, and narrative. These various dimensions were proclaimed in cyclic cere-monies which measured out the creative progress of manifest time in terms of seasonal changes and fertility cycles; the passage of time was celebrated in song and sacrifice which strove to close the gap between heaven and earth, picturing an ideal relationship between the manifest and the secret dimensions—a relationship rep-resenting a cosmic ritual unity between sacred place, sacred time, and sacred testi-mony, which together determined the continuity of Creation, agricultural plenty, and human fertility. The meaning of ritual in relation to the temple as microcosm has been aptly defined by a historian of religions, Jonathan Smith: 'Ritual rep-resents the creation of a controlled environment . . . [It is] a means of performing the way things ought to be in conscious tension to the way things are in such a way that this ritualized perfection is recollected in the ordinary, uncontrolled, course of things.'[28] The temple and its ceremonies represent the ideal world, ruled by the primary divine order. Hence, a disturbance of any one of its components—the pattern of sacred time, sacred place, or sacred ritual—bound up as they are in the numerical and ritual oneness of nature and culture, testimony and festivals, signs and covenants, religion and law, purity and impurity, life and death, is seen as having a calamitous effect on the cosmic order of things: it wreaks havoc with the mutual relationship between heaven and earth.

[27] See Elior, 'From Earthly Temple to Heavenly Shrines'.
[28] J. Smith, *Imagining Religion*, 63.

The secessionist priesthood whose works were discovered at Qumran considered the Temple of their times, throughout the Hasmonaean period and the previous two decades, as desecrating and violating the hallowed rules of purity, as impure, so defiled that they withdrew from its service. This follows from the letter known as *Miktsat ma'asei hatorah* (MMT), written at the beginning of the Hasmonaean period. In this work, which deals with the laws of purity in the Temple and recounts the various sins which brought about the defilement of the Temple, we read: 'And you know that we have separated from the mass of the people and from their impurity and from mingling with them in these matters and from being in contact with them in these matters.'[29] The same is stated explicitly in the Commentary on Habakkuk: 'As for that which he said, *Because of the blood of the city and the violence done to the land* [Hab. 2: 7]: interpreted, *the city* is Jerusalem, where the Wicked Priest committed abominable deeds and defiled the Temple of God.'[30] The target of the attacks in both works is most probably Jonathan the Hasmonaean, who defiled the Temple through his priesthood; in any event, the text is clearly referring to the Temple of the writer's time as defiled by the Hasmonaean priesthood. Similarly, we read in the Damascus Document: 'Moreover, they profane the Temple', 'they profaned the Temple', 'the third is profanation of the Temple', 'to defile the city of the sanctuary with their uncleanness',[31] and even more strongly in the Testament of Levi: 'You will be inflated with pride over your priesthood, exalting yourselves not merely by human standards but contrary to the commands of God; . . . you will deride the sacred

[29] *DJD* X, 27, 58, 59, 57 (4Q 397, frgs. 14–21). On this work, see n. 10 above. On the defiled Temple see Damascus Document IV, 15–18; V, 6–7; VI, 11–13; XI, 19. And cf. Community Rule, Temple Scroll, Testament of Levi.

[30] Commentary on Habakkuk XII, 8–9, 18; and cf. ibid. VIII, 4–5 (Nitzan (ed.), *Pesher Habakkuk*; Horgan, *Pesharim*). The identity of the Wicked Priest who persecuted the Teacher of Righteousness has been hotly contested: Vermes (*Dead Sea Scrolls: Qumran in Perspective*, 126–39), Milik (*Ten Years of Discovery*, 84–7), and Stegemann ('Qumran Essenes', 89, 152) identify the 'Wicked Priest' with Mattathias' son Jonathan, who officiated as high priest in 153/2–143/2 BCE, not long after the desecration of the Temple, the religious persecution, and the outbreak of the Maccabean revolt, in the wake of which the Hasmonaean dynasty came to power. The text of MMT, which has been dated to the beginning of the Hasmonaean period and is addressed to some leading priestly figure, supports this identification. Cross, however (*Ancient Library of Qumran*, 141–56; 'Early History'), suggests that he was Jonathan's brother Simeon, who ruled Judaea in 142–134 BCE. Another possible candidate for the role is the Hasmonaean king Alexander Yannai, who ruled the country and officiated as high priest during 103–76 BCE (so Flusser, 'Judaean Desert Sect'; Nitzan (ed.), *Pesher Habakkuk*, 132–5). The text of the Commentary on Habakkuk (VIII, 8–9) reads: 'Interpreted, this concerns the Wicked Priest who was called by the name of truth when he first arose. But *when he ruled over Israel* his heart became proud, and he forsook God and betrayed the precepts for the sake of riches.' See also ibid. I, 13; IX, 9; XI, 4; XII, 2, 8; and cf. Josephus, *Antiquities*, XIII. xiii. 5; *War*, I. iv. 4, 6; BT *Suk.* 48*b*; *Kid.* 66*a*. The Wicked Priest also figures in the Commentary on Psalms 37: 39–40: 'The wicked watches out for the righteous and seeks [to slay him . . .] . . . Interpreted, this concerns the Wicked [Priest] who sent (to the Teacher of Righteousness?) to put him to death . . .' (Licht, *Thanksgiving Hymns*, 243). See also Schürer, *History*, i. 174–88, 220–7.

[31] Damascus Document V, 6; VIII, 46; IV, 17–18; VI, 15–16; XII, 1–2; XX, 23.

things. Therefore the sanctuary which the Lord chose shall become desolate through your uncleanness.'[32]

As against the impure, defiled Temple from which they had withdrawn, administered as it was by 'Sons of Darkness' (implicitly identified as the priests of the Hasmonaean dynasty, of the division of Jehoiarib, who had usurped the high priesthood), those priestly circles who considered themselves to be the 'Sons of Light' and explicitly identified themselves as the priests of the House of Zadok (deprived of the priesthood in the Hasmonaean period), together with their allies, envisaged a super-temporal, heavenly Temple, drawing on traditions of the First Temple and Ezekiel's vision, as one deduces from the Songs of the Sabbath Sacrifice and from the Blessings Scroll, both found at Qumran.[33] Parallel to the heavenly Temple in the world of the Merkavah was a 'sanctuary of men' for the priests and other members of the Community—an expression occurring in 4QFlorilegium[34] and defined as follows: 'He has commanded that a Sanctuary of men be built for himself, that there they may send up, like the smoke of incense, the works of the Law.' The nature of this 'sanctuary of men' is described in detail in the Rule Scroll and in MMT. On the evidence of the scrolls, the members of the Community scrupulously observed the cyclic order of sabbaths and festivals according to the solar calendar, shared the cyclic celebrations of the sacred rites with the angels, and meticulously adhered to the stringent laws of purity and impurity that made it possible for them to keep angelic company. Before the schism became complete, probably in the early stages of the separation, when there was still some communication, the writers of MMT proposed the institution of alternative, pure rites, to replace the impure, false order prevailing in the earthly Temple;[35] elsewhere, however—as in the Temple Scroll, New Jerusalem, the Damascus Document, and the Rule of the Congregation of Israel at the End of Days—they appear to have lost hope of any further contact with the Temple of their times.

The works of this literature describe a different, gigantic, earthly Temple, or a future Temple built mostly according to a square plan measured in sevenfold

[32] Testament of Levi 14: 5–8; 15: 1–4; 16: 1; 17: 11. For further references to the defilement of the Temple see Jub. 23: 21; 1 En. 89: 73; Commentary on Habakkuk XII, 7–9; cf. Ezek. 23: 38; 4Q183, frg. 1 ii, 1; 4Q 390, frg. 2 i, 9–10.

[33] The description of the heavenly Temple in the Songs of the Sabbath Sacrifice, and of those serving in it, is based primarily on Ezekiel's vision of the Temple, on traditions relating to the desert sanctuary and the First Temple; see Strugnell, 'Angelic Liturgy'; Schiffman, 'Heikhalot Literature'; id., '*Merkavah* Speculation'; Newsom, *Songs*, 39–58; see also the references in n. 16 above. On the heavenly Temple in the liturgical work found at Qumran and known as the Blessings Scroll (4QBerakhot[a–e] = 4Q286–90) see *DJD* XI, 1–74, in particular pp. 12–13. Cf. Nitzan, *Qumran Prayer*, 112–24, 207–38.

[34] 4QFlorilegium (4Q174), frgs. 1–2 i: 7 (*DJD* V, 53; Vermes, *CDSSIE*, 493).

[35] On the proper cultic procedures see MMT, Messianic Rule, and the Temple Scroll. Based on stylistic and historical analysis of the mode of address, scholars believe that MMT was written in the early, formative stages of the Qumran Community, before the split became permanent; see *DJD* X, 109–21.

units, influenced by biblical traditions and by Ezekiel's vision of the Temple.[36] Between rejecting the contemporary, desecrated Temple, deploring the defiling rites performed in it by unworthy priests, and harbouring hopes for the reconstitution of the future Temple, with its legitimate cult restored, at the End of Days, the seceding priests seem to have focused their sacred service on the eternal heavenly Temple and its angelic cult.

The essential feature of the heavenly Temple—the world of the Merkavah—was its profound relationship with Ezekiel's Chariot Throne/Merkavah, the cherubim, and the sacred creatures, mounted in their four-faced spatial pattern and their sevenfold vertical pattern, representing sacred time measured in weeks/sabbaths and sacred place as embodied in seven *heikhalot* and seven *merkavot*. This chronotopic order, unifying time and place around a common sevenfold–fourfold axis, was associated with the mysteries of sanctity, eternity, communion, and life itself, with the mutual relationship between cycles of time, cycles of fertility, and tangible prototypes representing the mystery of hidden things. The concepts of season, cycle, sanctity, four/quarter, seven/week/oath (all three derive from the same root in Hebrew *sh–v–a*), purity and benediction, community and communion, all have double meanings, referring to sacred time and place alike and through them to the divine Covenant, to the cycle of seven festivals, to holiness and benediction. On the human plane, the same concepts are also associated with betrothal and union for purposes of fertility and reproduction, which involve cycles of ovulation counted in four-week periods, the seven-day term of purification, self-sanctification, covenant and oath, the seven benedictions of betrothal, the husband's conjugal duties, and the laws governing conjugal union.

Many of the spatial, temporal, ritual, and liturgical components of the heavenly Temple are arranged in a sevenfold pattern relating to time and place in a context of holiness: the seven days of Creation and their cyclic recurrence as fifty-two weeks, celebrated by the priestly courses performing their sacral duties in cycles of seven days and sequences of seven festivals; and by septuples of angels discharging their functions in similar fashion. Alongside this sevenfold motif, as noted above, was a fourfold motif: four seasons of the year, four points of the compass, twelve diagonal boundaries, twelve months of the solar year, and twelve signs of the zodiac. (Cultic representations in the earthly Temple of this sevenfold and twelvefold order, such as the seven-branched candelabrum, the twelve stones of the priest's breastplate, and so on, will be discussed later.) It was the task of the priests and their angelic counterparts to observe the seasons and festivals; that observance

---

[36] Ezek. 40–8. On the ideal Temple see Yadin (ed.), *Temple Scroll*; Broshi, 'Visionary Architecture'; Qimron, *Temple Scroll*. Cf. Herr, 'Jerusalem, the Temple, and the Temple Service'. For a summary of Temple Scroll research see Brooke (ed.), *Temple Scroll Studies*; Schiffman, 'Temple Scroll'; Qimron, *Temple Scroll*. The Temple Scroll is concerned with priestly halakhah in relation to the future Temple, along the lines of Ezekiel 40–8 according to the solar calendar, with paramount importance ascribed to the numbers seven and four. On the problematics of Ezekiel 40–8 see Zimmerli, *Ezekiel*.

was governed on the time axis by a synchronization of the calendar of sabbaths, divided into four equal quarters/seasons of thirteen sabbaths each, with the calendar of biblical festivals, which provided for seven festivals within a seven month period from Passover in the first month (Nisan) to the Festival of Ingathering in the seventh (Tishrei).[37] In this twenty-eight-week period there were four festivals of first fruits at intervals of seven sabbaths (the first two coinciding with the biblical festivals of Omer and Shavuot): the Festival of the First Barley (26 Nisan), the Festival of the First Wheat (15 Sivan), the Festival of the First Wine (3 Av), and the Festival of the First Olive Oil (22 Elul). They were always celebrated on a Sunday and involved pilgrimage to the Temple; they are detailed in the Temple Scroll and in MMT 4Q394, frgs. 1–2 i–v.

The components of the heavenly Temple constitute a multifaceted cosmic reality, unifying place, time, and ritual. The dimension of place is represented in myth and ritual, as we shall see later, by such elements as the Garden of Eden and the tree of life, Paradise (the mystical Pardes), the Merkavah, the Holy of Holies, the cherubim, conjugal union and communion; time is represented by the eternity of the cyclic laws of nature, which dictate, on the one hand, cycles of life and fertility and, on the other, the sequence of covenants and festivals; while ritual consists of sacred song, sacred service, blessing, and praise recited by priests and angels. The axis that holds all these disparate elements together is the number seven, which is common to the divine, sacred cycles of the seven days of Creation and the seven days of purification, the seven days of consecration (of the priests) and the seven appointed times, the seven benedictions, the seven branches of the candelabrum and the seven priestly vestments, and the whole complex of 'sevens' (or heptads) associated with the sacred service and specified in the Priestly Code.

All components of the Merkavah undergo a process of liturgical personification, by virtue of which they themselves become the bearers of sanctity and ritual. The ritual and liturgical elements were divided or multiplied by seven after experiencing a visionary metamorphosis that linked them to their divine origin, to become seven holy precincts, seven chariot thrones, seven *devirim* (Holies of Holies), seven *heikhalot*, and seven angelic priesthoods, in a vertical heavenly space comprising seven firmaments, as we read in the Songs of the Sabbath Sacrifice. This fixed *vertical* sevenfold axis of space is correlated with a cyclic *horizontal* axis of time: the sacred space is sliced, as it were, into horizontal septuples/heptads of time, invested with sanctity in accordance with the solar calendar, which itself is divided into sabbaths and weeks in a fixed, eternal, cyclic sequence preserved by angelic and priestly courses. This ritual and liturgical calendar, measured from the fourth day

---

[37] Here and at various other places throughout, the month names current in modern Hebrew have been included for the reader's convenience. These names, of post-exilic date and Babylonian origin, are well attested in the later books of the Bible, but it should be noted that in the Pentateuch and other priestly books, as in the Qumran literature, the months are identified not by name but by ordinal number ('the first month' etc.) or by reference to agricultural season.

of Creation—the day on which the heavenly luminaries were created—and onward, in regular, sevenfold cycles, is observed in the heavens by the princes of the angelic priesthoods, who recite the Songs of the Sabbath Sacrifice and continuously proclaim 'seven times with seven . . .'; and on earth by the twenty-four priestly courses, which share their sacral duties according to an immutable order, each for an appointed seven-day span. The names of the twenty-four priestly courses—whose number corresponds to the number of hours in a day—designate the order of succession of weeks in the ritual and liturgical calendar, in which each of the four seasons is a cycle of thirteen sabbaths.

The system of priestly courses was based on 1 Chronicles 24, where the Chronicler, expressing priestly tradition, describes how King David and two leading priests, Zadok and Ahimelech, divided the two families of Aaronide priests, the descendants of Aaron's sons Eleazar and Itamar, into twenty-four divisions or 'courses'. Various historical problems are presented by this biblical tradition and the lists of priestly courses in the Bible. Whether the priestly courses were indeed established only in the early days of the Second Temple, as claimed by modern scholars,[38] or whether they in fact go back to the time of David and Solomon, in accordance with biblical tradition, Qumran writings surely considered them of paramount importance. The various fragments of the so-called 'Calendars of Priestly Courses' (also referred to as the Scroll of Priestly Courses, known in Hebrew as *mishmarot*) describe a sequence of twenty-four priestly courses, officiating in rotation for one week each in a fixed liturgical order, thus attesting to the fixed, cyclic rhythm of cosmic and liturgical time. The Calendars specify the name of the officiating course on the first day of each month, at each appointed time, and on each sabbath in a concise formulation, for example 'The first year; the first month; on the fifth, in Jedaiah, on the thirtieth of the month', that is, 'In the first year of the six-year cycle, in the first month [Nisan], on the fifth day [= Thursday] of the week of [the course of] Jedaiah, which falls on the thirtieth of the first month.' Only the priestly courses serving in the first week of the month are named, as well as those serving on festivals; the other courses officiated consecutively in the prescribed order. Days of the week are also specified with reference to the priestly courses then on duty, for example 'Creation, on the fourth, in Gamul', that is, 'On the fourth day [= Wednesday] of the week of the course of Gamul will fall the New Year of the week of Creation.' The lunar phases (new moon, full moon, etc.) and times relating to sabbatical and jubilee years are also stated in that way. The underlying reference system is thus a sequence of six-year cycles, rigidly prescribed over periods of six jubilees.

---

[38] Both Liver, *History of the Priesthood and the Levites*, 33, and Japhet, *I and II Chronicles*, 429, argue, relying on critical analysis, that the division into priestly courses was not established until the Second Temple period, though Liver suggests that the Chronicler was relying on some kind of division that actually existed in the First Temple (op. cit. 49). The full editions of the lists of priestly courses from Qumran, which were published in the 1990s, may change these assessments.

In order to prevent any possible desecration of the sabbath, each course, having served its term of duty, was replaced by its successor on the morning of the Sunday of the new week.[39] Rabbinical tradition, in contrast, decreed that the rotation should take place on the sabbath itself, after the additional sacrifice of the sabbath had been offered.[40] Indeed, the Sages did not prescribe a fixed order of service; instead, lots were drawn during the pilgrimage festivals in Jerusalem to determine which priestly course would serve first, the rest continuing in order.[41]

The six-year cycle was necessary to correlate the calendar of priestly courses with the solar calendar. Indeed, elementary arithmetic shows that the lowest common multiple of the two numbers 24 (the number of courses) and 364 (the number of days in a (solar) year) is $2,184 = 6 \times 364$. Thus, for example, the priestly course on duty in the first week of the year (which began on a Wednesday) would come back to the same week after a cycle of six years, during which it would have served a total of thirteen times. The New Year festival—the first day of the first month—in the first and fourth years of the six-year cycle always fell on a Wednesday, the day on which the heavenly luminaries had been created. This was also the vernal equinox, when day and night are of equal length; and since the moon was created full, it is full on both those days. In other words, once in three years, on the first day of the first month (Nisan), the sun's and moon's paths return to their position at Creation; this event is referred to in Qumran literature as a sign, Heb. *ot*. According to Milik,[42] thirty days were added every three years to co-ordinate the paths of the sun and the moon ($364 \times 3 = 354 \times 3 + 30$). Another possibility, more plausible, is that a week was added every seven years in the sabbatical year (*shemitah*) ($7 \times 365 = 7 \times 364 + 7$).

As against the *mishmarot* scrolls with their twenty-four courses as in the Bible, the number prescribed in the War Scroll is twenty-six, which is half the number of weeks in the solar year:

The fathers of the Community are fifty-two. The chief priests shall be appointed after the High Priest and his deputy, twelve chiefs to serve always before God. And the twenty-six chiefs of the courses shall serve in the courses. After them the chief Levites, to serve always twelve, one for each tribe, and the chiefs of their courses shall serve, each in his place. And the chiefs of the tribes and fathers of the Community after them, to attend always at the gates of the Temple. And the chiefs of their courses, with their numbered men, shall attend at their appointed times, at the beginnings of months and on Sabbaths, and on all the days of the year.[43]

---

[39] See Talmon, 'Calendrical Calculation', 96.
[40] Mishnah *Tam.* 5: 1; *Suk.* 5: 8; see also Josephus, *Antiquities*, VII. xiv. 7.
[41] Mishnah *Ta'an.* 4: 2; BT *Suk.* 48a.
[42] *Ten Years of Discovery*, 110–13; *Books of Enoch*, 274–5.
[43] War Scroll II, 1–4 (Vermes, *CDSSIE*, 164).

This may be a reference to a system based on the number of weeks in a half-year.[44] Another possibility is that the War Scroll was referring to some ideal, eschatological situation featuring a sevenfold correlation between weeks, courses, and years.

Various inscriptions listing priestly courses have been found, both in the Land of Israel (Caesarea, Ashkelon, Kisufim, Beit El, Rehov, Nazareth) and elsewhere (Yemen); their presence is undoubtedly linked with the move of priests to Galilee after the Bar-Kokhba revolt. The question of the relationship between these inscriptions and the Qumran tradition of priestly courses and their preservation of liturgical order has yet to be studied. The same applies to a possible relationship with the evidence of priestly and liturgical traditions in Heikhalot literature, written long after the destruction of the Temple (see below, Ch. 10), when the priestly courses were meaningless as an organizational framework for Temple service. Their only possible significance then was to memorialize the sacred ritual and preserve its liturgical calendar.[45]

Sacred heavenly *space* exhibits a vertical sevenfold pattern; it is divided in the Songs of the Sabbath Sacrifice into 'seven lofty holy places', 'seven wondrous territories', 'seven holy mysteries', 'seven most holy precincts', 'seven *devirim* of the priesthoods', 'seven holy precincts', or into seven *heikhalot* in seven firmaments. But it also displays a fourfold pattern, exemplified by the four sides of the Chariot Throne, the four points of the compass, 'four foundations of the wondrous firmament'. In parallel to these spatial patterns the secessionist priests observed and preserved a fixed, eternal and continuous, cyclic, sevenfold pattern of sacred *time*, divided into four equal seasons. They regarded the cultic calendar that governed the sacred Temple services around the time of their secession—based on a lunar calendar of 354 days, counted in months of unequal length dependent on human discretion, based on variable human observations of the new moon—as false and arbitrary, an infringement of the Covenant, sinful and wicked. This newly imposed lunar calendar was to be replaced by the ancient priestly solar calendar, re-establishing the sacred ritual and liturgical calendar of divine origin, extant from the very beginning of time, characterized by a fixed, eternal, cosmic, sevenfold and fourfold symmetry, counted in sabbaths of days (= weeks) and cycles of annual seasons. The sacred divisions of the solar calendar are outlined by the Angel of the Countenance, speaking to Moses in Jubilees:

---

[44] See Yadin (ed.), *Scroll of the War*, 202–8; Talmon, 'Calendrical Calculation'; but cf. Talmon and Knohl, 'Calendrical Scroll', for a different explanation.

[45] For the fragmentary inscriptions see Klein, *Land of Galilee*, 64–70; Avi-Yonah, 'Inscription from Caesarea'; T. Kahana, 'Priests according to their Courses'. For a survey of scholarly views on the subject see Liver, *History of the Priesthood and the Levites*, 35–52; Trifon, 'Did the Priestly Courses Relocate . . .?'; Safrai, 'When did the Priests Relocate . . .?'

And all of the weeks which will be commanded will be fifty-two weeks of days, and all of them are a complete year. Thus it is engraved and ordained on the heavenly tablets. . . . And you, command the children of Israel so that they shall guard the years in this number, three hundred and sixty-four days, and it will be a complete year. And no one shall corrupt its (appointed) time from its days or from its feasts . . .[46]

This system was based on a solar calendar of 364 days, consisting of fifty-two weeks, whose sabbaths were counted in a fixed annual cycle, divided symmetrically among the four annual seasons, and on a prescribed mathematical calculation of the progress of the solar year: twelve thirty-day months, with four further days added to differentiate the four annual seasons. These 364 days were divided into four quarters, or seasons, each of thirteen weeks, which together constituted a year of fifty-two sabbaths.[47]

The principles of the beautiful, harmonic, mathematical calculation underlying the solar year, which according to priestly tradition derived from a divine origin, are enunciated in detail in 1 Enoch 72: 32, 74: 10–12; 75: 2; 82: 6; 2 Enoch 13–17, 41–8; Jubilees 6: 23–38; 4QMMT A II–III; Psalms Scroll 11QPsᵃ XXVII, 2–11; mention of these principles may also be found in the Temple Scroll, the Damascus Document, the Scroll of Priestly Courses, and the Songs of the Sabbath Sacrifice. The solar year began on the day on which the heavenly luminaries were created—Wednesday—and was divided into consecutive quarters of fixed structure: ninety-one days divided into thirteen weeks; the sabbaths fell on fixed dates—the same ones in each quarter; the days on which the first days of months and the festivals fell were also known in advance—always falling on the same day of the week, the festivals on the same day of the month and in the same position within the quarter. No festival could ever fall on a sabbath, and neither could the first day of any month; the solar calendar could be used to determine the cycles of service of the twenty-four priestly courses, in sevenfold cycles of sabbatical years and jubilees.

This calendar, 'ordained and written in the heavenly tablets' and imprinted in the cyclic laws of nature, divided into seasons and signs of the zodiac based on an underlying fourfold, annual principle, reflects the divine pattern of time—the

---

[46] Jub. 6: 30–2.

[47] On the calendar of the secessionist priesthood and the historical relationship between the solar and lunar calendars see Jaubert, 'Calendrier des Jubilées... Qumran'; id., 'Calendrier des Jubilées... semaine'; Talmon, 'Calendar of the Covenanters'; Milik, *Ten Years of Discovery*, 110–13; J. M. Baumgarten, 'Qumran Studies'; id., 'Beginning of the Day'; Talmon, 'Calendrical Calculation'; van Goudoever, *Biblical Calendars*; Yadin (ed.), *Scroll of the War*; id. (ed.), *Temple Scroll*, ii. 89–136; Ben-Shahar, 'Calendar of the Judaean Desert Sect'; Licht, 'Temporal Doctrine'; Herr, 'Calendar'; J. M. Baumgarten, *Studies in Qumran Law*, 101–42; VanderKam, 'Origin, Character and History'; J. M. Baumgarten, 'Calendars'; Talmon, *World of Qumran from Within*; VanderKam, 'Temple Scroll and Book of Jubilees'; Sussmann, 'History of Halakhah'; Sacchi, 'Two Calendars'; Maier, 'Shire Olat hash-Shabbat'; Stegemann, 'Qumran Essenes', 114–22; Chyutin, *War of Calendars*; VanderKam and Milik, '4Q Jub c(4Q218) and 4Q Jub e(4Q220)'; Talmon and Knohl, 'Calendrical Scroll'; Talmon, 'Calendar of the *yaḥad*'; VanderKam, *Calendars in the Dead Sea Scrolls*. For a brief account of various aspects of the solar calendar of Qumran, see pp. 82 ff. below.

The Solar Calendar: The First Seven Months According to the Priestly Calendar Scrolls

Katsir (harvest): First quarter

	Nisan: First month			Iyar: Second month			Sivan: Third month			Tamuz: Fourth	
I	**1** W	Vernal equinox; day of remembrance; start of Days of Consecration; start of first quarter		1 F			1 Su			**1** W	
	2 Th		V	2 **Sa**			2 M			2 Th	
	3 F			3 Su			3 T			3 F	
I	4 **Sa**			4 M			4 W		I	4 **Sa**	
	5 Su			5 T			5 Th			5 Su	
	6 M			6 W			6 F			6 M	
	7 T			7 T		X	7 **Sa**			7 T	
	8 W			8 F			8 Su			8 W	
	9 Th		VI	9 **Sa**			9 M			9 Th	
	10 F			10 Su			10 T			10 F	
II	11 **Sa**			11 M			11 W		II	11 **Sa**	
	12 Su			12 T			12 Th			12 Su	
	13 M			13 W			13 F			13 M	
	14 T	*Passover*		14 Th		XI	14 **Sa**			14 T	
	15 W	*Festival of Unleavened Bread*		15 F			**15** Su	*Shavuot; Festival of First Wheat*		15 W	
	16 Th		VII	16 **Sa**			16 M			16 Th	
	17 F			**17** Su	Start and end of Flood		17 T			17 F	
III	18 **Sa**			18 M			18 W		III	18 **Sa**	
	19 Su			19 T			19 Th			19 Su	
	20 M			20 W			20 F			20 M	
	21 T			21 Th		XII	21 **Sa**			21 T	
	22 W			22 F			22 Su			22 W	
	23 Th		VIII	23 **Sa**			23 M			23 Th	
	24 F			24 Su			24 T			24 F	
IV	25 **Sa**			25 M			25 W		IV	25 **Sa**	
	26 Su	*Omer (day of waving the sheaf); Festival of First Barley*		26 T			26 Th			26 Su	
	27 M			27 W			27 F			27 M	
	28 T			28 Th		XIII	28 **Sa**			28 T	
	29 W			29 F			29 Su			29 W	
	30 Th		IX	30 **Sa**			30 M			30 Th	
							31 T	Meeting Day			

Note: In each quarter there are thirteen Saturdays, marked with roman numerals; corresponding Saturdays in each quarter fall on the same date. Biblical festivals are marked in italic.

Left margin (continued): th — nmer stice; day of nembrance; rt of second arter

Av: Fifth month

Week	Day		Note
	1	F	
V	2	Sa	
	3	Su	Festival of First Wine
	4	M	
	5	T	
	6	W	
	7	T	
	8	F	
VI	9	Sa	
	10	Su	
	11	M	
	12	T	
	13	W	
	14	Th	
	15	F	
VII	16	Sa	
	17	Su	
	18	M	
	19	T	
	20	W	
	21	Th	
	22	F	
VIII	23	Sa	
	24	Su	
	25	M	
	26	T	
	27	W	
	28	Th	
	29	F	
IX	30	Sa	

Elul: Sixth month

Week	Day		Note
	1	Su	
	2	M	
	3	T	
	4	W	
	5	Th	
	6	F	
X	7	Sa	
	8	Su	
	9	M	
	10	T	
	11	W	
	12	Th	
	13	F	
XI	14	Sa	
	15	Su	
	16	M	
	17	T	
	18	W	
	19	Th	
	20	F	
XII	21	Sa	
	22	Su	Festival of First Olive Oil
	23	M	Start of Festival of Wood-Offering
	24	T	
	25	W	
	26	Th	
	27	F	
XIII	28	Sa	
	29	Su	
	30	M	
	31	T	Meeting Day

Tishrei: Seventh month

Week	Day		Note
	1	W	Autumnal equinox; day of remembrance; *Commemoration of Horn-Blowing*; start of third quarter
	2	Th	
	3	F	
I	4	Sa	
	5	Su	
	6	M	
	7	T	
	8	W	
	9	Th	
	10	F	*Day of Atonement*
II	11	Sa	
	12	Su	
	13	M	
	14	T	150 days from start of Flood
	15	W	*Sukkot (Festival of Booths)*; *Festival of Ingathering*
	16	Th	
	17	F	
III	18	Sa	
	19	Su	
	20	M	
	21	T	
	22	W	Eighth Day of Assembly
	23	Th	
	24	F	
IV	25	Sa	
	26	Su	
	27	M	
	28	T	
	29	W	
	30	Th	

seven days of Creation and the various sevenfold divisions derived therefrom—as well as the harmonic principle linking cosmic divine time, as revealed in nature, and cultic time, as entrusted to human beings.[48]

The sevenfold solar year, measuring time on the basis of a sacred principle amalgamating the cosmic, astronomical order and the ritual and liturgical order, was first learned from its guardians, the angels in heaven, who taught it to men in the time of Enoch, the seventh patriarch of the world, who in turn taught it to his descendants the priests Methuselah, Lamech, and Noah, as we read in the books of

---

[48] Jub. 32: 21; 1 En. 81: 1–2; 93: 1–3; 103: 2–3; etc. The opening part of Jubilees, as if complementing Exod. 24: 12–18, relates how the angels taught Moses the calendar one day after the theophany at Sinai. Opinions differ as to the date of composition of Jubilees, which was written in Hebrew, translated into Greek and Syriac, and then translated from the Greek into Latin and Ethiopic (Ge'ez). The only extant complete version is the Ethiopic, though some fragments of the Hebrew original were found at Qumran and Masada. Some authorities date the work to the beginning of the Hasmonaean period or thereabouts, between 170 and 150 BCE; some actually narrow the gap to 168–160 BCE. Nickelsburg dates it around 168 BCE. VanderKam favours the years 161–152 BCE, pointing to what he believes is an indirect reference to Judah Maccabee's battles in 161 (Jub. 34: 4–7). Mendels (*Land of Israel*, 57) rejects these early dates, holding that the book was written around 125 BCE. Wintermute, who translated the book from Ethiopic into English in Charlesworth (ed.), *OT Pseudepigrapha* (on the basis of the Charles edn. and comparison with the Syriac version and the Qumran fragments), reviews the palaeographic findings from Qumran; in his view, the Qumran fragments were written around 100 BCE, and the book itself in 152–140 BCE. A. Kahana dates the book after the death of John Hyrcanus (104 BCE), but before Herod's accession to the throne (37 BCE) (cf. *DJD* XIII, 6: 4Q216, frg. I, 3–12). Some indication of the work's date of composition may be the fact that the Ethiopian Jews (Beta Israel), who claim to be descended from Judahites exiled during the First Temple period, base their laws and festival calculations on the book of Jubilees.

For various aspects of Jubilees and its investigation see the following publications: A. Kahana (ed.), *Apocrypha*, i. 216–313; Jaubert, 'Calendrier des Jubilées... Qumran'; VanderKam, *Textual and Historical Studies*; Charlesworth (ed.), *OT Pseudepigrapha*; J. M. Baumgarten, 'Calendars'; Endres, *Biblical Interpretation*; J. M. Baumgarten, 'Qumran Sabbath *Shirot*'; VanderKam, 'Temple Scroll and Book of Jubilees'; id., *Book of Jubilees*; id., 'Jubilees Fragments'; id. and Milik, '4Q Jub c(4Q218) and 4Q Jub e(4Q220)'; *DJD* XIII; Kugel, 'Levi's Elevation to the Priesthood'; Werman, 'Attitude to Gentiles'.

Jubilees assigns particular sanctity to the tribe of Levi. It also hallows the sabbath and various sevenfold calculations in numerous contexts, and its laws concerning them are exceptionally strict. In Jubilees, the Hebrew word *shavua* means not, as often in the Bible, 'week', but a period of seven years (as in Dan. 9: 24–7); while the word *yovel*, 'jubilee', denotes a period of forty-nine years, in contrast to its biblical connotation of the fiftieth year, after seven sabbatical periods (Lev. 25). All these 'sevens' are derived from the verses telling of Sarah's death: 'And all the days of the life of Sarah were one hundred and twenty-seven. These are two jubilees and four weeks (of years) and one year. These are the days of the life of Sarah' (Jub. 19: 7), that is, $49+49+28+1=127$. Jaubert has pointed out the unique features of the priestly calendar of Jubilees, which recounts the dates of the Israelites' travels in the desert in order to prove that they did not travel on the sabbath. The important days in the festival calendar are Sunday, on which the elevation of the Omer (the first barley) falls, as well as the festivals of Shavuot and the first fruits of wine and oil; Wednesday, the day on which the luminaries were created, and on which Passover, Sukkot, and the first days of the four quarters fall; and Friday, on which the Day of Atonement falls. According to the solar calendar every month will start on one of these days in the order Wednesday, Friday, Sunday. As already mentioned, according to Jaubert's analysis, the books of Chronicles, Ezra, Nehemiah, and Ezekiel are based on a solar calendar of 364 days, as is the book of Jubilees.

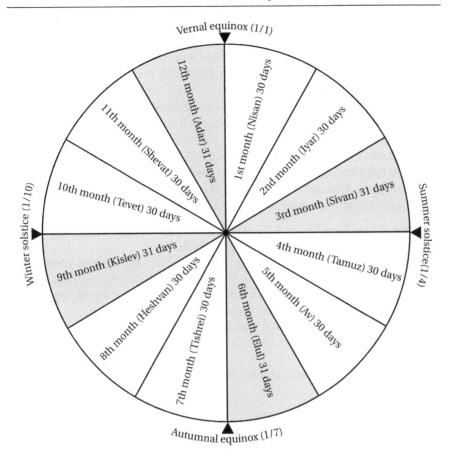

Vernal equinox (1/1)

12th month (Adar) 31 days

1st month (Nisan) 30 days

11th month (Shevat) 30 days

2nd month (Iyar) 30 days

10th month (Tevet) 30 days

3rd month (Sivan) 31 days

Winter solstice (1/10)

Summer solstice (1/4)

9th month (Kislev) 31 days

4th month (Tamuz) 30 days

8th month (Heshvan) 30 days

5th month (Av) 30 days

7th month (Tishrei) 30 days

6th month (Elul) 31 days

Autumnal equinox (1/7)

Schematic priestly solar calendar according to the Qumran Scrolls, Jubilees, and Enoch

Enoch. It was later learned in Moses' day too, for he learned it on Mount Sinai on the 16th of the third month, after being given the Torah on the 15th, from the Angel of the Countenance.[49] Qumran literature also refers in this way to the high priest, of whom it was said, 'May you be like an Angel of the Countenance in the Abode of Holiness, to the glory of God before you . . .'.[50] Moses then imparted what he had heard from the angel to his brother, Aaron the priest, who became the cultic guardian of that information, as we read in Jubilees. From then on the solar calendar of sabbaths and festivals, seasons and jubilees, was in the keeping of the witnesses to the Covenant, angels and priests—the ministering angels known as the 'priests of the inner sanctum' and the Zadokite priests serving in the sanctuary.

[49] 1 En. 72–3; Jub. 6: 17–29; 2 En. 13–17, 48 ff.; Jub. 1: 1.
[50] Blessings IV, 25 (cf. Vermes, *CDSSIE*, 376).

Subsequently, the order of sabbaths and festivals was observed by the twenty-four priestly courses in Solomon's Temple, until the time of the Second Temple. The fifty-two weeks of the solar year were named in a multi-annual cyclic order after the twenty-four priestly courses and correlated with the fifty-two 'fathers of the Community', as noted in the War Scroll.[51]

That there was a cultic link between the solar calendar and the high priesthood of First Temple times follows from the fact that the guardians of the Qumranic liturgical tradition of the Temple associated the psalms of David, which they believed to have been revealed to the seventh son of Jesse, a fourteenth-generation descendant of Abraham,[52] in a prophetic vision, on the one hand, and the sequence of sabbaths and festivals as recorded in the sacrificial order of Temple service according to the solar calendar, which was of divine origin:

David son of Jesse was wise and brilliant like the light of the sun; (he was) a scribe, intelligent and perfect in all his ways before God and men.

And YHWH gave him an intelligent and brilliant spirit, and he wrote 3,600 psalms and 364 songs to sing before the altar for the daily perpetual sacrifice, for all the days of the year; and 52 songs for the Sabbath offerings; and 30 songs for the offerings for the beginnings of months, for all the festivals and for the Day of Atonement.

In all, the songs which he uttered were 446, and 4 songs to make music on the intercalary days.

In all, they were 4,050.

All these he uttered through prophecy which was given him from before the Most High.[53]

The calendar alluded to in this passage—the earliest source ascribing the composition of the book of Psalms to David—refers to a year of 364 days on which the songs accompanying the daily sacrifice were recited; to fifty-two weeks on which the sabbath sacrifice was offered; and to thirty songs sung on the thirty days on which an additional sacrifice was offered: that is, the twelve first days of months and the seven Temple festivals celebrated between the first and seventh months— 'all the festivals' listed in Leviticus 23, on which sacrifices were offered to God, which amount to eighteen days (Passover—1, the Festival of Unleavened Bread— 7; the Omer—1; the Festival of Weeks (Shavuot)—1; the Day of Atonement (Yom

---

[51] War Scroll II, 1–4.   [52] 1 Chr. 2: 3–16.

[53] 11QPs[a] XXVII, 2–11 (cf. Vermes, *CDSSIE*, 307); see DJD IV, 48; Sanders, *Dead Sea Psalms Scroll*; Talmon, 'Apocryphal Psalms'; id., 'Covenanters' Calendar'; Flint, *Dead Sea Psalms Scrolls*. According to the Tosefta, 'The Hallel is recited on eighteen days of the year' (*Suk.* 3: 2; cf. BT *Arakh.* 20a–b). However, the number of festival days is different, as this includes Hanukah, which was not counted as a festival by the Qumran Community. (The War Scroll II, 1 ff., mentions fifty-two 'fathers of the Community', as against the fifty-two sabbaths, and twelve 'chief priests', as against the twelve months; see p. 43 above.) On the additional Temple festivals mentioned in the Temple Scroll and the Calendar of Priestly Courses see n. 59 below. However, these festivals did not have the same standing as those of Leviticus and therefore had no special songs. See further 11QPs[a] XXVII, 2–11 (*DJD* IV, 91–3), and the studies of the calendar cited in n. 47 above.

Kippur)—1; and the Festival of Ingathering—7). Special songs were composed for these eighteen days. Four further songs were added, for the days at the junctures of the four seasons; these days were known as 'meeting (day)s' (Heb. *peguim*: see Gen. 32: 2).[54] As stated, the calendar was divided into fifty-two sabbaths designating fifty-two weeks, each of seven days, amounting all in all to the 364 days of the solar year.

The 4,050 psalms and songs that David composed were divided into three groups: 4,050 = 3,600 + 446 + 4, representing a ritual and liturgical calendar: 3,600 psalms, that is, ten times the number 360 of days in the solar year ($4 \times 90 = 360 = 12 \times 30$), on each of which ten psalms were recited; 446 songs for the cumulative total of days on which sacrifices were offered: 364 days of the 'perpetual' daily sacrifice, fifty-two days of the sabbath sacrifice, and thirty days (the festivals and the first days of months) on which an additional sacrifice was offered ($364 + 52 + 30 = 446$); and, finally, the four 'meeting' songs for the days between each two of the four seasons. On the basis of this calendar, the Temple year was divided into four ritual and liturgical quarters, each with the same number of days, sabbaths, and months; accordingly, this rich poetic opus was also divided into four. Thus we find at Qumran thirteen Songs of the Sabbath Sacrifice, which were probably recited four times a year, on the fifty-two sabbaths. Most probably, the book of Psalms, both the familiar traditional text and the recensions found at Qumran, contained songs and hymns representing a fourfold division of the poems and songs to accompany the various sacrifices offered on weekdays, sabbaths, and festivals, and of the poems accompanying the cyclic sequence of the Temple service, which as we have observed was correlated with the cosmic order of the seasonal cycle.

The basic idea of the calendar of fifty-two sabbaths was to consecrate the pattern of time beginning with the seven days of Creation, extending in sevenfold cyclic symmetry over the whole year. In addition, the annual cycle of sabbaths and weeks was synchronized with the fourfold cycle of the year, by dividing it into four symmetric periods of thirteen sabbaths each, co-ordinated with the cycle of thirteen Songs of the Sabbath Sacrifice ($91 : 13 = 7$; $52 \times 7 = 4 \times 91 = 364$). Special importance attached to the seventh (middle) sabbath in each of the thirteen-sabbath cycles, which always fell on the 16th of the month in the second, fifth, eighth, and eleventh months of the year and was the midpoint of the division of the whole ninety-one-day season.

---

[54] The archaic 360-day Egyptian solar year added similar intercalary days, which were not counted as part of the year. Cf. 1 En. 72–82, which deal with these added days, and esp. 75: 1–2; 82: 4–6. Sanders, editor of the Psalms Scroll (see previous note), dates the manuscript of the scroll to the first half of the 1st century CE, in the Herodian period, but he does not discuss the possible date of composition of the apocryphal psalms in his edition. On David as the seventh see Ch. 8, n. 106. For the relationship between the psalms and songs that he composed and the calendar of festivals and sacrifices see 1 Chr. 23: 30–1; Ben Sira 47: 13–14.

The division into sabbaths was the basis for the division of twenty-four priestly courses, which served in the Temple twice a year in six-year cycles: each of the twenty-four courses served thirteen times in six years. As seen above, the division into thirteen sabbaths per quarter and thirteen cycles of service of the twenty-four priestly courses was a consequence of the fact that there were thirteen twenty-eight-day cycles in a solar year ($13 \times 28 = 364$), corresponding to thirteen lunar cycles—but also to thirteen cycles of fertility each year in a woman's body, as will be seen below. The product of the numbers 4 [annual cyclic seasons/quarters/annual liturgical and ritual units] and 7 [days of the week/seventh day/weekly liturgical and ritual units] is 28, which is counted 13 times [cycle/period = monthly cycle/lunar cycle/new moon] in the solar year of 364 days.

The priestly Temple calendar of the solar year, embodying the assumption that cosmic order was revealed through harmony as expressed in number, counting, and cycle, was associated with the mythological tradition of Enoch son of Jared, the seventh patriarch of the world;[55] with the perception of the sabbath as symbolizing the sanctity invested in the universe since the week of Creation and forming a link between the seventh day and the oath, 'a covenant for all time; it shall be a sign for all time';[56] with the seven days of ordination at the start of the year, beginning with the fourth day, on which the heavenly luminaries were created; and with Shavuot, the Festival of Weeks/Oaths, celebrated seven sabbaths after the elevation of the Omer. The continuous calculations of the solar calendar revolved around a seven-fold axis, associated with the fifty-two sabbaths of the year, on which the sabbath sacrifice was offered; with the seven Temple festivals—which, together with the fifty-two sabbaths, make up a total of seventy days of complete cessation of labour; and with festivals celebrating the first harvests of wine and olive oil and the Wood-Offering, all of which revolved around a pentecostal axis, each festival being celebrated on the fiftieth day, after seven sabbaths, that is, after seven complete weeks ($7 \times 7 + 1 = 50$).

The agricultural sacral year extended over the period elapsing from the elevation of the Omer to the Festival of Ingathering—seven months, from the first month (Nisan) to the seventh (Tishrei); or from the Festival of Unleavened Bread, which fell on the 15th of the first month and was celebrated for seven days (from the 15th to the 21st), to the Festival of Booths (Sukkot), which coincided with the seven days of the Festival of Ingathering in the middle of the seventh month. The festivals thus began in the middle of the first month with a seven-day festival and ended in the middle of the seventh month with another seven-day festival; they were celebrated at intervals of seven sabbaths (seven complete weeks), as described in the Temple Scroll[57] and in MMT.[58] Seven weeks elapsed from the elevation of the Omer (the sheaf of the wave-offering—the first produce of barley) on Sunday,

---

[55] Gen. 5: 21–4.   [56] Exod. 31: 13–17.
[57] XI, 10–13; XXXVIII, 4–5 plus 4Q 365; XVIII, 10–14; XIX, 9–16; XXI, 12–16; XXIII, 10–11; XLIII, 3–10.   [58] 4Q 394, frgs. 1–2 i–v (*DJD* X, 7, 45).

the 26th of the first month (Nisan), to Shavuot (marking the first wheat harvest) on Sunday, the 15th of the third month (Sivan). Another seven weeks separated the 15th of the third month from the first harvest of wine on Sunday, the 3rd of the fifth month (Av). Still another seven weeks elapsed until the first harvest of olive oil on Sunday, the 22nd of the sixth month (Elul), and the next day—Monday— was the time of the Wood-Offering, which began on the 23rd of the month and lasted six days. In other words, the Festival of the First Olive Oil and the Wood-Offering were consecutive, forming a seven-day festival, seven full weeks after the Festival of the First Wine.[59] The ritual year ended with the seven days of the Festival of Ingathering, halfway through the seventh month.

All these elements formed a link between two manifestations of sacred time. One was the permanent recurrence of the four seasons and the cycles of the agricultural year, whose first produce, of 'seven species' (barley, wheat, olive oil, wine, and the ingathering of fruit, completed by the addition of the Wood-Offering), was brought to the Temple at seven-week intervals, during the first seven months of the year. The other manifestation was the ritual determinism of the preordained

[59] Temple Scroll XVII, 10–XXIII, 9; see Yadin (ed.), *Temple Scroll*, i. 89–136; Qimron, *Temple Scroll*, 20, 28, 29, 54; and cf. *DJD* XXIII, 374–82, as well as the opening passage of MMT. On the Festivals of the First Olive Oil and the Wood-Offering see Wacholder and Abegg, *Preliminary Edition*, i. 86–7. The Festivals of the First Oil and the Wood-Offering, celebrated seven weeks (or fifty days) after the Festival of the First Wine and seven weeks apart from each other, are not explicitly mentioned in the Bible; nevertheless, it seems clear that they derive from the biblical sources referring to the privileges of the Levites serving in the Temple: 'All the best of the new oil, wine, and grain—the choice parts that they present to the Lord—I give to you. The first fruits of everything in their land, that they bring to the Lord, shall be yours' (Num. 18: 12–13); 'You shall also give him the first fruits of your new grain and wine and oil, and the first shearing of your sheep' (Deut. 18: 4). For the Wood-Offering, see Neh. 10: 34–40: 'to bring the wood-offering to the House of our God by clans annually at set times . . . We will bring to the storerooms of the House of our God the first part of . . . the fruit of every tree, wine and oil for the priests . . . For it is to the storerooms that the Israelites and the Levites must bring the gifts of grain, wine, and oil.' The biblical formulation should be compared with that of Qumran: 'Grain, wine, and oil, and all produce . . . and all elevated offerings of the world in twelve months' (4QBer^a (= 4Q286), frg. 5, 6–7: *DJD* XI, 22–3). See also Temple Scroll LIX–LX (García Martínez and Tigchelaar, *Study Edition*, ii. 1051; Yadin, *Temple Scroll*, i. 99–122), and the parallel 4Q 524 published by Puech in *DJD* XXV, 95: 'And he shall give the priest . . . and the first fruits of their grain, their wine and their oil (l. 6) . . . And for the Levites, a tithe of grain, wine and oil, which they consecrated to me at first (l. 10)'. Cf. Jub. 7: 36: 'And let one offer up the first fruits which are acceptable before the Lord Most High, Who made heaven and earth and everything, so that they might offer up as a whole-offering the first of the wine and the oil as first fruits upon the altar of the Lord, Who will accept it. And that which is left the servants of the house of the Lord will eat before the altar . . .'.

The calendar in MMT is consistent with the 364-day calendar mentioned in the apocryphal psalms (11QPs^a XXVII, 2–11), in Jubilees, in 1 Enoch 72–8, and in the Temple Scroll. Cf. Jaubert, 'Calendrier des Jubilées. . . Qumran'; id., 'Calendrier des Jubilées. . . semaine'; Maier, 'Shire Olat hash-Shabbat'. Philo, in his account of the *Therapeutae* in *De vita contemplativa*, describes their life as a continuous sequence of seven-week periods, with each fiftieth day sanctified (Philo, *On the Contemplative Life or Suppliants*, 65, in *Collected Works*, ix. 152–3). A celebration after fifty days is also mentioned in the apocryphal book of Tobit; see Ch. 6, n. 22. Yadin (*Temple Scroll*, i. 119–22) discusses other calendars based on counting consecutive sequences of seven weeks.

calendar, based on a divine sevenfold pattern of sacred heavenly time; this time, given the status of an oath and a 'covenant for all time', was measured in sabbaths and weeks in cycles of four seasons, representing the continuity of the cosmic order, but also in terms of times of first yields, weekly divisions, and seven days of ordination, representing the parallel cultic order.

The cosmic clock of nature as measured in the solar calendar, with time demarcated in multiples of 7, 13, and 4 ($4 \times 7 \times 13 = 364$)—each sabbath being the seventh day, thirteen sabbaths in each ritual quarter of the liturgical cycle, i.e. in each of the four seasons—also governed another set of thirteen: any woman's thirteen fertile periods, once every four weeks, in the 364-day year ($364 = 4 \times 7 \times 13$). These calculations were all based on the idea of an all-embracing divine presence, beyond the limits of human apprehension but manifested in a permanent, cyclic, numerical harmony—a harmony based on data not subject to erratic human observation. In other words, the priestly calculations were supposed to evoke an abstract, harmonic, cosmic order, revealed in cyclic relations and recurrences of numbers; whereas the calculations of the rival lunar calendar were founded on erroneous sensory data, dependent on the limits of human visualization.

All this seven-based counting, as we have seen, was associated on the one hand with sabbaths, festivals, and agricultural fertility as laid down in a permanent solar calendar. It represented divine, mathematical time flowing at a fixed rate, without regard for human comprehension, as reflected in the creative process of nature or the rhythm of fertility of Creation and Covenant, of nature and the seasons. On the other hand, every woman has a variable, personal calendar of weeks, which also involves counting in sevens. This personal calendar reflects the rhythm of human procreation—the cycle of fertility/infertility which a woman experiences every four weeks, which guarantees the fertile period following the seven days of purification and hence the very possibility of conception, birth, growth, and life. The synchronization achieved by such seven-based counting ensured fulfilment of the Covenant of continued life and procreation which, like nature itself, depended on a fixed number of cycles. As if to confirm this link between seven-based counting and procreation, only two commandments in the Bible are referred to as a 'covenant': the sabbath, which is called an 'everlasting covenant',[60] observed once every seven days and delineating the basic unit of the cosmic ritual order—the week; and circumcision, also called an 'everlasting covenant',[61] observed seven days after the birth of a son—the result of conception, which, too, occurs after the observance of seven days in the mother's personal calendar of purification, also measured in weeks. The two commandments involving the number seven, one termed 'a sign for all time' and the other an 'everlasting covenant', are associated with an eternal covenant between God and his people: for the sabbath, seven days are counted repeatedly, throughout the annual cycle of agricultural fertility; and

---

[60] Exod. 31: 12–17.   [61] Gen. 17: 12–13.

for the seven days of purification, seven days are counted repeatedly throughout a woman's personal cycle of fertility.

The rhythm of feminine fertility is associated with the cycle of the moon with its phases; indeed, the Hebrew word for the waxing of the moon, *ibur*, also means 'conception'; while the Hebrew word for the appearance of the new moon, *molad*, is of the same root (*w-l-d*) as the word *ledah*, 'birth', and its cognates; similarly, the words that refer to a woman's monthly cycle may also be applied to the lunar phases. Both cycles are associated with the passage of four weeks. A menstruating woman is forbidden to her husband until seven 'clean' days (i.e. days on which no blood whatsoever has been seen) have elapsed, and only then—when the probability of conception is highest—may cohabitation occur. The ritual calendar was concerned with the Temple and the Holy of Holies; with sabbaths, festivals, and sacrifices; with purity and impurity; with sabbatical years and jubilees. The personal calendar was associated with sanctification, betrothal, isolation (when a woman is menstruating or otherwise 'unclean'), purification, and cohabitation. Both calendars, as we have seen, were marked off in sevens; both guaranteed continued fertility, the eternal continuity of life as dependent on a sevenfold rhythm; and both involved counting and number, oath and covenant, testimony and set times, holiness and sanctification, unification and separation, the eternity of Creation. On the one hand, the year is divided into weeks, which delineate the cycle of fertility and agricultural yields, as well as the phases of the moon; on the other, the seven days of purification guarantee the maximum probability of conception, birth, and the continuation of life.

It is not insignificant that the sanctity and purity which condition manifestations of life and fertility are bound up with numbers and cycles, while impurity and death have no numerical or other measure. Very probably, the sacred creatures/cherubim, which various traditions portray as if their bodies were 'intertwined with one another', possibly alluding to sexual intimacy (see below), were originally a cultic representation of the secret of life and cycles of fertility. There is thus an affinity between the sanctity of the Temple, ceremonially expressed through interlocking septuples of time, place, and ritual in the Holy of Holies (*kodesh kodashim*) and symbolizing the link between the revealed and the concealed, and *kidushin*, 'sanctification', the Hebrew term for betrothal and conjugal union—a personal covenant whose purpose is to perpetuate life, also associated with ceremony and number, with cycle and counting, with sanctity and purity. Both the sanctity of the Temple and betrothal connect with the number seven, with oaths, with 'a covenant for all time', with blessing and fertility and the cycle of life.

The relationship between the divinely preordained, eternal, cosmic pattern of sacred time and the solar calendar representing it, on the one hand, and the tradition of covenants, sacrifices, and agricultural sacral festivals of sacred space and time, on the other, is described in Jubilees and the Temple Scroll. It is a deterministic relationship, linking the eternity of the natural cycles with the eternity of the

Deity; it posits a permanent, cyclic, sevenfold pattern of divine time, which governs both seasonal changes and agricultural yields, and the ritual of the priestly courses in the Temple, through the latter's dependence on the solar calendar. The cosmic time concept, reflecting a divine reality beyond the apprehension of human observation and based on a permanent, cyclic, mathematical calculation, was quantified by the endless recurrence of the calendar from beginning to end, demarcated in sevens and multiples of seven, in fourfold cycles of thirteen.

This numerical conception, rooted in the symmetric, cyclic recurrence of four seasons, but also associated with the cycles of continued life and reproduction in nature, celebrating the first fruits and other agricultural produce at seven-week intervals, supplanted the conception of human, variable time underlying the lunar calendar. Human time was based on the estimated sighting of the new moon—an act of human observation and discretion—and on historical and national vicissitudes, rather than on cosmic, cyclic events. This human element led the secessionist priesthood, as we shall see, to reject the cult based on the lunar calendar, as well as the familiar, historical reasons for the festivals. They abhorred a conception of time based on human sovereignty, relying on variable counting and thereby on humanly observable data, which were inherently changeable and subordinate to variable human needs. Instead, they advocated a cosmic conception of time, based on permanent numerical calculation and thereby rooted in a comprehensive, eternal, abstract, divine reality, beyond the reach of the senses and of human observation, but measured in the permanent numerical proportions of the elements of the solar calendar.

Thus, the seven-based solar calendar, fixed and stable since antiquity, was symmetrically, harmonically, and cyclically structured; it was based on synchronization of the four seasons with sevenfold cycles of sabbaths and festivals—all dependent on calculations reflecting a world whose laws and order were open to systematic discovery and expression. The keepers of sabbaths and festivals according to this calendar saw themselves as initiates privy to wondrous mysteries, or to a divine revelation that explicated the secrets of time. In their own eyes, they were the guardians of divine times and festivals, celebrating covenants and cycles of agricultural produce, testifying to the annual seasons and the sabbaths of the year; their task was to preserve the secret pattern of the order of divine time, with its implications for agricultural plenty and the continuity of life:

But with the remnant which held fast to the commandments of God He made His Covenant with Israel for ever, revealing to them the *hidden things* in which all Israel had gone astray. He unfolded before them His holy Sabbaths and His glorious feasts, the testimonies of His righteousness and the ways of His truth, and the desires of His will which a man must do in order to *live*.[62]

---

[62] Damascus Document III, 12–16 (Vermes, *CDSSIE*, 129; italics mine). In regard to those who 'had gone astray' in their understanding of the calendar cf. 1 En. 80: 2–8.

The unstable ritual year governing the sacred service in the Second Temple period—based on the false, variable, lunar year with its unreliable concept of time dependent on human observation, estimation, and discretion; a year in which the first days of months and festivals wandered from one day of the week to another— was condemned by the seceding priests as a sinful, blasphemous violation of the Covenant. The practices of the then officiating Temple priests were seen as impure and defiled: they had rejected the cyclic, cosmic, harmonic 'clock' of nature, measured by mathematical calculation, of the solar calendar, and the seasons counted in sevens ('mysteries of marvels'), in favour of an arbitrary 'clock', based on observation of the appearance of the new moon, which had nothing to do with the preordained and precalculated cyclic, symmetric, permanent, regular order of things. This condemnation is clearly implied by the highly polemical tone of Jubilees, MMT, the Damascus Document, the *pesharim*, the Rule Scroll, and the Temple Scroll.

As against the defiled Temple, distorted calendar, and sinful priesthood, which had arbitrarily caused this chaotic dislocation of the sacred service, defiled the Temple, and disturbed the synchronization of the set times of fertility and those of the Temple—as described in considerable detail in Qumran literature, both in terms of myth and vision and in terms of law and precept—the priestly authors envisioned a horizontal, seven-based pattern of divine time, reflecting a perfect, harmonic, world order and dictating a fixed, preordained continuum of appointed times, covenants, and oaths, as laid down in the solar calendar with its four seasons and twelve months of equal length. But their vision also included a vertical seven-based pattern of sacred, heavenly space, linked with the four cardinal directions that engender the universe and its fourfold and twelvefold divisions, in accordance with the tradition of the four-faced Merkavah and the diverse spatial elements associated with it: cherubim and sacred creatures, the Garden of Eden and Paradise, *peruyim* and *apiryon* (both words from a Hebrew root with the connotation of 'fertility'), the 'eternal plantation', 'sacred plantation', and 'plantation of righteousness'; and the seven-based sanctuary, the 'seven holy precincts', the seven Heikhalot, and the twelve diagonal boundaries. The third overarching component of the secessionist priesthood's vision was the ritual seven-based pattern of the angelic service and sacred song, also associated with the Merkavah tradition, with the sacred service and the Songs of the Sabbath Sacrifice sung by seven angelic priesthoods, with the 'seven words of wondrous exaltations' sung every seven days, in accordance with the weeks of the solar calendar, in the seven supernal sanctuaries.

Alongside the seven-based pattern, there was also a fourfold/twelvefold pattern: the four archangels Uriel, Raphael, Gabriel, and Michael; the four faces of the sacred creatures; the twelve heavenly gates, the twelve months and signs of the zodiac; the twelve tribes; the twelve gates of the Temple; the twelve stones of the breastplate; the twelve leaders of the Community; the twelve diagonal boundaries dividing the space of the universe into twenty-four parts, correlated with the twenty-four priestly courses; and so on. This ritual and chronotopic unity bound together sacred time and sacred space in a ritual continuum; it thus amalgamated the concepts of cosmic and earthly time, space, and ritual, around one single sacred prototype, all of whose components were interdependent and interlocked.[63]

These priestly circles expressed profound identification with the angels—guardians of the covenants and the oaths, the sabbaths, the weeks, and the festivals, as engraved on the heavenly tablets; guardians of the gates and entrances representing the days, months, and seasons of the year.[64] They described priestly and angelic liturgical ceremonies, organized in a sevenfold order according to the eternal, sacred solar calendar; they envisaged a community of angelic priests in the world of the Merkavah and in the 'sanctuary of man' (Songs of the Sabbath Sacrifice, Florilegium). In place of the arbitrary, sinful, chaotic, and distorting ritual of the human priests, which divorced time from space, disturbed ritual cosmic synchronization, defiled the Temple, and endangered the cycles of life and fertility, they envisaged a heavenly cult of angelic priests, a sacred ritual archetype, organized in an eternal, harmonic, seven-based pattern, in which the days of the year defined an orderly, symmetrical continuum in sacred space. This rite, with its cyclic, mathematical patterns delineated by the sabbaths and the festivals, rooted in divine paths of righteousness, observed in purity and sanctity by the priestly courses simultaneously with their angelic counterparts, was designed to uphold the Covenant, the blessing, the eternity of life and fertility for the guardians of the covenants and the festivals, of sanctity and purity.[65]

In the various Merkavah traditions and the writings of the Community (or, as already noted, the *yaḥad*, implying the simultaneity of heavenly and earthly worship), priests and angels were witnesses to sacred time, observing sabbaths and festivals *together* in accordance with the solar calendar; *together*, in the supernal worlds and the visionary Temple, at seven-day intervals, they chanted the 'seven

---

[63] One example of a chronotopic expression is the concept of *mo'ed*, which has the double sense of 'appointed or set time' (sacred time: 'These are the set times of the Lord'—Lev. 23: 37) and 'meeting', as in the term 'Tent of Meeting' (sacred place). For a chronotope combining static vertical space and the dynamic progress of time, see 'I wrote down the height from the earth to the seventh heaven . . . and put in the midst of them the sun, so that he might travel along the seven celestial circles' (2 En. 40: 12; 48: 1). The relationship between the twelve-month calendar and the administrative division of twelve tribes may be observed both in the division relating to Solomon's Temple (1 Chr. 27) and in Plato's observation: 'And not only is the whole number divisible by twelve, but also the number of each tribe is divisible by twelve. Now every portion should be regarded by us as a sacred gift of Heaven, corresponding to the months and to the revolution of the universe' (Plato, *Laws*, bk. VI, cited from Jowett translation).   [64] 1 En. 1: 72–82.

[65] For the prominence of angels at Qumran see Licht, *Rule Scroll*, index, s.vv. *benei or, malakhim, sar urim*; Yadin (ed.), *Scroll of the War*, 229–42; Noll, 'Angelology in the Qumran Texts'; Newsom, *Songs*, 23–38; ead., 'He has Established for Himself Priests'; Mach, 'Saints–Angels'; Dimant, 'Children of Heaven'; Elior, 'Mysticism, Magic and Angelology'; Nitzan, *Qumran Prayer*; Elior, 'From Earthly Temple to Heavenly Shrines', 224 n. 21.

wondrous songs' and 'seven psalms of magnification'—the Songs of the Sabbath Sacrifice. So priests and angels *together*, observing the holy appointed times in their preordained, cyclic, divine order, uttered words of praise and thanks, recited blessings and divine names, pronounced the Ineffable Name with its benedictions as done in the Temple—all in regular sevenfold formulations. The tradition of the priestly courses, succeeding one another at weekly intervals in a prescribed order, was scrupulously adhered to—it had been instituted by Zadok the priest during King David's reign,[66] and numerous lists of such courses have been discovered at Qumran, attesting to the observance there of the calendar of sabbaths and festivals and their regular liturgical order.[67] In parallel, the names of the angelic courses, divided into seven or twenty-four, were carefully preserved, as indicated by Josephus' reference in his account of the Essenes: 'They swear . . . to preserve the books of their sect and in the same way the names of the angels';[68] the chief priests on earth regularly chanted, in the prescribed order, the thirteen Songs of the Sabbath Sacrifice, each sung on one of the thirteen sabbaths of the recurring season, together with the heavenly 'priests of the inner sanctum'. Such formulas as

> Give thanks to God
> Bless His Holy Name always
> In the Heavens and their dominion
> All the angels of the holy firmament

or 'All the spirits of those who bring to the sanctuary . . . in their companies and in their dominions . . . all bless in community Your holy name'[69] may be found in a variety of versions, clearly demonstrating the participation of angels in the ritual and the interaction between heavenly and earthly worship. The holy names of the Deity are recited by angels and priests, just as the blessings, praises, and thanksgiving for the favour of Creation are uttered by those performing their sacral duties in both upper and lower worlds.

Angelic revelations, inscribed on heavenly tablets or imparted in dreams or mystical visions, recorded in holy books of divine origin, constitute the primary fount of religious validity and authority in this literature. They relate to the consecration of the priesthood, its affinity with the angelic world, the participation of angels in the cult, and the establishment of liturgical formulas recited jointly by

---

[66] 1 Chr. 24.

[67] See Milik, *Books of Enoch*, 59–69; Wacholder and Abegg, *Preliminary Edition*, i. 60–101, 103–18; Talmon and Knohl, 'Calendrical Scroll'; Chyutin, *War of Calendars*, 32–3. For a brief discussion of the biblical and later systems of priestly courses, see pp. 42–3 ff. above.   [68] *War*, ii. viii. 7.

[69] Words of the Heavenly Lights (4Q504, frgs. 1–2, VII, 4–6; cf. García Martínez and Tigchelaar, *Study Edition*, ii. 1017); 4QBer[a], frg. 2, 1–4 (*DJD* XI, 17); cf. 'He distinguishes light from darkness; He establishes the dawn by the knowledge of His heart. Then did all His angels see and sing, for He showed them that which they had not known' (11QPs[a] XXVI, 9–12: *DJD* IV). For other English translations of these verses see *DJD* IV, 90; García Martínez and Tigchelaar, *Study Edition*, ii. 1179.

the earthly guardians of the Covenant and their heavenly counterparts. All this revolves around the solar calendar, which sanctifies heavenly time in the Heikhalot, the supernal sanctuaries.

*

The alternatives proposed by the proponents of the secessionist priestly rite in these three areas—sacred time, sacred place, and sacred ritual, intertwined in a complex system of mutual relationships—were closely associated with the seven days of Creation, so that seven became a sacred typological number, an archetypal numerical model of divine origin governing time, place, and ritual. The priestly opposition venerated the number seven with all its derivatives and multiples, its mythical and mystical manifestations. It became a distinctive, identifying label, a sacred typological number pervading the universe and dictating the cultic rhythm of life, an eternal, ritual and liturgical axis combining septuples of time, of place, and of sacred ritual, and interchanging them in mystical metamorphoses. The number seven—dictating the span of time needed for the transition from chaos to Creation, from impurity to purity, and from death to life, associated, linguistically and conceptually, with oath, week, sabbath, the calendar, and the priestly courses—thus assumed a transcendental, cosmic, cultic significance, bridging the gap between the heavenly and the earthly through sacred sevenfold formulas.

The liturgical axis engendered mystical metamorphoses that unified cosmic, heavenly, angelic time and earthly, cultic, priestly time—both measured in multiples of seven: sabbaths and weeks; the seven Temple festivals, seven weeks apart; seasons, sabbatical years, jubilees—with cosmic space as manifested in seven sacred precincts, seven *merkavot*, seven *devirim*, and seven *heikhalot*. All these components were reflected in the angelic priestly ritual observed in the 'sanctuary of man' by the 'seven chief princes' and the priestly courses, and in the supernal sanctuaries by the seven 'priests of the inner sanctum' and the angelic courses. The sacred service was performed by the priestly courses, succeeding one another at weekly intervals, thus observing the order of sabbaths. Among its main elements were the oaths of the guardians of the Covenant and the sacred song, sung every sabbath by septuples of angels and priests. These metamorphoses, which will be discussed below, created a link between the Chariot Throne of the cherubim in the ruined earthly Temple and its heavenly memorialization, Ezekiel's Merkavah, on the one hand, and Shavuot, the festival of the Covenant of fertility and first fruits, of Temple pilgrimage, celebrated in heaven by the angels and on earth by the priests, on the other. A mutual relationship, or interaction, was thus established between angelic worship in the heavenly sanctuaries and worship by priests and Levites singing in the earthly Temple, beyond the limits of time and space.

These seven-based traditions, consecrating cosmic time and place and their terrestrial representations, revolved around several elements: the focus of that sanctity was the Merkavah, the Chariot Throne of cherubim that had stood in the *devir* or Holy of Holies since the time of the desert sanctuary[70] and the time of Solomon's Temple,[71] and whose memory was perpetuated in various priestly traditions.[72] The solar calendar hallowed by Merkavah traditions had probably been observed as a cultic and liturgical calendar by the Zadokite priests, who had officiated as high priests from the time of the First Temple until the middle of the Second Temple period.[73] It was certainly regarded as the definitive ritual calendar by the priestly opposition circles of the Second Temple period and the Qumran priests, who identified themselves with the Zadokite priests; and it was the exclusive basis for the heavenly worship of the ministering angels, the priests of the inner sanctum, and chief princes as described in Songs of the Sabbath Sacrifice and in Enoch literature.

The circles among whom proto-Qumran and Qumran literature was composed, edited, preserved, and ultimately canonized proposed to replace the Temple cult of their time with three central priestly mystical traditions:

1. the Merkavah/Chariot Throne of the cherubim in the *devir*/Holy of Holies of the desert sanctuary and of Solomon's Temple, built according to a heavenly prototype, and Ezekiel's Merkavah in its visionary transformation, as prototypes of sacred heavenly space;

2. the calendar of sabbaths—the solar calendar, as revealed in the tradition of Enoch, Jubilees, the Qumranic Psalms of David, and Songs of the Sabbath Sacrifice and preserved in the Temple Scroll, the Calendars of Priestly Courses, and MMT, as the prototype of sacred heavenly time; and

3. the angelic priesthood and the worship by the creatures of the Merkavah, described in the Songs of the Sabbath Sacrifice and the Blessings Scroll, as the prototype of the sacred heavenly ritual.

These three traditions of sacred time, place, and ritual were associated with the tradition of covenants, Shavuot, and the overarching predominance of the number seven, with regard both to numbers reflecting the laws and eternal order of the universe, which are open to systematic discovery and expression, and to abstract ideas concerning the mystery of life and blessing of fertility and procreation, reflecting divine law with its concrete manifestations and its cultic representation. The eternity of the divine order with its mysteries, referred to in the secessionist priestly literature as 'wondrous mysteries' or similar expressions, and with its complex manifestations in terms of calculation and number, everlasting ages, seasons, and appointed times, is described in the Thanksgiving Hymns:

---

[70] Exod. 15: 18–22.   [71] 1 Kgs. 6: 23–8; 2 Chr. 8: 18.
[72] Temple Scroll VII, 10–12; Songs of the Sabbath Sacrifice.
[73] See VanderKam, 'Origin, Character and History'.

> All things are graven before Thee
> on a written Reminder
> for everlasting ages,
> and for the numbered cycles
> of the eternal years
> in all their appointed times. . . .[74]

I shall now examine each of these three traditions and the seven-based meta-morphoses associated with them, in connection with Chariot Throne and Temple, calendar and Covenant, priests and angels.

[74] Thanksgiving Hymns I, 24 (cf. Vermes, *CDSSIE*, 254).

From Temple to Merkavah: From the Chariot Throne of the Cherubim to Ezekiel's Vision

Bless the one who does amazing wonders and shows the might of his hand, sealing up mysteries and revealing hidden things . . . confirming majestic mysteries and establishing glorious wonders.[1]

THE secessionist priestly literature treated Ezekiel's Merkavah as a prototype of sacred heavenly space, because the Merkavah was portrayed and interpreted as a visionary, mystical transformation of the Holy of Holies, a composite of details from the Temple which expressed the very essence of the sacred precinct. The roots from which Jewish mysticism sprang lie in the Merkavah vision of the priest Ezekiel son of Buzi, composed in exile while Nebuchadnezzar was laying waste to Jerusalem and the First Temple. The prophet-priest, exiled from Jerusalem together with King Jehoiachin, envisioned the ruined earthly Temple as an eternal, heavenly Chariot Throne, transcending the bounds of time and place. The *four*-winged cherubim of the Holy of Holies,[2] the copper wheels of the stands in the Temple court, the *four* threesomes of creatures on all four sides of a square structure (facing all four points of the compass), the lions, oxen, cherubim, and *ofanim*—all cultic objects, made of burnished bronze[3]—became *four* sacred winged creatures, sparkling with that same bronze lustre, with the faces of lions, oxen, eagles, and human beings. They stood on *four* wheels (Heb. *ofanim*) which had the appearance of 'two wheels cutting through each other' and faced all four points of the compass,[4] like their counterparts in the Temple.

The gold-plated winged cherubim in the sanctuary, whose wings were extended and 'touched each other', and which stood on their feet,[5] were transformed in Ezekiel's vision into sacred, sparkling, winged creatures, 'each of whose wings touched those of the other'[6] and whose legs 'were fused into a single rigid leg';[7]

---

[1] Thanksgiving Hymns, 4Q427, frg. 7 i, 18–20 (*DJD* XXIX, 110, 112–13; cf. Vermes, *CDSSIE*, 298–9). [2] 1 Kgs. 6: 23–8; 8: 6–8; 2 Chr. 3: 10–13.

[3] 1 Kgs. 7: 23–37; 8: 6–9; 2 Chr. 4: 3–4. [4] Ezek. 1: 4–11, 16–21.

[5] 1 Kgs. 6: 23–8; 8: 6–8; 2 Chr. 3: 10–13. [6] Ezek. 1: 9. [7] Ezek. 1: 7.

their appearance was 'like burning coals of fire . . . torches'.[8] The cherubim, lions, and palms referred to in the biblical account of Solomon's Temple[9] also figure in Ezekiel's vision,[10] as do the sapphire and beryl (*tarshish*) associated with the image of the Deity and his seat in the Temple rites.[11] There is thus a whole system of correlations between the ideal picture of the destroyed earthly Temple and the visionary Temple revealed in heaven.

Such was the interpretation of Ezekiel's vision by the contemporaries of the Second Temple. Following the Chronicler, they associated Ezekiel's account of the sacred winged creatures standing on wheels[12]—described as cherubim with extended wings[13] after the fashion of the cherubim in the desert sanctuary[14]—with the divine prototype (or pattern) of the Chariot Throne of winged cherubim in the Holy of Holies, shown to David from heaven and transmitted to Solomon, who was to build the earthly Temple: 'the weight of refined gold for the incense altar and the gold for the pattern [Heb. *tavnit*] of the chariot—the cherubim—those with outspread wings screening the Ark of the Covenant of the Lord; all this that the Lord made me understand by His hand on me, I give you in writing—the pattern of all the works'.[15]

Readers and listeners in antiquity were presumably aware that the cherubim with outspread wings in the biblical traditions of the Holy of Holies were identified with the sacred creatures or cherubim, they too with outspread wings, in the priestly prophetic tradition of Ezekiel's vision. Here was a link between the gold 'pattern of the chariot, the cherubim', the very core of the earthly Temple, revealed to David before its construction, and Ezekiel's Merkavah, the essence of the heavenly Temple, revealed to him after the destruction of its earthly counterpart.

---

[8] Ezek. 1: 13.   [9] 1 Kgs. 6: 32, 35; 7: 36.   [10] Ezek. 41: 18–19, 25–6.
[11] Ezek. 1: 16, 26; 10: 1, 9.   [12] Ezek. 1; 10: 9–15.
[13] Ezek. 10: 15–17.   [14] Exod. 25: 17–20.
[15] 1 Chr. 28: 18–19. On the Merkavah see Tur-Sinai, 'Problem of the Ark', 5; Haran, *Temples and Temple Service*, 247–59. There is no agreement among Bible scholars as to the date of the book of Ezekiel and its affinities with earlier priestly sources; see Cassuto, 'Ezekiel', 637–9; Zimmerli, *Ezekiel*; Haran, 'Topics in Bible'; Greenberg, *Ezekiel 1–20*; Brooke, 'Ezekiel in Some Qumran and NT Texts'; Halperin, *Faces of the Chariot*. Whatever the case, Ezekiel's vision is a pivotal element of the mystical literature under discussion here. Whether Ezekiel's prophecies were based on the eyewitness evidence of a priest who had actually served in the Temple, on written priestly traditions, or on a combination of sources deriving from different sources of inspiration, the direct affinity between the earthly Temple and the exiled priest's Merkavah vision was obvious to his readers. On the mystical interpretation of Ezekiel's Merkavah vision see Gruenwald, *Apocalyptic and Merkavah Mysticism*, 32–3; Newsom, 'Merkabah Exegesis'; Halperin, *Faces of the Chariot*; Elior, 'From Earthly Temple to Heavenly Shrines'. On the replacement of earthly ritual by the Merkavah and the heavenly sanctuary after the destruction of the First Temple, see Maier, *Vom Kultus zur Gnosis*, 103–6; and cf. Aptowitzer, 'Heavenly Temple'. On the Temple and the priesthood see Büchler, *Die Priester und der Cultus*; Haran, *Temples and Temple Service*; Herr, 'Jerusalem, the Temple, and the Temple Service'.
    Note the Hebrew word *tavnit* in the above verse from 1 Chronicles, here translated as 'pattern', denoting the heavenly pattern or prototype of the sanctuary and its cultic representation, as it does in the divine revelation to Moses (Exod. 25: 9, 40); cf. Heb. 8: 5.

The Septuagint renders Ezekiel 43: 3 as 'the vision of the chariot [*merkavah*] which I saw was like the vision which I saw at the River Chobar', whereas the Masoretic text has 'the vision was like the vision [*mareh*] I had seen'—in a verse that uses the word 'vision' four times! Ben Sira—also a priest in Jerusalem when the Zadokite priests were ministering in the Temple—states the association briefly at the beginning of the second century BCE: 'Ezekiel saw a vision and he recounted the varieties of *merkavah*';[16] his wording attests to his use of *merkavah* as a common priestly term whose significance was quite clear in the context of Ezekiel's vision.

An unknown work, of which several copies were discovered at Qumran, has been named 'Second Ezekiel' as it revolves around the figure of the prophet, his prophecies, and his visions. This work contains a unique version of the Merkavah vision—not a duplication of the traditional text but an abbreviation or reworked version—an ancient attestation of the tradition, comprising about ten fragmentary lines:

5　The vision that Ezek[iel] saw

6　a radiance of a *chariot* and four living creature[　and while walking they would not turn]

7　backwards; upon two each living creature was walking, and its two le[gs

8　[le]g [　was spiritual and their faces were one joined to the oth[er. And the shape of the]

9　fac[es, one of a lion, and on]e of an eagle and one of a calf, and one of a man, and each [one had a hand of]

10　of a man joined from the backs of the living creatures and attached to [their wings] and the whe[els . . .]

11　wheel joined to wheel as they went, and from the two sides of the whe[els were streams of fire]

12　and there was in the midst of the coals living creatures, like coals of fire[, like torches in the midst of]

13　the whe[e]ls and the living creatures and the wheels; and there wa[s over their heads a firmament like]

14　the terri[ble] ice. [And there w]as a sound[from above the firmament.[17]

The phrase *nogah merkavah*, 'radiance of a chariot', is unknown elsewhere (the parallel phrase in the Masoretic text is 'surrounded by a radiance'), but the association with Ezekiel's vision is obvious from the wording and structure of the text. One might say that tradition referred to Ezekiel's vision as 'vision of the Merkavah' or 'Ezekiel's Merkavah' because the prophet, in that vision, dismantled and reconstituted the sacred space of a lost composite of cultic objects, the prototype being

---

[16]　Ben Sira 49: 8.

[17]　4Q 385, frg. 4 (*DJD* XXX, 42–4). On the Qumran Merkavah text see Halperin, *Faces of the Chariot*, 50, 55; Dimant and Strugnell, 'Merkabah Vision'; Brooke, 'Ezekiel in Some Qumran and NT Texts'.

the Chariot Throne in the Holy of Holies. The vision of the Merkavah was a synec-dochic description of the earthly and heavenly Temple—the part representing the whole, a limited weave of details expressing the whole composite in its entirety. The wings, cherubim, creatures and wheels, the fire and sounds, all associated with the Temple and its cult, together with the four-sided, many-faced cultic structure from the Temple courts and the Chariot Throne of winged cherubim from the Holy of Holies, came together to form a living, visionary, heavenly reality. The vision, creating a visual and verbal metamorphosis of the memory of the cult, reproduced the heavenly prototype of the Merkavah and the sublime, numinous beauty with which it was imbued, beyond the limits of time and place. However, it should be noted that the cultic tradition associated with the Temple and the Merkavah assigned different meanings to the sanctity of time, of place, and of life, and to their dialectical relationship with the concealed and the revealed.

The various traditions that describe the Merkavah, implicitly and explicitly, clearly involve two elements: a composite structure facing four directions, forming as it were a microcosmic model of the universe with its four cyclic seasons and four spatial directions relating to the divine set times, that is, to *sacred time*; and a winged, angelic model, encompassing the ark-cover and the cherubim, the sacred creatures, and the wheels, all mythically and mystically expressing the affinity between the hidden divine essence and its cultic representations, thus representing the place of divine revelation, that is, *sacred place*. This hallowed place, built according to a divine plan,[18] was explicitly associated with divine revelation: 'There I will meet with you, and I will impart to you—from above the cover, from between the two cherubim . . .',[19] and implicitly associated with the secret of life, with eternity and fertility, 'the eternal plant', Garden of Eden and Paradise, Temple, Chariot, Holy of Holies, sanctification, and betrothal. The affinities between concealed and revealed in these areas are probably reflected by a mythical representation of the *sacred act of Creation* through the sacred creatures/cherubim and the creatures of the Merkavah. In biblical tradition, the cherubim marked the place of the Deity's self-revelation in the desert sanctuary,[20] they adorned the laver stands in the Temple court[21] and stood in the Holy of Holies.[22] They are men-tioned again in the ornamentation of the cloth strips for the desert sanctuary, the engravings on the Temple walls, and the decorations of the curtain in the Temple;[23] in other traditions, they were part of the winged divine retinue and served as guardians of the Garden of Eden.[24]

The cherubim in the Holy of Holies are always referred to as 'two cherubim of gold',[25] sometimes as standing;[26] an obscure term in one reference[27] is generally

[18] Exod. 25: 40.   [19] Exod. 25: 22; 1 Kgs. 8: 11.   [20] Exod. 25: 18–22; 37: 6–9.
[21] 1 Kgs. 7: 29.   [22] 1 Kgs. 6: 23–9; 8: 6–7; 2 Chr. 3: 10–13; 5: 7–8.
[23] Exod. 26: 1, 31; 36: 8, 35; 1 Kgs. 6: 28, 32, 35; 7: 29, 36; 2 Chr. 3: 7, 14.
[24] Gen. 3: 24.   [25] Exod. 25: 18–22.
[26] 1 Kgs. 6: 23; 2 Chr. 3: 13.   [27] 2 Chr. 3 :10.

translated as 'sculptured'. Descriptions of them usually imply a posture characterized by reciprocity or contact: 'They faced each other',[28] or also 'their wings
touched each other'[29] or were even joined together.[30] The Temple Scroll contains
a fragmentary description of the cherubim in the Holy of Holies: 'And the cover
that is above . . . two cherubim . . . the second end, spreading their wings . . . above
the ark and their faces were toward each other',[31] paraphrasing the biblical account
of the attitude of the cherubim facing each other: 'The cherubim shall have their
wings spread out above, shielding the cover with their wings. They shall confront
each other, the faces of the cherubim being turned toward the cover'.[32]

It is clear from the various traditions that the cherubim, sculpted, engraved, and
painted, were of paramount importance in the Temple, and moreover that the disposition of their wings towards each other, covering and revealing, was particularly
significant. In biblical tradition, the phrase 'to spread wing(s)' is used both of the
cherubim[33] and of the shelter given to a woman by a man, as when Ruth addresses
Boaz: 'Spread your robe [Heb. *kenafkha*, lit. 'your wing'] over your handmaid'[34]—
an idiom based on the semantic range of the Hebrew word *kanaf*, 'wing', which
also means, by extension, 'extremity, corner', especially of a piece of clothing (and
also of the earth). Sometimes *kanaf* is used synecdochically to denote an entire
garment, as in the idiom 'to expose, remove another person's *kanaf*', which is associated with uncovering another person's genitals and hence with the sexual act,
permitted or otherwise.[35]

While these traditions only alluded to this aspect of the cherubim and refrained
from explaining the secret meaning of the touching wings—the various verbs
used, both in the Bible and elsewhere, imply varying degrees of proximity and
contact—later tradition was more explicit, clearly indicating the identity of the
cherubim as a mythical symbolization of reproduction and fertility, expressed in
the form of the intertwined male and female:

Whenever Israel came on pilgrimage on festivals [to the Temple in Jerusalem], the curtain would be removed for them and the cherubim were shown to them, whose bodies
were intertwined with one another, and they would be thus addressed: Look! You are
beloved before God as the love between man and woman.[36]

---

[28] Exod. 37: 9.   [29] 1 Kgs. 6: 27; Ezek. 1: 9.   [30] 2 Chr. 3: 12.   [31] VII, 9–13.
[32] Exod. 25: 20.   [33] Exod. 25: 20; 1 Kgs. 6: 7; 8: 7; 2 Chr. 5: 8.
[34] Ruth 3: 9.   [35] See Deut. 23: 1; 27: 20; Temple Scroll LXVI, 12–13.
[36] BT *Yoma* 54a. Cf. Rashi's interpretation of this talmudic verse: 'The cherubim are united one
with the other, and cleaving to each other and intertwining one with the other as a male hugs a female.
Intertwining is a language of conjugal union.' The root *d-b-k* or *d-v-k*, signifying 'conjugal union'
(Gen. 2: 25), is associated with the cherubim in the sanctuary in 4Q405, frg. 19, 2–7 (*DJD* XI, 339,
341), where they are called 'figures of godlike beings' or 'images of living godlike beings'. Newsom
translates *kodshei dibkei pele* as 'holy wondrous mosaic', noting (*Songs*, 343) that it is uncertain. In my
view it should be translated according to the biblical meaning of the root *d-b-k* (Gen. 2: 25) as 'holy
wondrous union'.

This description echoes a mythical mystical tradition associating the implied intimacy of the cherubim with the act of pilgrimage; the tradition is most probably very early and refers to the First Temple, for in the Second Temple the Chariot Throne of the cherubim was no more than a mythical memory.[37] Although the above passage is taken from tractate *Yoma*, which is concerned primarily with the Day of Atonement, the description explicitly refers to pilgrimage on a festival. I believe the festival intended is Shavuot, the Festival of Weeks/Oaths, the Covenant festival described in later mystical tradition as celebrating betrothal, on earth and in heaven, or *hieros gamos*, the sacred union, as we shall see later. Perhaps the expression 'intertwined [Heb. *me'urim*] with one another' is akin to another obscure biblical expression used in connection with the engraving of the cherubim in Solomon's Temple: *kema'ar-ish veloyot saviv*,[38] the word *ma'ar* understood as referring to an exposed, naked area (New Jewish Publication Society Translation: 'as the clear space on each allowed . . .'). The expression is also reminiscent of the term *berit maor* occurring in commentaries on the ancient mystical work *Sefer yetsirah* (Book of Creation), associated there with nakedness and sexual union and hence with reproduction and fecundity.[39]

Apparently, then, the Chariot Throne of the winged cherubim alluded to the secret of procreation and the continuity of life, through the symbolization of sexual union by the wings of the cherubim, and to the unity of time and place, appointed time and purity, as manifest in the affinity between holiness (*kodesh*) and betrothal (*kidushin*), a holy communion or sexual act which is a precondition for the continuity of life in the context of seven days of purification after menstruation and a seven-based cycle. These mysteries were bound up with the three dimensions

---

[37] BT *Yoma* 21*b*.   [38] 1 Kgs. 7: 36.

[39] See Liebes, *Creation Doctrine*, 229–37, and index, s.v. *maor*. Nevertheless, a late tradition cited in the Book of the *Zohar* associates the cherubim with the Day of Atonement: 'When [the high priest enters the Holy of Holies on the Day of Atonement], he hears the sound of the wings of the cherubim, who sing and beat their wings that are stretched out towards the heavens. He burns the incense-offering; the sound of their wings subsides and they cleave together in silence . . . When he has finished, the cherubim lift up their wings as they did before and begin to sing. Then the priest knows that it has been accepted, and it is a moment of joy for all' (*Zohar* III, 67*a*; translation cited from Tishby, *Wisdom of the Zohar*, iii. 92–3). There is some similarity in the *Zohar* between Shavuot and the Day of Atonement. On the latter, as on Shavuot, the Deity is coupled with the Shekhinah, and the ritual immersion practised on the eve of the Day of Atonement has the same motive as on Shavuot, which as it were prepares the 'bride' for the wedding (*Zohar* III, 214*b*). I cannot discuss here the question of the ancient priestly traditions which gave rise to the late mystical tradition of the *Zohar*; at any rate, it seems plausible that the mystical tradition of the divine nuptials on Shavuot is indirectly related to the ancient substrate of traditions concerning the coupling of the cherubim during pilgrimage. Perhaps it is not insignificant that the time span from the Day of Atonement to Shavuot is *nine months*, the length of human pregnancy; and it also parallels the time span from sowing to harvest, from the seventh month to the third month of the next year according to the solar calendar. On mystical traditions associated with Shavuot and the Day of Atonement and their possible antiquity see Liebes, 'Messiah of the Zohar', appendices 1 and 2 (pp. 74–84). On the *Zohar* tradition in relation to Rabbi Joseph Karo and Shavuot see Elior, 'R. Joseph Karo and R. Israel Ba'al Shem Tov'.

of the Chariot Throne: (1) its four-sided *microcosmic pattern*, reflecting the four seasons of the year and the four directions of the universe, which represented the sanctity of time and its cyclic nature through number, counting, appointed time, and cycles of fertility and agricultural yields, based on synchronization between quadruples and septuples, between seasons and sabbaths, and associated with the appointed times for the offering of sacrifices; (2) its *winged pattern*, represented by the cherubim, the wheels, and the sacred creatures, which signified the sanctity and purity of space, the secret of life and procreation, uncovering and covering, communion and sexual union, Paradise and the Garden of Eden, the sacred plant, the tree of life and the fragrance of the incense, the Holy of Holies and betrothal, the sanctification of nature and the promise of fertility, and the Song of Songs (which Rabbi Akiva called 'Holy of Holies'); and (3) its *ritual and liturgical pattern*, sanctifying time in a heavenly ambience associated with angelic worship, described as

the mystery/council of *elim* [godlike beings] of purification with all those who have eternal knowledge, to prai[se and to bles]s Your glorious name in all [ever]la[sting ages]. Amen. Amen . . . [And] they shall again bless the God [of Israel] . . .[40]

—and with song and blessing, praise and holiness of the '*elim* of knowledge' and 'priests of the inner sanctum', the worship of the guardians of purification and sanctification, of sabbaths and festivals in their sevenfold order perpetuating Creation.

In the priestly literature of antiquity, the visionary Merkavah, combining mythical, cultic, and liturgical elements and replacing their concrete and abstract realities with a multifaceted mystical vision, was a heavenly representation of the ruined earthly Temple: 'the pattern of the chariot—the cherubim—those with outspread wings screening the Ark of the Covenant of the Lord', handed down from David to his son Solomon as a heavenly testimony anticipating the actual construction: 'All this that the Lord made me understand by His hand on me, I give you in writing—the pattern of all the works.'[41] This vision presents the eternal heavenly prototype of the Holy of Holies in the earthly Temple, revealed to Ezekiel in its glorious existence in heaven even after its destruction.

The sacred heavenly space, representing the heavenly Holy of Holies, the seat of the God enthroned on the cherubim, was portrayed in songs, hymns, thanksgiving, and blessings discovered at Masada and at Qumran, all showing a distinct affinity with the language of Ezekiel's Merkavah as perpetuated in angelic song and imbued with life in mystical vision:

1. The throne of Your splendour and the footstool of Your glory in the heights of Your standing and

2. Your holy stepping-place. And Your glorious chariots, their cherubim, their wheels and all their councils;

---

[40] 4Q286, frg. 7, 6–8 (*DJD* XI, 25–6).   [41] 1 Chr. 28: 18–19.

3. foundations of fire and flames of brightness and shinings of majesty and str[eams] of fire and wonderful luminaries;

4. [majes]ty and splendour and glorious height, holy foundation and sou[rce of] majesty and height of glory . . .[42]

The terms 'footstool', 'standing', and 'stepping-place' recall the description of the sacred creatures' legs in Ezekiels vision[43] and the reference to the cherubim in the Holy of Holies.[44] The wings of the cherubim are referred to in various traditions as the seat of the Deity, while the mystery, the wonder, the shining light, the fire, and the brightness reflect the beauty of the Deity in its various manifestations, manifest and concealed, in the world of the Merkavah. Many of the terms featured in this text—*kavod, yekar,* or *tiferet*, 'glory', *rom* or *marom*, 'height', *kodesh*, 'seats of holiness', *merkavah* and *merkavot, keruvim*, 'cherubim', *ofanim*, 'wheels', *sod*, 'secret', *demut*, 'figure' or 'form', *esh*, 'fire', *nogah*, 'brilliance', *hod* or *hadar*, 'majesty, splendour', *or*, 'light', and *pele*, 'wonder', with their derived forms and unique combinations—figure in Ezekiel's vision.[45] These formulations became one half of the abstract–concrete verbal fabric which, in a language of mystery and allusion, erected the heavenly Holy of Holies and established the splendour of the sacred space, represented in cultic terms by the Temple and its rites. The other half comprised song, voice, name and sound, praise and thanksgiving, number and cycle in the world of those who frequented the world of the Merkavah, who counted the cycles of time and participated in the eternally ongoing cyclic sacred service and, through their praises, song, and blessings, constructed the heavenly reality and cosmic cyclic existence dependent on sacred time, as reflected in the priests' sacred service in the earthly Temple.

Just as the earthly sanctuary was a microcosmic reflection of its macrocosmic counterpart, the heavenly sanctuary was pictured through a mystical metamorphosis of its earthly parts, the details and precise dimensions of whose earthly prototype, as well as the materials from which they are made, are provided in Exodus, 1 Kings, and 1 and 2 Chronicles, in accordance with God's injunction concerning the heavenly prototype ('exactly as I show you . . . so you shall make it'[46]). These instructions, minutely detailed, are concerned with the representation of holiness in accordance with complex cosmic patterns, as may be inferred from statements by the priest Josephus Flavius,[47] who was born in 37 CE and served

---

[42] 4Q286, frg. 1 ii, 1–4 (*DJD* XI, 12; cf. Vermes, *CDSSIE*, 378). (Interestingly, some elements in this text are reminiscent of the *Aleinu* prayer recited daily to this day by observant Jews, and of literature relating to *ma'aseh merkavah*.) For discussion of the phraseology see B. Nitzan in *DJD* XI, 12–17; ead., *Qumran Prayer*. One Qumran fragment dealing with the Temple states that the *ofanim* were not visible outside (4Q365a, frg. 5, 3–4: *DJD* XIII, 331–2).

[43] Ezek. 1: 7; 10: 9–15; Second Ezekiel (*DJD* XXX, 43–4).   [44] 1 Kgs. 6: 23; 2 Chr. 3: 13.

[45] Cherubim: Ezek. 19: 1–22; *ofanim*: Ezek. 1: 15–21; 10: 9–15; *esh, nogah*: Ezek. 1: 18; 10: 2; 'Your glory . . . Your standing': cf. 'the glory of the Lord . . . stood', Ezek. 10: 18; 'glorious height': cf. Ezek. 10: 4; 3: 12.   [46] Exod. 25: 9.   [47] *War*, V. v. 4–5.

in the Temple before its destruction, and by Philo in the first century CE. The heavenly cultic elements of the Temple—including, besides the Chariot Throne and the Holy of Holies, the sanctuary (*heikhal*) and curtain, lavers, posts, walls, halls, gates, and doors, many of them decorated with cherubim and flowers, recalling the Garden of Eden—became a sublime, wondrous presence, through a liturgical metamorphosis. These elements, which had been from the start reflections of a heavenly prototype, became agents performing the sacred service, praising, blessing, and singing in the supernal worlds, where sacred place and sacred time coalesced in a heavenly ceremony modelled on the priestly service. Descriptions of the sanctity of space, measured in terms associated with the Temple and its rites, with their heavenly prototype and its earthly reflections, featuring singing and chanting angels, may be found in fragments of the Blessings Scroll, opening with fragmentary lines referring to sacred time, which, marked off by ecstatic 'amens', was measured in cosmic measures involving luminaries and constellations (represented in the Temple in terms of the numbers seven and twelve, recalling the seven planets and the twelve signs of the zodiac):

]and (the) lights
]their . . . in their constellations
]their . . . in all the set times
]all of them. Amen. Amen[48]

]their . . . and[ ] their engraved forms[
]their . . . [ ] their splendid [pa]tterns
[walls of] their glorious [hal]ls, their wondrous doors [
 ]their . . ., angels of fire and spirits of cloud [
  bri]ghtness of the embroidered spirits of the Holy of Ho[lies
   ] . . . and firmaments of holy[
  [spirits of the Holy] of Holies [will sing in joy] at all the set time[s
and they will bless]the name of Your glorious divinity [
  ]their . . . and all the ministers of ho[liness
   ]in the perfection of th[eir] works
    holi]ness in the temples of [Your] k[ingdom and . . . won]ders of
    ]all [Your] minister[s in] their [beautiful]splendour, angels of
spirits of]Your holiness in [their wondrous] habita[tions, a]ngels of Your righteousness.
in] their [awes]ome deeds, and they will bless Your holy name with
 blessings of[the holiest of the holy ones[49]

References to going out and coming in, portals and gates guarded by the angels describing the changes of the cosmic order, the sun's advance through the four seasons and the twelve months of the year, may be found in the Book of Heavenly Luminaries[50] and in various Qumran scrolls referring to the twelve gates of the

[48] 4Q287, frg. 1, 1 (*DJD* XI, 50).   [49] 4Q287, frg. 2a, b, 1–13; 3, 1 (cf. *DJD* XI, 51–2, 54).
[50] 1 En. 72: 3–33; 74: 10–13; 33: 3–4.

Temple and correlating them with the months and the names of the tribes.[51] The Temple with its twelve holy gates, portals, and exits is featured in the Songs of the Sabbath Sacrifice in the context of angelic worship, in terms borrowed from the earthly service of the priests and the Levites:

6 The godlike beings praise Him [when they fi]rst arise, and all the s[pirits] of the pure firmame[nts]
7 Rejoice in His glory; and there is a sound of blessing from all its divisions, which tells of His glorious firmaments; and His gates praise
8 with a voice of song. Whenever the *elim* of knowledge enter by the portals of glory, and whenever the holy angels go out to their dominion,
9 the portals of entrance and the gates of exit make known the glory of the King, blessing and praising all the spirits of
10 God at (their) going out and at (their) coming in by the gates of holiness. . . .[52]

Like the liturgical work quoted previously,[53] with its descriptions of the seat of the Deity, the Merkavah, in the plural—'Your glorious chariots'—in language mingling concrete and abstract and deriving from Ezekiel's vision, the Songs of the Sabbath Sacrifice, describing the sacred service of the angels in the seven supernal *heikhalot* in language replete with sublime mysteries, repeatedly employ a wealth of otherwise unknown combinations of the word *merkavah*, in singular and plural, in relation to Ezekiel's vision: 'The pattern of the Chariot Throne do they bless', 'and the chariots of his *devir* give praise together and their cherubim and their *ofanim* bless wondrously', 'the spirits of living godlike beings which move continuously with the glory of the wondrous chariots', 'his glorious chariots as they move'.[54] The plural form *merkavot*, 'chariots, chariot thrones', may be due to the plural 'cherubim'; or else the plural reflects the sevenfold replication of the world of the Merkavah. We find in these songs many descriptions that personify all the components of Ezekiel's vision, endow them with a ritual meaning, and portray the heavenly entities of the world of the Merkavah, fashioned in accordance with the prototype of the Holy of Holies, as reciting the liturgy of the Temple rites, performing the priestly service and the levitical song:

6 By the instr[uctor. Song of the sacrifice of] the twelfth [sa]bbath [on the twenty-first of the third month. Praise the God of]
7 wondrous [years] and exalt Him according to the Glory. In the tabern[acle of the God of] knowledge, the [cheru]bim fall before him, and they bl[es]s as they rise, the sound of divine stillness

---

[51] 4Q365a (*DJD* XIII, 327–8).
[52] 4Q405, frg. 23 i, 6–10 (cf. *DJD* XI, 356–7).   [53] 4QBerᵃ = 4Q286.
[54] Cf. 4Q403, frg. 2 ii, 15 ('chariots of his *devir*'); 4Q405, frg. 20 ii, 21–2, 3, 5 ('glorious chariots'); 4Q405, frg. 20 ii, 21–2, 8 ('pattern of the Chariot Throne'); 4QBerᵃ I, ii, 2 ('chariots of your glory'). See Newsom, *Songs*, 303; ead., *DJD* XI, 345, 346–7.

8 [is heard], and there is a tumult of jubilation as their wings lift up, the sound of divine [stillnes]s. The pattern of the Chariot Throne do they bless, above the firmament of the cherubim.

9 [And the splendou]r of the luminous firmament do they sing, beneath His glorious seat. And when the wheels move, the holy angels return. They go out from between

10 its glorious [h]ubs. Like the appearance of fire (are) the most holy spirits round about, the appearance of streams of fire like *ḥashmal*. And there is a radiant substance

11 with glorious colours, wondrously hued, purely blended, the spirits of living godlike beings which move continuously with the glory of the wondrous chariots.

12 There is a still sound of blessing in the tumult of their movement. And they praise His holiness as they return on their paths. As they rise, they rise marvellously; and when they settle,

13 they [stand] still. The sound of glad rejoicing falls silent, and there is a stillness of divine blessing in all the camps of the godlike beings; [and] the sound of prais[es]

14 ... from all their divisions on the[ir] si[des ... and] all their mustered troops rejoice, each o[n]e in [his] stat[ion].[55]

This song, opening with the date on which it is to be recited—the twelfth sabbath in the quarterly cycle of thirteen sabbaths, which will invariably fall on the 21st of the third month in that quarter—reflects a heavenly, angelic reality consisting of several simultaneous layers. In this mythical mystical existence, the common meanings of terms were transformed by restoring them to their heavenly roots and charging them with new meaning, based on a super-temporal understanding of an earthly and heavenly cultic reality. The song perpetuates the cult in a variety of ways: (1) it refers to a sublime realm, suffused with or representative of sanctity: the *devir*, the sanctuary, the embroidered curtain, the Chariot Throne of the cherubim, the wings of the cherubim, and the incense altar,[56] all of which represent the sacred place and the bond between heaven and earth; (2) it links up with the sacred cyclic ritual which re-establishes this bond every sabbath; (3) it recalls the poetic language of the sacred service in Psalms, as recited by the worshippers on high and those who serve in the Temple (exalt, bless, chant, praise, sing; songs and praises; contrasted with the silence and stillness characteristic of divine revelation);[57] and

---

[55] 4Q405, frg. 20 ii, 21–2 (cf. *DJD* XI, 345–55); cf. Newsom's 1985 edn. of *Songs of the Sabbath Sacrifice*, 303, pl. IX. The first part of the song clearly refers to Ezek. 3: 12–13. See Strugnell, 'Angelic Liturgy'; cf. *DJD* XXIII, 283–4, 285.

[56] Cf. 'In the *devir* he made two cherubim . . .' (1 Kgs. 6: 23); 'the weight of refined gold for the incense altar and the gold for the pattern of the chariot—the cherubim—those with outspread wings screening the Ark of the Covenant of the Lord' (1 Chr. 28: 18; cf. Ezek. 1: 26; 1 Sam. 4: 4). The desert sanctuary and the Temple are synonymous in Ezek. 37: 26–7. On the embroidered curtain at the entrance to the Tent of Meeting see Exod. 26: 34–6; 36: 37.

[57] Pss. 33: 1–3; 66: 1–2; 81: 2–3; 84; 98: 4–6; 100; 105; 106: 1; 117; 118: 29; 148; 150. For levitical song accompanied by cymbals, harps, and lyres see Neh. 12: 27–47; 1 Chr. 15: 16–24; 25: 1; 2 Chr. 5: 12–13; 29: 25–7; Pss. 88: 4–5; 149: 3; 150: 3–5. On singers reciting psalms in the Temple see Mishnah *Tam.* 7: 4, *RH* 4: 4; and cf. Gunkel's thesis that the whole book of Psalms represents a ritual situation: Gunkel, *Introduction to Psalms*; cf. also Dahood, *Psalms I*.

(4) it harks back to the priests' ceremonial preparation of incense in the Tent of Meeting and in the Temple (which was associated with the solar calendar[58]), and to the various ceremonies connected with prostration in the Temple.[59]

All these elements, on their different levels—mythological, mystical, historical, written, and ritual—subsisted in a super-temporal, heavenly ambience, in an eternal, mythical, mystical, liturgical presence beyond the limits of reality, preserved by angels and priests. Ezekiel's Merkavah was the visionary foundation of this song, describing the sacred space which itself was originally meant to represent a heavenly prototype; while the tradition of the sacred service in the Temple, most probably itself based originally on an angelic prototype, was the

[58] Indeed, an early *baraita* (tannaitic teaching) relating to the Temple ritual reflects a tradition that depends essentially on the solar calendar: 'Our rabbis taught: The incense was made of 368 *manehs*. Three hundred and sixty-five corresponded to the number of days in the solar calendar; of the three remaining *manehs*, the high priest took his hands full on the Day of Atonement' (BT *Ker.* 6a). This prescription for making incense in the Temple is clearly in keeping with the solar calendar. It involves preparation of 368 measures of incense, of which 365 were meant for the daily offering: one *peras* (half a *maneh*) in the morning and one *peras* in the evening. Three further measures were earmarked for the special incense offered on the Day of Atonement.

[59] '. . . incense, a compound expertly blended, refined, pure, sacred' (Exod. 30: 35). Incense was burned on the golden altar in the sanctuary (Exod. 30: 1–8) and in the Temple (1 Kgs. 7: 48), and its ritual use was the exclusive privilege of the priests (Exod. 30: 37–8). Cf. Ben Sira 49: 1: 'like blended incense prepared by the skill of the perfumer'. On incense and the Temple see Haran, *Temples and Temple Service*, 231–45; Newsom, *Songs*, 297–8; ead., *DJD* XI, 342. On prostrating oneself in the Temple on the Day of Atonement see Mishnah *Yoma* 10: 2; JT *Yoma* 3: 7 [40d].

The rites accompanying the burning of incense in the Holy of Holies on the Day of Atonement were a prominent bone of contention between the Pharisees and the Sadducees (BT *Yoma* 19b), perhaps also echoed by the *baraita* cited in the previous note. The literature of the secessionist priests associates the origins of incense-burning with Noah's sacrificial worship upon leaving the ark after a full solar year: 'And he made atonement with its blood for all the sins of the land . . . and he placed incense upon it' (Jub. 6: 2–4). The fragrant odour of incense prepared the way for the Covenant that God made with humanity concerning the eternal order of time and the cosmic laws of Creation (Jub. 6: 1–4). The Aramaic Genesis Apocryphon found at Qumran states regarding Noah: 'I atoned for the whole earth, all of it . . . I burned all their flesh on the altar . . . On it I put . . . together with frankincense as a meal-offering . . . the scent of my incense rose up to heaven' (X, 13–17). The parallel version in Gen. 8: 20 mentions neither incense nor the concept of atonement by burning incense—the ritual priestly element has disappeared.

An interesting passage in Jubilees describes the incense as made up of seven ingredients, thus associating it with septuples of sacrifices, as well as with the seven days of Sukkot (the Festival of Booths) celebrated in the seventh month and instituted by Abraham at Beersheba, for he was 'the first [to observe] the feast of the booths on the earth. And in these seven days he was making offering every day, day by day, on the altar . . . seven lambs, one kid, on behalf of sins, so that he might atone thereby on behalf of himself and his seed. And for a thank offering: seven rams . . . and their grain-offerings and their libations and all their fat he offered upon the altar as chosen burnt offering to the Lord for a sweet-smelling odour. And in the morning and evening he offered incense, frankincense and galbanum and stacte and nard and myrrh and spices and costum. All seven of these he offered, crushed, mixed in equal parts (and) pure . . . And Abraham took branches of palm trees and fruit of good trees and each day of the days he used to go around the altar with branches' (Jub. 16: 21–31). For incense as originating in the Garden of Eden see 1 En. 29–31; Book of Adam and Eve 29. Cf. the processions around the altar on Sukkot: Mishnah *Suk.* 4: 5; BT *Suk.* 43b.

cyclic liturgical foundation for the service of the beings of the Merkavah in the supernal Holy of Holies. The angelic song known as Songs of the Sabbath Sacrifice, alluding to the sacrificial rites that bound heaven and earth together with cultic ceremony and sacred song, correlated with the solar calendar of the year, wove the two realms together.

The cosmic voices, the indistinguishable sound and confusion of the cherubim and the sacred creatures, are described dramatically in the sources as thundering divine voices in the prophet-priest's vision—'When they moved, I could hear the sound of their wings like the sound of mighty waters, like the sound of Shaddai, a tumult like the voice of a host. . . . From above the expanse over their heads came a sound';[60] 'And there, coming from the east with a roar like the roar of mighty waters, was the Presence of the God of Israel, and the earth was lit up by His Presence';[61] 'the sound of the wings of the creatures beating against one another, and the sound of the wheels beside them—a great roaring sound';[62] 'The sound of the cherubim's wings could be heard as far as the outer court, like the voice of El Shaddai when He speaks.'[63] All these sounds were transformed in the Songs of the Sabbath Sacrifice into angelic voices which bless, sing, praise, and exalt in a well-defined cyclic liturgical order, preserving the harmony, pattern, and continuity of the ritual calendar and of cosmic order. The stormy movement of the cherubim and the sacred creatures in Ezekiel's vision, involving similes of thunder and lightning and the sound of beating wings, are translated in the Songs of the Sabbath Sacrifice into stately, measured, regular ceremonial movement, into the sounds of a sublime sacred service, weaving together stillness and song in the annual cycle of sabbath songs. Josephus Flavius associates the tinkling of the bells and pomegranates on the high priest's vestments with thunder and lightning: '[The high priest] officiated in breeches . . . with a linen shirt and over that an ankle-length blue robe, circular and tasselled; to the tassels were attached alternately golden bells and pomegranates, thunder being signified by the bells, lightning by the pomegranates.'[64] The authors of the songs combined the prophet's language with that of the book of Psalms and with the ceremonial language of the priestly courses and the levitical singers, the language of benediction and praise, song and music, holy names and prostration, based on a fixed ritual order, musical tradition, and a hallowed liturgy.

The cherubim were associated with the mythological world of the Garden of Eden,[65] the realm of eternity and sanctity, the beginning of Creation, abundance, the mystery of life and fertility where death had no dominion, and with the cultic representation of the revealed God seated on the cherubim.[66] They constituted an iconic cultic representation in the sanctuary and the Temple—as in the 'two

---

[60] Ezek. 1: 24–5.   [61] Ezek. 43: 2.   [62] Ezek. 3: 13.
[63] Ezek. 10: 5.   [64] *War*, v. v. 7.   [65] Gen. 3: 24.
[66] 1 Sam. 4: 4; 2 Kgs. 19: 15; Isa. 37: 16; Ps. 80: 3; 1 Chr. 13: 6; 1 En. 14: 18.

cherubim of gold' on the cover of the Ark[67] and the Chariot Throne;[68] this representation also alluded to their association with conjugal love and the continuity of life and procreation, through their physical contact as observed during the festival pilgrimage (on the festival of first fruits; see above). Ezekiel's vision transforms these diverse images into sacred creatures, Chariot Throne, and cherubim, described in alternating feminine and masculine words and constructions: *ḥayot*, 'creatures' (feminine); 'each (*aḥat*) had four faces and each (*aḥat*) had four wings' (feminine); *ragleihem*, 'their legs' (masculine); *kanfeihem*, 'their wings' (masculine); *ḥoverot ishah el aḥotah*, 'touched those of the other' (feminine); *lekhtan*, 'when they moved' (feminine), 'each (*ish*) could move in the direction of any of its faces' (masculine) (and many other examples throughout the first chapter of Ezekiel). The result is a multifaceted, heavenly, visionary reality, a combination of mythical, mystical, and cosmic dimensions.

The earliest part of 1 Enoch, describing the first vision of the Merkavah after Ezekiel, alludes to the cosmic character of the cherubim in the supernal sanctuary, presenting them as the seat of the Godhead:

And I came into the tongues of the fire and drew near to a great house which was built of white marble, the floor of crystal, the ceiling like the path of the stars and lightnings, between which (stood) fiery cherubim . . . And I observed and saw inside it a lofty throne—its appearance was like crystal and its wheels like the shining sun, and there were[?] cherubim . . .[69]

The last clause has been translated in different ways. Charles, translating from the Greek, adds the word 'vision' and proposes 'There was [the vision of] cherubim'; Milik and Nickelsburg translate 'and its sides were cherubim'; Knibb's version is 'and the sound of cherubim'; while Isaac (in the Charlesworth edition) translates 'and [I heard?] the voice of the cherubim'.

In the Blessings Scroll and the Songs of the Sabbath Sacrifice the appearance and sounds attributed to the cherubim in the different traditions are combined and invested with a mystical liturgical aura, described in enigmatic language suggesting a connection between their position in the Holy of Holies, their voices and the sacred service associated with them, and their appearance, in the context of the Chariot Throne and Ezekiel's Merkavah:

6 . . . Praise the God of]

7 wo]ndrous [years] and exalt Him according to the Glory. In the tabern[acle of the God of] knowledge, the [cheru]bim fall before Him, and they bl[es]s as they rise, the sound of divine stillness

8 [is heard], and there is a tumult of jubilation as their wings lift up, / the sound of divine [stillnes]s. / The pattern of the Chariot Throne do they bless, above the firmament of the cherubim.

---

[67] Exod. 26: 1, 31; 36: 35; 1 Kgs. 6: 23–8; 8: 6–8; 2 Chr. 3: 10–13.   [68] 1 Chr. 28: 18.

[69] 1 En. 14: 10–20 (Charlesworth (ed.), *OT Pseudepigrapha*, i. 20–1).

Or: 'and their cherubim and *ofanim* bless wondrously'; 'Holy cherubim, luminous *ofanim* in the *devir*'; 'above the firmament of the cherubim'; 'chariots of Your Glory, their cherubim and their *ofanim*'.[70]

A characteristic feature of the priestly mystical tradition is the multiplication by seven in the heavenly cult of almost every element of the earthy cult once performed in Solomon's Temple,[71] or its visionary transformation in Ezekiel's Merkavah;[72] from a cultic object or structure, destroyed and no longer existent, it is transformed into an eternal, heavenly, liturgical entity in the supernal sanctuary—singing, chanting, blessing. This tradition structures sacred space in a vertical sevenfold pattern, based on song and voice, chant and sound, and founded on structures from the earthly sanctuary, attesting to a sevenfold, kaleidoscopic, visionary refraction of super-temporal reality through a sevenfold replication of the sacred.

The Mishnah divides the Temple Mount into seven domains, each within another, increasing in sanctity as one approaches the Holy of Holies,[73] and various traditions speak of an association, implicit or explicit, between the Temple and a sevenfold division, referring to seven gates and seven steps in the Temple, or to the seven-branched lampstand and the seven planets,[74] as well as various other septuples associated with the Temple. Perhaps these septuples are simply a representation of sacred time, divided into sevens or sabbaths of days, parallel to the seven days of the week. Perhaps, moreover, the mystical tradition preserved in literary works of the last centuries BCE and the first centuries CE, referring at different stages to seven firmaments and to one or more Heikhalot in the seventh firmament;[75] to seven Chariot Thrones, seven Heikhalot and their cosmic multiples, picturing the heavens as a Temple consisting of seven sanctuaries—perhaps this tradition is alluding to the memory of some sevenfold perception of an actual cultic reality: 'And above the heavens there are in it seven *heikhalot* of fire and seven altars of flame'; 'For who can think on seven *heikhalot* and gaze on the highest heavens . . . in the seventh *heikhal* there stand one hundred thousand thousand myriad *merkavot* of fire'; 'And these are the names of seven princes, the guards of the seven portals of the *heikhalot*'; or 'Seven firmaments did the Holy One create and in them seven *merkavot*'.[76]

---

[70] 4Q405, frg. 20 ii, 21–2 (cf. *DJD* XI, 345–55; and see ibid., concordance, s.v. *keruv*).

[71] 1 Kgs. 6–8; 1 Chr. 28.   [72] Ezek. 1; 3: 12–13; 8: 2–4; 10.

[73] *Kel.* 1: 8–9; *Mid.* 2: 3.   [74] Josephus, *Antiquities*, III. vi. 7; *War*, V. v. 5; VII. v. 5.

[75] 2 En. 20 ff.; Testament of Levi 3: 4–8.

[76] Schäfer (ed.), *Synopse*, §§772, 554; ibid., §414; Gruenwald (ed.), *Re'uyot yehezkel*, 119, l. 45. Seven firmaments also figure in contemporary apocryphal literature: the Vision of Isaiah 7; Book of Adam and Eve 35; Apocalypse of Abraham 19: 4. The sevenfold structure of the heavens, a basic tenet of ancient cosmology, left its mark on many cultures. It is generally linked with the seven planets; Josephus, for example, associates the seven branches of the lampstand with the seven planets (*Antiquities*, III. vi. 7). Babylonian temples often reflected a seven-based pattern of sacred space, having

These and similar traditions, stressing not only the reflection of the earthly sanctuary but also the sevenfold structure of the heavens—as a Garden of Eden with seven firmaments, or as a universe with seven stars, seven heavenly circles, seven heavenly ages, seven appointed angels, seven mountains, and seven thunders[77]—postulate a general link between the cosmic order, counted in the sabbaths

seven floors, as in the Mesopotamian ziggurat, or the temples of Hadad and Assur by the Gate of Ishtar. For a survey of various sources relating to the seven firmaments see Cumont, *Astrology and Religion*; A. Y. Collins, 'Seven Heavens'; Arbel, 'Mythical Elements'.

The special attitude to seven as a typological number with occult properties, and the consequent preference for subdivisions of seven, may be traced to ancient sources. Seven was considered an ambivalent number in Egyptian mythology, i.e. it could bring good luck (seven Hathors) or bad (the seven arrows of Sekhmet). There are numerous Assyrian and Babylonian sources for the sanctity of the number seven. In the first centuries CE it was prominent in Gnostic and Mithraic cosmology, which, among other things, associated the seven planets with seven firmaments and with the fate of the soul after death. Jewish tradition, too, attaches importance to various numbers and to allusions based on the numerical values of the Hebrew letters (*gematriyah*). Thus, for example, it is perhaps no accident that the numerical value of the word *gad*, 'luck', is seven, while that of another word with the same connotation, *mazal*, is seventy-seven. Philo, in his discussion of the Creation, elaborates on the sanctity of the number seven; see Chyutin, 'Numerical Mysticism'. The number seven plays a major role in the New Testament Revelation of St John, which shows many points of contact with Ezekiel's vision and Temple traditions: 'I saw seven golden lampstands' (1: 13); 'seven stars' (1: 20); 'before the throne burn seven torches of fire, which are the seven spirits of God' (4: 5); 'Then I saw the seven angels who stand before God, and seven trumpets were given to them' (8: 2); 'the seventh angel . . .' (11: 15).

For numerology in general and the occult significance in the ancient world of the number seven in particular, see Schimmel, *Mystery of Numbers*, 127–55; Lurker, *Gods and Symbols of Ancient Egypt*, 88.

Despite the considerable attention given to the number seven in antiquity, Jewish tradition is alone in the ancient world in its conception of the seven days of the week and hence also of the sabbath, a conception based, of course, on the seven days of Creation. Even more important in the context of mysticism is the common root of the Hebrew words *sheva*, 'seven', and the word *shevuah*, 'oath'—a link of which the Qumranite writers were clearly aware, as noted by Yadin (ed.), *Dead Sea Scrolls*, 168. The earliest allusion to this link is the aetiological explanation of the name of the city of Beersheba—meaning either 'well of seven' or 'well of oath'—in Gen. 21: 28–31. The medieval commentator Ibn Ezra, commenting on Zech. 4: 10 ('Those seven are the eyes of the Lord, ranging over the whole earth'), notes the connection between 'seven' and 'oath', and then goes on to offer an occult interpretation of the verse, referring among other things to the sacred (seventh) *heikhal*, 'palace' or 'sanctuary', at the centre of Creation. The association is also made by Nahmanides, commenting on Num. 30: 3 ('If a man . . . takes an oath . . .'). Incidentally, according to the classical *Dictionary of the Hebrew Language* by E. Ben-Yehuda (Jerusalem, 1980), vol. iv, s.v., while the cognate root exists in all the Semitic languages in the sense of 'seven', the connotation of 'oath' or 'swear' is unique to Hebrew and to Jewish Aramaic.

The special importance and sanctity of the number seven in the Bible are undeniable, beginning with the count of seven days of Creation, through God's appearance to Moses on Mount Sinai on the seventh day ('On the seventh day He called to Moses from the midst of the cloud'—Exod. 24: 16), to the seven-times repeated ceremonies of purification, atonement, and benediction and the description in Prov. 9: 1: 'Wisdom has built her house, she has hewn her seven pillars.' Seven is the most prominent number in various priestly ceremonies and rituals (e.g. Lev. 4: 6–17), the sacrificial rites, the days of the pilgrimage festivals, and calculations of sabbatical years and jubilees. It is the number of 'princes of God, the archangels' (1 En. 20), and the number of angelic companies (2 En. 19: 1).

[77] 1 En. 20–1, 24, 43; 2 En. 3–22; Rev. 1. Biblical references to altars and sacrifice frequently involve the number seven. See, for example: 'Build me seven altars here . . .' (Num. 23: 1); 'Its staircase consisted of seven steps' (Ezek. 40: 26). The order of bulls offered as sacrifices on the seven days of

of the year, and the mythical space in which this order is preserved as seven Heikhalot in the Songs of the Sabbath Sacrifice by septuples of angels. They point to a perception of the heavens as a Temple of sevenfold structure.

This perception reaches its climax in the Songs of the Sabbath Sacrifice, in which the seven-based traditions of sacred time observed by angels, and the sacred place with its representation of the angels in the Chariot Throne of the cherubim, are combined with a seven-based tradition of a sacred service performed by angels. This is linked with the sublime components of the supernal sanctuary, which are described in terms of mystery and wonder, representing mystical metamorphoses coupling together the earthly and heavenly cults in sevenfold patterns:

> Psalm of praise-song by the tongue . . . The sev[enth of the chief princes] {{will sing}} a mighty praise-song to [the God of Holiness]
> [a] powerful [son]g to [the God of Holiness]
> [with seven wond]erful [songs] to bless the [King of Holiness seven times with seven] wonder[ful so]ngs
> [ ] Seven psalms of bl[essing of the glory of the Lord of all *elim*, sev]en psa[lms of magnification of]
> [His justice, seven] psalms of exal[tation of His kingdom, seven psalms of praise of His glory, seven psalms]
> [of thanksgiving for] His [won]ders [seven psalms of rejoicing in His power, seven psalms of songs of His holiness,
> [ ] seven times se[ven wonderful words, words of exaltation. [The sixth] of the deputy princes one will bless in the glorious]
> [name of the L]ord of a[l]l *el*[*im*, all the powerful of intellect with seven wonderful words, to bless all]
> [the priests of the] inner sanctum in the [wonderful] dwel[ling   with seven]
> wonderful [words] to praise [with seven]
> [won]derful [words and] he will praise a[ll   ][78]

Sukkot (Num. 29: 13–32) prescribes a descending number sequence, from thirteen on the first day, twelve on the second, and so on, to seven on the seventh day, for a total of seventy bulls (cf. the quotation from Jubilees, n. 59 above). See Chyutin, 'Numerical Mysticism'. The seven-branched lampstand in the Temple is linked by Philo and Josephus to the seven planets, but a more significant association would be to the seven days of Creation, as a link of sevenfold time and space. Many of the measurements in the Temple Scroll are based on multiples of seven, and the same is true of the dimensions in the scroll known as the New Jerusalem. In the early mystical work *Sefer yetsirah* (4: 3) we read: 'Seven directions and the Holy [seventh] Sanctuary [*heikhal*] precisely in the centre, and it supports them all'; the author then goes on to describe the affinities between seven days in the time dimension, seven planets, seven firmaments, seven sabbaths, seven sabbatical years, and further septuples or heptads, creating links between the universe and the world of humanity (ibid. 4: 4). A wall painting on the western wall of the ancient synagogue at Dura Europos portrays a heavenly Temple with seven walls, each behind another, surrounding a central sanctuary; perhaps there is some connection between this 3rd-century depiction and priestly traditions of septuples in the style of Heikhalot literature (see Goodenough, *Jewish Symbols*, xiii, pl. 9, and discussion ibid. x. 42–73).

[78] 11Q17 III, frgs. 4a–e, 5 (*DJD* XXIII, 271, 273). (Words in double braces are my clarifying additions, with no textual basis.)

This song is an invocation in which priests invoke angels (perhaps this is the ancient meaning of the word 'Hallelujah'), designated as 'chief princes', 'godlike beings of knowledge', 'God of holiness', and 'the powerful of intellect'; they describe their worship in such phrases as 'seven times with seven wonderful words', 'seven priesthoods in the wondrous sanctuary for the seven holy councils', 'seven mysteries of knowledge in the wondrous mystery of the seven precincts of the Holy of Holies'.

Besides these liturgical septuples of angelic song, which interweave secret and manifest, mystery and knowledge in song and praise, we find references to 'seven lofty holy places', 'seven *devirim* of the priesthoods', 'seven wondrous territories according to the ordinances of his sanctuaries', and the like.[79] Such phrases, evoking the different connotations of the word *da'at*, 'knowledge', and echoing the language of *Sefer yetsirah*—which refers to 'twelve diagonal boundaries', 'sanctuary of holiness', and 'seventh sanctuary' in its account of cosmic order, perhaps alluding to the relationship between sexual urge (*yetser*) and creation (*yetsirah*), covenant (*berit*) and Creation (*beriah*)—structure the sacred space in a sevenfold pattern. These spatial patterns represent the sanctity of place in its relation to the Chariot Throne, the sanctuary, the Holy of Holies, the *heikhal*, the Temple, and the priesthood; in combination, they yield liturgical formulas which, in the Songs of the Sabbath Sacrifice, directly invoke the heavenly Temple; there the earthly sanctuary is transformed into seven supernal Heikhalot, pictured in the plural in terms clearly pointing to Ezekiel's Merkavah. As we have observed, the Merkavah tradition of mystical liturgy personifies the cultic structures of the Holy of Holies and the Temple courts, metamorphosing them into the cosmic space of the Merkavah and its creatures, which minister in the heavenly Temple, singing, praising, chanting, prostrating themselves, and blessing after the fashion of priestly and levitical worship.

The heavenly Temple is referred to in the Songs of the Sabbath Sacrifice and the Blessings Scroll, among other works, in a variety of terms: '*heikhalot* of His Glory', '*heikhalot* of the King', and described as 'the splendidly shining firmament of [His] holy sanctuary . . . the firmament of the uppermost heaven, all [its beams] and its walls, a[l]l its [form], the work of [its] pattern', 'in all heights of the sanctuaries of His glorious kingdom', 'from the source of holiness to the holy sanctuaries', 'walls of their glorious halls, their wondrous doors', 'the temples of Your kingdom . . . their wondrous abodes'. It is intimately bound up with the world of the Merkavah, all of whose elements bless, praise, and sing on high, sabbath after

---

[79] Newsom, *Songs*, concordance, 389–465. Maier, 'Shire Olat hash-Shabbat', 554, analysing the frequency of occurrences of words in the Songs, has found that the word *sheva*, 'seven', variously declined, occurs 116 times, out of 325 characteristic linguistic formations in these works. This is the largest number of occurrences compared with any other word. For comparison: the word *kodesh*, 'sanctity/holiness', occurs 97 times; *kavod*, 'glory'—100 times; *pele*, 'wonder'—101 times; *elohim*, 'God'—115 times.

sabbath. Such utterances as 'And the chariots of His *devir* give praise together, and their cherubim and thei[r] *ofanim* bless wondrously [. . .] the chiefs of the divine pattern. And they praise Him in His holy *devir*', 'the pattern of the Chariot Throne do they bless above the firmament of the cherubim', 'the cherubim fall before Him and bless, as they rise, the sound of divine stillness', 'move continuously with the glory of the wondrous chariots', 'for all His majestic chariots and His holy *devirim*', 'of wonder, *devir* to *devir* with the sound of holy multitudes, and all their crafted furnishings', 'with these let all the foundations of the Holy of Holies praise the uplifting pillars of the supremely lofty abode, and all the corners of its structure sing', 'Give praise to Him, O you godlike spirits, in order to thank for ever and ever. . . . The spirits of holiest holiness, the living godlike ones, the spirits of eternal holiness above . . . in all the wondrous sanctuaries', scattered throughout the Songs of the Sabbath Sacrifice,[80] and similar phrases in the Blessings: 'And all spirits of the sanctum who uplift (the praise) . . . all will bless together Your holy name', 'the mystery/council of the *elim* of purification with all those who have eternal knowledge, to praise and to bless Your glorious name in all everlasting ages', 'spirits of the holiest holiness will sing in joy in all the set times and they will bless the name of Your glorious divinity'[81]—such language unifies sacred space, portrayed in terms of *devir* and *heikhal*, of Merkavah and Temple, all multiplied by seven, with sacred ritual, represented in terms of song, chant, benediction, and praise in priestly-angelic worship, arranged in accordance with the cycle of sabbaths and in sevenfold multiples. These liturgical expressions turned the invisible world of the Chariot into an audible and verbal ritualized mystical reality. The world of the Merkavah pictured in the vision of the priest Ezekiel in relation to the Holy of Holies and the Temple was transformed in Qumran literature in terms of a heavenly ritual, to become a mystical reality, a liturgical entity, clearly demonstrating that wherever a secret reality occupies centre stage, a new verbal world will be created to make it manifest, recalling a penetrating insight of Mircea Eliade:

In mythical geography, sacred space is the essentially real space, for in the archaic world the myth alone is real. It tells of manifestations of the only indubitable reality—the sacred.[82]

---

[80] Newsom, *Songs*, 209–10, and concordance; *DJD* XI, 445–72.

[81] 4Q286, frg. 7 i, 6–7; ii, 1–2 (*DJD* XI, 17, 25, 26).   [82] Eliade, *Images and Symbols*, 40.

THREE

The Solar Calendar as Pattern of Sacred Time

And you, command the children of Israel so that they shall guard the years in this number, three hundred and sixty-four days, and it will be a complete year.[1]

... at the end of a full year of three hundred and sixty-four days.[2]

THE divine origin of time, its sacred cyclic pattern attesting to the eternity of the cosmic order, its regular, cyclic rhythms in time with the changes of nature, are described in the Thanksgiving Hymns. The poet describes a full twenty-four-hour day from end to end, from sunrise to sunrise, picturing the regular, eternal beat of divine time underlying the laws of heaven and earth:

Bowing down in prayer I will beg Thy favours
from *kets* to *kets*[3] always:
when light emerges from [its dwelling-place]
in the cycles [*tekufot*] of day as preordained
in accordance with the laws of the Great Light when evening falls
and light departs at the beginning of the dominion of darkness,
at the hour appointed [*mo'ed*] for night in its cycle, when morning dawns,
and at the end of its return to its dwelling-place before the approach of light;
always at all *moladei et, yesodei kets*
and the cycle of the appointed times as they are established
by signs [*ot*] for their entire dominion
established faithfully from God's mouth, by predestination [*te'udah*] of being
and it will be [for ever] and without end.
Without it nothing is nor shall be,
    for the God of knowledge established it
    and there is no other beside Him.[4]

---

[1] Jub. 6: 32.   [2] Genesis Commentaries, 4Q252, II, 2–3 (*DJD* XXII, 198–9).
[3] A term used in Qumran literature to denote a recurrent, measured, unit of time (in this case a twenty-four-hour day); it may sometimes be translated as 'age'. The usual meaning of the word in Biblical Hebrew is 'end' (e.g. Gen. 6: 13; Eccl. 4: 8); it took on the meaning of 'time' in later periods (and particularly in Aramaic).
[4] Thanksgiving Hymns XII, 4–11 (cf. Vermes, *CDSSIE*, 290–1). Cf. 4Q427, col. ii, 10–16 (*DJD* XXIX, 110–12).

The various time-related terms occurring here, in poetic language, represent the basis for the numerical calculation of the cyclic pattern of divine time: *kets* = recurrent time unit (such as, in the above passage, a twenty-four-hour day); *tekufah* = cyclic period (relative to the daily and annual course of the sun); *mo'ed* = divinely appointed time, attesting to God's decree; *moladei et, yesodei kets* = measurable and countable units of time: day, week, month, year, and the four intercalary days when the sun turns round in the heavens; *ot* = sign, a visible divine time marker, such as the sun, or a God-given invisible marker, such as the sabbath, attesting to and designating the fixed, divine, cyclic order; *te'udah* = preordained heavenly statute, destined to exist for ever and attesting to the laws of nature.

Alongside the cycles of transformations in nature reflecting the eternal divine order in the *revealed* dimension, the priestly tradition counted the ritual cycles of *mikra'ei kodesh* (holy convocations and appointed times, when rest was imposed and no work was done), monitoring the *concealed* sevenfold cycles of sabbaths and festivals, sabbatical years and jubilees. The sevenfold cycles of holy days of rest and no work, reflecting divine sovereignty and human resignation in favour of sanctity, have no visible testimony in nature or any revealed expression other than the audible divine decree taught by the angels and kept by the priests. Observing the sevenfold holy cycles of human resignation and rest, cessation of labour and abstention from mundane interests (sabbaths, *shevitah, shemitah, yovel, shivah mo'adim*) is the divine precondition for the continuity of the eternal cycles of nature, the cycle of fertility, procreation, and life promised in the covenants.

As noted previously, the literature of the secessionist priesthood envisaged the solar calendar, based on a cyclic seven-based calculation, as a paradigm of sacred time, combining cosmic and ritual time; or as an axis linking heaven and earth, defining the shifting seasons of the year, its sabbaths and appointed times as observed in the terrestrial Temple by the priests, guardians of the sacred service and witnesses to time, and in the heavenly Temple by the angels, guardians of the heavenly tablets. The priestly circles among whom these traditions emerged held the solar calendar to be sacred, eternal, and divine; it had governed pre-calculated, recurrent units of time since the seven days of Creation and symbolized the intrinsic holiness of the universe. It was imprinted upon nature as a divine sign, from God's sanctification of the first sabbath to the sanctification of the appointed times. This calendar, evidence of the divine origin of time and of its eternal sevenfold structure, linking the cyclicity of the cosmic order with that of the ritual order, was engraved on heavenly tablets and preserved and observed by the angels, as recounted in Enoch and Jubilees. The calculation of the calendar had been revealed to humans by the angels, so that mortals, too, would testify to the sanctity of time and its eternal cyclic structure, observing the sabbaths and the appointed times on earth in seven-weekly cycles *together with* the denizens of heaven.

Written in part in the heat of polemics and controversy over the sanctity of time, place, and ritual, the secessionist priestly literature, partly preserving ancient traditions, highlighted the heavenly origin of time. The continuity, uniformity, infinity, and preordained cyclic subdivision of time in heaven and earth bore witness to its divine origins. The seven-based pattern, deriving from the seven days of Creation, was associated with the eternal essence of the divine Creator, as reflected in the cosmic determinism of the cyclic natural laws that governed the four seasons of the solar year and the cyclic motions of the celestial bodies, which could be predicted and calculated with extreme mathematical precision.

The question of the different calendars of the Second Temple period and their relationship to biblical calendars has been discussed extensively in the literature[5] and in studies of the various works in which the Qumran calendar appears. Opinions are divided between two basic theses. The first claims that the Qumran calendar reflects a solar calendar dating to biblical times; in fact, in light of findings at the site, it has been conjectured that the solar calendar of the Qumranites was essentially that of the Bible.[6] Opponents of this thesis hold that the 364-day calendar has no foundation in biblical tradition and in fact was unusable in real life, arguing, among other things, that with passing time the discrepancy between this calendar and the true solar year, whose length is approximately 365¼ days, would have distorted the relationship between the festivals and the seasons.[7] This argument has been met with the suggestion that seven-day units were added (perhaps in the sabbatical year) to adapt the schematic Qumran calendar to the true solar calendar; alternatively, it has been suggested that the Qumranites used a lunar–solar calendar, or a synchronistic calendar.[8] Evidence of the latter has been found in some Qumran fragments,[9] implying that thirty days were added every three years to correlate the paths of the moon and the sun ($364 \times 3 = 354 \times 3 + 30$; the sun and moon return to the same position and the same configuration every three years, on the first day of the first month (Nisan)).

There is no doubt, however, that the different views of the calendar and the calculation of its subdivisions were hotly debated in the Second Temple period.

---

[5] See Ch. 1, n. 47.

[6] For this group see Jaubert, 'Calendrier des Jubilées... Qumran'; van Goudoever, *Biblical Calendars*; Milik, *Ten Years of Discovery*, 110; Jaubert, 'Calendar of Qumran'; Talmon, *World of Qumran from Within*; VanderKam, 'Origin, Character and History'; Chyutin, *War of Calendars*. Jaubert, 'Calendrier des Jubilées... Qumran', 256, arguing that the solar calendar of Qumran reflects a First Temple tradition, suggests that it was displaced by the lunar calendar owing to Greek influence (in 175 BCE, Antiochus IV Epiphanes instituted a lunar calendar throughout his kingdom). Nowhere in biblical tradition is the number of days in a year explicitly indicated, whereas the parallel traditions in the literature of the secessionist priesthood emphatically speak of a year of 364 days and 52 weeks. According to Jaubert, the books of Chronicles, Ezra, Nehemiah, and Ezekiel, which are attributed to priestly authorship, seem to be based on the solar calendar.

[7] See e.g. Herr, 'Calendar', and bibliography ibid. 862–4. J. M. Baumgarten, 'Calendars', holds that the lunar calendar was always the basis of religious life in Israel.

[8] The seven-day units were suggested, *inter alia*, by e.g. Talmon and Knohl, 'Calendrical Scroll'. For the alternative solution see e.g. Milik, *Books of Enoch*, 274–5, 429; id., *Ten Years of Discovery*, 110–11.   [9] 4QEnas7; cf. *DJD* XXXVI, 97–9, 108–10.

One theory actually traces the roots of the controversy to the Bible itself, where two different systems of counting seem to be reflected by the biblical prescriptions for Shavuot, the elevation of the Omer, and the seven-week period between them—one counting 'sabbath weeks', each beginning on Sunday and ending on the sabbath, as in Leviticus 23: 15–16; and the other counting in seven-day units, regardless of the first day of reckoning, as in Deuteronomy 16: 9. There is a striking correlation between these systems and the well-known controversies of the Second Temple period: counting in 'sabbath weeks' would seem to recall the tradition of the (priestly) Qumran calendar, while counting in seven-day units, disregarding the sabbath, conforms to rabbinic tradition.[10]

However, it is more generally believed that a split took place in the priesthood at some time in the fifth century BCE. One of the factions thus formed exhibited marked prophetic and priestly tendencies, while the other was more rationalist; ultimately, the first group evolved into the Qumran community, while the other was the basis of rabbinic Judaism. The frequency with which the solar calendar is mentioned and its obvious centrality in such works as 1 and 2 Enoch, Jubilees, the Temple Scroll, *Miktsat ma'asei hatorah*, the Scroll of Priestly Courses, the Thanksgiving Hymns, and the Flood fragments, as well as indirect evidence from the Songs of the Sabbath Sacrifice and the Commentary on Habakkuk, invite the plausible hypothesis that it was indeed used in the Temple by the pre-Hasmonaean Zadokite priests. The alternative versions of the Flood narrative, as to the number of days and their subdivision, as recounted in Genesis, on the one hand, and Qumran and Septuagint traditions, on the other, imply that the question was debated in the last centuries BCE, as is shown in detail in this study (see Chapter 6).

Among the indications that the solar calendar might well have been the official calendar of the First Temple or of the Second Temple in its earlier stages are the following: (1) According to mainstream tradition, the Temple day began in the morning, at sunrise, and the night was counted after the day—a characteristic of the solar year and calendar. (2) The liturgical traditions associated with the priestly courses are arranged according to the 'sabbath weeks' of the solar calendar.

In any event, as envisaged by the authors of the secessionist priestly literature, heavenly time, measured in weeks/sabbaths and guarded by angels, governed the liturgical appointed times of the Temple ritual, which were observed by priests. It described a sevenfold rhythm around a symmetric, fourfold division into liturgical quarter-years, correlated with the four seasons of the year and with the continuity of the cycle of life and fertility: twenty-four hours in a day, seven days in a week, thirteen sabbaths in a quarter; this rhythm was maintained by twenty-four priestly courses, serving thirteen cycles in weekly rotation in a recurrent, six-yearly cycle, as seen previously.[11]

This division of time was established on earth by the angelic revelation of the liturgical and ritual calendar, in which all days, appointed times, and dates were

---

[10] See Na'eh, 'Did the *tana'im* . . . ?', 424–39.   [11] See pp. 42–3 above.

predetermined and immutable: festivals never fell on the sabbath, but festivals and sabbaths were symmetrically synchronized from one quarter-year to the next, in a fixed schedule maintained by the guardians of the sacred service. The sanctity of time (appointed time; covenant; oath; sabbath); its divine origin (testimony; heavenly statutes; heavenly tablets; heavenly signs; seven days of Creation; 'wondrous mysteries'); its revelation by angels, witnesses to the Covenant, who taught humanity the proper sequence of sabbaths, weeks, seasons, festivals, months, sabbatical years, jubilees, and their fixed arithmetical relationships; and the priestly custodianship of divine time (the tablets of testimony; the tablets of the Covenant; the Tent of Meeting; the sacred service; priestly courses; seven days of ordination; sevenfold repetition of the rites of atonement and purification; priestly and angelic 'togetherness' or community (*yaḥad*); 'seven chief princes')—all these were the subject of three myths around which revolved the entire literature of the secessionist priesthood. These myths, each from a different perspective, postulated links between, on the one hand, the solar calendar, representing the cyclic pattern of cosmic order ('heavenly chariots', 1 Enoch 75: 3) and angelic testimony to heavenly time through observation of the liturgical order ('praise together the chariots of his inner sanctum') , and, on the other, the fixed, cyclic, cultic order and the priestly courses who expressed that order through narrative, number, and book.

A myth is the lens through which a society relates its own workings and order to the nature of things itself, to its divine origins, and to its representative concepts of sanctity. Myth defines a relationship between nature and the laws governing the universe, on the one hand, and history, religion, and cult, on the other; between the divine and the human. The three myths may be summarized as follows:

1. The sanctity of the solar year and its heavenly origin are reflected in the story of Enoch son of Jared, the seventh patriarch of the world, who ascended to heaven, learned the secrets of the calendar and its calculation from the angels, and witnessed the pattern of time and its eternal order. This order was associated with the seasons of the year, the laws of nature recorded in the heavenly tablets, and the preordained, cosmic, symmetric, mathematical cyclicity of nature, which found expression in the cult of the Sons of Light and the sons of Zadok, performed by priests and angels in concert, who thereby preserved the numerical aspects of the cycles of fertility and procreation, purification and sanctity, and thus the continuity of life itself.

2. The impure nature of the lunar calendar and its sinful origin are embodied in the myth of the descent of the 'sons of God' to earth, also known as the rebellion of the 'Watchers', who followed their wilful hearts, and 'the sin of the fallen angels', who corrupted the land. This rebellion constituted a violation of the sanctity of time and the divine order, a desecration of the sanctity of life; an eruption of evil forces that sought to disrupt the natural order and engaged in the most heinous crimes, it stemmed from misinterpretation and idolatrous knowledge of the ways

of the stars and the constellations, from espousal of the lunar calendar, which infringed upon the proper sequence of time. This confusion of the proper order was associated with Sons of Darkness, sons of iniquity, and the fate of Belial—the direct and indirect causes of impurity, oblivion, and death.

3. The eternal nature of the cultic solar calendar, its angelic origins, and its sevenfold structure are presented in the myth of the sabbath and Shavuot, celebrated together by septuples of angels in the seven supernal Heikhalot and by priestly courses serving weekly shifts in the terrestrial Temple. The sun, the great luminary,[12] sabbath, the seventh day,[13] the seven-coloured rainbow,[14] and Enoch, the seventh patriarch of the world,[15] are all called signs in parallel traditions in Genesis, Exodus, and Jubilees. The solar calendar attests to the eternal, divine order, which depends on heavenly signs, to the cosmic liturgical cycle of time counted in sabbaths, to the Covenant and eternal oath and the continuity of life. Signs also relate to cosmic and ritual testimony as to the eternity of oath and promise, which depend on a sevenfold cyclic order.

The next three chapters will consider a few aspects of these three myths, which concern the establishment and later violation of the divine order; the foundations of good and evil, sanctity and impurity, innocence and guilt; the struggle between light and darkness, between the solar calendar and the lunar; the conflict between immutable mathematical knowledge, which reflects an abstract, divine reality and cosmic cycles, and computation resting on variable, humanly observed data, limited by the powers of human apprehension and by concrete reality. In these myths, angels and human beings find themselves challenging the forbidden heavenly knowledge associated with the Watchers and the Sons of Darkness; they confront the fluctuating lunar calendar and temporary knowledge, based on human observation, with permitted heavenly knowledge coming from the angels, relating to the Sons of Light, the eternal solar calendar, and fixed arithmetical knowledge.

[12] Jub. 2: 8–9; Gen. 1: 14.   [13] Exod. 31: 13, 16.
[14] Gen. 9: 13–17.   [15] Jub. 4: 23–4.

FOUR

Enoch Son of Jared and the Solar Calendar

Enoch was found to be perfect and walked with the Lord and was taken, a sign of knowledge to all generations.[1]

He was the first among the sons of men who were born upon earth and who wrote in a book the signs of heaven according to the order of their months, so that the sons of man might know the appointed times of the years according to their order with respect to each of their months.[2]

TIME, as conceived by the authors of Qumran literature (in particular, the Temple Scroll, *Miktsat ma'asei hatorah* (MMT), Songs of the Sabbath Sacrifice, the Damascus Document, Blessings, the Psalms Scroll, the Calendars of Priestly Courses) and certain pseudepigraphic works (Jubilees, 1 and 2 Enoch), was not an arbitrary, man-made structure or human order, dependent on unstable observations and determinations influenced by external conditions, adjustments, and errors. It was of divine origin, a cosmic pattern obeying preordained, immutable laws, a cycle that had been recurring since sacred time was imprinted on nature during the seven days of Creation and consecrated through the sabbath day. Time was envisaged as the reflection of divine order in the universe, so designed as to perpetuate the cycle of life, blessing, and fertility, an order in which time and space are sanctified and interdependent from the earliest stages of Creation, which took place in time divided into seven days and in the space formed during those seven days.

The calendar was not entrusted to man, subject to adjustment and change, dependent upon human calculations or terrestrial considerations; for it represented the concept of a profound, comprehensive reality, a divine reality beyond the reach of the senses but reflected in the cyclic, numerical harmony revealed in the passage and changes of time. The calendar, based on a cycle of sabbaths and seasons, embodied the eternity of the primeval order, based on the eternal cycle of the sun and the cyclic motion of the celestial bodies, which could be precisely predicted by numerical calculation. The calendar also related to the secrets of the cyclic nature of procreation, dependent on counting and calculation, purification

---

[1] Ben Sira 44: 16.   [2] 11Q12, frg. 4, 1–3 (*DJD* XXIII, 213).

and oath, ensuring the continuity of abundance, life, and fertility. Any infringement of this sacred cyclic pattern, as expressed in the fixed numerical proportions of its component parts, any attempt to ignore the divine pattern based on number and counting, would generate impurity, bringing in its wake curse, death, and oblivion.

The calendar of weeks and seasons, of sabbaths and covenants, with its eternal cyclic, numerical pattern, was taught to human beings by divine, angelic revelation. The goal of this revelation—variously designated in Qumran literature as 'wondrous mysteries', 'the secret of Your wonder', 'the mystery of Your knowledge'[3]— was to teach the founders of the priestly dynasty the proper order of heavenly, cosmic time, and its terrestrial counterpart in a cyclic cultic order, reflected in liturgy, that testified to the seven-based divine pattern of time and to its cyclic nature, in terms of sabbaths and festivals, as well as cycles of life and fertility. This is the message of the books named after the archetypal mystical hero, Enoch son of Jared, who was taken up to heaven[4] to observe the cosmic regularity of the laws of nature, to witness the heavenly structure of time as manifested in the solar calendar, and to bring heavenly time down to terrestrial space and introduce the order of Creation into the cultic order.[5]

We possess four works known as 'the Book of Enoch', reflecting both parallel and distinct traditions concerning Enoch, his ascent to heaven, and the myth of the calendar and the priesthood.

I. The *First*, or *Ethiopic*, *Book of Enoch* (1 Enoch) was written in the second century BCE, translated from Hebrew or Aramaic into Greek and then into Ethiopic (Ge'ez). Some scholars favour an even earlier date of composition, assigning some parts of it to the third century BCE and others to the first century BCE.[6] Comprising 108 chapters and preserved in its entirety in Ethiopic, the work consists of five 'books':

(a) *The Book of the Watchers* (= angels), chs. 1–36, parts of which, in Aramaic, have been found at Qumran.

(b) *The Book of Similitudes*, chs. 37–71, also known as *The Similitudes of Enoch*, composed at a later date, possibly late first century BCE. Some authorities date this part as late as the third century CE;[7] no part of it was found at Qumran.

(c) *The Book of the Course of Heavenly Luminaries* (or *Astronomical Book*), chs. 72–82, assigned by some scholars to the third century BCE. Sizeable parts of this 'book', in Aramaic, were found in Qumran Cave 4, in four copies. There are significant differences between the Aramaic original and the Ethiopic version; the Aramaic is longer and more detailed, providing more astronomical information concerning the solar year of 364 days and the lunar year of 354 days.

---

[3] Thanksgiving Hymns XII.　　　　　　　　　　　　　　　　　　　[4] Gen. 5: 24.
[5] On the figure of Enoch see Schürer, *History*, iii. 269–75; A. Segal, 'Heavenly Ascent'; Elior, 'Jewish Calendar and Mystical Time'.
[6] See Greenfield and Stone, 'Enochic Pentateuch'.　　　　[7] Milik, *Books of Enoch*, 89–98.

(*d*) *The Book of Dreams* (or historical events), chs. 83–90, was found in Aramaic in Qumran Cave 4; it has been dated to the early Hasmonaean period (the sixties of the second century BCE).

(*e*) *The Epistle of Enoch* or *Apocalypse of Weeks* (Enoch's account of future events, delivered to his sons), chs. 91–107. The book ends with the miraculous birth of Noah, the successor to the priestly dynasty. Parts of the Epistle of Enoch, also in Aramaic, were found at Qumran; it has been dated to *c.*170 BCE. (Chapter 108 is not included in the early versions of the book and is apparently quite late.)

The First Book of Enoch was translated from Ethiopic back into Hebrew in modern times, by Jacques Faïtlovitch and Abraham Kahana (before the discovery of the Qumran fragments); the joint translation was published in the latter's edition of non-canonical literature.[8]

II. The *Second*, or *Slavonic, Book of Enoch* (2 Enoch), probably written in Hebrew in the first century CE (the original is lost), was translated into Greek and then into Church Slavonic. There are two recensions, one long and one short, based on five manuscripts discovered by a Russian scholar, M. Sokolov, in the 1880s and published by one of his pupils in 1910. The long recension was translated into Hebrew from the Belgrade manuscript by A. Kahana in 1937 and published in his edition of non-canonical works.[9] Various hypotheses have been put forward about the origin and date of composition of this work. Kahana believes that the work was written in Hebrew in Jerusalem while the Second Temple was still standing, and only translated into Greek in Egypt; while Charles dates the composition of the work to 30–70 CE in Alexandria. Andersen, introducing his modern English translation in Charlesworth's *Old Testament Pseudepigrapha*, insists on the basically Jewish ambience of the work, though other scholars claim to have identified Christian traces. Scholem, too, attributes the work to a Jewish author of the first century CE, advocating ideas close to Gnosticism and Heikhalot literature; Pines, VanderKam, and Charlesworth also believe that the author was Jewish and wrote in Hebrew in the first century CE; he was acquainted with the Temple service but had Hellenistic leanings. Most scholars believe the shorter recension

---

[8] A. Kahana (ed.), *Apocrypha*, i. 19–101. For modern English translations see Charlesworth (ed.), *OT Pseudepigrapha*; Black, *Book of Enoch*. For the reader's convenience, here is a representative selection of scholarly literature on 1 Enoch: Milik, *Books of Enoch*, with bibliography on pp. 59–69; Greenfield and Stone, 'Enochic Pentateuch'; Stone, 'Books of Enoch'; Knibb, *Ethiopic Book of Enoch*; Gruenwald, *Apocalyptic and Merkavah Mysticism*; Nickelsburg, 'Apocalyptic and Myth'; Isaac in Charlesworth (ed.), *OT Pseudepigrapha*, i. 5–12; Black, *Book of Enoch*; Gil, 'Studies in the Book of Enoch'; VanderKam, *Enoch and the Growth of an Apocalyptic Tradition*; Sacchi, 'Two Calendars'; VanderKam, *Enoch—A Man for All Generations*; id., *Calendars in the Dead Sea Scrolls*. Black, 'Bibliography on 1 Enoch', provides a bibliography of scholarship up to the end of the 1980s; further bibliography may be found in Boccaccini, *Beyond the Essene Hypothesis*, 349–56.

[9] A. Kahana (ed.), *Apocrypha*, i. 102–41.

to be closer to the original and date it around the first century, while the long recension is associated with the Greek translation of the work in the fifth century CE.[10]

III. The *Third Book of Enoch* (3 Enoch), also known as *Sefer heikhalot*, was written in Hebrew in the period of the Mishnah and the Talmud. It has survived in its original language in manuscripts of Heikhalot literature. Much of the work is based on earlier Enoch traditions.[11]

IV. The *Fourth Book of Enoch* (4 Enoch), found at Qumran in Aramaic in eleven manuscripts, was published by Milik in his *The Books of Enoch*. This work, the earliest of the surviving Enoch books, includes parts of 1 Enoch—from all parts of it except the Book of Similitudes. As already noted, no fragments of the Book of Similitudes, whose content and style mark it as a late addition to the original work, have been discovered at Qumran. On the other hand, Qumran finds include nine manuscripts of what has been called the Book of Giants, a sequel to the Book of the Watchers. Milik conjectures that this was the second part of the Enoch 'anthology' before it was replaced by the Book of Similitudes. The Qumran (Aramaic) version of the Book of Heavenly Luminaries includes important additions, not found in the Ethiopic version or its translations.[12]

Enoch traditions may also be found in Jubilees, the Genesis Apocryphon, the Testaments of the Twelve Tribes, and various Qumran fragments, touching among other things on the origins of the priesthood and the birth of Noah. Enoch is mentioned, for example, in 5Q13, in a passage alluding to God's election of *benei elim*, Enoch, Abraham, Jacob, Levi, and his sons as keepers of the covenants and

---

[10] For 2 Enoch in general see A. Kahana (ed.), *Apocrypha*, introduction (pp. 102–4); Odeberg, *3 Enoch*, 43–63; Scholem, *Jewish Gnosticism*, 62 ff.; Rubinstein, 'Observations'; Pines, 'Eschatology and the Concept of Time'; Milik, *Books of Enoch*, 109–12; Andersen in Charlesworth (ed.), *OT Pseudepigrapha*, i. 91–213; Böttrich, *Weltweisheit* (the last-named is the most thorough study to date of Slavonic Enoch, including a comprehensive history of research in the field, including the Russian manuscripts). Milik, *Books of Enoch*, 110, relying on the references in the last chapters to the story of Melchizedek and the lineage of the priesthood, ascribes the book to a Byzantine Christian monk, but his thesis has not found support in the scholarly world. A. M. Wagner, in a recent doctoral dissertation on 2 Enoch ('Zwischen Engeln und Menschen'), has argued that the longer recension is superior to the shorter one.

[11] 3 Enoch was first published by Odeberg, *3 Enoch*, in 1928 (but based on a corrupt manuscript), and reprinted in 1973, with a 'Prolegomenon' by Greenfield. The complete text, in different versions, may now be found in Schäfer (ed.), *Synopse*, §§1–80. A new English translation was published by P. S. Alexander in Charlesworth's *OT Pseudepigrapha*, i. 223–316, with an introduction summarizing the research history of the work up to the early 1980s. See Odeberg, *3 Enoch*; Scholem, *Jewish Gnosticism*, 43–55; Milik, *Books of Enoch*, 126–35; Alexander, 'Historical Setting', 156–80; Gruenwald, *Apocalyptic and Merkavah Mysticism*, 191–208; Schäfer, *Hidden and Manifest God*, 123–38; Elior, 'Mysticism, Magic and Angelology'.

[12] For 4 Enoch and its affinity with 1 Enoch see Milik, *Books of Enoch*, 273–8; VanderKam, *Enoch and the Growth of an Apocalyptic Tradition*; Gil, 'Studies in the Book of Enoch'; Black, *Book of Enoch*; id., 'Bibliography on 1 Enoch'; Stone, 'Enoch, Aramaic Levi and Sectarian Origins'; *DJD* XXXVI, 3–171.

the appointed times. He is also referred to implicitly in 4Q 534, in an allusion to Enoch the scribe: 'a man who knows nothing until the time when he knows the three books'; and in the so-called Book of Noah, in a Hebrew fragment (1Q19) referring to 1 Enoch 8: 4.

The aim of Enoch literature—whose hero, described as 'Enoch have you chosen from among the sons of A[da]m' and called a 'righteous man, scribe of righteousness',[13] repeatedly transcended the boundaries of time and place—was to link cosmic with ritual cyclicity, to elucidate in detail the relationship between the divine sevenfold structure of heavenly time, as reflected by sign and oath (sabbath, sun, seven, sun of righteousness), and the pattern of weeks of the cyclic earthly calendar, as reflected in the cultic calendar and attested by the priestly courses as they observed the appointed times, kept the oath and the Covenant, and pursued the paths of righteousness. Enoch literature also delineated the sevenfold pattern of sabbaths of years, sabbatical years, jubilee years, and ages (*kitsim*) of the deterministic, linear calendar—the calendar of years of continuous history, preordained from beginning to end in multiples of seven. This pattern was embodied in the myth recounted by the priests and angels who were responsible for preserving the sequence of sabbatical and jubilee years, it too designated by the names of the priestly courses.

Enoch son of Jared was, as already noted, the seventh in the list of generations from Adam to Noah; this is stated in the biblical 'record of Adam's line'[14] and in the list of patriarchs of the world in a prayer found at Qumran: 'Kenan was from the fourth generation and Mahalel his son was the fifth generation . . . and Jared his son was sixth generation and Enoch his son; Enoch was seventh generation.'[15] The length of his mortal life—365 years[16]—exactly parallels the number of days in the solar year, specified sometimes as 364 and sometimes as 365 in the various calendar traditions.[17]

---

[13] 5Q13: 5 (cf. Kister, '5Q13 and the Avoda'); 1 En. 15: 1.   [14] Gen. 5: 1–33.

[15] 4Q 369, frg. 1 i, 9–10 (*DJD* XIII, 353–5; cf. Vermes, *CDSSIE*, 511). Cf. Jub. 7: 39: 'as Enoch commanded his son in the first jubilee, being the seventh in his generation'; 1 En. 37: 1–2: 'The vision which Enoch saw the second time—the vision of wisdom which Enoch, son of Jared, son of Mahalel, son of Kenan, son of Enosh, son of Seth, son of Adam, saw'; and cf. 1 En. 93: 3; 60: 8. On Enoch see also Ben Sira 44: 16; 49: 14; Heb. 11: 5–6. Qumran traditions on Enoch may also be found in the fragment 5Q13 (cf. 11Q12, frg. 4, 1–3: *DJD* XXIII, 213; see Kister, '5Q13 and the Avoda'), which deals with the list of keepers of the Covenant and the festival calendar, as well as in passages relating to the birth of Noah in the Genesis Apocryphon. For Mesopotamian traditions of one Enmeduranki, the seventh of a line of ten Sumerian kings, who ruled before the Flood in Sipar, the city of the sun god, and possessed divine knowledge, and the comparison with Enoch, the seventh patriarch of the world, who brought the solar calendar to earth and was granted divine visions, see Lambert, 'Enmeduranki'; VanderKam, *Enoch—A Man for All Generations*, 7–14; Arbel, 'Mythical Elements'.   [16] Gen. 5: 23.

[17] 1 En. 1: 1–36; 2 En. 14: 1; 16: 4; 68ᵃ: 1; Jub. 6: 32. The real solar year comprises 365¼ days (that is, a full cycle of the sun's apparent motion), but the schematic year in the Qumran calendar consists of 364 days (= fifty-two weeks). The number of days in the solar year was quite well known in antiquity, as we learn from Egyptian literature and 2 Enoch, and the authors of Enoch and Jubilees were well aware of the discrepancy. We do not know how the priestly community actually co-ordinated the real

The story of Enoch is the story of a human being transported from the realm of life and death ordained for ordinary mortals: he did not die like any other mortal but was taken to God: 'All the days of Enoch came to 365 years. Enoch walked with God; then he was no more, for God took him.'[18] As we learn from the four books named after Enoch, it was God's will that he become immortal, so that he should be able to observe and study heavenly time and its structure, its regularity and continuity, and report the mutual relationship between the realms of time and Creation to his sons, the founders of the priesthood, who were entrusted with preservation of the testimony and the appointed times. He became a prototype of the mystical priestly hero who transcended the boundaries of time and place, ascending from earth to heaven by divine will; he rose above the limits differentiating man and angel in order to learn the divine secrets of time and place. Enoch was 'taken to God' to be a sign, an eternal witness, beyond the confines of time and place, to the laws of heaven and earth.

Two special numbers, of crucial significance for the solar calendar, were associated with the figure of Enoch: seven, the number of days of Creation and the number signifying the sabbath, and 364/365, the number of days in the solar year. There may also be some significance to the numerical value (*gematriyah*) of his name, $84 = 7 \times 12$, the product of the number of days in the week and the number of months in a year. By virtue of these two numbers, and of course his signal righteousness, he alone was granted eternal life and heavenly knowledge of the mysteries of the universe and its cyclic nature. The first literate and numerate person in human history according to priestly tradition, he crossed the lines from mortality to immortality, to be a sign like the sabbath, the rainbow, and the sun, permitted to move back and forth between the realms of earthly and heavenly time and space and the realms of past and future, between the realms of human knowledge and the infinity of divine knowledge—in order to learn the secrets of the solar calendar and the order of sabbaths and festivals.

and ritual numbers, but their cyclic calculations involve a calendar of 364 days and an additional day, not included in the ritual count, which was perhaps added once in four years to compensate for the difference (or perhaps added as an extra week in the sabbatical year, once in seven years). The various traditions refer to both numbers and to the additional, uncounted, day. The number 365 occurs in many traditions: 3 Baruch 6: 13–14 mentions 365 gates through which the sun goes in and out, recalling the description in 2 Enoch. A similar tradition may be found in the Jerusalem Talmud, *RH* 2: 5 [58*a*]: 'The Holy One, blessed be He, created 365 windows to be used by the world, 182 in the east, 182 in the west and one in the centre of the firmament, from which the act of Creation first proceeded.' The number also figures in Heikhalot literature in relation to the purification rites performed before the ceremony of heavenly song, which are modelled on the rites performed by the priests before performing their service in the Temple (see Mishnah *Tam.* 1: 2, 4; *Yoma* 3: 3): 'Forthwith the . . . angels descend into rivers of fire and rivers of flame and immerse themselves seven times and test themselves in fire 365 times . . . When the time comes to sing, they ascend to heaven and purify themselves in fire' (*Seder raba divreshit* 47, p. 46; see Schäfer (ed.), *Synopse*, §§180, 810). An association is thus created between the heavenly purification rites and the number of days in the solar year.

[18] Gen. 5: 23–4.

All these elements combined to make the righteous Enoch the hero of the central myth of this literature, a super-temporal witness, beyond the limits of knowledge dependent on sensory perception, attesting before the denizens of terrestrial space to the cyclic nature of heavenly time revealed to him by the angels, to its eternal numerical pattern and its infinite sanctity, measured in number, perpetuated in sign and book, preserved in a cultic cycle, and recounted in an angelic priestly narrative. Enoch was a 'sign of knowledge from generation to generation', a 'scribe of righteousness', who counted the cycles of divine time, measured in hours of the day, seasons of the year, its months and weeks. He wrote books about angels, told stories about heavenly calendars, and counted celestial numbers. His salient characteristics were righteousness, knowledge and testimony, covenants and oaths; he founded the myth of the priesthood and established the cultic solar calendar of sabbaths and appointed times, linking heaven and earth, Creation and cult, book, narrative, and number. Transcending history, an immortal figure from the mythological antediluvian generation, Enoch was spared the fate of all mortals as an eternal *witness* in the heavens, attesting to the progress of divine time and the march of history, which was preordained from beginning to end, assuring the righteous of recompense and the wicked of retribution. Weaving together heavenly knowledge and testimony, an eternal eyewitness to the order of Creation and of time, he upheld the cyclic order of laws and appointed times that link terrestrial and heavenly time.

This wondrous knowledge, the basis of the priestly cultic calendar, was concerned with several elements: (1) *te'udot*, divinely appointed times and their confirmation by heavenly testimony; something destined to exist for ever and laid down in the heavenly statute of Creation, like sunrise and sunset;[19] (2) *mo'adim*,

---

[19] For the concept of *te'udot* in the sense of preordained temporal regularity, sanctified by God and remembered by humanity, see: 'and in the wisdom of Your knowledge You have determined their preordained course [*te'udatam*] before they came to exist and without You nothing is done' (Thanksgiving Hymns IX, 19–20 (cf. Vermes, *CDSSIE*, 254); cf. 4Q402, frg. 4: *DJD* XI, 228–9, 240–2); 'they shall write the *te'udot* of God' (War Scroll III, 4; cf. Vermes, *CDSSIE*, 165); 'seasons and eternally preordained appointed times [*mo'adei te'udot*]' (ibid. XIV, 13; cf. Vermes, *CDSSIE*, 179); 'as He commanded for His preordained appointed times [*mo'adei te'udotav*]' (Community Rule III, 10; cf. Vermes, *CDSSIE*, 101); 'When, as ordained for them [*lite'udatam*], they come into being, it is in accord with His glorious design that they accomplish their task without change' (ibid. 16; cf. Vermes, *CDSSIE*, 101); 'You made a Covenant with our fathers and established it for their descendants for eternally appointed times, and in all Your glorious *te'udot* there has been remembrance of Your kingship' (War Scroll XIII, 7–8; cf. Vermes, *CDSSIE*, 177); 'glorious appointed times in their *te'udot*' (4Q286, 1a, ii,b, l. 10: *DJD* XI, 12–13); 'For from the God of knowledge came into being everything which exists forever. And from His knowledge and His purposes have come into existence all things which were eternally appointed (*te'udot olamim*)' (Newsom, *Songs*, 168); 'what will happen in all the divisions of the days according to the Torah and the *te'udah*, and throughout their weeks (of years) and jubilees for ever' (Jub. 1: 26). Typical of Qumran literature is the exceptional number of terms denoting time as a divine cyclic manifestation: *ad, olamim, netsaḥ, idanim, maḥlekot ha'itim, tekufot, tekhunam, te'udah, te'udot el, mo'adim, mo'adei olamim, mo'adei kodesh, kitsim, itim, shanim, shavuot, yovelim, shemitot, shabetot kodesh, otot*, etc.

'appointed times of His glory, testimony of His righteousness' (cultic times of heavenly origin, connected or associated with *edut*, 'testimony', from which the word *edah*, 'community, the *yahad*'),[20] referring to the festivals and other set times in heaven and on earth, which themselves bear witness to cyclic divine time and the laws of nature; (3) *otot*, 'signs' (the covenants relating to heavenly time and to 'seventh' entities, such as the sabbath and Enoch); (4) *tekufot*, the cycles of the sun and the celestial bodies and their relationship to the seasons of the year, divided into four symmetric thirteen-week periods correlated with liturgy and cult; and (5) *sabbaths*, constituting a kind of cyclic seven-based framework, the basic pattern of the solar calendar since the seven days of Creation—signifying rest, cessation of labour and other secular occupations, or, in other words, resignation of human sovereignty in favour of sanctity, in a regular, sevenfold cycle.

Enoch was 'taken up to God' in order to observe the proper sequence of sabbaths and weeks, of years, festivals, luminaries, and days, so that he would be able to understand their cosmic laws and their affinity with the laws of nature, their cyclic calculations and the arithmetical relation between time and space. The angels were to teach him the correlation between visible and invisible, between testimony and number; he would then return to earth and testify to the synchronization between the laws of nature and the numerical divine order, on the one hand, and the rules of the ritual, on the other. Thus, divine order, based on seven, four, and twelve, was represented by the solar calendar: 364 *days*, each counting twenty-four hours; fifty-two weeks/sabbaths, each counting seven days; twelve *months*, each counting thirty days; four intercalary days (known as days of meeting) which, when added to the four three-month-long seasons, brought the total per season to ninety-one days; while the seven-based ritual order was represented by sabbaths grouped in four quarters or seasons of thirteen sabbaths, each entrusted to one of the twenty-four priestly courses ($13 \times 7 \times 4 = 364$; $52 \div 4 = 13$). Enoch learned this synchronic relationship between nature and cult, between sevenfold cycles and quarterly seasons; he could thus attest to the heavenly appointed times and teach his priestly sons the secret of their cyclic calculation: 'While he was alive

---

[20] The biblical word *mo'ed* (pl. *mo'adim*), which is related to the word *te'udah* discussed in the previous note, refers both to *ohel mo'ed*, 'the Tent of Meeting'—the place where God places his name and meets prophets and priests—and to a fixed, cyclically occurring appointed or set time, a festival or holiday, on which pilgrims seek to appear before him. Both connotations link up with the concepts of testimony (*edut*) and eternity (*ad*). It appears dozens if not hundreds of times in Qumran writings, sometimes in phrases unknown from any other source, denoting a fixed, divinely appointed time, calculated in advance, linked in some way with the laws of nature and with cultic testimony entrusted to the priests. See, for example: 'They shall arrange all these things in the appointed time of the sabbatical year' (War Scroll II, 6; cf. Vermes, *CDSSIE*, 165); 'at the divinely appointed time His exalted greatness shall shine' (ibid. I, 8; cf. Vermes, *CDSSIE*, 163–4); 'in the course of appointed times in their order' (Thanksgiving Hymns XX, 8; cf. Vermes, *CDSSIE*, 291); 'they shall not be late for any of their appointed times' (Community Rule I, 14–15; cf. Vermes, *CDSSIE*, 99); 'at the end of their appointed times, when the law is fulfilled' (ibid. X, 7; cf. Vermes, *CDSSIE*, 112); and there are countless more instances.

in his *seventh* generation, he commanded and bore witness to his son and his grandsons until the day of his death.'[21] Enoch is mentioned as a witness both to cosmic time as divided into appointed times, and to historical time, divided into sabbaths of years, sabbaticals, and jubilees: 'for the work of Enoch had been created as a witness to the generations of the world so that he might report every deed of each generation in the day of judgement'.[22]

Enoch, upon ascending to heaven and observing the divine origin of time impressed in the laws of nature, the eternal cyclic pattern of fertility and death, the synchronization between the diverse components of the cosmic calendar, and the relationship between the mysteries of the divine order and the wonders of the cyclic numerical harmony, testified at length to the heavenly solar calendar:

I saw how the stars of heaven come out; and I counted the gates out of which they exit and wrote down all their exits for each one: according to their numbers, their names, their ranks, their positions, their periods, their months, as Uriel, the holy angel who was with me, showed me. He showed me all things and wrote them down for me—also in addition he wrote down their names, their laws and their companies.[23]

In this manner the year is completed scrupulously in three hundred and sixty-four fixed stations of the cosmos. Thus the signs, the durations of time, the years, and the days were shown to me by the angel Uriel, whom the Lord, God of eternal glory, has appointed over all the luminaries of heaven—in heaven and the world—in order that the chariots of heaven . . . should rule in the face of the sky and be seen on the earth. Likewise Uriel showed me twelve wide openings in the sky, along the course of the chariots of the sun.[24]

The year is completed in 364 days. True is the matter of the exact computation of that which has been recorded; for Uriel—whom the Lord of all the creation of the world has ordered for me in order to explain the host of heaven—has revealed to me and breathed over me concerning the luminaries, the months, the festivals, the years, and the days.[25]

And the Lord summoned one of his archangels, (Vrevoil) [Uriel] by name, who was swifter in wisdom than the other archangels, and who records all the Lord's deeds. And the Lord said to [Uriel], 'Bring out the books from my storehouses, and fetch a pen . . . and give it to Enoch and read him the books . . . And he was telling me all the things of heaven and earth and sea and all the elements and the movements and their courses, and the living thunder, the sun and the moon and the stars, their courses and their changes, and seasons and years and days and hours . . . and the number of the angels and the songs of the armed troops; and every kind of human thing, and every kind of language (and) singing, . . . and everything that it is appropriate to learn.[26]

The Damascus Document explains the secret, divine nature of the appointed times revealed by angels, as well as the meaning of the observation of these testimonial times:

---

[21] Jub. 7: 39.   [22] Jub. 10: 17.   [23] Book of the Watchers: 1 En. 33: 3–4.
[24] Book of Heavenly Luminaries: 1 En. 75: 2–3.
[25] Ibid.: 1 En. 82: 6–7.   [26] 2 En.[J] 22: 10–23: 2.

for they can neither [come b]efo[r]e or after their appointed times . . .
[and He established times of favour for those that see]k his commandments and for those
   that walk on the path of integrity.
[And He uncovered their eyes to hidden things and] they opened their[e]ars and heard
   profundities, and they understood
[all that is to be before it comes upon them].[27]

The 364 days of the year and their numerical divisions, as described above, constitute the axis that distinguishes this tradition from the conventional biblical
tradition, which does not specify the number of days in a year; neither does it count
a fixed number of weeks, nor explicitly refer to the number of hours, seasons, or
days per month. The number 364, so prominent in all writings of the secessionist
priests found at Qumran, the basis for the synchronization of the two divisions of
the time continuum—four- and twelve-based, as against seven- and thirteen-
based—was brought by Enoch from heaven.

   Enoch, who transcended time, to whom the mysteries of the heavens, the laws
of nature, and the secrets of the calendar were revealed by Uriel, the archangel of
the 'Sons of Light', whose scrolls were discovered in the Qumran caves, was also a
scribe, prophet, and priest in his earthly life, the source of testimony and human
knowledge concerning the eternal calendar and the heavenly secrets relating to
priesthood and cult, to angelic companies and cosmic order. A tradition from the
first century CE cites Enoch's detailed account of the numerical cosmic knowledge
he had learned and its written transmission in book and number:

I know everything, and everything I have written down in the books, the heavens and
their boundaries and their contents. And all the heavenly hosts and their movements I
have measured. And I have recorded the stars and the multitude of multitudes innumer-
able. . . . The solar circle I have measured. . . . I appointed four seasons, and from the
seasons I created four cycles, and in the cycles I appointed the year, and I appointed
months, and from the months I counted days, and from the days I measured off the
hours. . . .[28]

He is described in similar terms in an ancient tradition found in the book of Ben
Sira (Ecclesiasticus), written at the beginning of the second century BCE by a priest
who described the Temple and its rites in the time of the Zadokites: 'Enoch [was
foun]d to be perfect and walked with the Lord and was taken, a *sign of knowledge* to
all generations.'[29] Ben Sira sings his praises among the patriarchs of the world and
alludes to his relationship with the angels of the Countenance: 'Few like Enoch
have been created on earth; he also was taken up to the Presence.[30] In the fragments
of Jubilees found at Qumran, the angels describe Enoch's role, linking heaven and
earth with knowledge of *te'udah*, 'predestined time', *mo'ed*, 'appointed time', and
edut, 'testimony', connecting visible signs of nature and invisible sevenfold divisions:

[27] 4Q266, frg. 2, 2–6 (*DJD* XVIII, 34–5).   [28] 2 En.[J] 40: 1–6.
[29] Ben Sira 44: 16.   [30] Ben Sira 49: 14.

[And he wrote down in a book the signs of the sky, according to the order of their months, so tha]t [the sons of men] would know [the cycles of the years, according to the orders of all their months. He was the] [fir]st [to write a *te'udah*, and he testified to the sons of men in the generations of the earth, the weeks of] the [jubilees].[31]

Testimony and knowledge of heavenly origin, writing and counting to angelic dictation, memorialization and computation of time by divine decree—such are the characteristic traits of Enoch the scribe, who knew the laws of heaven and the history of earth and time, who saw past and future, remembered, testified, and recorded in writing the laws of heaven and earth and the statute, commandment, and justice founded upon those laws. The details of his testimony and his computations are set out at length in many chapters of the book of Enoch. The end of his terrestrial life, which took place beyond time and place, is recounted in the Genesis Apocryphon from Qumran and told by the angels in Jubilees:

And he was taken from among the children of men, and we led him to the garden of Eden for greatness and honor. And behold, he is there writing law and judgment forever . . . for he was put there as a sign and so that he might bear witness to all of the children of men, so that he might relate all of the deeds of the generations until the day of judgment.[32]

The concept of 'sign' is associated with Creation and signs in the heavens, with the order of time, with the sign of the Covenant, with sabbath and cosmic testimony, with an oath dependent on cyclic seven-based order, with heavenly knowledge and measurement of time; the root of the Hebrew word for sign, *ot*, is related to that of the Aramaic verb *ata*, 'to come', alluding to Enoch, who constantly comes and goes.

When Enoch ascended to heaven, the angels imparted to him divine knowledge of the laws of nature, the secrets of the heavenly signs (astronomy), the changing of the seasons (meteorology), the secrets of the computation, history, and pattern of cosmic time. Thus Enoch holds within himself all knowledge of the orderly march of time in the divine and human world alike. He himself is a bond between this heavenly knowledge and earthly testimony, or between knowledge, predestined history, testimony, and appointed times. Like the eternal signs of the heavens, he bears witness to the relationship between heavenly and earthly time and the cultic calendar; he guarantees the realization of the march of history, just as the laws of nature, the signs of the heavens, and the cycles of fertility and procreation are constantly acting, for it is he who testifies in his super-temporal life to their progress. Enoch forms a link between the eternal heavenly calendar—correlated with the laws of nature and the four seasons of the year, divided into weeks of days and attested by the cyclic calendar of the Temple, divided into sabbaths of days and appointed times in a fixed liturgical and cultic order—and the historical

[31] 11Q12, frg. 4 (*DJD* XXIII, 213).   [32] Jub. 4: 23–4.

and eschatological terrestrial calendar, divided into sabbaths of years, of sab-baticals and of jubilees, attested by the heavenly tablets and the myths of angelic priests.

In the world of the priests of righteousness, who inherited the teaching of Enoch—the righteous scribe,[33] father of the eternal, infinite signs and numbers, which subdivide and recombine *ad infinitum* in a predestined, cyclic, divine order—history, past and present, as recorded in the heavenly tablets, is immutable, thus ensuring justice and proper recompense as a basic principle for those who walk in the paths of righteousness.

Diverse traditions recorded in the Enoch literature describe how Enoch testi-fied concerning the knowledge and justice imprinted in the calendar of sabbaths and seasons, in the history and laws written on the heavenly tablets, to his children, guardians of that knowledge, founders of the priestly line—Methuselah, Lamech, and Noah.[34] Other traditions in the same works, which describe at great length the circumstances under which the angels revealed the solar calendar and the meaning of its seven-based pattern, imply a relationship between the divine origins of time, its fixed seven-based pattern derived from the seven days of Creation and the fifty-two weeks of the solar year, divided into four symmetric seasons of thirteen sab-baths each, on the one hand; and the eternal, cyclic laws of nature, as represented by the twenty-four hours of the day, the four seasons of the year, and the thirteen cycles of the waxing and waning moon and of human fertility ($7 \times 4 \times 13 = 364$), on the other. This relationship is embodied in the unchangeable, numerically and computationally based solar calendar, which is regarded as testimony to the divine march of sacred time and scrupulously observed by the guardians of the sacred rites, by divisions of angels in heaven and twenty-four priestly courses on earth. Adherence to the solar calendar, first communicated to humanity by angels who imparted it to a man who became an angel, was construed as *imitatio angelorum*, imitation of the angelic sacred service in sacred heavenly space—the service that brought together eternal knowledge, testimony, predestined history, mission, sign, and appointed time with Covenant, sabbaths, and weeks, as reported by the angels who tell the mythological story of Enoch, attesting to the heavenly origins of the solar calendar, in the book of Jubilees.

The book of Jubilees, devoted entirely to the sevenfold structuring of historical and cultic time,[35] retells the story of Enoch, seventh patriarch of the world—scribe and narrator, who learned the mysteries of the universe and the secrets of its numbers from the angels; founder of the priesthood and father of cultic terrestrial time—from the angelic viewpoint of the guardians of the seasons and appointed times in the heavens:

---

[33] 1 En. 12: 4; 2 En.[J] 33: 3–36: 1; Jub. 4: 23.

[34] 1 En. 79: 1; 81: 6; 82: 1–20; 83; 92; 93; 2 En.[J] 39–55; Jub. 7: 38–9; and the Enoch fragments from Qumran.   [35] See Ch. 1, n. 48.

This one was the first who learned writing and knowledge and wisdom, from among the sons of men, from among those who were born upon earth. {[And he wrote down in a book the signs of the sky, according to the order of their months, so tha]t [the sons of men] would know [the cycles of the years, according to the orders of all their months. He was the] [fir]st [to write a *te'udah*, and he testified to the sons of men in the generations of the earth, the weeks of] the [[jubilees].} He recounted the days of the years, and the months he set in order, and the Sabbaths of the year he recounted, just as we made it known to him. And he saw what was and what will be in a vision of his sleep as it will happen among the children of men in their generations until the day of judgment. He saw and knew everything and wrote his testimony and deposited his testimony upon the earth against all the children of men in their generations.[36]

The seven divisions of time—signs, months, seasons, weeks, days, sabbaths of the year, and weeks of jubilees—are associated with testimony and predestination, book and knowledge. The association with the tablets of the testimony and the order of sabbaths and festivals immediately suggests itself; here, however, the origin of these divisions of time is angelic, and their revelation predated the traditional historical order, which links the tablets of the testimony with the theophany at Sinai, by about forty-nine jubilees. A fragment of Jubilees found at Qumran preserves the remnants of a similar formulation, which also indicates the angelic origin of that knowledge and Enoch's testimony thereto:

[E]noch after we taught him . . . six jubilees of years . . . {{returned to}} [the e]arth among the sons of mankind. And he testified against all of them . . . and also against the Watchers. And he wrote all the {{laws of}} the sky and the paths of their host and the [mon]ths . . . [so] that the ri[ghteous] should not err. . . .[37]

The thirteen Songs of the Sabbath Sacrifice, which are arranged according to the thirteen sabbaths of the quarters/seasons in the solar calendar and repeated cyclically in set order four times a year, provide numerous indications of the profound affinity between the concepts of *da'at*, 'knowledge', *edut*, 'testimony', *te'udah*, 'predestined history', *mo'adim*, 'appointed times', *ad*, 'eternity'—words with the same or similar roots in Hebrew. They clearly show that the order of time, its cyclic pattern, and its perpetual subdivision—'things which are eternally appointed'— derive from a fixed, divine order, preordained from beginning to end, and from

---

[36] Jub. 4: 17–19 (Charlesworth (ed.), *OT Pseudepigrapha*, ii. 62; passage in braces corrected after *DJD* XXIII, 213). In Qumran literature the words here translated as 'know' (*yada*) and 'testimony' (*edut*) are related, as testimony is about heavenly knowledge (*te'udah*) brought by a witness (*ed*) from heaven to earth.

[37] *DJD* XIII, 173 (4Q227, frg. 2; cf. Vermes, *CDSSIE*, 510), combined with the version in 11Q12, frg. 4 (*DJD* XXIII, 213); phrases in double braces are my clarifying additions, with no textual basis. Some words are deciphered otherwise in Wacholder and Abegg, *Preliminary Edition*, ii. 211; they read *hakedoshim* (= the holy ones) where *DJD* reads *heḥodashim* (= the months); they also omit the word 'righteous'.

eternal celestial lore or 'wonderful mysteries', imprinted in nature and kept by the angels:

For from the God of knowledge came into being everything which exists forever. And from His knowledge and His purposes have come into existence all things which were eternally appointed. He makes the former things in their *seasons* and the latter things in their due time.[38]

or:

When, as ordained for them, they come into being, it is in accord with His glorious design that they accomplish their task without change.[39]

Similar formulations, associating the eternity of the laws of nature with that of the laws of time, occur in the War Scroll and the Thanksgiving Hymns:

at every moment and at the times indicated [*mo'adei*] by your eternal preordinations [*te'udot olamim*] at the onset of day and at night at the fall of evening and at dawn.[40]

of the sacred appointed times [*mo'adei kodesh*], of the cycle of years [*tekufot shanim*] and the ages of eternity [*kitsei ad*] . . . We have known these through Your knowledge . . .[41]

And you will share it out among all their offspring according to the number of their eternal generations and for all years continuously . . . and in the wisdom of Your knowledge You have determined their preordained course [*te'udatam*] before they came to exist . . . These things I know through Your knowledge.[42]

Heavenly knowledge of the divisions of time and its cyclic nature, the eternal, deterministic aspect of Creation, of the laws of nature and its cosmic order, divided into quarters/seasons and eternally appointed sevenfold festivals, preordained by God since the beginning of time, was inscribed in the heavenly tablets and imparted to Enoch by the angels. This knowledge, expounded, as we have already observed, in Enoch and Jubilees and in Qumran literature, is the source of the testimony for the cyclic weekly worship of the twenty-four priestly courses, celebrated in a continuous, seven-based cycle of fifty-two weeks, divided into four thirteen-week seasons—'all their sevenfold predestined histories', 'holy weeks in their fixed order . . . sabbatical years of the earth in their divisions'—this knowledge bears witness to the mystery of the order of divine time:

8 . . . kind deeds and virtuous humility, and true kindness and eternal mercies. And wo[ndrous] mysteries

9 when th[ey app]ear and holy weeks in their fixed order, and divisions of months, [

10 beginnings of y]ears in their cycles and glorious festivals in times ordained [for them,

---

[38] Newsom, *Songs*, 170.   [39] Community Rule III, 16 (Vermes, *CDSSIE*, 101).
[40] War Scroll XIV, 15 (cf. Vermes, *CDSSIE*, 179).
[41] Ibid. X, 15–16 (cf. Vermes, *CDSSIE*, 174).
[42] Thanksgiving Hymns IX, 18–21 (cf. Vermes, *CDSSIE*, 254).

11   ]and the sabbatical years of the earth in [their] divi[sions and appo]inted times of liber[ty

12   ]eternal generations and   [

13   ]light and reck[onings of . . .[43]

Such phraseology, creating an association between the division of heavenly and earthly time—'their divisions/their cycles'—and the division of set times in the sacred service—'glorious festivals in times ordained'—indicates the preordained regularity of divine time, its relationship with the eternal laws of nature, its deterministic significance, the eternity of the calendar ('everything which exists for ever'), and the role of the calendar, as testimony to the divine Covenant that weaves together natural and metahistorical order. This cultic pattern of time links heaven and earth in angelic and priestly worship, comprising a recurrent cycle of testimony, remembrance, observance, and perpetuation, of sabbaths and festivals, weeks and months, changes of time and cycles of years, preordained since the beginning of Creation.

The history of the earth, as recounted in sequence, from beginning to end, in terms of years, sabbaths of years, sabbaticals, jubilees,[44] and ages; and the cyclic division of time into sabbaths of days, months, appointed times, and days—both are associated with the seven-based divine order and heavenly testimony. The seven-based relation between sabbatical and jubilee years ($7 \times 7 + 1$) is the same as the relation between sabbath and festival; the Temple festivals were celebrated at intervals of seven weeks after seven sabbaths, on the fiftieth day, as we shall see. The seventh day is the axis around which the solar calendar, measured out in sabbaths of the year and learned from the angels of the Countenance, was calculated. For the seventh day, the sabbath, is the consecrated day, signifying—as has already been pointed out—cessation of routine, resignation of human sovereignty and the natural cycle of nature, for a sevenfold routine of heavenly time, measured in a regular cycle of days of rest and sanctity. The sabbath is observed every seven days—together with the angels—in heaven and earth, in an ongoing sequence of days of rest, perceived as days on which angelic presence is anticipated on earth, purity is strictly observed, and all worldly engagement is halted in the consecrated Community. Such is the description of the seventh day of the week in the Qumranic version of Jubilees:

He gave us a great sign the] Sabbath [day] on [which] He ceased . . . and that we should keep Sabbath on the se[venth] day [from all work. For we—all the angels of the Countenance and all the angels of holiness]—these [two] kinds—He to[ld us to keep Sabbath with Him in heaven and on earth. He said to us: 'I will now separate for Myself]

---

[43] 4Q286, frg. 1 ii, 8–13 (*DJD* XI, 12–16).

[44] The seventh (sabbatical) year in each cycle is called 'sabbath [Heb. *shabat*] of the Lord' (Lev. 25: 2, 4) or 'sabbath [= year of complete rest] for the land' (Lev. 25: 6). A cycle of seven years is also referred to in Hebrew as *shabat*, and each cycle of seven such 'sabbaths of years' is followed by a jubilee year (Heb. *yovel*) (Lev. 25: 8; 26: 34, 35, 43).

a people among My nations. And [they will keep Sabbath. I will sanctify them as My people and I will bless them. They will be My people and I will be their God.] And He chose the descendants of Jacob . . . [. . . I . . . have sanctified them for Myself] for all the age(s) of eternity. The [seventh] day [I will tell them so that they keep Sabbath on it from everything', as He blessed them and sanctified them for Himself as a special people] out of all the nations and to be [keeping Sabbath] *together* [with us].[45]

The solar calendar is portrayed in Qumran literature as a kind of window between divine space-time and human space-time; between angelic time in sacred heavenly space and priestly time in sacred terrestrial space. It reflects a preordained, cyclic schematization of time: sabbaths, first days of months, and festivals, always falling on fixed, predetermined days of the week, never clashing with one another, preserving the unique sanctity of the sabbath. The 364 days of the year are divided into twelve heavenly 'gates', through which the sun enters and leaves,[46] in parallel to the twelve months of the year (or 365 days, where the added day, the 'Day of the Lord', is not counted and was probably used to make up the discrepancy between the ritual figure of 364 and the actual figure of the earth's revolution around the sun in 365¼ days).[47] The year divides into two equal parts, each twenty-six weeks long, counted from the 1st of the first month and from the 1st of the seventh month, respectively; and into four annual seasons, whose computation derives from the story of the Flood. In fact, the Flood episode provides the calendar with a computational substrate, inasmuch as it describes a 364-day year divided into four quarters,[48] each of which comprises thirteen sabbaths; the Flood story also refers to twelve months in a year, each consisting of thirty days. (The four missing days will be discussed below.)

The months of the year are specified by numbers, not by names, so that the liturgical order of the thirteen sabbaths may be repeated, and in fact on the same dates, in each of the four seasons. Each month of the solar calendar is thirty days long except for those ending the four seasons—the third, sixth, ninth, and twelfth—which have an added, intercalary day, counted as the day before the first day of the new season (the 1st of the first, fourth, seventh, and tenth months). The first day of a new season is called a 'sign' or 'day of remembrance'. Thus the year comprises 364 days, counted in cycles of thirteen sabbaths in each of the four ninety-one-day seasons.[49]

The four days of remembrance, also called *degalim* (a word relating to angelic beings associated with the months), mark the division of the year according to the Flood story; they are the first days of the astronomical seasons of the sun's progress through the heavens and separate the four annual seasons. The days of

---

[45] 4Q216, VII, 5–13 (*DJD* XIII, 19). Cf. 'to those who share a common lot with the angels of the Countenance' (Thanksgiving Hymns XIV, 13). Cf. Doering, *The Concept of the Sabbath*.

[46] 1 En. 72: 3–33; 74: 1–13; 75: 4.   [47] See n. 17 above and Ch. 1, n. 48.

[48] Jub. 6: 23–9; Gen. 5; Genesis Commentaries. See Ch. 6, n. 10.

[49] 1 En. 82: 14–20; 75; Jub. 6: 23–30.

remembrance in the first and seventh months mark the equinoxes, when the sun stands vertically above the earth's equator and day and night are of equal length— these days mark the beginnings of the respective half-years. The days of remembrance in the fourth and tenth months mark the solstices: the summer solstice, the longest day in the year; and the winter solstice, the shortest.

Each of these four seasons begins on a Wednesday—the day on which the luminaries were created, and divides, as already noted, into thirteen weeks, the basis for the cyclic liturgy of the thirteen Songs of the Sabbath Sacrifice.[50] All these fourfold divisions, relating to the astronomical seasons of the sun's progress through the heavens, taken together, reflect fifty-two sabbaths, designating the weekly units of time, arranged in sevenfold cycles in an inviolable, divine, cosmic structure:

And on the first of the first month and on the first of the fourth month and on the first of the seventh month and on the first of the tenth month are the days of remembrance and they are the days of appointed times in the four parts of the year. They are written and inscribed for an eternal witness. . . . And they set them upon the heavenly tablets. Each one of them is thirteen weeks from one to another of the remembrances, from the first to the second, and from the second to the third, and from the third to the fourth. And all of the weeks which will be commanded will be fifty-two weeks of days, and all of them are a complete year. Thus it is engraved and ordained on the heavenly tablets, and there is no transgressing in a single year, from year to year. And you, command the children of Israel so that they shall guard the years in this number, three hundred and sixty-four days, and it will be a complete year. And no one shall corrupt its appointed time from its days or from its feasts because all (of the appointed times) will arrive in them according to their testimony.[51]

This calendar, based on a fixed mathematical computation of weeks, guarantees that the thirteen sabbaths of each season will fall on fixed, identical dates every three months (ninety-one days), each three-month period constituting one of the four agricultural seasons: early harvest, summer time, sowing, and grass.[52] It also guarantees that the festivals will fall on fixed days not only in each month but also in each week; for it is based on the principle that the first day of each quarter (i.e. season) always falls on Wednesday, the day on which the heavenly bodies were created; of these, the first day of the third quarter (called 'New Year' in later, tannaitic tradition) is known as 'commemoration of the horn-blowing', and the same is true of the Festival of Unleavened Bread and Sukkot; the Day of Atonement always falls on Friday and Shavuot on Sunday, the 15th of the third month, on the morrow of the sabbath, seven weeks after the elevation of the Omer—counted in this calendar from the first sabbath after the end of the Passover festival and invariably celebrated on Sunday, 26th of the first month. The three pilgrimage

---

[50] Jub. 6: 29; Newsom, *Songs*, concordance, s.vv. *shabat, shavua'*, and cf. *DJD* XI, concordance, 445–72.

[51] Jub. 6: 23–32.

[52] Community Rule X, 7.

festivals thus always fall on the 15th of the month, in the first month, the third, and the seventh.

The first sabbath of each quarter will always fall on the 4th of the first month, the second sabbath on the 11th of the first month, the third on the 18th, and so on, in cycles of seven days, up to the twelfth sabbath, which will fall on the 21st of the third month, and the last, thirteenth sabbath, which will always fall on the 28th of the third month. Thus the sabbaths occur on the same dates in all four seasons, and no festival (or other 'appointed time') will ever coincide with a sabbath. It is striking that the number of days in a season, ninety-one, obtained as a product of the thirteen weeks in each season by seven, is also the number obtained when one adds up all the natural numbers from 1 to 13 $(1 + 2 + 3 + \ldots + 13 = 91)$. The ninety-first day of each season, the meeting day, is always a Tuesday, after which the new season begins, with an identical count: ninety-one more days, divided into thirteen sabbaths, and so on.[53]

Thirteen is also a number of cardinal importance in calculating the times of the new moon and its full phase, and in calculating the cycles of feminine fertility: every four weeks, thirteen times a year, these cycles are repeated $(13 \times 28 = 364)$, marking the waxing and waning of the moon, on the one hand, and the peak of fertility in a woman's body, on the other, after the seven days of post-menstrual purification incumbent in Jewish law on every woman.

In this calendar, with its underlying mathematical beauty, harmonic symmetry, and eternal, preordained cyclic pattern, the dates of sabbaths and festivals and cycles of years can be calculated in advance, as can the terms of office of the priestly courses, which give their names to the weeks. The sanctity of the seven-based calendar, a divine gift to humankind from on high, observed in heaven and on earth by divisions of angels and priests, week after week, is celebrated in Enoch, Jubilees, the Songs of the Sabbath Sacrifice, the Psalms Scroll, MMT, the Calendars of Priestly Courses, the War Scroll, and in fact throughout Qumran literature, the literature of the seceding priests who fought to uphold the sanctity of their solar calendar of 364 days. The Masoretic text of the Bible makes no explicit reference to the number of days or weeks in the year; as told in Jubilees, the story of the Flood, the basis for computations of the structure of the year, differs in certain numerical respects from the biblical account: in Genesis the story extends over 364 days, from the 17th of the second month to the 27th of the second month in the next year, comprising one (lunar) year plus ten days $(364 = 354 + 10)$; Jubilees, in contrast, counts 364 days beginning and ending on the same date, the 17th of the second month, and counted as a full year $(12 \times 30 + 4 = 364)$, a subdivision confirmed in Qumran traditions as well.

For the authors of this literature—the members of the *yahad*-Community, who pictured angels and priests as *joint* (= *yahad*) custodians of the calendrical order—

---

[53] For the calendar, see the studies cited in Ch. 1, n. 48.

any violation of the sequence of properly dated sabbaths in each season, or of any other aspect of calendrical regularity, was sinful. It was a breach of cosmic order and divine law, a desecration of the cult, of the oaths and covenants concluded between heaven and earth, which are celebrated by predetermined priestly courses on special festivals—always falling on the same, preordained days of the week and of the month. Their liturgy assigned the Songs of the Sabbath Sacrifice and the Psalms of David to fixed days in a sevenfold and fourfold cyclic order: a full cycle of the Songs of the Sabbath Sacrifice comprises one-quarter of the year's sabbaths so that they are recited four times in a fixed cyclic order. In addition, the Psalms may also stand in some such cyclic relationship to one-quarter of the year's days; thus, in combination with the songs for the first days of months, festivals, and the days of remembrance (see above), the members of the Community envisaged a complete liturgical calendar, prescribing a regular, permanent cycle of songs over each season, repeated four times a year. Violation of this all-embracing, fixed ritual order would be punished by a parallel, divinely wrought disturbance of nature, bringing doom and destruction on earth.

Diverse problems relating to this calendar—historical, ritual, mathematical, and practical—have been dealt with in the scholarly literature. What still awaits discussion, however, is its mystical significance: a seven-based pattern or proto-type linking heavenly with earthly, buttressing the correlation between the divine origin of time and its cosmic heavenly prototype, dependent on the seasonal solar cycle, on the one hand; and its cultic representation, repeated every seven days in a cycle of thirteen sabbaths in all four seasons of the solar year, on the other. This eternal order was maintained by the priestly courses, each serving in rotation for one particular week, from sabbath to sabbath, and by septuples of angels in heaven; priests and angels together sang their sacred songs in a cycle of thirteen sabbaths. The seven-based solar calendar, demonstrating the continuity of the structure of divine time in a cyclic, horizontal sequence, was a crux of mythical and mystical identification, a major bone of halakhic and cultic contention between the secessionist priesthood, who held fast to their fixed solar calendar of sabbaths, and the official priests of the Temple, faithful to their variable lunar calendar.

The literature of the secessionist priesthood waged war, both directly and indirectly, against the lunar calendar—an arbitrary calendar of days based on changeable human discretion, dependent on the senses. Instead, the priesthood championed the solar calendar—a sacred calendar of sabbaths founded on a fixed seven-based computation of divine origin, an abstract numerical principle con-firmed by angelic testimony. In this context they assigned a central role to the figure of Enoch, who himself, in his admonition to his sons the priests, declares his 'sabbatical' and sevenfold identity: 'I was born the *seventh* during the first week, during which time justice and righteousness continued to endure',[54] and then

[54] I En. 93: 3.

goes on to describe how he acquired angelic knowledge of the solar calendar and imparted that knowledge on his sons.[55] Enoch is referred to in Jubilees[56] as a sign, a term normally reserved for the sabbath,[57] the sun, the Covenant, and the eternity of natural laws.

What was at stake was not the calendar *per se*, but the very foundations of the perception of sacred time, place, and cult. The secessionist priesthood *rejected* an unstable time concept, based on arbitrary human determination, on unreliable human observation of the new moon; on erroneous, fluctuating calculations of the appointed times of the calendar, deriving from human consecration of time and adjustment of time to changing realities. It *advocated* a time concept founded on the laws of nature, on divine revelation as reflected in the cosmic order of annual seasons and hours of light; a cyclic time, measured out in sabbaths, featuring an eternal, immutable, mathematical structure, whose liturgical and cultic cycles were witnessed, celebrated, and preserved by priests and angels in concert, *yaḥad*.[58]

Priests and angels alike consecrated this heavenly time, maintaining an eternal, unbroken continuity in a prescribed order, through a system of covenants, through an immutable, harmonic, symmetric mathematical calculation, to which they bore witness in the words of their cyclic liturgy. The priests, perpetuating the continuum of weeks through the designations of the twenty-four courses, in cyclic sequences recurring every seventh year, offered up the sabbath sacrifice once every seven days, as well as the sacrifices prescribed for the seven Temple festivals, celebrating first fruits and agricultural yields, which fell once every seven weeks on fixed dates in the first seven months of the year; in parallel, the angels performed their heavenly rites, observing the sabbaths and the appointed times in the supernal worlds.

The lunar calendar of antiquity was not a fixed calendar; neither months nor years were of fixed length, and festivals did not fall on fixed days, for the month was consecrated on the basis of visual observations. The calendar was calculated each time anew, depending on the astronomical situation, relying on recurrent sightings of the moon and hence on human eyesight, individual discretion, and the decision of a human court, which had to make allowance for various circumstances when determining the new moon and hence the festivals.[59]

The struggle between the lunar and solar calendars was a struggle between a flexible, human calendar, not bound by a fixed, cyclic, numerical pattern but dependent on the inconstant, unpredictable human reading of nature and sub-

---

[55] 1 En. 79–82; 92–3.   [56] Jub. 4: 23–4.   [57] Exod. 31: 13; Ezek. 20: 12.

[58] For the service of seven companies of angels in parallel to the priestly service, see 2 En. 19: 1–6. On Enoch imparting the knowledge to his sons the priests see 2 En. 47–54; 1 En. 106; Jub. 6. On the priestly service see Community Rule, MMT, Temple Scroll, Psalms Scroll, Calendar of Priestly Courses; and see Ch. 8 below.

[59] Gen. 1: 14; Ps. 104: 19; Mishnah *RH* 1: 3–3: 1; BT ibid.; BT *San.* 10b. See Herr, 'Calendar'; Tabori, *Jewish Festivals*, 19–34.

ordinate to changing earthly needs; and a mythological calendar, at one with the laws of nature, dependent on the divine reading of nature, predetermined from beginning to end, eternally correlated with the four seasons, the solstices, and the equinoxes. Put differently, it was between a *changeable* calendar based on unstable human observation and eyewitness reports, on variable calculations and sanctification by human beings, and an *unchangeable* calendar of heavenly origin, based on a fixed mathematical calculation of the eternal cyclic pattern of the cyclic motions of the sun, relying on consecration by angels and priests. This sacred calendar synchronized the natural progress of time (day, night, month, season) with a seemingly abstract pattern of regular, cyclic, cessation of manual labour in particular and of secular occupations in general (sabbaths, festivals, sabbatical years, etc.).

The solar calendar, representing an immutable relationship between sabbaths and festivals in heaven and on earth, was agriculturally based, marking such events as the first produce of barley, grain, wine, and olive oil, the harvesting and ingathering of crops; it bound together nature and ritual, being founded on the postulate that time and its divisions were divine, that the abstract sabbath had been imprinted upon visible nature since the seven days of Creation. The adherents of the solar calendar argued that the festivals fell on days prearranged by divine decree, in keeping with the biblical verse, 'These are the set times of the Lord, the sacred occasions, which you shall celebrate each at its appointed time';[60] 'appointed time', they argued, implied an eternally fixed date, dependent on the cyclic movements of the sun and observed in heaven and on earth. By contrast, the believers in the sanctity of the lunar calendar stressed the second person plural, '*you* shall celebrate', implying human determination of the times of the festivals, as expressed by consecration of the new month on the basis of human sightings of the crescent moon, which was not subject to any priestly angelic pattern of cyclic recurrence. It was a human court that heard the human witnesses and on that basis, by consecration of the new moon, established the dates of the festivals. The disagreement is clearly reflected in the following passage of the Mishnah, which specifically concerns the determination of the Day of Atonement:

'These are the appointed times of the Lord, holy convocations, which ye shall proclaim'[61]—whether at their proper time or not at their proper time, I have no appointed times save these.[62]

According to some authorities, the author of this statement, Rabbi Akiva, made the inference from the defective spelling of the Hebrew word *otam*, 'them', referring to the 'set/appointed times', which could also be read as *atem*, 'you'. This is the gist of a *baraita* (tannaitic teaching) cited in the talmudic exposition of the above Mishnah passage:

---

[60] Lev. 23: 4.

[61] The text omits the last word of the verse Lev. 23: 4, *bemo'adam*, 'at their appointed time'; the omission is highly significant.   [62] Mishnah *RH* 2: 9.

The text says, 'you', 'you', 'you', three times [i.e. the word *otam* (them) in Lev. 22: 31, 23: 2, and 23: 4 is read as if vocalized *atem* (you) for homiletical purposes], to indicate that 'you' [may set the appointed times] even if you err inadvertently, 'you', even if you err deliberately, 'you', even if you are misled.[63]

A similar exposition is offered in the halakhic midrash *Sifra*: 'If *you* proclaim them, they are my set times; if not, they are not my set times'.[64] In other words: there are no appointed times (*mo'adim*) other than those announced and celebrated by the sages of the court, regardless of whether they have been set for the 'proper' time.

The cardinal religious importance that the Sages attached to the consecration of the appointed times by the court—a human agency—emerges from many traditions and is in direct contrast to the priestly position. Sages in the Land of Israel fought for centuries to maintain this exclusive right. Vestiges of the controversy echo in the well-known polemic between the Pharisees and the Sadducees (or between the Sages and the Boethusians, *beit tsadok*, the Zadokites) as to the meaning of the expression 'the day after the sabbath',[65] which determines when the counting of the Omer begins and hence when Shavuot is to be celebrated:[66] the Sadducees count from the day after the first sabbath after Passover, i.e. from 26 Nisan (the first month), and Shavuot is celebrated seven weeks later, on Sunday, 15 Sivan (the third month). It is also reflected in the Qumranic Commentary on Habakkuk in relation to persecution of the secessionist priesthood and calendrical controversy.[67]

All these manifestations of the controversy may be summarized as follows. On the one hand was a deterministic perception of time, of heavenly origin, bound up with the cyclic laws of nature as reflected in a fixed solar calendar whose festivals fell not only on fixed dates of the month but also on fixed days of the week, a calendar maintained unchanged by angels and priests who attested to its divine origin, recording its heavenly character in their written documents and citing the full text of the verse Leviticus 23: 4 (see above), thus declaring, as it were, 'It is in the heavens' (contrary to Deuteronomy 30: 12). On the other was a perception of time dependent on variable, human decisions, governed by observations made by ordinary mortals, as reflected in a changeable, lunar calendar, maintained by leaders who derived their authority from the people as a whole, by a court which heard testimony from any witness, took terrestrial interests and the good of the

---

[63] BT *RH* 25a. The word *otam*, 'them', is written *otema* in a particular full spelling in the Temple Scroll, with vav and heh, which excludes the possibility of reading *atem*, 'you': cf. Temple Scroll XXIX, 2 (Qimron, *Temple Scroll*, 44).

[64] *Sifra*, 'Emor', 10: 2.   [65] Lev. 23: 11, 15.   [66] BT *Men.* 65b–66a.

[67] '[He] makes them drunk, to gaze upon their appointed times' (a non-Masoretic version of Hab. 2: 15). 'Interpreted, this concerns the Wicked Priest who pursued the Teacher of Righteousness to the house of his exile that he might confuse him with his venomous fury. And at the time appointed for rest, for the Day of Atonement, he appeared before them to confuse them, and to cause them to stumble on the Day of Fasting, their Sabbath of repose.' Commentary on Habakkuk XI, 3–8 (Vermes, *CDSSIE*, 484); cf. Nitzan (ed.), *Pesher Habakkuk*, 190.

Community into consideration, and invoked, as a crucial principle, 'It is not in the heavens.'

The primeval roots of the conflict lie in two myths: one describing the establishment of the laws of nature and the founding of the cycles of Creation on opposites and their separation; and the other concerned with the violation of the proper natural order by failure to recognize and separate those opposites. These myths recount the spiritual co-operation between angels and human beings, the separation of unlike and incomparable entities; they tell the story of Creation and Flood, order and chaos, righteousness versus evil, sanctity and purity as against impurity and corruption. The first element in each of these pairs is based on delimitation, on the recognition of boundaries, on the precise measurement of quantities and numbers upon which life itself depends; while the second represents confusion and disorder, blurring of boundaries, and disregard of measurement and number, leading to death. These are myths of life and fertility, of cyclic recurrence and eternity adhering to a divine order based on separation, division, and counting, on differentiation between permissible and forbidden (calendar and law, set time and testimony, sanctity and purity); but they are also concerned with death and oblivion due to infringement of that divine order, anarchy and chaos, violation of boundaries, corrupt counting, defiance of authority, and disregard of prohibition (false calendar, arbitrariness, impurity, and corruption). These myths, relating to priests and angels, are set in the context of the first chapters of Genesis, which describe a time when the passageways between heaven and earth were still open. They aim to explicate the establishment of the basic patterns of sanctity and purity, on the one hand, and sin and impurity, on the other; they describe the formation and violation of the divine order and discuss the holy origin of the solar calendar, representing the existence and maintenance of divine order, and the sinful origin of the lunar calendar, representing the violation and corruption of that order.

FIVE

The Sin of the Watchers and the Lunar Calendar

You see what Azazel has done; how he has taught all (forms of) lawlessness upon the earth.[1]

And lawlessness increased upon the earth, and all flesh corrupted its way.[2]

IN order to endorse the sanctity of the solar calendar, to confirm its divine source and eternal validity, attributed to angelic testimony, to affirm the consecrated appointed times, purity, sanctity and blessing, fertility and the cycle of life—all associated with fixed, cyclically repeating abstract numbers and calculations—the secessionist priesthood told and retold the story of Enoch son of Jared. Enoch, who 'walked with God', was transformed from human being to divine creature and ascended by God's will from earth to heaven to learn heavenly knowledge from the angels, to testify to the sanctity of the appointed times, the fixed cycles, numbers, and calculations, and to teach the secrets of the solar calendar. The lunar calendar, on the other hand, derived from a sinful source, associated with the Watchers (Aramaic *irim*) and forbidden sexual acts (*arayot*; the Hebrew roots of these two words share the consonants ayin and resh), with curses and sins, with impurity and blasphemy—all due to unsanctioned sighting and variable observation, confined by the limits of sensory perception. In order to denounce this source the seceding priests told and retold the story of the divine beings who 'saw the daughters of man',[3] also known as the story of the angels of destruction who 'followed the wilfulness of their hearts', the story of the fallen angels, or the rebellion of the Watchers, who taught humans the lunar calendar.

This myth is concerned with 'divine beings' (Heb. *benei elohim*, lit. 'sons of God'), who breached the barriers that separate mortals from immortals, descended in contravention of God's will from heaven to earth, were transformed from spiritual beings to flesh and blood, violated the limits of the taboo, and 'took wives from among those that pleased them'.[4] They committed forbidden acts of sexual union with the daughters of man and fathered monstrous giants known in Hebrew as *nefilim*. They disobeyed God and his commands, disrupted the order of nature,

---

[1] 1 En. 9: 6.   [2] Jub. 5: 2.   [3] Gen. 6: 1–7.
[4] Gen. 6: 2. In Hebrew, literally 'took wives among all those that they chose'.

and taught men forbidden knowledge, derived from observations of the moon and the stars. While the Enoch myth is recounted at length and in detail—in contrast to the brief allusions in Genesis 5: 22–5—as a tale of conversion (sacred transformation, sanctioned by God's will), transcending the bounds of the senses and entering the realm of divine knowledge, the story of the fallen angels—alluded to in Genesis 6: 1–7—is a tale of inversion (reversion to sin, contravening God's will), of transgression of the flesh, of sensual error and the power of lust.

The myth of Enoch's ascension to heaven is a foundation story concerning the knowledge revealed to humanity by divine authority, knowledge that transcends the bounds of sensory perception and relates to the eternal order of Creation, to sanctity and purity as defined by cycle, counting, and number, sacred interruption of routine, and cessation of labour. The establishment of law and order, appointed times and testimonies, derives from an abstract principle and from heavenly revelation, based on counting and calculation, distinction and separation, prohibition and permission, associated with covenants and oaths, light and good, angels and priests. The story of the fallen angels, on the other hand, is a foundation narrative in which knowledge confined by human senses and desires, implying a violation of natural order, is seen as the source of evil and sin, a challenge to divine authority. This violation of law and order entails impurity without measure, expressed through rebellious, chaotic forces that breach barriers, ignore distinctions and separations, violate prohibitions, and disrupt counting, number, and cycle. It is a myth of carnal desire, of the forbidden cohabitation of the sons of God and the daughters of man, a brief account of the sin incurred by disobeying God, acting wilfully against the laws and order of Creation, and maliciously commingling the disjoint domains of heavenly and terrestrial, of spirit and flesh, of immortal and mortal. As a result, the earth became filled with lawlessness, polluted with forbidden unions, bloodshed, and idolatry—disastrous consequences washed away only by the Flood:

The sons of God saw how beautiful the daughters of men were and took wives from among those that pleased them. . . . It was then, and later too, that the *nefilim* appeared on earth—when the sons of God cohabited with the daughters of men, who bore them offspring. They were the heroes. . . . The Lord saw how great was man's wickedness on earth. . . . The Lord said, 'I will blot out from the earth the men whom I created.'[5]

The literature of the secessionist priests expands upon this obscure story, one of the most puzzling elements of which is the fact that while the sinners are the sons of God, it is humanity that is punished: lawlessness and disorder on the polluted earth are obliterated by the cleansing flood, which lays the foundations for a re-established order. The story is placed in the context of a theodicean myth, an attempted explanation of the origins and nature of evil in the world. It is 'seeing',

---

[5] Gen. 6: 1–7.

observation through the senses, that generates the primeval error and all its terrible consequences.

But the story is not only a foundation myth about beginnings, about a distant mythological past; it is a tale told from the vantage point of an elite laying claim to supernatural authority, authority which they once lost, along with their role as leaders responsible for decisions shaping the face of culture, memory, law, and ethics; that role was usurped by other elites, whose world view was based on the senses, and their authority therefore dependent on personal experience, human intelligence, and fickle, variable human governance. The first elite derived its authority from divine election and angelic knowledge; its tasks, as it saw them, were to maintain divine order, to consecrate nature, and to delimit it through sign and number, through eternally valid law and calendar. The usurping elite originated, so claimed the displaced leaders, in infringement of divine order, through action based on sensory perception that violated natural laws, wrought havoc with law and calendar, breached boundaries, and disseminated forbidden heavenly knowledge contrary to the rules of nature and cultic order.

By choosing the language of myth, placed in a misty, distant past, the displaced priests more easily expressed their rage and hatred in their anonymous pseudepigraphic and polemical literature. The Enoch literature,[6] Jubilees,[7] and various Qumranic works[8] tell of the angels of destruction who tampered with the laws of Creation, also called 'sons of defilement', who corrupted the continuity of life,[9] 'sinning angels' who sinned by consummating forbidden sexual unions,[10] and Watchers, most probably because of their association with the danger of perdition due to forbidden sexual relationships which curtail procreation. The Watchers are associated in great detail with Azazel and Belial, with the very origin of evil and corruption, with acts of abomination and darkness, wickedness and impurity.[11] The Testament of Reuben refers to them as *nefilim*,[12] and the Testament of Naphtali blames them for the curse of desolation and barrenness. Chapters of Enoch found at Qumran, known as the Book of Giants, relate the history of the forbidden unions that corrupted the earth, filled it with wickedness, and brought about the Flood; and various narratives in 2 Enoch[13] recount the detailed circumstances of the sin of the Watchers, their punishment, and their past and present history.

As against the myth of the Watchers, who personify sin and impurity, the violation of eternal divine, natural order, the story of the Flood represents the victory of purity and number; for in the literature of the secessionist priesthood the Flood and its aftermath provide the basis for the calendar, and the different phases of the

---

    [6] 1 En. 6–16; 19: 1–3; 64: 2–4; 65: 6–11; 69: 1–12; 106: 13–15; 2 En. 18.
    [7] Jub. 5: 1–2; 7: 21–6; 8: 3.   [8] Community Rule II, 1–3; IV, 9–14; Damascus Document II, 6.
    [9] Community Rule II, 1–3; IV, 9–14; Blessings 4Q286.   [10] 1 En. 1: 15–16.
    [11] War Scroll XIII, 12; Damascus Document II, 6; III, 17; 1 En. 63: 1; Blessings 4Q286; Community Rule II, 1; III, 16–25. On the name 'Watchers' see Mach, 'Saints–Angels', 306–7.
    [12] 4: 6–7.   [13] Chs. 7, 18.

Flood, as enumerated in detail in Jubilees,[14] is the numerical basis for the calculations of a calendar whose harmonious structure is guaranteed by the eternal, divine
rules of arithmetic. The dates figuring in the story of the Flood in the Jubilees fragments found at Qumran are based on a 364-day year, divided into four quarters or
seasons, each a cycle of thirteen sabbaths, associated with the dates of covenants, as
we shall see below. Besides its role as a foundation narrative for sin and punishment, the Flood is also a paradigmatic, apocalyptic prefiguration of the flood that,
at the End of Days, will enfold the violators of the Covenant, cleansing the land and
saving only those who remain loyal to the Covenant.

The narrative of the Watchers' sin figures in this literature as a counterfoil to the
narrative of Enoch son of Jared, who 'walked with God'; it is told from his super-
temporal vantage point as the background for the sin and corruption that could be
cleansed and purified only by the Flood:

For in the generation of Jared, my father, they (= the heavenly angels, the Watchers)
transgressed the word of the Lord, (that is) the law of heaven. And behold, they commit
sin and transgress the commandment; they have united themselves with women and
commit sin together with them; and they have married (wives) from among them, and
begotten children by them. . . . And upon the earth they shall give birth to giants, not of
the spirit but of the flesh. There shall be a great plague upon the earth, and the earth
shall be washed clean from all the corruption.[15]

The forbidden sexual unions and the concomitant violation of limits and boundaries, as related in the story of the Watchers, are of considerable significance, for
the forbidden carnal knowledge that had such calamitous consequences on earth is

[14] Chs. 6, 7.

[15] 1 En. 106: 13–17. For different versions of the story of the fallen angels see Cassuto, 'Story of the
Sons of God'; Dimant, 'Sinning Angels'; Hanson, 'Rebellion in Heaven'; Suter, 'Fallen Angel, Fallen
Priest'; Molenberg, 'Roles of Shemihaza and Asael'; cf. 4Q180, frg. 1, 7–10 (*DJD* V, 78). Traditions
concerning this story and its overtones of sin, violation of forbidden boundaries, the root of evil, and
the Flood may be found in 1 and 2 Enoch, Jubilees, the Book of Giants, the Damascus Document, the
Testament of Reuben, and many of the Dead Sea Scrolls; traces may also be found in Josephus, in the
New Testament (Second Epistle of Peter), and in Tertullian, among others. For the carnal sins of the
Watchers see Dimant, 'Sinning Angels', 30–44. The Midrash preserves detailed traditions of these
sins, including rape and other forms of sexual assault, which were punished by the Flood: 'The sons of
God saw the daughters of man—This means that they would seize women and assault them in public'
(*Sifrei zuta* 11). Or, in *Genesis Rabbah* 26: 5: '"... that they were fair"—Said Rabbi Yudan: ... Hence
we learn that when a woman was beautified for her husband, a great one would enter and have inter-
course with her first. Thus Scripture says, "that they were fair", referring to the virgins. But "they
took wives from among those that pleased them" refers to married women. "From among those that
pleased them" refers to homosexuality and bestiality.' In regard to 'they *took* wives etc.' as referring to
violent seizure of beautiful women from their husbands, recalling the medieval institution of *droit du
seigneur*, cf. Pharaoh's abduction of Sarah in Gen. 12: 15: 'The woman was *taken* into Pharaoh's
palace'; or David's seizure of Bathsheba: 'David sent messengers to *take* her . . . and he lay with her'
(2 Sam. 11: 4). Scholars discussing the myth of the Watchers have not realized its significance for the
secessionist priests, its polemical context, and its inverse affinity with the Enoch myth.

associated with forbidden knowledge that had calamitous results beyond the bounds of time and place.

The story of the 'sons of God' and the 'daughters of man' figures in the Bible in a very brief version, as a background to the Flood narrative; it alludes obscurely to breaching of limits, challenging of authority, commingling of separate realms, and infringement of taboo. The story is much expanded in the secessionist priestly literature; it begins with forbidden observation and illicit coveting, continuing with added details of the forbidden knowledge involved, carnal and other. Because of the deeds of the sons of God, who rebelled against their Creator, wilfully came down to earth without divine sanction, and behaved promiscuously,[16] deliberately committing the cardinal sins of forbidden incest, bloodshed, and idolatry— because of these misdeeds, humankind learned forbidden divine knowledge, based on the observation of nature, namely, the perverse, inherently sinful, lunar calendar, with its dependence on seeing:

> And there was much wickedness and they committed adultery and erred, and all their conduct became corrupt. Shamhazai [lit. 'there he saw'] taught incantation and the cutting of roots; and Aramaros the resolving of incantations; and Baraqiel astrology, and Kokabiel observation of the stars, and Tamiel taught the seeing of the stars, and Sahariel taught the course of the moon. And it came to pass, when the people died, they cried out and their voice reached up into heaven.[17]

According to Jubilees, the forbidden knowledge was associated with forbidden sighting or observation: 'the teaching of the Watchers by which they used to show the sorceries of the sun and moon and stars and all the signs of heaven'.[18] The determination of the calendar and the festivals via human observation of heavenly signs, of the constellations, or of other natural phenomena is referred to here, when ascribed to the Watchers, the changing phases of the moon, the angel Sahariel, and those who determine the calendar by human sight, as 'sorceries'. Similar determination associated with calculation and number is designated in such terms as set or appointed times (*mo'adot, mo'adim*) of the Lord, testimony (*edut*), and predestination (*te'udah*)—as observed previously, all three Hebrew words derive from similar roots. For such calculation and number derive from angelic knowledge and priestly testimony; they represent the regular, cyclic measures of an abstract divine order, unseen arithmetical principles engraved on the heavenly tablets and associated with the angel Uriel, the solar calendar, and the priesthood. Determination of the calendar by observation is referred to as 'ways of wickedness', in contrast to calculation of the calendar by the fixed course of the sun, which is 'ways of righteousness'.

The essence of the sin committed by the Watchers or fallen angels seems to involve knowledge obtained by astronomical observation of the heavenly bodies,

---

[16] 1 En. 6–8; 15–16.
[17] 1 En. 8: 2–4; text according to A. Kahana. Cf. Charlesworth (ed.), *OT Pseudepigrapha*, i. 16.
[18] Jub. 8: 3. Cf. *DJD* XIII, 173; *DJD* XVIII, 37; *DJD* XXXVI, 20.

based on an erroneous conception in which the abstract, divine, numerical rhythm of time is replaced by human sighting and visible natural signs. The variations of nature are gauged by the senses (phases of the moon, variable observations, changeable numbers of days and weeks in the lunar year), which create confusion and corrupt calculations of the march of time—all anathema to the secessionist priests:

And there will be those who will examine the moon diligently because it will corrupt the (appointed) times and it will advance from year to year ten days. Therefore, the years will come to them as they corrupt and make a day of testimony a reproach and a profane day a festival, and they will mix up everything, a holy day profaned and a profane day for a holy day, because they will set awry the months and Sabbaths and feasts and jubilees.[19]

Thus, observation dependent on the senses in relation to the realm of the sacred—such as the cultic calendar—was repudiated: subjective estimation and the resulting false calendar were negated, in favour of a calendar based on systematic numerical rules derived from Creation, on fixed calculation, cycle, and counting, independent of human observation. Such an attitude to the evidence of the senses should be seen in the context of religious thought envisaging an infinite God, with no observable, visible attribute other than the cyclic regularity of the natural world, of the laws of the universe, as a totality of data open to exact prediction and calculation. This abstract, divine being has an aspect that is embodied in the mathematical rules, fixed durations and fluctuations represented by the creative progress of nature and its cyclic events; it possesses a rhythm measured in terms of cycle and revolution, sign and number, arithmetic and knowledge, the determination of the sevenfold appointed times and the secrets of the fourfold changing seasons and ages, all infinite and of divine origin.

But there seems to be another side to this manifestation of the struggle of the deposed priesthood, deprived of its prerogative of dictating the basic order and schedule underlying religion and cult. This myth echoes the claim of the Zadokite priests to possess the exclusive right to this knowledge, the knowledge of 'wondrous secrets', and to the arithmetical principles upon which it is based (the solar year; the fixed cyclic calculation of 364 days and their division into units of four and seven). Indeed, the calculation of seasons, appointed times, months, and years was long entrusted to them by virtue of heavenly authority, as guardians of the sequence of times observed in the Temple, which had all been calculated on the basis of the solar calendar until Hasmonaean times.

The myth associates the dissemination of forbidden divine knowledge with disobedience of God's command, with violation of the strict separation between spiritual beings and flesh-and-blood, as decreed by heavenly laws, through forbidden carnal knowledge of sexuality. These elements, which represent confusion between the manifest and the hidden, are considered sacrilegious, as they obscure

---

[19] Jub. 6: 36–7.

the limits between what is permitted and what is forbidden in the relationship between heaven and earth. They also blur the distinction between forbidden and permitted sexual relationships, observance of which is crucial for the perpetuation of the cosmic cycle, while their violation disturbs the cycles of sanctity and purity and corrupts life itself. The calamitous results of the sin of forbidden sexuality are described briefly in the mythical language of a fragment of Jubilees found at Qumran:

[. . . and these are the gi]i[ant]s. And [lawlessness] increased [on the earth, and all flesh corrupted its way, from man to]animals . . . [and they all c]orrupted their way and [their] or[dinance, and they began to eat one another. And lawlessness increased on the earth . . .].[20]

The word *ḥamas*, translated here as 'lawlessness', is derived from a root meaning to violate or profane;[21] there may also be a connection between the words 'for the earth was filled with lawlessness',[22] which refer to the biblical account of the sin of the 'sons of God', who violated the limits between forbidden and permitted sexual union (associated indirectly with the sin of blasphemy imputed to the contemporary Temple priesthood), and Ezekiel's trenchant censure of a similarly sinful priesthood:[23] 'Her priests have violated [Heb. *ḥamesu*] My Teaching: they have profaned what is sacred to Me, they have not distinguished between the sacred and the profane, they have not taught the difference between the unclean and the clean, and they have closed their eyes to My Sabbaths. I am profaned [Heb. *va'eḥal*] in their midst' (*va'eḥal* is derived from the root *ḥ-l-l*, implying profanation of the sacred, sacrilege).[24]

A further echo of this episode, described in a fragment of the Damascus Document found at Qumran, notes the fate of those sinful 'sons of God' who broke down the barriers between forbidden and permitted, deliberately rejected the ways of God, and disobeyed their Creator's command:

Hear now, my sons, and I will uncover your eyes that you may see and understand the works of God, that you may choose that which pleases Him and reject that which He hates, that you may walk perfectly in all His ways and not follow after thoughts of the guilty inclination and after eyes of lust. For through them, great men have gone astray and mighty heroes have stumbled, from former times till now. Because they walked in the stubbornness of their hearts the Heavenly Watchers fell; they were caught because they did not keep the commandments of God. And their sons also fell, who were tall as cedar trees and whose bodies were like mountains. All flesh on dry land perished; they were as though they had never been, because they did their own will and did not keep the commandments of their Creator, so that His wrath was kindled against them.

---

[20] *DJD* XXIII, 215 (11Q12, frg. 7, 1–4); other cardinal sins are listed in the same context in 1 En. 7: 1–6.   [21] See Ezek. 22: 26; Zeph. 3: 4; Pss. 11: 5; 55: 10; MMT C = 4Q 397 (*DJD* X, 58).
[22] Gen. 6: 13.   [23] Ezek. 22: 26.   [24] Cf. *Genesis Rabbah* 26: 4.

Through it, the children of Noah went astray, together with their kin, and were cut off.[25]

'Guilty inclination', 'eyes of lust', and 'stubbornness of the heart' refer to forbidden sexuality, profane and impure, ignoring the sacred constraints of matrimony ('and took wives from among those that pleased them'[26]) and of the purifying numbers that provide the basis for the constraints of divine law and order. Such commissions of the most cardinal sins are opposed to sanctified sexuality, whose object is procreation; that goal is pursued through symbols of sanctity and purity, founded on sanctification and the drawing of proper boundaries, conditional upon counting seven days of purity.

The two myths—Enoch son of Jared who ascended to heaven to 'see' the invisible divine division of time, and the sons of God who descended from heaven to earth to 'see' the visible but forbidden humans—are clearly intended to constitute an antithetical pair: in both, the boundaries between the heavenly and the earthly are transcended, a relationship is established between angels and humans, and hidden knowledge is acquired; and in both, boundaries are drawn between forbidden and permitted perceptions of time. The heavenly knowledge is concerned with permitted liaisons, supernatural authority, sanctity, purity, benediction, and life, on the one hand; or with forbidden liaisons, the violation of authority, impurity and blasphemy, corruption, malediction, and death, on the other hand—all described in such terms as light and darkness, good and evil, innocence and stubbornness, knowledge and corruption.

In the story of Enoch, a human being ascends to heaven as willed by God, experiences conversion from man to angel, from mortal to immortal, and receives from the angels divinely sanctioned heavenly knowledge that reveals the eternal divine order. Instructed by the angels, he takes this knowledge down to earth and,

---

[25] Damascus Document II, 14–21 (cf. Vermes, *CDSSIE*, 128–9); Broshi (ed.), *Damascus Document Reconsidered*, [13]; see also J. M. Baumgarten, *The Damascus Document (DJD* XVIII), 4Q266, frg. 2 ii, ll. 13 ff. (pp. 34–6); Wacholder and Abegg, *Preliminary Edition*, i. 6, frg. 2, col. 2, ll. 16–20. For 'stubbornness of heart' (Heb. *sherirut lev*) representing evil and rebellion against God see Deut. 29: 18. This expression always occurs in the Bible in the context of the Israelites' worship of foreign deities and their disregard for the duty of ongoing remembrance and testimony incumbent on the participants in the oath and the Covenant (Ps. 83: 6–15). Walking in the stubbornness of one's heart is the reverse of remembrance and observance; abandoning the Covenant is associated with forgetting the past, turning one's back on the binding oaths and the circumstances in which the Covenant was concluded (Jer. 3: 17; 7: 24; 9: 12–13; 11: 18; Ps. 83: 6–15). A highly charged expression, it occurs in all the writings of the secessionist priests as a synonym for the sins of the Watchers and, in addition, for any infringement by an individual of the rules of the Community. See Community Rule VI, 4; VII, 19, 24, etc.; Thanksgiving Hymns XII, 15; Damascus Document III, 5; VIII, 32–3; Dimant, 'Sinning Angels'. The opposite expression is 'to walk perfectly (also: wholeheartedly or blamelessly, Heb. *tamim*) in all his ways', which may be linked with the figure of Enoch, who walked 'with God', and with that of Noah, who was 'a righteous man, blameless in his generations' (Gen. 6: 9)—the two major heroes of this literature, who are associated with the solar calendar and with paths of righteousness and integrity.

[26] Gen. 6: 2.

fulfilling the divine command, imparts it to humankind, in order to establish true ways and to constitute the sacred priesthood, which relies on the solar calendar and testifies to the eternity of divine order.

In the fallen angels story, the divine beings descend from heaven in their stubbornness, contravening God's will. They experience reversion from holy, heavenly beings to sinful earthlings, who deliberately and rebelliously disobey God's commands. They disrupt the proper order, violate the boundaries and distinctions of Creation, lust after every desire and covet what is not theirs, enter into forbidden liaisons that commingle the upper and lower realms, mortals and immortals. These forbidden liaisons produce uncontrollable, monstrous creatures, giants, *nefilim*, who devastate life and vegetation and disrupt world order, transgress the laws of forbidden sexual unions, and commit various carnal sins; they teach people heavenly knowledge that is not properly theirs, as well as idolatry; they promote the worship of heavenly bodies and introduce the lunar calendar. The result is death, destruction, and bloodshed.

The two myths are concerned with the most elemental pairs of opposites: life and death, Creation and chaos, light and darkness, good and evil, permitted and forbidden things, observance and infringement of taboos, purity and impurity, blessing and curse, counting and calculating in fixed proportions as against disregard of number and variable counting, licit and illicit knowledge, sanctified and forbidden sexual unions.

In the first myth, Enoch, the 'righteous', virtuous, 'seventh', who walked with God in sanctity, was taken up to heaven by God ('then he was no more, for God took him') to learn the secrets of the solar calendar from an angel named Uriel (the prince of the Sons of Light; the Angel of the Presence or Countenance; the Hebrew word *or*, from which the angel's name is derived, means 'light') and to testify to these secrets before his sons—the founders of the priestly dynasty that was to culminate in the 'Sons of Light', the 'righteous plantation', the 'eternal righteous plantation', the 'sons of Zadok', the priests.[27] These children of the Covenant, who observe purity and sanctity and walk in the ways of truth and righteousness, are the faithful guardians, together with the angels, of the cyclic enumeration of days reflecting the order of Creation, the covenants between heaven and earth, as celebrated in the heavenly sequence of sabbaths and appointed times (sabbath is a 'sign', an 'eternal covenant').

In the second myth, the 'sons of God', Watchers, or 'angels of destruction' first come down to earth on their own sinful initiative, as stressed in the account of the recognition of sin and of shared guilt, expressed in their oath by *ḥerem* taken on Mount Hermon.[28] In the second stage of their rebellion they disrupt the laws of

[27] Expressions similar to 'righteous plantation' occur in Enoch and Jubilees; see e.g. 1 En. 10: 16; 93: 9–10; Jub. 16: 26; and see below.

[28] 1 En. 6: 1–7; 2 En. 18: 3–5; *ḥerem* denotes not only a curse, but also sacrilege and infringement of taboo, as in Arabic *ḥarām*.

nature, disregard the boundaries between forbidden and permitted things, ignore faith and law, the laws of impurity and forbidden sexual unions, sign and number: '[They] took for themselves wives from all whom they chose and made a beginning of impurity';[29] 'They commit sin and transgress the commandment; they have united themselves with women and commit sin together with them; and they have married (wives) from among them, and begotten children by them.'[30] The sinful angels upset the natural and proper order of things, deliberately violating divine law and order, breaching the laws of separation and the taboos that govern the relationships of nature and civilization, heaven and earth; they teach heavenly secrets, idolatry and worship of the heavens, sorcery and forbidden knowledge involving sensory observation, carnal sin, and bloodshed. An angel named Sahariel (*sahar* = moon) teaches the secrets of the lunar calendar, whose revelation involves the cardinal sins.[31] The result of the violation of boundaries, the commingling of incompatibles, and the disruption of the order of Creation is the birth of the *nefilim*, born in sin, uncontrollable monsters who devastated the world of man and the kingdoms of the animals and the plants, spreading evil, lust, idolatry, and bloodshed, a situation described in the Bible as 'and the earth was filled with *ḥamas*, lawlessness'. The traditions concerned with the forbidden carnal knowledge involved in the Watchers' misdeeds speak of heavenly knowledge imparted by the sinful angels, stressing the affinity of that knowledge with the realms of darkness and night, with forbidden observation relying on the fallible human senses, and with the forbidden realm of idolatry, sorcery, and secrets: 'incantation . . . astrology . . . the seeing of the stars . . . the course of the moon'.[32]

As I have already stated, this knowledge produced destruction, miscegenation, impurity, evil, lust, forbidden sexuality, stubbornness, and idolatry: 'because they have acquired the knowledge of all the secrets of the angels, all the oppressive deeds of the Satans, as well as all their most occult powers, all the powers of those who practise sorcery, . . . all the powers of those who make molten images'.[33] The teachings of Enoch, by contrast, dwell upon an abstract calculation, independent of human observation but reflected in the order of Creation; they are concerned with divine knowledge of the sun's course, of light and the domain of day, with adherence to divinely appointed times and ways of righteousness, purity, and sanctity.

Enoch represents the divine knowledge of Creation and the cyclic order of nature, founded on angelic authority and recognition of limits and boundaries, reflecting sanctity and light, eternal order, the legal delineation of permitted and prohibited things, testimony and righteous conduct—associated with counting, number, and cycle, the abstract numerical principle sanctifying seven-based cycles. The Watchers, on the other hand, represent forbidden knowledge, founded on rebellion and breaching of boundaries, associated with impurity and

[29] Jub. 7: 21.   [30] 1 En. 106: 14.
[31] 1 En. 6–15; 19; 65; Jub. 7.   [32] 1 En. 8: 2–4.   [33] 1 En. 65: 6.

disregard for number, counting, and cycle. Implicit in such knowledge are death and destruction, a lawless world bereft of natural order, a world of sin and rebellion in which there is no judgement or morality, a world of violence and unrestrained lust, disregarding the injunctions of taboo, number, and counting; a world without sanctity and purity which closes its eyes to knowledge beyond sensory perception.

The evil world revealed through the forbidden deeds of the sons of God affords a glimpse into the darkest recesses of the human soul: forbidden carnal knowledge and forbidden divine knowledge, founded on seeing and lust, sorcery and mystery, tyranny, licentiousness, impurity, and stubbornness; a world of idolatry, bloodshed, and incest. These three cardinal sins are associated with the sin of the Watchers, for they, too, set aside the sanctions and boundaries set by society, religion, and culture: the boundaries between man and God defined by the injunction against idolatry; the boundaries between human beings defined by the prohibition of murder; and the boundaries forbidding sexual relationships between consanguineous relatives and different or distinct species.

In the language of myth—which tells the story of Creation, the initiation of life, and the establishment of natural order, on the one hand, and the story of death, destruction, and the disruption of natural order, on the other—Enoch is the human epitome of light, benevolence, wisdom, knowledge, eternal order, oath and Covenant, counting and number, precept and law, sanctity and purity, entailing blessing and fertility, innocence, integrity, and righteousness, all representative of the sacred, angelic source of the solar calendar. All these elements are embodied in Enoch, the seventh patriarch of the world, the first literate and numerate human being, founder of the priesthood, agent of eternal life; he represents fulfilment of the precepts and ways of integrity, observance of seven days of purity and seven days of the week.

At the other extreme lie darkness and evil, sin and injustice, promiscuity and violation of boundaries and of natural order, commingling of the diverse and the distinct, numberless chaos, blind lust, lawlessness and wickedness, impurity and destruction, malediction, abomination and corruption, incest, sacrilege, forbidden knowledge, disruption of the calendar of sabbaths and appointed times, neglect of the seven days of purity. All these, and in particular the sinful angelic origin of the lunar calendar, are embodied in the myth of the Watchers' sin, which brought about the Flood and the destruction of the earth. The struggle between Enoch's teachings, the precondition for life, and those of the Watchers, which lead inevitably to death, is a struggle between subordination to an abstract principle of knowledge, law, and number, transcending the limits of the human senses (represented, for example, by the number of days in the year, fixed at 364 and divided into fixed numerical divisions, independent of human observation), on the one hand, and subordination to a material principle, dependent on sight and sensory perception (such as the determination of the first days of months by human observation, with twelve months making up a year of 354 days divided into months with fluctuating numbers of days).

As we have seen, the secessionist priests of Qumran believed that the teachings of the Watchers originated in the three cardinal sins, which are punishable by what the Bible calls *karet*, 'to be cut off'. These sins were implicitly associated with the reality against which those priests were struggling, with their time and place and the history of the earlier controversies between different priestly houses. Traces of those earlier struggles are to be found in biblical literature, in the book of Ezekiel, who waged the war of the sons of Zadok against an impious, sacrilegious priest-hood,[34] from which we learn of the existence of an alternative priestly law, distinct from that formulated in the Bible. It was the use of mythical language and pseudepigraphic attribution, in a story purporting to describe primeval times, in terms of protagonists who had already played a part in the sacred scriptures and in cultic awareness, that enabled the rejected priests—deprived of their hegemony, painfully conscious of injustice and lawlessness, aghast at depravity and sacri-lege—to come to terms with the reality of their situation (in other words, the Qumranite 'Zadokite' priests as it were took over Ezekiel's championing of the bib-lical Zadokite priests in order to justify their own stand against their opponents). One might say that the ancient myth of the origin of evil and the violation of sacred boundaries, of profanation and chaos corrupting the order of Creation, was revived and retold with respect to the teachings of the sacrilegious ruling priesthood, which was disrupting the old, natural order, disturbing the proper order of sab-baths and festivals. These rival priests are known in the literature of the secession-ist priesthood as 'sons of wickedness', 'sons of Belial', 'house of rebellion' and 'Sons of Darkness'.

The antithetical relationship between life and death, purity and impurity, fertil-ity and destruction, light and darkness, good and evil, permitted divine knowledge and forbidden carnal knowledge, abstract hearing and material, sensual percep-tion, is clearly brought out in the injunctions formulated in Jubilees and in the Community Rule. Permitted relationships, typified by sanctity and sanctification, dependent on counting and enumeration, on calculating the days of the week and the seven days of purification, condition the promise of seed and fertility, the con-tinuity of generations. While forbidden relationships, defined as incest, abomina-tion and promiscuity, impurity and depravity devoid of sanctity or sanctification, disregard for enumeration and numbers, and associated with 'watching' or the sin of the Watchers, inevitably produce calamity and oblivion, drought and barren-ness, aridity and desert, curse and death.

Promiscuity and incest stem from unbridled sexuality not directed towards reproduction and continuity, and from violation of civilized limits and taboos—

---

[34] Ezek. 40–8.

including the cardinal sins of idolatry, bloodshed, and incest, which should not be committed even upon pain of death. They were prohibited in order to avert death and ensure life, to ward off the danger of loss of seed and annihilation which would follow inevitably from forbidden relationships, commingling of opposites, and infringement of taboo. Forbidden relationships and incest, unrestrained human desire dependent on sensory perception, had to be proscribed in order to guarantee maintenance of the cycle of life, blessing and fertility through sanctification and sanctity, purity and observance of the Covenant, counting and number, sabbath and oath, appointed times and calendar—all based on a principle transcending the human senses. The story of the ascent of Enoch, the seventh, and his study of the calculation of the calendar of sabbaths that safeguards the eternal order of Creation and establishes blessing, purity, and the continuity of life, is concerned with these elements; while the story of the fall of the Watchers, a story rooted in forbidden sexuality, idolatry, and bloodshed and culminating in violation, destruction, and flood, in curse and death, in barrenness and desert, is thus concerned with the antithesis of the previous elements and clearly illustrates the implications of breached boundaries.

The myth of the Watchers describes violation of that cosmic order in which separation is a precondition for harmony in Creation; it also teaches a lesson, namely, that the disruption of natural order unavoidably entails disruption of social order, which is also based on separation, on established limits of permitted and forbidden, of possible and impossible. It is a story of forbidden sexual unions between distinct species, originating in forbidden observation ('the sons of God saw how beautiful the daughters of men were'), lawlessness and forbidden seizure ('and took wives from among those that pleased them'), aimed not at procreation and continuity but at satisfaction of lust and therefore considered impure, depraved, and culminating in death. The whole story is presented as an antithetical demonstration of the value of sanctified conjugal life, between permitted partners of the same species, within the constraints of civilized contract based on sanctity and law (sanctification = betrothal, matrimony). Such permitted bonds, aimed at procreation, at continuity of generations and the life cycle, depend on the con-servation of purity, cycle, and number (oaths, seven days of purification). The obligatory separation of consanguineous relatives, prohibiting sexual relations between such relatives (incest) or between Jews and gentiles, is emphasized throughout the literature of the secessionist priests. The preferred conjugal rela-tionship in that literature is that of a man with his father's sister's daughter, which was thought to preserve the familial, dynastic framework, as against the forbidden union with his mother's sister's daughter, which was considered as incest, or with a gentile woman—these forbidden unions were thought to threaten the purity of the dynasty and the uniqueness of the nation.

The Hebrew root *z-n-h*, which has the sense of harlotry or forbidden sexuality, appears only twice in Genesis in relation to a woman of a different nation, namely,

Tamar;[35] while the biblical narrative has nothing to say of the various episodes of forbidden unions (the sons of God and the daughters of man; Pharaoh and Abimelech with Sarah and Rebekah, respectively; Reuben and Bilhah) and incest (Noah and his son Ham; the first generations of the patriarchs; Lot and his daughters); these episodes are treated as isolated cases, tests or mishaps, whether reported or suppressed, without broad implications and without any obligatory legal conclusion. Jubilees, however, which retells the Genesis stories with the express purpose of deriving all possible precepts and injunctions from the patriarchs' lives, interprets them in great detail and is much concerned with such forbidden unions with foreign partners[36] or incestuous unions, all of which violate boundaries and disrupt numerical relationships. The author of Jubilees presents the various illustrations of such forbidden unions, beginning with the episode of the sons of God and the daughters of man,[37] which is also treated at length in both books of Enoch; continuing with the story of Sodom, which involves a variety of forbidden sexual acts,[38] the story of Abraham's farewell testimony, in which he forbids his sons to marry Canaanite women and instructs them to burn women who have 'fornicated';[39] and culminating in the episode of the rape of Dinah, which inspires the injunction against marrying foreign partners and is held to justify the killing of the Shechemites, for violation of these prohibitions is unpardonable.[40]

The prohibition of incest also figures in the episodes of Lot's daughters and their father, of Noah's sons, of Reuben and Bilhah,[41] and of Judah and Tamar. Each of these episodes is narrated as a background to the divine injunctions against various patterns of incest and forbidden sex, which reflect the story of the Watchers and their disruption of the proper natural order and the harmonic rhythm of Creation associated with the number seven. All these offences—incest, abomination, fornication, impurity—are interrelated, all involving forbidden proximity between kin or between members of different categories, impurity, curse, and death. Contrasted with such forbidden sexual unions are the sanctified bonds directed towards fertility, procreation, and the continuity of life, which depend on a careful balance between nearness and distance: close relatives must be kept apart, and on the other hand so must members of different species.

The antithesis between impurity, lawlessness and abomination, incest and promiscuity (which represent disregard for measure, number, or limit) and purity (which maintains measure, number and limit, cycle and sanctity) is the mythical antithesis between chaos and Creation, death and life, enslavement and freedom; between the march of time without beginning and end, without enumeration and cycle, without seasons and appointed times signifying respite and interruption of routine, and time that has been enumerated in septuples ever since the seven days of Creation and is governed by cycle, epoch, season, and sabbath. The sevenfold

---

[35] Gen. 38: 24.   [36] e.g. Jub. 30: 8.   [37] Jub. 7: 20–33.
[38] Jub. 16: 5–9.   [39] Jub. 20: 3–10; 25: 4–7.   [40] Jub. 30: 5–23.   [41] Jub. 33: 15–16.

regulation that guarantees Creation, purity, sanctity, and the continuity of life was the responsibility of the priesthood, which associated it with Enoch the seventh patriarch, with the sabbath and the seven days of purification, with the seventy days of rest every year, with the cultic and cyclic representations of the number seven in the calendar, the Temple, and with the very boundaries of civilization and life. Hence the seven days of the week, the seven days of purification, the seven weeks between the appointed times of the Temple, the seven festivals in the first seven months of the year, and the oath of holy betrothal guarantee the continuity of life and procreation. The sanctity of the sabbath and that of Shavuot (see below), both bound up with sevenfold order, constitute a central axis of Jubilees, which is entirely dedicated to expounding this sevenfold regularity. The seven days of purification and the laws of impurity and of the menstruating woman are presented in the context of Eve in the Garden of Eden, in her capacity as both born and giving birth; that is, these laws date to the very beginning of Creation. Enumeration, calculation, number, cyclic counting associated with seven (*sheva*) and oath (*shevuah*) represent the difference between purity and sanctity, sacred connubiality, the blessing of fertility and guaranteed continuity of life, on the one hand, and impurity and depravity, promiscuity and incest, curse, barrenness and the destruction of life, on the other. All such manifestations of sanctity, conjugal relations, purity and sabbath, blessing and fertility are subordinate to an abstract principle and dependent on number, calculation, enumeration and cycle, fixed regulation; they are subject to rigidly defined concepts of permitted and forbidden nearness and distance. At the other extreme are impurity, abomination, incest, and sin, all linked with relationships free of restraint, devoid of enumeration, number, cycle, limitation, and regulation—behaviour ruled only by the limits of sensory and sensual perception.

We thus have a clear-cut antithetical relationship. On the one hand: the divinely sanctioned ascent of Enoch, the righteous, who 'walked with God', learned from the angels, and testified to the sanctity of time and the divine source of the number, to the eternal order of Creation and the heavenly source of the sequence of sabbaths and seven appointed times. Enoch thus brought about the divine revelation of the solar calendar, and its acceptance by the Zadokite priests, the Sons of Light, who testified to its sanctity through their loyalty to the Covenant with God and their observance of its appointed times,[42] precepts, and injunctions in accordance with the solar calendar, in a pure human Temple. Their counterparts are the angels who serve as 'priests of the inner sanctum' in the heavenly Temple, the 'lot of the Sons of Light'. On the other hand: the descent, against God's will, of the sinning 'sons of God' who 'walked in the stubbornness of their heart', disrupted divine order, learned forbidden knowledge, and brought about the sinful revelation of the lunar calendar and its acceptance by the Sons of Darkness, who violated

---

[42] Lev. 23.

the divine Covenant, distorted God's commands, and perverted his appointed times in their waywardness by following the lunar calendar. Their counterparts are the 'angels of destruction', priests of iniquity, the 'lot of the Sons of Darkness', in a defiled Temple. This antithetical relationship is the driving force behind many narratives in the literature of the secessionist priesthood, which established a dualistic, mythological world view as the background of and justification for segregation and secession. This myth is a foundation narrative for the distinction between good and evil, knowledge and lust, for the presence of evil in the world; it attributes the disruption of the proper order of heaven and earth to stubbornness, violation of boundaries, promiscuity, injustice, represented by the idolatry, incest, and bloodshed caused by the Watchers' descent. But the constant concern with the myth is due not merely to its role as foundation narrative, but also to its sequel.

The Watchers, as 'sons of God', were immortal, so that the flood that annihilated their mortal offspring had no effect on them or on their spiritual offspring—spirits of evil and injustice, who subsist in the realms of heavenly and terrestrial existence, bearing punishment or bound and imprisoned, according to various traditions, in the realms of darkness, wilderness, desolation, impurity, the region of Azazel, the land of the shadow of darkness, corruption, and Belial (a combination of two Hebrew words meaning: 'the place from which no ascent is possible'). Chapters 15 and 16 of 1 Enoch deal with the fate of the descendants of the Watchers' sin, the evil spirits 'born from (the union of) the spirits and the flesh',[43] and Qumran literature discusses the curses imposed on these evil spirits, which shaped the lot of the Sons of Darkness and threatened that of the Sons of Light.[44]

The secessionist priests who related these myths of the establishment and violation of divine order, of light and darkness, of sun and moon, of Enoch and the Watchers, of life and death, divided the earthly and heavenly world into two realms of light and darkness, righteousness and wickedness, purity and impurity, truth and falsehood, observance and violation of the Covenant, calculation and observation, permitted knowledge and forbidden sorcery, holy angels and angels of Belial, cultivation and wilderness, fresh water and desert. They distinguished between those who undertook to 'walk in perfection in all his ways', to live by knowledge, number, the laws of purity, and the sevenfold Covenant, and those who 'walked in the stubbornness of their heart' and violated that order. This is known from the writings of the secessionist priesthood in general and in particular from the War of the Sons of Light against the Sons of Darkness and the Community Rule. The conflict between the two realms continues without end.

From the God of Knowledge comes all that is and shall be. Before ever they existed He established their whole design, and when, as ordained for them, they come into being, it is in accord with His glorious design that they accomplish their task without change. The laws of all things are in His hand and He provides them with all their needs.

---

[43] 1 En. 15: 8–9.   [44] 1 En. 9: 6–9; cf. 4Q180, frg. 1, 7–10 (*DJD* V, 78–80).

He has created man to govern the world, and has appointed for him two spirits in which to walk until the time of His visitation: the spirits of truth and injustice. Those born of truth spring from a fountain of light, but those born of injustice spring from a source of darkness. All the children of righteousness are ruled by the Prince of Light and walk in the ways of light, but all the children of injustice are ruled by the Angel of Darkness and walk in the ways of darkness. The Angel of Darkness leads all the children of righteousness astray, and until his end, all their sin, iniquities, wickedness, and all their unlawful deeds are caused by his dominion in accordance with the mysteries of God. Every one of their chastisements, and every one of the seasons of their distress, shall be brought about by the rule of his malevolence; for all the spirits of his lot seek the overthrow of the Sons of Light. But the God of Israel and His Angel of Truth will succour all the Sons of Light.[45]

The Community, which refers to its members as 'those who turn from transgression'[46] and 'those who enter the Covenant',[47] Sons of Light and Sons of Righteousness, was headed by a leader known as the Priest of Righteousness, Master/Teacher of Righteousness, or Chief Priest. This leader was the counterpart of the Prince of Light, that is, Uriel, who is featured in Enoch literature as having revealed the calendar to Enoch and is also called his Angel of Truth or the Angel of the Countenance. The community [of the] faithful, the Sons of Righteousness (Heb. *benei tsedek*, cf. *benei tsadok* = sons of Zadok, Zadokites), observed the solar calendar, and adhered to the ways of the lot of the Sons of Light, who relied on calculation and number. Their opponents were led by the Wicked Priest, counterpart of the Prince of Darkness, Belial, or Mastemah (the prince of malevolence), while they themselves were called Sons of Injustice or Sons of Lawlessness, who followed the lot of the Sons of Darkness and observed the lunar calendar, which relies on human observation. The Sons of Light or Sons of Righteousness observed the Covenant, counting sabbaths and appointed times as they should be counted; they were blessed, entered into the Covenant, lived in concert with the angels of light and priests of righteousness; they testified to the Covenant and considered themselves as the 'eternal plantation' and 'shoot of justice and integrity', in an affinity with Paradise, the cherubim, and the source of life and eternity. The Sons of Darkness or Sons of Injustice, however, were the accursed violators of the Covenant, who lived in concert with the angels of darkness, Azazel, Belial, and Mastemah, with the priests of injustice, who walked in the stubbornness of their hearts, and disrupted the sequence of sabbaths and appointed times through dependence on

---

[45] Community Rule III, 15–25 (cf. Vermes, *CDSSIE*, 101). Cf. 4QBer, frg. 6, 1–11 (*DJD* XI, 57–8), and various passages in the War Scroll. For the 'two ways' see also 4Q473 in *DJD* XXII, 292. The Slavonic Book of Enoch preserves evidence of the obligation to know divine law in relation to the laws of nature and heavenly knowledge, in the Creation story as recounted by God: 'And I called his name Adam . . . and I pointed out to him the two ways—light and darkness. And I said to him, "This is good for you, but that is bad" . . . And ignorance is more lamentable than sin' (2 En. 30: 14–16).

[46] Damascus Document II, 5.   [47] Ibid. 2.

human observation, testifying to the chaos associated with wilderness and desert, death and destruction.

A cultic echo of this dualism, signifying the struggle between life and death, fertility and barrenness, cultivation and desert, purity and impurity, may be traced in the scapegoat ceremony on the Day of Atonement, when repentant sinners were absolved of their sins by sending a goat to Azazel in the wilderness, the realm that represents impurity, curse, darkness, wilderness, and the shadow of death, the realm of chaos without measure or number.[48] At the same time, incense was burned in the Holy of Holies, the realm associated with the Garden of Eden and representative of purity, sanctity, blessing, growth, eternity, and life dependent on number and cycle. Azazel is the name of the leader of the rebellious angels in the myth of the Watchers, of whom it is said, 'You see what Azazel has done, how he has taught all (forms of) oppression upon the earth; and he revealed eternal secrets which are revealed in heaven'.[49] The punishment meted out to this immortal and his cronies, who taught oppression, evil, transgression, and sin,[50] was eternal imprisonment and exile to the desert, to the province of darkness, death, corruption, and desolation;[51] the various phases of this punishment, relating to the Watchers and their sons, were implemented by Uriel, Raphael, Michael, and Gabriel,[52] the four chief angels of the Sons of Light. The Damascus Document associates atonement with the angels' sin: 'They will serve Him, patience is with Him, and much forgiveness, to atone for those who repent sin; but power, might and great flaming wrath are with Him, by the hand of all the Angels of Destruction, toward those who depart from the way and abhor the law.'[53]

In this literature, the atoning incense originates in the Garden of Eden, the source of life; it is associated with blessing, with the mystery of eternal natural growth and the eternity of life. Made from seven ingredients, the incense is prepared in advance in accordance with the number of days in the solar year.[54] In the various traditions, the seven aromatic ingredients are saffron, spikenard, reed, cinnamon, myrrh, frankincense, and mastic (alternative ingredients are balsam, galbanum, aloe, and aromatic gum), extracted from plants grown in the Garden of Eden[55] and kept exclusively by the priests. Jubilees lists seven ingredients of the

[48] 1 En. 10: 4–16.   [49] 1 En. 9: 6.
[50] 1 En. 13: 1.   [51] 1 En. 10: 4–16.   [52] 1 En. 10: 1–9.
[53] Damascus Document II, 4–6 (cf. Vermes, *CDSSIE*, 128). Evidence of these ancient traditions may also be found in rabbinic literature. Commenting on the biblical term 'Azazel' in connection with the scapegoat ceremony, the Babylonian Talmud (*Yoma* 67b) cites a tradition that '[Azazel was so called] because it atones for the affair of Uza and Aza'el'. This obscure reference is explained by the medieval commentator Rashi as follows: '[These were] the angels of destruction who came down to earth in the time of Na'amah, sister of Tubal Cain, of which Scripture says, "[They] saw how beautiful the daughters of men were" [Gen. 6: 2]; that is to say, it atones for incestuous relationships.' We thus have an association, on the one hand, with the fallen angels, i.e. the Watchers, and, on the other, with the sin of forbidden, incestuous relationships. See also R. Margaliot, *Heavenly Angels*, 274 ff.; Tabori, *Jewish Festivals*, 292 n. 134.   [54] BT *Ker.* 6a.
[55] Life of Adam and Eve 29: 3–7; 1 En. 29–32; Jub. 3: 27; Ben Sira 30: 7.

incense,[56] but rabbinic tradition specifies twelve. The high priest enters the Holy of Holies on the Day of Atonement and stands before the cherubim—associated, as seen in a previous chapter, with the mystery of life, blessing, and sacred union—in a cloud of incense, burned on this day in a special ceremony on the gold (incense) altar, or on an incense pan in the Holy of Holies.[57] He does so after having dispatched the goat to the wilderness, the realm of Azazel, leader of the sinful angels, who is associated with forbidden incest, with curse, darkness, and death. The contrast between the high priest's entry into the Holy of Holies, representing the Garden of Eden and associated with palm trees, flowers, cherubim, gold, and incense, representative of light and the mystery of life, on the one hand, and the dispatching of the goat to the wilderness, representing death and desolation, darkness and bloodshed—that is the contrast between benediction and malediction, life and death.

The Qumran community held a dramatic ceremony of imprecation, which is described in terms referring explicitly to the story of the Watchers. It may well have been connected with the ceremony of blessings and curses at the time the Covenant was concluded on Shavuot (see below). In this ceremony, the Levites set a curse on the lot of Belial and the lot of darkness, the angel of corruption, hatred, evil spirits, impurity, and abomination, all associated with the evil spirits that emerged from the sin of the Watchers, all eager to destroy the divine Covenant and the law of the Torah:[58]

the council of the community, all of them will say together: 'Amen. Amen'. And then [they] will curse Belial and all his guilty lot. And they will speak up, saying: 'Cursed be [B]elial in his hostile [sc]heme, and damned is he in his guilty authority. And cursed are all the spir[its] of his [lo]t in their wicked scheme, and they are damned in the schemes of their [un]clean impurity; for[they are the lo]t of darkness, and their punishment is in the eternal pit. Amen. Amen.

And cursed is the Wick[ed One during all periods] of his dominions; and damned are all the sons of Beli[al] in all their periods of service until their consummation [forever. Amen. Amen.]

And [they will say again: 'Cursed are you Ange]l of the Pit and Spir[it of Aba]ddon in al[l] the schemes of [your] g[uilty] inclination [and in all (your) abomin]able [purposes] and [your] wicked counsel; [and da]mned are you in [the] d[omi]n[ion of] [your pervers-ity and in yo]ur [wicked and guilty authority] with all the con[taminations of Sheo]l and wit[h the disgraces of the pi]t [and with the humi]liations of destruction with [no rem-nant, with no forgi]veness, with the anger of [G]od's wrath [for all the ages of eternit]y. Amen. A[men].'

[And cursed are a]ll who execute their [wicked schemes] and confirm their evil pur-pose [in their hearts by plotting evil] [against the covenant of Go]d and by[the words of the seers of] His [tru]th and by exchanging the judgem[ents of the Law].[59]

---

[56] Jub. 16: 24. See Ch. 2, n. 59.   [57] Mishnah *Tam.* 6: 2; *Yoma* 1: 5.

[58] 1 En. 10: 4–16; 15: 1–12; 16: 1–2; Jub. 48: 2, 9; 49: 2.

[59] 4Q286, frg. 7 (*DJD* XI, 27–8, 57).

Parallels to this ceremony, which is based on the ceremonial proclamation of curses on Mount Ebal,[60] may be found, as noted, in the Covenant in the Community Rule, where 'the Levites shall curse all the men of the lot of Belial . . . And after the blessing and the cursing, all those entering the Covenant shall say, Amen, Amen!',[61] in the similar ceremony described in the War Scroll,[62] and in the narrative in the Damascus Document[63] concerning the developments associated with Prince Mastemah and his wrath against 'those who depart from the way and abhor the precept'.

The frequency with which the myths of Enoch's ascent and the descent of the Watchers, as well as the associated myths of the sanctity and the establishment of the solar calendar and the opposing myth of the source of all evil and impurity, appear implicitly or explicitly in Qumran literature is a clear indication that they are significant and meaningful for the writers, far beyond the literal meaning of the texts themselves. The roots of that deeper, old-new, meaning lie in the contemporary struggle between light and darkness, good and evil, blessing and curse, purity and impurity, life and death, in the writers' own times, as they fought for the sanctity of the solar calendar and the tradition of the Zadokite priests, originating in the First Temple period, and against the iniquity that they perceived in the lunar calendar and the alternative priestly tradition of the Hasmonaean dynasty in Second Temple times. The secessionist priests, in their own mind the keepers of the Covenant, the true sons of Zadok and the blessed 'lot of light', considering their opponents violators of the Covenant, sons of evil and the accursed 'lot of darkness', expanded the mainly allusive biblical narrative, interpreting it as an account of the very origin of evil and indeed of a host of sins and transgressions. Through mythical personification, they portrayed their antagonists as the sons of Belial, reflections of the sinning angels, who had violated the Covenant and instructed others in the errant ways of the lunar calendar and other forbidden knowledge, defiling the Temple and establishing the domination of the 'lot' of the Sons of Darkness, Belial, and the Prince Mastemah. They themselves, in contrast, were the counterparts of the Sons of Light, keepers of the Covenant, 'plantation of righteousness', privy to divine knowledge associated with sanctified angelic traditions dating back to Enoch, the Angel of the Countenance, and the Prince of Light, with the heavenly tablets, the cherubim, and the Merkavah, with the holy testimony of the solar calendar, observed in a pure Temple in the spiritual world of the Sons of Light.

The struggle over the calendar was the struggle of the Sons of Light and the Sons of Darkness for validation, legitimization, and authority; a struggle over the origins of cultic knowledge concerning the workings of nature, over whether that knowledge is sacred, or corrupt and distorted: light and darkness, sun and moon, divinely inspired calculation of the sun's unchanging course in heaven as against

---

[60] Deut. 27: 13–26.   [61] Community Rule II, 5–10.

[62] XIII, 1–17.   [63] VIII, 2; and *passim*.

human observation of the shifting cycles of the moon; a struggle between calendars based on these two kinds of knowledge. This struggle and the consequent cultic order and dualistic symbolism received mythical descriptions in the context of the halakhic and cultic disputes between the two contradictory religious world views, as reflected in the controversy between the two competing priestly groups.

The heavily polemical tone of this literature involves not only denunciation of the moon, with emphasis on the astronomical fact that the sun's light is seven times that of the moon,[64] but also, at times, exclusion of the moon from the company of the heavenly signs taken into consideration in calendrical calculations. Jubilees, in its Qumranic version, demands a special status for the sun, as a reference point for calculating the entire cycle of time, divided into seven different periods, saying (the text uses the term *ot*, 'sign', in reference to the sabbath, Enoch, and the rainbow, all associated with the number seven): '[He appointed the sun as a gre]at [sign above the earth] for day[s], for [sa]bbaths, for [months, for appointed times, for years, for the weeks of years, for jubi]lees, and for all the cy[cles of the years]',[65] while the parallel text in Genesis uses the plural (in all textual witnesses): 'Let there be lights . . .; they shall serve as signs for the set times—the days and the years.[66] The Hebrew original, however, presents a linguistic difficulty of possible significance: the singular verbal form *yehi* translated here as 'let there be', clashing with the plural 'lights', raises questions as to this traditional text, as already noted by Onkelos, who changed the verb to the plural in his Aramaic translation. The Community Rule, too, refers only to the 'greater light' in connection with calculations of the festivals and other appointed times: God, it says, created 'the greater light for the Holy of Holies . . . for the beginnings of the appointed times in every period . . . at the beginnings of the years and in the course of their appointed times . . .'.[67] In the Book of Heavenly Luminaries, in the chapter devoted to the lunar cycle and its sevenfold pattern, in relation to the solar year, 'In one-seven-seven parts it completes all its light in the east and in seven-seven parts completes all its

---

[64] According to Isa. 30: 26; 2 En. 11: 2; 1 En. 78: 4.

[65] 4Q216, VI, 7–8 (= Jub. 2: 9); *DJD* XIII, 16–17. Cf. Jub. 4: 23–4, concerning Enoch: 'For he was put there for a sign and so that he might bear witness against all of the children of men so that he might relate all of the deeds of the generations until the day of judgment.' For the sabbath as a sign see Exod. 31: 13, and cf. Ezek. 20: 12. The Hebrew word *ot* is reserved for cosmic cycles associated with light and dark, or with the rising and setting of a heavenly luminary, as in Qumranic liturgy: 'who has created the morning as a *sign* to reveal the dominion of the light as the boundary of the daytime . . . for their work. To bless Your holy name You have created them, for the light is good . . . who has created the evening as a *sign* to reveal the dominion [of darkness] (as the boundary of the night-time) . . . from labour. You have created them to bless [Your holy name]' (4Q408, frg. 1; cf. Vermes, *CDSSIE*, 373; italics are mine).   [66] Gen. 1: 14–15; Ps. 104: 19.

[67] Community Rule X, 4–6; Talmon, 'The Calendar of the *yaḥad* Community', 111 (cf. Vermes, *CDSSIE*, 111–12). Rabbinic tradition emphasized the Genesis version, 'God made the two great lights' (Gen. 1: 16) (*Midrash Psalms*, ed. Buber (Vilna, 1891), 230). In the Aramaic version of the Book of Heavenly Luminaries (1 En. 72–82) there are important additions concerning the relationship between the sun and the moon. For the Aramaic manuscripts 4Q208–9 see now *DJD* XXXVI, 95–171.

darkness in the west', we read: 'The sun and the stars bring about all the years punctiliously, so that they forever neither gain upon nor fall behind their fixed positions for a single day, but they convert the year with punctilious justice into three hundred and sixty-four days.'[68] Jubilees describes the fundamental error incurred by basing the sequence of time on the moon's course and on inherently erroneous human observation, in terms of various words derived from the root *sh-ḥ-t*, which is usually reserved for the misdeeds of the Watchers, for impurity and death:

And there will be those who will examine the moon diligently because it will corrupt [*yashḥit*] the (appointed) times and it will advance from year to year ten days. Therefore, the years will come to them as they corrupt [*yashḥitu*] and make a day of testimony a reproach and a profane day a festival, and they will mix up everything, a holy day profaned and a profane day for a holy day, because they will set awry the months and Sabbaths and feasts and jubilees.[69]

'The day of testimony' is Shavuot, the Festival of Weeks/Oaths, as follows from Jubilees 6: 12—the festival associated with the Covenant at Sinai, whose determination was in dispute: the principle of the calculation, based on the regular, sevenfold rhythm of agricultural produce according to the solar calendar, was in danger of violation. One Qumranic psalm, whose main topic is evident despite formidable textual difficulties, describes the divine order of natural fertility as dependent on correctly counted periods and appointed times:

As for YHWH, how mighty   marvels. He, by an oath, made heaven and earth . . . the s[un?], its lights . . . night and st[ar]s and constellations . . . trees and every fru[it of the vineya]rd and all the produce of the field. And according to His words . . . and by His spirit He made them stand, to rule over all these on earth and over all [. . .] [mon]th by [m]onth, appointed time by appointed time, day by day, to eat its fruit (that) [the land] makes flourish . . . and all His hosts and His angels . . . to serve humankind and to minister to them . . .[70]

Nature, through the cyclic repetition of agricultural produce, reflects God's blessing, which transcends human action. There is a relationship—of cardinal importance in the priestly myth of the guardians of sanctity—between this aspect of nature, on the one hand, and such human actions as calculation, number, enumeration, and appointed times, based on the movements of the heavenly bodies and the cycles of the sun and the moon, which delineate the various measures of time and attest to its eternal order. These human actions are entrusted for safekeeping to priests, angels, and their allies, and they find expression in testimony and appointed times (festivals), in the counting of sabbaths and months. It is the priests and angels entrusted with such calculations who forge the link between the eternity of cosmic order and the continuity of cultic order; they achieve this supreme end by coupling the hidden with the manifest, the calculated with the visible, by upholding

---

[68] I En. 74: 11–12.   [69] Jub. 6: 36–7.   [70] 4Q 381, frg. 1, 2–11 (*DJD* XI, 92–4).

justice, knowledge, testimony, covenants, counting and enumeration, wondrous mysteries and eternal light, on earth as in heaven. Characteristic expressions of this perception, through which the passage and division of time are made independent of human observation and its arbitrary determinations, but founded instead on divine calculation, on a conception of sacred patterned time obeying the divine law observed by angels and priests, may be found in the priestly literature from Qumran in general and in the Blessings Scroll in particular:

And wo[ndrous] mysteries when th[ey app]ear and holy weeks in their fixed order, and divisions of months,

[beginnings of y]ears in their cycles and glorious festivals in times ordained [for them,]and the sabbatical years of the earth in [their] divi[sions and appo]inted times of liber[ty]eternal liberties and [   ]light and reck[onings of[71]

for you have created [   ] at their appointed times; and renews [   ] for satiating them . . . and al]l their elect ones [   ] and all those who have [k]nowledge in psalms of [   ] and blessings of truth in the times of fe[stivals. . . .[72]

[spirits of the holiest]holiness [will sing in joy] in all the due time[s and they will bless] the name of Your glorious divinity[73]

The regular, eternal order associated with God's ways and the cultic order, with divine testimony and appointed times, with stable calculation of weeks and seasons, with symmetry, harmony, and cyclic order of sabbaths and sevens, with seasons and fours, as the foundation for sanctity and purity, blessing and life—such an order could be founded only on the eternal laws of nature, on the unchangeable course of the sun, which alone permits a fixed, cyclic calculation of sabbaths and appointed times based on an abstract numerical principle. In contrast, disorder and disruption of the flow of time and cultic occasions—associated with sin, impurity and death, injustice and arbitrariness, randomness devoid of cycle and accounting, instability and non-enumeration, with chaos and darkness—were all attributed to sinful knowledge, to 'the secrets which the Watchers disclosed'[74] and to the false march of time, based on the limits of sensory perception, on inaccurate estimation and arbitrary observations of the waning and waxing moon.

According to fragments of the Calendars of Priestly Courses discovered at Qumran, the members of the Community made detailed calculations of the phases of the moon, with complete disregard for any testimony dependent on sighting; they prescribed a predetermined calendar of 364 days, divided into weeks of the priestly courses. These calculations of the time of the new moon and the other lunar phases were based on a fixed sequence of lunar months alternately twenty-nine and thirty days long, counting thirteen days between the full moon and its

---

[71] 4Q286, frg. 1, 8–13 (cf. *DJD* XI, 12–13). It seems that the word missing after 'divisions of months' is *bemo'adeihem*, 'in their appointed time'.

[72] 4Q286, frgs. 6, 1–3; 7, 2–4 (*DJD* XI, 24–6).

[73] 4Q287, frg. 2a, b, 7–8 (*DJD* XI, 51–2).   [74] I En. 10: 8.

disappearance. The calculations referred to a cycle of three years, in order to arrive at a time when the beginning of the solar year and the full moon fell on the same day, as had happened in the week of Creation.[75] The purpose of these calculations had to do with the fixed cyclic relationship of the light and dark parts of the different days of the month, symbolic of the relationship between good and evil; there was no connection, however, with the determination of seasons, sabbaths, and appointed times (festivals), which were established according to the aforementioned computational principle, fixed from the beginning to the end of time in accordance with a solar calendar of sabbaths totalling 364 days. The light periods—or 'gates of light'—which varied in a fixed cycle each day of the month, constituted the basis for the daily prayer, mentioned in the Book of Heavenly Luminaries, with blessings recited each day—special blessings for each 'gate of light'.

Thus a cosmic order, based on predictable, predetermined processes, and a cultic order, based on precise, cyclic calculation, were harmonized with one another and placed in a causal relationship. Such precise calculation, fixed and predetermined order, schematic accuracy, cyclic repetition, and eternal regularity in regard to the courses of the sun and the moon—reflecting the solar calendar with its symmetric, fourfold and sevenfold divisions, observed in the succession of sabbaths by the priestly courses—constituted the basis for testimony to the divine order of Creation, the eternity of divine law, predetermined in heaven and earth, and to the cultic order attuned with it. This sequence of regular, fixed, continuous arithmetical units, relating to one another in a fixed cyclic order, determined the succession of sabbaths and festivals, weeks and seasons, reflecting the sanctity of the Covenant. It was also associated, however, with the Merkavah, facing all four points of the compass and representing the seasons in their fourfold order, the eternity of natural order; and the Heikhalot, which in their sevenfold numbers (seven *heikhalot*, seven firmaments, seven *merkavot*) represent the cycle of sabbaths, the cycle of 'appointed times of liberty'[76]—times of sacred rest, of resignation of human sovereignty, when humans resign their part in the creative process of nature and, together with the angels, cease their activities in the sacred space of time and place—and the cycle of the seven days of Creation underlying the cultic order.

---

[75] See Wacholder and Abegg, vol. i, pp. x, 68–71, 74–6; and cf. Talmon and Knohl, 'Calendrical Scroll'; Talmon in *DJD* XXI, 320–94; Chyutin, *War of Calendars*, 32–3. The system of priestly courses was based on 1 Chr. 24.   [76] See 4Q286, frg. 1a, col. ii b (*DJD* XI, 12–13).

SIX

Covenants, Oaths, Sevens, and the Festival of Shavuot

Visible things are proofs of the invisible.[1]

ACCORDING to the authors of Jubilees and the Apocalypse of Weeks,[2] not only does cyclic time, as represented in the calendar, flow in an eternal sevenfold rhythm through the sabbaths of the year—but the whole of history, from beginning to end, marches forward in recurrent cycles of sabbaths, years, sabbaticals, jubilees, and ages (*kitsim*). Heaven and earth have thereby been linked together since the seven days of Creation, through signs, covenants, and oaths that constitute bonds between God and man, through the sacrifices that man offers God, in a fixed, sevenfold progression governed by the solar calendar and observed by the angels.

Alongside cultic time, reflected in the solar calendar with its subdivision into sabbaths of days, i.e. weeks, there is a concept of deterministic, historical, linear time, measured in past, present, and future in terms of sabbaths of years and jubilees, which add together to form long periods known in Qumran terminology as *kitsim* (sing. *kets*) or ages: 'Interpretation considering the ages made by God, all ages for the accomplishment [of all the events, past] and future. Before He ever created them, He determined their works age by age, and it was engraved upon the heavenly tablets, the ages of their domination';[3] 'all their appointed t[imes] in their ages, ... [ag]e of your marvel, for from old you have engraved for them His judgement until the ordained time of judgement in all the eternal predestinations'.[4]

In the book of Jubilees, a jubilee is a period of forty-nine years, and a 'week [of years]' or 'sabbatical', Heb. *shavua*, is a period of seven years. The author divides history, from Creation to the theophany at Sinai, into forty-nine jubilees, or forty-nine periods of seven *shavuot*, 'sabbaticals', each. The ages, engraved on heavenly tablets, marked and measured in terms of sabbaticals, jubilees, and their multiples,

---

[1] Anaxagoras, frg. 21a.   [2] 1 En. 93.

[3] *Pesharim* 4Q180 (*DJD* V, 77–9; cf. Vermes, *CDSSIE*, 520).

[4] 4Q369 (*DJD* XIII, 354). The messianic hopes of the Covenanters related to a continuum of pre-ordained historical periods referred to as divine ages (*kitsei el*) or eternal ages (*kitsei olamim, kitsei netsah*).

a system of multiples of seven, were a major element in the controversy between two conflicting ideologies: a cosmic, ahistorical world view, founded on signs and oaths, ages and covenants, and the predestined march of time, entrusted to heaven and extending from beginning to end in a fixed, regular continuum; contrasted with a terrestrial, realistic world view, founded on a perception of time entrusted to man, measured in terms of historical dates referring to earthly and national events, time consecrated by human deliberation, hence a world view that denies the idea of a predestined, eternally known course of events. The fact that the calendar is founded on the laws of nature, on absolute cosmic sequences reflected in whole sabbaths and weeks, a cyclic cultic calendar measured in sabbaticals and jubilees, a linear, predetermined calendar—this fact conditions the structuring of a deterministic history, paving the way for an attempt to decipher the mysterious divine intention hidden therein as time marches on from beginning to end.

The section of 1 Enoch known as the Apoclypse of Weeks is concerned with the angelic revelation of the division of continuous time into seven historical periods called 'weeks [of years]' or 'sabbaths of years',[5] that is, 'sabbaticals', beginning with the birth of Enoch, the seventh patriarch of the universe, and ending with the seventh week, at whose completion 'there shall be elected the elect ones of righteousness from the eternal plant of righteousness, to whom shall be given sevenfold knowledge concerning all His creation'.[6] Jubilees, on the other hand, expounds the details of the seven-based calendar, in which time is measured, on the one hand, along a continuous, metahistorical, linear, deterministic axis stretching from Creation to the theophany at Sinai, divided into sabbaticals and jubilees (cycle of seven years = sabbatical; seven sabbaticals = jubilee), and, on the other hand, along a cultic cyclic axis—the solar year, divided into seven-day weeks, seasons, and units (*degalim*). In this calendar, which associates the festivals with the beginning of history, the various appointed times depend on the system of covenants concluded with the patriarchs before the theophany at Mount Sinai—a system quite different from the traditional one, in which the festivals are associated with the historical events of the Exodus from Egypt and the Israelites' peregrinations in the desert after Sinai.

All the events in Jubilees relevant to the continuity of the covenant between divine time and earthly time and place occur in the third month, generally on Shavuot on 15 Sivan,[7] seven weeks after the beginning of the counting of the Omer on the 26th of the first month (Nisan)—the time at which the first covenant was concluded and the covenantal oath renewed in heaven and on earth. However, unlike the standard tradition, in which the Covenant at Sinai is paramount and the commandments given on Mount Sinai are radically new, while the exact date of the theophany is never specified or explicitly associated with the Festival of Weeks, the tradition of Jubilees considers this covenant the last in a chain of oaths and

[5] Lev. 25: 1–9.   [6] 1 En. 93: 9–10.   [7] Jub. 16: 13.

covenants, all concluded in the third month. All the covenants are associated with oaths and promises relating to the continuity of life, with angels, and with the Festival of Weeks, whose Hebrew name may be vocalized in two ways: *shavuot*, meaning 'weeks' and thus alluding to the aforementioned seven weeks following the Omer, and *shevuot*, meaning 'oaths' or 'covenants'.[8] Jubilees is referred to in the Damascus Document as the 'book of the divisions of times in their jubilees and their weeks', dealing with the 'determination of their ages',[9] that is, the principle governing the calculation of the passage of years. Its aim is to recount the mythical, mystical, and angelic nature of the oaths and the covenants, to demonstrate their cultic nature and the eternal validity of the commandments associated with them, to indicate their relationship with the sevenfold structure of the solar calendar, which links the heavens with the earth, the angels ministering in heaven with the priests ministering on earth, through the succession of weeks and sabbaths, sabbaticals and jubilees.

Thus, the theophany at Sinai is not a beginning, but a renewal of previous covenants, all concluded in the third month, and a summation of customs, appointed times, and commandments proclaimed through divine angelic revelation since the beginning of time; the Covenant at Sinai loses its historical and national significance as the foundation event of the Covenant between God and his people. Jubilees reiterates the mythical, metahistorical significance of the archetypal cultic simulation, repeated at set times, of covenants and oaths already concluded between heaven and earth, between angels—witnesses to heavenly time, keepers of sabbaths and oaths—and priests—keepers of terrestrial time, guardians of the sacred service, who change guard every seven days, burn incense according to the solar calendar, and offer earthly sacrifices according to the liturgical calendar of 52 sabbaths, 52 weeks, 364 days, and 70 days of cessation of labour.

The first covenant, the Rainbow Covenant, was made with Noah when he emerged from the ark after a whole year, counted as four seasons and divided into twelve months of days, each thirty days long, as related in Jubilees 5–6.

The Genesis Commentaries, a Qumranic work which deals with the chronology of the Flood,[10] provides details of this year and the calculation of its parts:

In] the year four hundred and eighty of Noah's life, Noah reached the end of them. And God said: 'My spirit will not reside in man for ever. Their days shall be fixed at one hundred and twenty years until the end of the waters of the flood.' And the waters of the flood burst over the earth.

In the year six hundred of Noah's life, *in the second month, on the first (day) of the week, on its seventeenth (day)*, on that day all the springs of the great abyss were split and

---

[8] Cf. Temple Scroll XIX, 11–13; XXI, 12–14; cf. Qimron, *Temple Scroll*, 29.　　　[9] XVI, 2–4.

[10] The Qumranic *pesher* known generally as 'Genesis Commentaries', which deals *inter alia* with the chronology of the Flood, survives in only a few fragments: 4Q252, cols. I–II, frgs. 1–3 (*DJD* XXII, 193–4, 198–9), and 4Q254a, frg. 3 (ibid. 235). For the exceptional research history of these fragments see Brooke in *DJD* XXII, 185, who also comments extensively on the text, ibid. 193–200, 235–6.

the sluices of the sky opened and rain fell upon the earth forty days and forty nights, until the *twenty-sixth day of the third month, the fifth day of the week*. One hundred and fifty days did the wate[rs] hold sway over the [ea]rth, until *the fourteenth day in the seventh month, the third (day) of the week*. At the end of one hundred and fifty days, the waters subsided (during) two days, the fourth day and the fifth day, and on the sixth day, the ark rested in the mountains of Hurarat, *i[t was] the seventeenth [da]y of the seventh month*. And the waters continu[ed] diminishing until *the [te]nth month, on its first (day), the fourth day of the week*, the peaks of the mountains began to be visible. And at the end of forty days, when the peaks of the mountain[s] had become visible, Noah [op]ened the window of the ark *the first day of the week, which is the tenth day of the el[eventh] month*. And he sent out the dove to see whether the waters had diminished, but it did not find a place of rest and returned to him, [to] the ark. And he waited yet a[nother] seven days and again sent it out, and it returned to him, and in its beak there was a newly plucked olive leaf. [It was *day twenty-]four of the eleventh month, the first (day) of the wee[k*. And Noah knew that the waters had diminished] from upon the earth. And at the end of another seven days, [he sent] the [dove out, but it did not] come back again. *It was the fi[rst] day [of the twelfth] month, [the first day] of the week*. And at the end of the thir[ty-one days after having sent out the dov]e which did not come back again, the wat[ers] dried up [from upon the earth and] Noah removed the cover of the ark and looked, and behold [they had dried up *on the fourth day of the week,*] *on the first (day) of the first month*.[11]

In the year six hundred and one of Noah's life, *on the seventeenth day of the second month*, the land dried up, *on the first (day) of the week*. On that day, Noah went out of the ark, at the end of a complete year of three hundred and sixty-four days, on the first (day) of the week. On the seven[teenth of the second month in the year] one and six [hundred] [   ] Noah from the ark, at the appointed time of a complete year.[12]

This account of the Flood narrative specifies ten explicit dates, given in terms of day, month, and year (of Noah's life; indicated by italics), including the day of the week and the number of days elapsing from each date to the next, in relation to a year of 364 days. It is instructive to list them in order, in modern notation:

17/2/600	Sunday
26/3/600	Thursday
14/7/600	Tuesday
17/7/600	Friday
1/10/600	Wednesday

---

[11] 4Q252, I, frgs. 1, 2: 1–22 (*DJD* XXII, 193–4; the translation here follows that of García Martínez and Tigchelaar, *Study Edition*; the italics are mine).

[12] 4Q252, II, frgs. 1, 3: 1–5 (*DJD* XXII, 198; cf. Vermes, *CDSSIE*, 461–2); 4Q254a, frg. 3: 1–3 (*DJD* XXII, 235). See also Wacholder and Abegg, *Preliminary Edition*, ii. 212–15. Cf. MMT = 4Q 394, frgs. 3–7: 2 (*DJD* X, 8): 'And the year is complete, three hundred and sixty-four days.' Cf. also Jub. 5: 23–32; 6: 23–33; 11QPs^a XXVII, 6–7. For the significance of these versions of the Flood narrative in relation to solar-calendar calculations in the literature of the secessionist priesthood see Werman, 'Structure of the Events'; Zipor, 'Flood Chronology'.

10/11/600   Sunday

24/11/600   Sunday

1/12/600   Sunday

1/1/601   Wednesday

17/2/601   Sunday

According to this schedule, the Flood began on Sunday, after the seventh sabbath in the first quarter of the 600th year, and ended on Sunday, after the seventh sabbath in the first quarter of the 601st year. The date 17/7 marks the passage of half a year since Noah entered the ark, while 1/10 (the winter solstice) is the beginning of the fourth quarter and 1/1 (the vernal equinox) is the beginning of the first quarter—the New Year according to the solar calendar.[13] Thus, the text specifies detailed dates in the course of one year, permitting calculation of an exact calendar for that year, thus providing a detailed basis for all calculations of the solar calendar. The biblical account, however, does not name the days of the week, so that no such calculation is possible.

As the story is told in Genesis, the Flood began on the 17th of the second month in the six hundredth year of Noah's life, and the earth dried up on the 27th of the second month;[14] that is, the duration of the Flood amounted to one year and ten or eleven days more than a (lunar!) year, measured as 354 days, for a total of 364/5 days, i.e. a solar year. Thus the biblical and Qumran traditions agree as to the total duration of the Flood, but the internal division is different, the Bible simply adding ten days to the lunar year to get 364, while the Qumran priests, Jubilees, and the Qumranic Genesis Commentaries explicitly specify 364 days, from the 17th of the second month to the same date one year later. The Septuagint version gives the 27th of the second month as the beginning of the Flood and the same date one year later as its end, thus agreeing with the biblical account as to the end of the Flood but placing the beginning ten days later in order to preserve the one-year time frame.[15] It seems evident that the different recensions of the Flood narrative

---

[13] Some of these dates figure in Jubilees in connection with events in the Garden of Eden: 'in the second month, on the seventeenth day, the serpent came and drew near the woman' (3: 17); 'And on the first of the fourth month, Adam and his wife went out from the Garden of Eden' (3: 32). The first of the fourth month is explained as referring to the Flood story in Jub. 5: 29: 'And in the fourth month the springs of the great deep were closed and the floodgates of heaven were held shut.' Jub. 6: 26 narrates the parallel tradition: 'And on the first of the fourth month, the mouths of the depths of the abysses which were beneath were shut.' Hence, the date on which the Flood began also marks the origin of sin in the Garden of Eden, and the date of Adam and Eve's departure from the Garden of Eden is exactly that on which the springs of the great deep were closed in the Flood story—the summer solstice, according to the solar calendar.   [14] Gen. 5: 14.

[15] Josephus (*Antiquities*, I. iii. 3) agrees with the Septuagint, specifying the 27th of the second month as the beginning of the Flood. It should be remembered that, while the biblical text was considered sacred, it was not completely finalized until the end of the canonization process, towards the end of the 1st century CE; see Talmon, 'Old Testament Text'; Beckwith, *Old Testament Canon*; Haran, *Biblical Anthology*.

reveal the struggle between the solar and lunar calendars: of the four known traditions, the Masoretic (biblical) one is based on the lunar calendar, whereas those of the Septuagint (and Josephus), Jubilees, and the Genesis Commentaries rely on the solar calendar and give the Flood the duration of one complete solar year.

Having emerged from the ark in the third month,[16] Noah, Enoch's great-grandson, built an altar, burned fragrant incense, offered sacrifices, pronounced an oath, undertook to observe certain prohibitions, and laid the foundation for the priestly cult that linked earthly sacrifice with heavenly covenant at a sacred time. This covenant, whose sign was the (seven-coloured) rainbow, assured man of the eternal continuity of the laws of nature.[17] In the Jubilees version, however, this covenant, at this particular time, had been observed in heaven since Creation:

> Therefore, it is ordained and written in the heavenly tablets that they should observe the Feast of Weeks in this (the third) month, once per year, in order to renew the covenant each and every year. And all of this feast was celebrated in heaven from the day of Creation until the days of Noah.[18]

With this covenant, Noah and his household joined the ranks of the angels, who had been observing the Covenant since Creation and bore witness to the eternal continuity of the cyclic laws of nature.

Examining the different covenants described in Jubilees, one sees that God's part in the Covenant is his commitment to ensure continuity and eternity, to establish for man a law based on number and divine blessing, marked and commemorated by a special sign. The human obligation, on the other hand, is to swear an oath of allegiance to the divine decree of sanctity of time, to accept the yoke of commandments and prohibitions, to observe the sabbaths and the appointed times, and to write down and preserve the testimony. Those who fulfil the covenantal terms, including observance of the commandments, maintenance of strict purity, and the proper sequence of time, indicate that they have joined the ranks of the angels, the guardians of the divine order of time, witnesses to the eternity of the cosmic order in time and space, observers of the sabbath and Shavuot. They are upholding the Covenant between heaven and earth that guarantees the continuation of life in concordance with sevenfold order.

It should now be clear why Noah, upon conclusion of the Covenant, received seven commandments—which reversed the sins of the Watchers that brought about the Flood. He was thereby removed from the chaotic, sinful, and corrupt world of the Watchers, who had violated the divine boundaries of time and place, to a world founded on sacred, divine order, associated with oath and bound by

---

[16] Jub. 6: 1–4. Jubilees distinguishes between the day the earth dried (the 17th of the second month, 601), the day Noah opened the ark for the animals (the 27th of the second month), and the day he himself departed from the ark and built an altar (the 1st of the third month). This is contrary to the Qumran tradition (4Q252–4) according to which he departed on the 17th of the second month.

[17] Jub. 6: 4–16.   [18] Jub. 6: 17.

Covenant,[19] inhabited by angels and priests, witnesses to divine time and guardians thereof, who helped to perpetuate the cosmic order of natural laws through a sacred cult performed in a sacred place at a sacred time. The cult was based on the sabbaths and weeks of the solar year, enumerated according to a liturgical calendar that marked their order in four equivalent quarters of a year. Sacred time, place, and cult were bound together by the rotating priestly courses, which changed places every week and perpetuated the sacred service in seven-year units.

God's part in the Covenant was to establish a permanent, eternal order of natural laws and seasons, which guaranteed the recurrent cycles of the agricultural year and, together with it, abundant produce and fertility, the continuity of life:

And He made a covenant with him so that there might not be flood waters which would destroy the earth. All the days of the earth, seed (time) and harvest will not cease. Cold and heat and summer and winter and day and night will not change their ordinances or cease for ever.[20]

The human obligation, on the other hand, involved testimony and predestination, *sefer, mispar, vesipur*—'book, number, and narrative'—to use (we recall) the phrasing of the Book of Creation; it added a dimension that remembered and protected, attested and created, counted, enumerated, and narrated—a dimension not present in nature, dependent on letters and numbers, on narrative, enumeration, and number, on memory and language, on testimony and set time. The Covenant depended on oath and remembrance, knowledge and testimony—remembering the Covenant and observing its proper time in the cultic calendar, re-establishing the Covenant through sacrifices and offerings brought at a set time, Shavuot, and renewing the oath of the Covenant or its finalization; such were the tasks of those with whom the divine Covenant was concluded, or those destined for that mission from birth, by natural law, to serve in the sacred precincts, to observe the sabbaths and the Temple festivals—the priests. The object of the promise and the blessing was to ensure the continuity of procreation and life, of testimony and cult; for Shavuot, celebrated seven whole weeks after the elevation of the Omer,[21] was also the festival of the first wheat harvest and the time of the new grain-offering.[22] So,

---

[19] On the relationship between the seven Noahide laws and the sins of the Watchers, see Dimant, 'Sinning Angels', 50–1. On the connection between the concepts of oath and prohibition as binding human existence and limiting nature and its laws and cycles, see pp. 147–8 below. For different views of the sin of the Watchers see Hanson, 'Rebellion in Heaven'; Molenberg, 'Roles of Shemihaza and Asael'. Milik has argued that the original version of Enoch comprised, in place of the so-called Book of Similitudes (chs. 37–71), the work called the Book of Giants; see p. 91 above.

[20] Jub. 6: 4. The translation here follows A. Kahana's Hebrew translation, rather than the Charlesworth English version. Cf. also Gen. 8: 22.   [21] Lev. 23: 15–16.

[22] Exod. 23: 14–16; 34: 22; Lev. 23: 15–21; Num. 28: 26; Deut. 16: 9–12. Cf. the Temple Scroll fragments from Cave 11 (11Q20) III, frgs. 3 ii, 5, 6, 7 (*DJD* XXIII, 372–3): '[they shall lift . . . The first fruits] shall be for the priests, and they shall eat them in the [inner] courtya[rd] . . . new bread, ears of grain [and soft grain. And this day will be proclaimed holy, an eternal precept for their generations. T]he[y] shall [do] no [men]ial work [at all, for it is the Festival of Weeks/Oaths, and the Festival of the

too, each of the other agricultural pilgrimage festivals: the first produce of barley, wine, olive oil, and the harvest, celebrated from the first month to the seventh at seven-week intervals, was accompanied by offerings from the various types of produce, brought to the Temple on the fiftieth day, the first Sunday seven sabbaths/weeks after the previous festival, as stipulated in Leviticus,[23] the Temple Scroll, Jubilees, and the Scroll of Priestly Courses.

The second covenant, the Covenant between the Pieces,[24] was made with Abram/Abraham, again in the third month; the angels explain it as a renewal of the divine/angelic covenant with Noah:

And on that day we made a covenant with Abram just as we had made a covenant that month with Noah. And Abram renewed the feast and the ordinance for himself for ever.[25]

Abram, observing the Covenant, celebrates the first fruits of the grain harvest halfway through the third month and offers up a new sacrifice on the altar. God appears to him and commands him to circumcise himself and the males of his household as a sign that his progeny has been specially chosen, sanctified, and likened to the angels; at this time, too, his name is changed to Abraham.[26] The birth of Isaac during Shavuot, halfway through the third month, is a sign that the

First Fruits as an eternal memorial . . .]'. In the Bible, Shavuot occurs between the festivals of Passover and Sukkot, but the exact date is not specified. Some scholars believe it was omitted from the original text of Exod. 19: 1. M. Breuer, for example, suggests on the basis of a textual analysis that the date of the festival, omitted in our text, should have been the 15th day of the third month; he points out the similar omission of the date on which the Torah was given at Sinai; see Breuer, *Festival Chapters*, 369–77. Nevertheless, the connection between the festival of the first harvest, at the time of the Festival of Unleavened Bread, and the second harvest festival, that of Shavuot, is made clear, and the time elapsing between the two is given as seven sabbaths or seven weeks. On the significance of the different enumerations, in sabbaths or in weeks, see Na'eh, 'Did the *tana'im* . . .?', 424–39. The Pentateuch does not associate this festival with any specific historical or religious event; the linkage with the theophany at Sinai and the giving of the Torah is explicitly mentioned only in Jubilees and in Qumran literature, and alluded to in the biblical Psalms, as has been shown by Weinfeld, 'Pentecost'. It appears explicitly in a tannaitic tradition cited in the Babylonian Talmud, *Pes.* 68a. For a summary of research in this area see Breuer, *Festival Chapters*, 347–78; Weinfeld, 'Pentecost'; and Tabori, *Jewish Festivals*, 146–55. Tabori, however, does not discuss the special features of the festival as described in Jubilees or its relationship with the Pentecost tradition in the New Testament book of Acts, and he ignores its mystical, priestly, and polemical context. The question of the traces of priestly tradition in the New Testament and its position in early Christianity, in relation to atoning offerings and oaths, to sanctity and participation in angelic song, is of considerable interest, but outside the scope of the present study. Weinfeld, 'Pentecost', has touched upon the subject.

A tradition relating to Shavuot and pilgrimage when the Temple was still standing is cited in the apocryphal book of Tobit, which has been dated to the 4th–3rd centuries BCE: 'Only I alone came up to Jerusalem many times for the festivals, as is written for all Israel as an eternal law, with first fruits in my hands . . . And I gave them to the priests, the sons of Aaron, for the altar. Of all kinds of grain I gave the tithe to the sons of Levi who serve in Jerusalem . . . When I returned to my home . . . On the festival of the fifty, which is a sacred festival every seven weeks, I had a feast' (Tobit 1: 6–8; 2: 1; A. Kahana (ed.), *Apocrypha*, ii. 313, 316); the long version reads: 'On our festival of Pentecost, which is the sacred festival of seven weeks'.

[23] Lev. 23: 15.   [24] See Gen. 15: 9–21.   [25] Jub. 14: 20.   [26] Jub. 15: 1–15; 27.

divine promise made through the Covenant between the Pieces has been fulfilled, and he is circumcised. Further celebrations of Shavuot by members of Abraham's family entering the Covenant are described in chapters 17, 22, 32, and 44 of Jubilees; many events in the lives of Isaac and Jacob, involving oaths, promises, celebrations, sacrifices, and covenants, are associated with the time appointed for the renewal of the Covenant—celebrated annually on Shavuot, which thus guarantees transmission of the Covenant to their offspring.

The transmission of the Covenant progresses from the general to the particular, its scope being gradually narrowed down to an increasingly select group, which is enjoined to observe the relevant commandments and prohibitions. Thus, the covenant with Noah embraces the totality of humankind; the covenant with Abraham concerns him and his progeny; the covenant with Isaac—only part of the descendants of Abraham, namely, Jacob's sons. The covenant with Jacob is confined to the tribe of Levi, which is consecrated to the priesthood.[27]

The beginning of Jubilees[28] and its end[29] are concerned with the covenant made with Moses and Israel on Mount Sinai in the third month; this covenant is of a rather different nature, as it is reported from an angelic point of view, associated with the sanctity and subdivision of time, and with the associated covenants and oaths. In the world of the secessionist priests, the Covenant with the people of Israel as a whole reduces to a covenant between the angels and the 'community of God', descendants of the Zadokite priests, guardians of the Covenant, and their followers. These alone are considered among the ranks of the righteous, Sons of Light, observers of sabbaths, weeks, and festivals, the inheritors of the solar calendar entrusted to them by the seventh patriarch of the world, as against the violators of the Covenant, Sons of Darkness, who follow the lunar calendar with its confusion of the proper Covenant renewal times and festivals, partners to the angels of malevolence and the prince Belial.

The first covenant is recounted in Jubilees as follows: 'And Noah and his sons *swore* that they would not eat any blood which was in any flesh. And he made a covenant before the Lord God forever in all of the generations of the earth in *that month*';[30] but the next verse recounts an angelic injunction relating to the last covenant, that concluded with Moses: 'Therefore, he [the angel on Mount Sinai] spoke to you [Moses] so that you also might make a covenant with the children of Israel with an *oath* in *this month* upon the mountain. And you will sprinkle blood upon them on account of all of the words of the covenant.'[31] There follows a list of the prohibitions imposed by the covenant, which ends as follows: 'Therefore, it is ordained and written in the heavenly tablets that they should observe the feast of *Shavuot/Shevuot* [= Weeks/Oaths/Covenants] *in this month*, once per year, in order to renew the Covenant each and every year.'[32]

---

[27] Jub. 28: 16; 29: 5; 44: 1, 8.   [28] Jub. 1: 1; 6: 11.   [29] Jub. 50: 1–2.

[30] Jub. 6: 9–10. Here and in the next two quotations the italics are mine.

[31] Jub. 6: 11.   [32] Jub. 6: 17.

In parallel to the eternal divine oath addressed to Noah on Shavuot, which is renewed annually through the cycles of natural events and the order of the universe, the human oath is also renewed annually, in a ceremony held on that same festival. The renewal of the Covenant implies renewal of the ancient oath, which involved divine promises to those who kept the Covenant and the threat of punishment to its violators—blessings as against curses. Qumran literature highlights the continuity and similarity between patriarchs and their annual renewal of the Covenant, as described in Jubilees,[33] on the one hand, and the members of the Community, who refer to themselves in the Community Rule and the Damascus Document as 'keepers of the Covenant', 'those who enter into the Covenant' (sometimes referred to in the scholarly literature as 'Covenanters'), who observe the 'oath of the Covenant'. They re-enact the Covenant ceremony at this time, following in the patriarchs' footsteps, and again swear an oath to observe the laws of the Torah in the strict Qumranic formulation: scrupulous observation of the sacred appointed times, as well as the oaths and Covenant associated with them. The patriarchs' annual observance of the Covenant on the 15th of the third month is a model emulated by the members of the Community as they renew the Covenant at the same time each year, repeating the oath and ceremonially obeying the biblical injunction associated with the blessing and the curse: 'to enter into the Covenant of the Lord your God, with its sanctions'[34] or its parallel in Jubilees 6: 17 quoted above.

Scholars of the Bible and the ancient Near East have pointed out the practice, common to many religions of the ancient Near East, of observing an annual celebration symbolizing the renewal of the covenant with their god(s). Moshe Weinfeld, suggesting that the same was true of the Israelites, has noted several psalms particularly apt for such a ceremony. In view of various allusions to Shavuot in these psalms, he in fact conjectures that that festival was the time appointed for the ceremony.[35] A further allusion to the covenantal tradition of Shavuot may be

---

[33] Chs. 6, 14, 15.   [34] Deut. 29: 11.

[35] Weinfeld, 'Pentecost', points out that Pss. 50 and 81 refer to a theophany resembling that of Sinai (with Zion replacing Sinai), as well as a few of the Ten Commandments and a festival of 'testimony' (*edut*), in relation to a covenant, the blowing of a ram's horn, and a book of law. Comparison with Exod. 19: 15–20 and the Covenant-renewal ceremony in 2 Chr. 15: 10–19 (see below), with their references to swearing an oath, supports his thesis. An ancient tradition celebrating the renewal of a covenant or oath has been preserved among the Jews of Ethiopia (Beta Israel), who celebrate a festival called *sigd*, essentially re-enacting the Covenant-renewal festival celebrated in Jerusalem at the time of Ezra and Nehemiah (Neh. 9: 1–3). During the festival, the whole community assembles to read the Ten Commandments, symbolizing Moses' ascent to Mount Sinai. According to the elders of the community, the festival is related to Shavuot in connection with the biblical offering of new grain and the 'two loaves of bread' (Num. 28: 26; Lev. 23: 15–16) taken from the first wheat harvest, seven weeks after the Omer. Because of climatic differences, the time of the festival was moved from the third month to the season in which wheat ripens in Ethiopia—on the 29th of the month of Heshvan (in biblical parlance—the eighth month), seven weeks after the Day of Atonement. On another plane, it is conceivable that the reading of the Tokhehah (the admonitory verses in Lev. 26: 14–43) before Shavuot is also related to the concept of that festival as marking the renewal of the Covenant and thus a festival of blessing and imprecation; see Bar-Ilan, 'Interpretation of a *baraita*'.

found in Chronicles—a book of distinctly priestly nature—which describes a traditional covenant ceremony observed in the third month in the First Temple period. This tradition is probably associated with the pilgrimage to the Temple on that festival, and presents several elements that clearly indicate renewal of a covenant: worshipping (*derishah*) God, swearing an oath, loud voice, trumpeting, blasts of the horn—reminiscent of the theophany on Mount Sinai:

> They were assembled in Jerusalem in the third month of the fifteenth year of the reign of Asa. They brought sacrifices to the Lord on that day; . . . They entered into a covenant to worship the Lord God of their fathers with all their heart and with all their soul. Whoever would not worship the Lord God of Israel would be put to death. . . . So they took an oath to the Lord in a loud voice and with shouts, with trumpeting and blasts of the horn.[36]

The Aramaic Targum to Chronicles, known as the Targum of Rav Joseph, explicitly specifies the time of the covenant concluded during Asa's reign, translating the words 'they brought sacrifices to the Lord on that day' as 'they brought sacrifices before the Lord on that day, on the Festival of Weeks'.

The Covenant ceremony, associated from the start with angelic presence, with sacrificial offerings and an injunction against the consumption of blood, with oath and promise, with blessing and curse, is described as such in the first three columns of the Community Rule.[37] There we read of a typically priestly rite, in which blessing and curses are pronounced by the priests and the Levites, to which all those present answer 'amen' in token of their acceptance of the Covenant and their undertaking to honour the oath. Though the account does not specify a date, this detail is supplied by a passage in the Damascus Document: 'And all [the inhabitants] of the camps shall assemble in the third month and shall curse him who turns aside, to the right [or to the left, from the] Law.'[38] This parallels the description, in the Community Rule, of the Levites who curse and admonish: 'straying neither to the right nor to the left, and transgressing none of His words . . .'[39] (compare also the curse ceremony described towards the end of the previous chapter). All these accounts recall the biblical ceremony of blessing and curses at Mount Gerizim and Mount Ebal,[40] which is essentially a covenantal ceremony

---

[36] 2 Chr. 15: 10–14.   [37] I, 16–II, 25.

[38] 4Q270, frg. 7 ii, 11–12 (*DJD* XVIII, 166) (cf. 4Q266, frg. 11, II; Vermes, *CDSSIE*, 153). See also Wacholder and Abegg, *Preliminary Edition*, i. 47; Broshi (ed.), *Damascus Document Reconsidered*, D^{e}11ii: 11–15 = D^{b}18v: 16–20. This is in all probability the unpublished fragment whose discovery was announced many years ago by Milik (*Ten Years of Discovery*, 113–17), who claimed that it associated the Covenant-renewal celebration with Shavuot. See also Licht, *Rule Scroll*, 55–6. The fragment continues as follows: 'And this is the interpretation of the laws which they shall observe in all the age [of visitation] . . . when they will stand during all the age of wrath and in their marches for all those who dwell in their camps and all their towns. Behold, all this is according to the last interpretation of [M]oses' Law.' Perhaps the reference is to Deut. 29: 11–12, 'You stand this day, all of you, before the Lord your God . . . to enter into the Covenant of the Lord . . .'.

[39] Community Rule III, 11 (cf. Vermes, *CDSSIE*, 101).   [40] Deut. 27: 12–26.

deriving from the verses, 'to enter into the covenant of the Lord your God, which the Lord your God is concluding with you this day, with its sanctions; to the end that He may establish you this day as His people and be your God, as He promised you and as He swore to your fathers, Abraham, Isaac, and Jacob'.[41] That ceremony lists the blessings to be enjoyed by those who keep the Covenant[42] and the transgressions for which the curses described in the next verses[43] will be imposed.

The Community's ceremony ends with the statement, 'Thus shall they do, year by year, for as long as the dominion of Belial endures.'[44] The parallel in Jubilees reads: 'Therefore, it is ordained and written in the heavenly tablets that they should observe the Festival of Weeks in this (the third) month, once per year, in order to renew the covenant each and every year'.[45] It seems highly probable that the blessing and curses pronounced with regard to God and the angels, on the one hand, and to Belial and his cohorts, on the other, in the Blessings Scroll,[46] which end with the call 'The Council of the Community, all of them will say together: "Amen, Amen"',[47] are also part of the Covenant-renewal ceremony, with the objects of the blessings and the curses being heavenly beings.[48]

In the Qumran community, the renewal of the Covenant in the third month, or of the oath on the Festival of Weeks/Oaths (referred to at Qumran as both *shavuot* and *shavuim*[49]), was of central significance. The covenantal oath was a ceremonial expression of religious identification, consolidating and unifying the Community, on the one hand, and distinguishing and isolating the blessed Covenanters from the accursed violators of the Covenant, on the other. Both the Community Rule and the Damascus Document treat the Covenant as an oath sworn by the members of the Community once a year, on a fixed date. The ceremony in which the celebrants 'entered the Covenant' in the third month was an undertaking to observe the whole complex of injunctions received from heaven in the earlier covenants, as expressed in the oath taken publicly at Shavuot. This oath, symbolizing the continuity of the Covenant and its annual renewal at the festival, pertained to the corpus of prohibitions and restrictions assumed by the members of the Community, to the segregation of the Sons of Light, the keepers of the Covenant, who were granted God's blessing, from the Sons of Darkness, violators of the Covenant, who received his curse. The ceremony, probably held in the putative presence of the heavenly hosts—who, according to Jubilees, had participated in the previous

---

[41] Deut. 29: 11–12.   [42] Deut. 28: 1–14.   [43] Deut. 28: 15–69.

[44] Community Rule II, 19 (Vermes, *CDSSIE*, 100).   [45] Jub. 6: 17.

[46] 4Q286–8 (*DJD* XI, 1–65, esp. 27–8).   [47] *DJD* XI, 27–8; cf. also 25–6, 57–8.

[48] The editor of the work in *DJD* XI, Bilhah Nitzan, merely comments: 'The text of 4QBerakhot consists of a series of liturgical blessings and curses and a series of laws for an annual covenantal ceremony of the community' (ibid. 1), but does not discuss the possible time and context of the ceremony.

[49] For the festival of *shavuim* (perhaps derived from the Hebrew noun meaning 'those who swear' or 'those who are adjured'), as a regular feature of the Scroll of Priestly Courses, see Wacholder and Abegg, *Preliminary Edition*, i. 71–2 (cf. *DJD* XXIII, 372). The fragments of the Temple Scroll from Cave 11 refer to the festival as *shavuot*: see n. 22 above. Cf. Temple Scroll XVIII–XIX, XXI, XLIII.

covenants—was a ritual occasion, on which the members of the Community renewed their Covenant with God and proclaimed their distinctness from its violators. During the ceremony, blessings were invoked upon those entering the Covenant—the Sons of Light—in parallel to curses pronounced on those who had excluded themselves—the Sons of Darkness. As described in the Community Rule, the earthly oath had a divine counterpart, as specified in the covenants concluded between heaven and earth in the third month, while the Damascus Document adds the information that the ceremony was held on Shavuot.

The root *sh-v-ʿ* in biblical Hebrew is associated both with the sacred number seven (*sheva*) and the sacred, eternal oath (*shevuah*) connected with the invocation of God's name (as, for example, in the name Beersheba in Gen. 21: 29-31; 26: 23-33; cf. 'an oath before the Lord' in Exod. 22: 10).[50] The name of the festival of Shavuot/Shevuot (i.e. Weeks/Oaths[51]) derives from the same root, in the meaning of oath/covenant/testimony, referring to the system of covenants concluded on that day, and to the testimony to those covenants; but it also derives from the other meaning of 'seven', referring to the sacred count of seven weeks between the two harvesting times. In addition, the festival is referred to in Qumran literature as *mishneh ḥag*, '(the) twofold festival', as embodying both of the above meanings, which bind heaven and earth and are publicly celebrated upon renewal of the Covenant—the latter known variously as 'Covenant of God', 'oath of the Covenant', 'oath of binding prohibition', 'Covenant for eternal law', and 'new Covenant'.[52] Thus, the word *shevuah*, which links the eternity of time, as counted in weeks, with the eternity of the undertaking accepted during the Covenant ceremony or the sacred service associated with multiples of seven and signifying the regular succession of time—this word creates a bond between God and man, between God and Moses' Torah, as we read in the Community Rule: 'Whoever approaches the Council of the Community [Heb. *yahad*] shall enter the Covenant of God in the presence of all who have freely pledged themselves. He shall undertake by a binding oath to return with all his heart and soul to every commandment of the Law of Moses in accordance with all that has been revealed of it to the sons of Zadok, the Priests, Keepers of the Covenant and Seekers of His will, and to the multitude of the men of the Covenant who together have freely pledged themselves to His truth and to walking in the way of His delight.'[53] It is also associated in the Book of Similitudes with the secret name of the Creator, which is entrusted to the angels,

---

[50] See also Ch. 2, n. 76.   [51] See also p. 146 above.

[52] Damascus Document VI, 19; VIII, 35; XV, 1–2, 6–8; Commentary on Habakkuk II, 3; Community Rule VIII, 10; see also Habermann, *Judaean Desert Scrolls*, concordance, s.v. *berit*. The expression 'new Covenant', Heb. *berit hadashah*, occurs in Jer. 31: 31–4, where Jeremiah, the prophet-priest, develops the idea of a new covenant, inscribed upon the people's hearts, describing a time when the entire people, as it were with a single heart, will recognize God's kingship. This idea was adopted by the secessionist priests as referring to themselves and those who accepted their ideology. Jeremiah (33: 17–22) links the redemption of Israel with observance of God's covenant with the House of David, with the priests, and with the Levites.   [53] Community Rule V, 8–11 (Vermes, *CDSSIE*, 104).

and with the eternal regularity of Creation, which is bound and limited in time and place by an oath:

> He spoke to Michael to disclose to him his secret name so that he would memorize this secret name of his . . . He revealed . . . this power of this oath, for it is power and strength itself . . . These are the secrets of this oath . . . The heaven was suspended . . . By it the earth is founded upon the water . . . from the beginning of creation and forever! By that oath, the sea was created; and He put down for it a foundation of sand which cannot be transgressed. . . . By the same oath the sun and the moon complete their courses of travel, and do not deviate from the laws (made) for them, from the beginning (of creation): and forever![54]

Though no parts of the Book of Similitudes have been found at Qumran, it figures in some recensions of the apocryphal book of Enoch; while it may represent a late tradition, the cosmic significance of the divine oath associated with God's name and the number of days of Creation, with the foundation of natural order, its perpetuation by oath and covenant that maintain its cyclic regularity 'from the beginning of creation and forever', may surely be traced in the background of the Covenant and oath ceremony celebrated at Qumran. As already noted, this ceremony renewed and confirmed anew all the previous covenants, promises, undertakings, and cosmic and historic oaths relating to the continuity of the order of Creation; but it was also celebrated in the context of a time concept defined by sabbaths and appointed times, oaths and covenants, signs and commandments.

The earliest of those previous covenants was the Rainbow Covenant, concluded by God with Noah[55] when he emerged from the ark in which he had been living for a whole solar year. Noah learned the details of the calendar and initiated the sacrificial cult, atoning with blood for the land, offering up sacrifices in the third month, and entering into a covenant proclaiming the permanence of the laws of nature.[56] The covenants then continued with that concluded with Abraham and his progeny, also halfway through the third month, in the so-called Covenant between the Pieces,[57] which guaranteed the eternity of his progeny; and with the covenants with Isaac and Jacob, concluded on the same date;[58] finally, they were renewed again at Sinai, once again in the third month, with the participation of Moses and the Israelites,[59] where the biblical account sets forth the eternal Law and the content of the oath undertaken by all those entering the Covenant. The order and mutual relationships of the covenants are recounted by the Angel of the Countenance to Moses on Mount Sinai, after the theophany:

> And Noah and his sons swore that they would not eat any blood which was in any flesh. And he made a covenant before the Lord God forever in all of the generations of the earth *in that month*. Therefore, he [the angel on Mount Sinai] spoke to you [Moses] so

---

[54] 1 En. 69: 14–21. [55] Gen. 9: 12–17. [56] Gen. 7: 11; 8: 14; Jub. 6: 1–5.
[57] Jub. 14: 8–20. [58] Jub. 16: 13–14; 22: 1, 10–15. [59] Jub. 1: 1; 6: 11; 50: 1.

that you also might make a covenant with the children of Israel with an oath *in this month* upon the mountain. And you will sprinkle blood upon them on account of all of the words of the covenant which the Lord made with them for all time. This testimony is written concerning you so that you might keep it always. . . .

And he gave a sign to Noah and his children that there should not again be a flood upon the earth. He set his bow in the clouds for a sign of the covenant which is forever, that the water of the Flood should therefore not be upon the earth to destroy it all the days of the earth. Therefore, it is ordained and written in the heavenly tablets that they should observe the Festival of Shavuot *in this month*, once a year, in order to renew the Covenant each and every year. And all of this festival was celebrated in heaven from the day of Creation until the days of Noah, twenty-six Jubilees and five weeks of years. And Noah and his sons kept it for seven Jubilees . . . until the day of the death of Noah. And from the day of the death of Noah, his sons corrupted it until the days of Abraham. . . . But Abraham alone kept it. And Isaac and Jacob and his sons kept it until your days, but in your days the children of Israel forgot it until you renewed it for them on this mountain. And you, command the children of Israel so that they might keep this festival in all of their generations as a commandment to them. One day per year in this month they shall celebrate the festival, for it is the feast of Shavuot and it is the festival of the first fruits. This festival is twofold and of two natures. Just as it is written and engraved concerning it, observe it.[60]

An unusual description of the Covenant enacted at Sinai with Moses and the children of Israel was found among the Qumran scrolls. It relates a version of the numinous covenantal moment in the third month, previously described in Exodus 19 and 24 and Deuteronomy 4, 5, and 18:

[. . .] and your wonders . . . [. . .] they will have understanding in the statutes of Moses [. . .] And he answered [and] said: He[ar] congregation of YHWH and pay attention all the assembly . . . [. . .]

[　] Cursed is the man who will not stand and keep and d[o] all the la[ws of Y]HWH through the mouth of Moses his anointed one, and to follow YHWH, the God of our fathers, who m[　] to us from Mount Sinai. And he spoke wi[th] the assembly of Israel face to face, as a man speaks with his friend. And as[　] He showed us in a fire burning above [from], heaven [　] and on the earth, he stood on the mountain to make known that there is no God beside him and there is no Rock like him. [And] the assembly {the congregation} they answered. Trembling seized them before the glory of God and because of the wondrous sounds [　] and they stood at a distance. And Moses, the man of God, was with God in the cloud. And the cloud covered him because [. . .] when he was sanctified, and like an angel he would speak from his mouth, for who of fles[h] is like him, a man of faithfulness and [　] who were not created from eternity and forever.[61]

---

[60] Jub. 6: 10–22 (the italics are mine).

[61] 4Q377, frg. 2 ii, 1–12 (*DJD* XXVIII, 213–14; cf. García Martínez and Tigchelaar, *Study Edition*, ii. 744–5).

In this priestly version of the Covenant at Sinai, God was known directly to the assembly of Israel at the time when the divine law was given in the middle of the third month. The *mysterium tremendum* expressed in the divine revelation—the theophany of the giving of the law—is described as a numinous pattern of the annual covenantal ceremony of the keepers of the law.

Among the secessionist priests, those 'entering' the Covenant or observing the Covenant were the Covenanters, the members of the Community, who worshipped and celebrated together with the angels, or the 'Sons of Light', who adhered to the sacred calendar of weeks, that is, the solar calendar, which is based on a covenant between heaven and earth and represents the eternity of cosmic and cultic order linked together in the annual cycle. The solar calendar testifies to the continuity of the covenants and the appointed times, in a deterministic order engraved on the heavenly tablets from beginning to end, in an eternal, predetermined sequence; the faithful who lived by it were thereby granted hidden knowledge concerning the commandments and the appointed times. The Community is described in the Damascus Document in connection with the observance of sabbaths, festivals, and commandments, upon which the fulfilment of the Covenant depends: 'But with the remnant which held fast to the commandments of God He made His Covenant with Israel for ever, revealing to them the hidden things in which all Israel had gone astray. He unfolded before them His holy Sabbaths and His glorious feasts, the testimonies of His righteousness and the ways of His truth, and the desires of His will which a man must do in order to live.'[62] The violators of the Covenant were the Sons of Darkness, who held fast to the lunar calendar, which corrupts the covenantal festivals and the appointed times, as described in Jubilees;[63] they 'walk in the stubbornness of their heart',[64] in the sense of Deuteronomy 29: 18, and permitted themselves all the things forbidden in the books of the secessionist priests that set forth the sacred order: 'As for the exact determination of their times to which Israel turns a blind eye, behold, it is strictly defined in the *Book of the Divisions of the Times into their Jubilees and Weeks*.'[65]

The difference in the number of days and sabbaths in the year; the different principle underlying the calculation of the number of days in the month, whether a fixed number or dependent on variable observation; and the consequent differences in the sequence of festivals and their relationship with the Covenant

---

[62] Damascus Document III, 12–16 (Vermes, *CDSSIE*, 129). For those sinning and going astray in regard to the calendar cf. 1 En. 80: 2–8; 82: 5; Jub. 6.

[63] Jub. 6: 36–7.   [64] Damascus Document II, 18; Community Rule II, 14.

[65] Damascus Document XVI, 2–4 (Vermes, *CDSSIE*, 137). The reference is to Jubilees (1: 26–8; see also 4Q216, IV, 4–8), where God says to Moses: 'And you write down for yourself all of the matters which I shall make known to you on this mountain: what was in the beginning and what will be at the end, what will happen in all of the divisions of the days which are in the Law and in predestined history [Heb. *te'udah*], throughout the weeks of years according to the jubilees for ever, until I descend and dwell with them in all the ages of eternity. And he said to the Angel of the Countenance: "Dictate to Moses from the first Creation until My sanctuary is built in their midst for ever and ever."'

festivals—it was such differences that made it impossible for those who consecrated the solar calendar to share their cult, and indeed their lives, with the believers in the lunar calendar. The ultimate result was segregation and secession.

The festival of Shavuot, celebrating the renewal of the Covenant and the oath,
the central festival of the Zadokites' calendar, determined by counting seven
weeks/sabbaths after the elevation of the Omer, coupling together oath (*shevuah*)
and seven (*sheva*), sabbath and Covenant, survived only in writing, in the works of
the secessionist priesthood, and in echoes of the disputes between the Pharisees
and the Sadducees (= Zadokites!) concerning the time to count those seven weeks
and the proper time of the Festival of Weeks thereby determined. In early rabbinic
tradition there is no trace of the name Shavuot/Shevuot (Weeks/Oaths) for the
festival celebrated at the end of those seven weeks: it is referred to as *atseret*, meaning 'assembly', a term which obliterates any allusion to oaths and Covenant renewal;
the date of the festival was changed to obscure the underlying cycles of seven sabbaths and the fixed date in the solar calendar, according to which the weeks were
always counted beginning on the Sunday after Passover (26 Nisan), so that the
festival always fell on a Sunday, seven weeks later (15 Sivan). No memory remained
of the ceremonial significance of the festival as a re-enactment of the Covenant
ritual, renewing covenants and oaths solemnized from the days of the patriarchs
until the theophany at Sinai and memorialized through sabbaths and festivals in a
sevenfold cycle.[66]

There is no doubt that the complex association with the solar calendar—based
on fixed numerical calculation and on identification of cosmic and cultic order,
perpetuating the tradition of covenants and set times—and the association with the
ahistorical, predetermined calendar of sabbatical years and jubilees, with its identification of divine order and historical sequence of 'weeks of years', is the central
axis and major polemical characteristic of the literature of the priestly opposition.
The ideal portrait of these priestly circles is drawn in the Community Rule, with
its account of a stratified society headed by priests, their lives the very embodiment
of principles of unity, communal life, and social inequality; their leaders were
witnesses to the cosmic order and keepers of the cultic order that attested to it.
These circles, engaged in a halakhic and cultic dispute, fortified their position by a

---

[66] It is surely significant that Shavuot is not associated in the mainstream (rabbinic) tradition with
any particular precept incumbent upon the individual, other than the specification of the day—which
it shares with the other biblical festivals—as a day of holy assembly (*mikra kodesh*). For that reason the
festival received no special treatment in rabbinic literature, and there is indeed no special tractate of
the Mishnah or the Talmud devoted to it, unlike the other biblical festivals. For the meaning of the
term *atseret* in relation to the theophany at Sinai and the 'day of assembly' (Heb. *yom hakahal*, Deut. 9:
10; 18: 16), see Weinfeld, 'Pentecost'; Breuer, *Festival Chapters*, 347–78; Tabori, *Jewish Festivals*,
146–7. The lack of a date for this festival in biblical tradition, as well as its omission both from the
priestly enumeration of festival offerings in the book of Ezekiel and later from mishnaic tradition, may
presumably be associated with its centrality in the literature of the secessionist priesthood and Jubilees
as signifying the renewal of the Covenant, and its links with Merkavah tradition in general; see pp.
225, 226, 227 below.

myth of cosmic, angelic, liturgical, and mystical dimensions, 'so that the children of Israel might keep the Sabbath according to the commands of the Sabbaths of the land just as it was written in the tablets which he placed in my hands so that I might write for you the law of each time and according to each division of its days'.[67]

[67] Jub. 50: 13.

SEVEN

Ezekiel's Vision and the Festival of Shavuot

Glorious spirit, wondrous likeness, most holy spirit . . . [to]ngue of blessing . . . and the likeness of living godlike beings is engraved in the vestibules where the King enters, figures of luminous spirit, [ ] figures of glorious light [. . .], figures of living godlike beings [in the] glorious shrines, the structure of the most holy sanctuary in the shrines of the Kings, figures of the godlike beings . . . and from the likeness of holiest holiness.[1]

THE literature of the secessionist priesthood attaches paramount importance to Shavuot (the Festival of Weeks/Oaths), understood both as the time the Covenant was concluded with the patriarchs and as a celebration of the renewal of the oath and the acceptance of the Covenant, emulating the angels who celebrate the festival in heaven as a testimony to the tradition of covenants and oaths. In addition, the festival is also a sacred, basic model for the seven-week harvest and crop cycles and the pentecostal pilgrimage axis of the solar calendar observed in the Temple in the first seven months of each year. The priestly courses entrusted with its safekeeping, each serving out its appointed week, celebrated the appointed times (festivals) once every seven weeks from the first month to the seventh month, adhering to the continuous sevenfold cultic and liturgical calendar. The crucial significance of the festival is obvious in light of the great number of times the third month and the festival itself, which symbolize the continuity and renewal of the Covenant, are referred to in Jubilees, in different contexts—Covenant, cult, angels, and oaths. Further evidence is provided by the Community Rule and the Damascus Document, in their accounts of the acceptance of the Covenant and the accompanying pronouncement of blessings upon the adherents of the solar calendar and the heavenly tablets, curses being heaped upon those who dare to violate them.

However, there are two further contexts with which Shavuot is implicitly associated; one assumes significance in relation to the biblical past and the origins of mystical tradition, the other—in relation to the later mythical mystical tradition. The first context is the intriguing affinity between Ezekiel's vision and the festival, binding sacred place to sacred time in the tradition of covenants and signs; the

---

[1] Songs of the Sabbath Sacrifice, 4Q405, frgs. 14–15 (Newsom, *Songs*, 280).

other is the relationship between oath and Covenant, on the one hand, and the vigil (*tikun*) on the night of the festival, linking the sacred appointed time with the sacred act of union associated with the oath and the Covenant.

Various traditions hint at a complex relationship between Ezekiel's vision, the tradition of the Merkavah—the Chariot Throne—and Shavuot.[2] The penta-teuchal reading for that festival, as dictated by Jewish law since the time of the Mishnah and Tosefta, is the passage describing the theophany on Mount Sinai (Exodus 19), the divine revelation of the past, signifying the oath and the accept-ance of the Covenant. Remarkably, the prophetic reading (*haftarah*) for the fest-ival, even today, is Ezekiel's vision of the Merkavah,[3] the visionary metamorphosis of the Holy of Holies revealed to the prophet on the festival itself, as we shall see presently, attesting to the continuation of divine revelation and thus to the eternity of the oath and renewal of the Covenant, despite the destruction of the Temple and the exile to Babylonia. This coupling of the two readings is surely an indication of the ancient origins of the relationship between the two traditions that link sacred time with the sacred place where heavenly and earthly were bound together in oath and Covenant.[4]

The relationship between the two theophanies, both read on Shavuot, or between the two readings—the pentatuechal reading concerning the theophany at

---

[2] Lieberman, 'Mishnat shir hashirim'; Halperin, *Faces of the Chariot*, 262–88, and see also ibid., index, s.v. *Shavuot*. See such sources as the following: 'During the giving of the Torah, twenty-two thousand chariots came down with the Holy One, blessed be he, each one like the vision that Ezekiel saw' (*Pesikta rabati*, ch. 21, p. 103b); or: 'God's chariots are myriads upon myriads, thousands of angels [Ps. 68: 18]—this teaches us that twenty-two thousand chariots came down with the Holy One, blessed be he, and each and every chariot [was like the chariot?] seen by Ezekiel' (*Pesikta derav kahana*, pp. 219–20); and various parallels. The tradition of prophetic readings (*haftarot*) also attests to the link between the theophany and the angels: the reading for the sabbath on which the Ten Commandments in Exodus are read is Isaiah 6, which *inter alia* describes the *serafim* in the heavenly sanctuary (the *heikhal*). The New Testament preserves a tradition of similar import: 'you who received the Law as delivered by angels and did not keep it' (Acts 7: 53); the same source (2: 1–4) also states that the apostles were inspired by the Holy Spirit on the festival of Pentecost = Shavuot. The traditional tomb of Ezekiel in Iraq (first mentioned in *Igeret rav sherira gaon* and described as a holy place by medieval Jewish travellers) was visited in particular on Shavuot; see *Mamlekhet kohanim* (Baghdad, 1873), which prescribes special prayers to be recited on the occasion.   [3] Ezek. 1; 10.

[4] One view in the Tosefta (*Meg.* 3: 5) prescribes Exodus 19 as the pentateuchal reading for Shavuot; while a *baraita* in the Babylonian Talmud (*Meg.* 31*a–b*) prescribes Ezekiel's vision as the *haftarah* for that festival. The time at which the *haftarot* were established is not known; the practice itself of reading a passage from the Prophets after the pentateuchal reading is already referred to in literature from the end of the Second Temple period. Rabbinic literature contains echoes of a tradition that the practice was established during the persecutions instituted by Antiochus IV Epiphanes, whose desecration and spoilage of the Temple triggered the Hasmonaean revolt (167–164 BCE): when reading of the Torah was forbidden, the Jews began to read prophetic passages that were related in some way to the weekly portion of the Torah, and this practice remained in force even after the pro-hibition had been lifted. For these traditions, besides the sources cited at the beginning of this note, see also BT *Meg.* 23*a*–24*b*; *Soferim* 12–13. For the link between Shavuot and Ezekiel's vision, in the con-text of the 'descenders to the Merkavah' and later mystical tradition, see Liebes, 'Messiah of the Zohar', 74–84; id., *Sin of Elisha*; and see below in relation to Shavuot and sacred conjugality.

Sinai and the prophetic reading concerning Ezekiel's Merkavah or Chariot Throne—is established by the verses 'God's chariots are myriads upon myriads, thousands of angels; the Lord is among them as in Sinai in holiness. You went up to the heights, having taken captives, having received tribute of men.'[5] These verses, which associate the Merkavah—'God's chariots'—and the angels, on the one hand, with the theophany at Sinai—'in Sinai in holiness'—and Moses' ascent to the summit to receive the Torah—'You went up to the heights, having taken captives' (recalling 'Moses went up to God . . .' in Exodus 19: 3), on the other, create a link between the two theophanies and the two priestly prophetic traditions about Mount Sinai, the giving of the Torah, the making of the Covenant,[6] the Covenant-renewal ceremony (Community Rule), oaths (Jubilees, Damascus Document), the vision of the Merkavah, the cherubim and angels, and the festival of Shavuot on Sunday, the 15th of the third month.

We have already seen that, according to Jubilees, Shavuot celebrated the covenants that God made with man on the 15th of the third month—covenant as an eternal divine oath or promise—beginning with the Rainbow Covenant concluded with Noah, through the Covenant between the Pieces made with Abraham in a cloud of smoke and fire, and culminating in the Covenant concluded with Moses and Israel at Sinai in cloud and fire. It would appear that the vision of the Merkavah, revealed to Ezekiel in a cloud of fire and flaming torches,[7] accompanied by the appearance of a rainbow—the only rainbow mentioned in the Bible after Noah—may also be seen as part of the tradition of Covenant renewal in the third month. Indeed, according to the calculation of the Metonic cycle (the nineteen-year cycle that provides a commensurable basis for the solar and lunar calendars), Ezekiel's vision took place on Shavuot, the festival of pilgrimage to the earthly Temple which the exiled prophet-priest transformed into a heavenly Chariot Throne. The puzzling date at the beginning of the biblical text, which is incomprehensible as it stands, was explained by Michael Chyutin, who has examined the various dates in Ezekiel and interpreted them according to the correspondence with the solar calendar in relation to the Metonic cycle: 'The beginning of Ezekiel's prophecy (1: 1), according to calculations synchronizing [the lunar calendar] with the solar calendar, was on the eve of Shavuot, the fourteenth of the third month, or on the festival itself, on the fifteenth, as believed by the members of the Qumran sect.'[8]

---

[5] Ps. 68: 18–19.   [6] Exod. 24: 8.   [7] Ezek. 1: 4, 13.

[8] See Chyutin, *War of Calendars*, 75, for the detailed calculation. The Athenian astronomer Meton (fl. 432 BCE) devised a cycle of 19 years, consisting of 12 years of 12 lunar months each and 7 years of 13 lunar months, for a total of 235 lunar months, after which the moon's phases recur on the same days of the solar year. This cycle makes it possible to establish some commensurability between the solar year and the lunar year, by laying down a definite rule for a lunar calendar with intercalary months, to keep in step with a cycle of solar years. Some authorities hold that a 19-year cycle had already been known previously, in Babylonia. The author of 2 Enoch was certainly acquainted with the Metonic cycle, as evident from 2 En. 16: 8. Jaubert, 'Calendrier des Jubilées... Qumran', 260–1, points out that Ezekiel's

In other words, on the festival marking the renewal of the Sinai Covenant, celebrated in the Temple on Shavuot, or the priestly festival celebrating the acceptance of the Covenant, the exiled priest Ezekiel experienced the opposite
event—the destruction of the Temple and the Exile, as follows from the beginning
of his prophecies.[9] In the course of his 'visions of God' he saw the vision of the
Merkavah, the Chariot Throne, which eternalizes the destroyed earthly Temple
through a visionary metamorphosis of its component parts. Moreover, not only
does he perceive the sacred place—his vision also includes sacred time, namely,
the appointed time at which all the covenants were made and in addition the signs
of those covenants. Like Noah, who saw the rainbow in the third month as a sign of
the Covenant, Ezekiel, too saw a rainbow: 'Like the appearance of the bow which
shines in the clouds on a day of rain, such was the appearance of the surrounding
radiance. That was the appearance of the semblance of the Presence of the Lord.[10]
Like the cloud and flaming fire referred to in the Covenant between the Pieces[11]
made with Abraham 'in the third month, in the middle of the month',[12] and like
the Sinai Covenant made 'in the third month',[13] in which God came down on the
mountain 'in a thick cloud'[14] accompanied by 'thunder and lightning and a dense
cloud . . . smoke . . . and fire . . . thunder and flaming torches'[15]—Ezekiel too saw in
his vision 'a huge cloud and flashing fire',[16] 'burning coals of fire . . . suggestive of
torches' as well as 'fire and lightning'[17] and heavenly sounds.[18] Like the vision of
'the God of Israel, under His feet . . . the likeness of a pavement of sapphire, like
the very sky for purity'[19] that Moses saw at the end of the theophany on Mount
Sinai, after the sprinkling of 'the blood of the covenant that the Lord now makes
with you'[20]—a vision thought by various scholars to be an alternative account of
the theophany—Ezekiel saw at the climax of his vision 'the semblance of a throne,
in appearance like sapphire'[21] and 'something like a sapphire stone . . . resembling
a throne'.[22] Like 'the Presence of the Lord [appearing] in the sight of the Israelites
as a consuming fire',[23] Ezekiel saw at the end of his vision 'the semblance of the
Presence of the Lord' as a 'surrounding radiance'.[24] Like the vision described by
Moses as 'The Lord our God has just shown us His majestic Presence, and we have
heard His voice out of the fire',[25] Ezekiel, having seen 'the radiance of the Presence
of the Lord',[26] describes the appearance of the 'Presence of the Lord': 'I saw a

visions generally take place on a Sunday, but never on the sabbath, and that the dates in the book of
Ezekiel conform to the priestly calendar observed in Chronicles, Ezra and Nehemiah, and Jubilees (see
also id., 'Calendrier des Jubilées... semaine', 36–42). See VanderKam's reassessment of Jaubert's
hypotheses, with whose main arguments he fully agrees, in 'Origin, Character and History'.

[9] Ezek. 1: 1.	[10] Ezek. 1: 28.	[11] Gen. 15: 17–18.
[12] Jub. 15: 1.	[13] Exod. 19: 1.	[14] Exod. 19: 9.
[15] Exod. 19: 16, 18; 20: 18.	[16] Ezek. 1: 4.	[17] Ezek. 1: 13–14.
[18] Ezek. 1: 24–5.	[19] Exod. 24: 10.	[20] Exod. 24: 8.
[21] Ezek. 1: 26.	[22] Ezek. 10: 1.	[23] Exod. 24: 17.
[24] Ezek. 1: 28.	[25] Deut. 5: 21.	[26] Ezek. 10: 4.

gleam as of amber—what looked like a fire . . .; and from what appeared as his loins down, I saw what looked like fire, and there was a radiance all about him.'[27]

There is no denying the similarity of various elements in the biblical accounts of the two theophanies—on the one hand Ezekiel's Merkavah vision, and on the other hand the various divine revelations associated with the covenants made in the middle of the third month, marked by cosmic signs reflecting the sublime beauty and glory of the forces of nature in all their awe-inspiring grandeur. Reading the biblical descriptions of the covenants and their signs, linking divine set times with cosmic testimony and creating the awesome, mysterious splendour that Rudolph Otto called *mysterium tremendum*, one is reminded of Rainer Maria Rilke's line, 'For beauty is nothing but the beginning of the awesome.' It is no accident that Ezekiel's Merkavah vision, a text of incomparable numinous quality describing a divine revelation which took place, according to the solar calendar tradition, on Shavuot in the middle of the third month, was prescribed, as already noted, to be recited on Shavuot as the prophetic reading accompanying the divine covenantal revelation on Mount Sinai in that same month.

Ezekiel's vision may be perceived as a priestly prophetic tradition of a mystical and visionary metamorphosis of the Holy of Holies in Solomon's Temple, or as a heavenly memorialization of the ruined earthly Temple in a heavenly counterpart and an archetypal cosmic model; but it is also, albeit implicitly, a mystical, visionary metamorphosis of the tradition of the signs of divine revelation and the covenants concluded between heaven and earth on Shavuot. In other words, the exiled prophet-priest's vision binds together sacred time (Covenant, oath, seven weeks, third month, testimony, sign) and sacred place (Sinai, Merkavah, Temple, earthly and heavenly Holy of Holies, implicitly related to the Garden of Eden and the seven Heikhalot), but beyond the boundaries of time and place. Not surprisingly, this vision, with its intimation of Covenant renewal referring to the most sacred time and place became the basis of priestly mystical thought in antiquity; each of its components became part of the fabric of heavenly reality in the tradition of angelic priests and the mystical experience that form part of the Merkavah tradition.

Various traditions, both early and late, link Shavuot, the festival of the Covenant and the Temple, with the perception of the Covenant between heaven and earth as a pact or oath of betrothal, matrimony, and sacred conjugality in the supernal worlds. These traditions are associated with the time of the theophany at Shavuot, that is, with the theophany at Sinai, with Ezekiel's Merkavah and the Chariot Throne of the cherubim in the Holy of Holies. Shavuot, one of the three

---

[27] Ezek. 1: 27. A liturgical text for the festivals discovered at Qumran, in a passage associated with Shavuot, links the renewal of the Covenant with the vision of God's glory or Presence (*kavod*) referred to at Sinai and in Ezekiel's vision: 'You have renewed your Covenant for them in a vision of glory' (4Q509, frgs. 97–8 ii: *DJD* VII, 199). Cf. Schiffman, 'Heikhalot Literature', 132. Incidentally, it is intriguing that the rainbow—the sign of the Covenant—and the vision of the divine Presence seen by Noah and Ezekiel are associated with the appearance of the high priest in Ben Sira 50: 8.

pilgrimage festivals,[28] is explicitly associated with first fruits and thereby with fertility and the cycle of crops and procreation. This cycle depends, as we have seen, upon the counting of seven weeks and is associated, explicitly and implicitly, with the most profound meaning of such concepts as purity, sanctity, oath, covenant, union, creation, and matrimony—with the seven-day transition from chaos to Creation, from impurity to purity, from separation to union, and from barrenness to fertility.

Earlier on, in my discussion of the cherubim and their Chariot Throne, I mentioned the tradition associating pilgrimage with the sacred union on that occasion:

> Whenever Israel came on pilgrimage on festivals [to the Temple in Jerusalem], the curtain would be removed for them and the cherubim were shown to them, whose bodies were intertwined with one another, and they would be thus addressed: Look! You are beloved before God as the love between man and woman.[29]

Perhaps we hear in this description an echo of an ancient tradition of the First Temple, for there were neither cherubim nor Chariot Throne in the Second Temple, only a mythical memory (although there may have been paintings or reliefs reflecting that tradition in later periods too).[30]

The description of the intertwined cherubim, revealed to the pilgrims when the curtain was removed from the Holy of Holies, offers some striking linguistic allusions. The rather unusual Hebrew verb describing the removal of the curtain (*megalelin*) is related to the verb in the standard rabbinic phrase for forbidden sexual unions (*giluy arayot*; their roots, *g-l-l* and *g-l-h*, respectively, have the two consonants *g* and *l* in common); the literal meaning of the latter phrase is to uncover and expose what is normally covered and concealed, in an erotic context. In addition, the word *me'urim*, translated above as 'intertwined', has the root *a̔-r-h*, which is precisely the root of the noun in the above phrase, *arayot*. The latter, in turn, recalls an allusive phrase of sexual connotation referring to the upper worlds, '*arayot* are the King's sceptre'—a phrase found in late mystical tradition; and it is also reminiscent of an expression used in *Sefer yetsirah, berit maor*, referring to the sexual organs, which are variously called *eryah/ervah/arayot* (nakedness with an erotic connotation), and thus alluding to procreation as associated with exposure and covering. The description in the Talmud, therefore, suggests a cultic, mystical representation of myths of *hieros gamos*, the sacred union or heavenly matrimony, probably in the context of the pilgrimage on Shavuot, the festival of the Covenant and the occasion on which the Chariot Throne of the cherubim is revealed. Moreover, the grammatical relationship between the Hebrew words for the Holy of Holies—*kodesh hakodashim*—and for betrothal—*kidushin*—suggests an ancient common ground of heavenly and earthly union.

In this context, the scene of the theophany at Sinai was the sacred union or marriage of the community of Israel (*keneset yisra'el*, or its female hypostasis, the

---

[28] Exod. 23: 14–17.   [29] BT *Yoma* 54a.   [30] See BT *Yoma* 21b.

Shekhinah, described as a bride) and God (likened to a bridegroom) in an esoteric rabbinic tradition, as pointed out by Saul Lieberman in a now classic article.[31] This tradition links the Songs of Songs, said by various *tana'im* to have been given to the Israelites at Sinai, with gazing at the sacred, as in the verse 'Let me see your face',[32] which is interpreted as an allegorical reference to the theophany at Sinai.[33]

As we shall see later, Rabbi Akiva is associated with 'entering the Pardes', the mystical Holy of Holies, and 'descending to the Merkavah', the heavenly Holy of Holies, as described in the Babylonian Talmud in tractate *Ḥagigah* and in *Heikhalot zutarti*. It is surely no accident, therefore, that he is the sage who establishes the link between the theophany at Sinai (the time and place of the Covenant or holy union between God and Israel), the Song of Songs (a love song referring to conjugal union), and the Holy of Holies (the place of the intertwined, 'betrothed' cherubim, likened to male and female): 'Rabbi Akiva says: This [= 'Let me see your face'] was said precisely at Mount Sinai.'[34] Rabbi Akiva, too, affirms the hallowed status of the Song of Songs: 'Said Rabbi Akiva: The entire world is not as worthy as the day the Song of Songs was given to Israel; for all the Scriptures are holy, but the Song of Songs is the Holy of Holies.'[35] Various midrashic expositions of the Song of Songs explicitly and implicitly associate the ideas of procreation and matrimony, plainly alluded to in the Song of Songs, with the Covenant at Sinai, the Throne of Glory, the Chariot Throne, the cherubim, and Shavuot.[36]

The relationship between weeks, oaths, Sinai, the Chariot Throne, and Ezekiel's Merkavah may also be found in a maxim of an *amora* named Rabbi Avdima (or Avdimi) of Haifa: 'I learned in my teaching that twenty-two thousand of ministering angels came down to Sinai with the Holy One, blessed be He. . . . Alternatively: "God's chariots are myriads upon myriads, thousands of angels" (Ps. 68: 18)— twenty-two thousand chariots came down with the Holy One, blessed be He, and each and every chariot (was like the chariot?) seen by Ezekiel.'[37] Lieberman showed that in antiquity and the Middle Ages, alongside the literal interpretation of the Song of Songs, there also existed a mystical interpretation, citing Rabbi Joshua ibn Shu'eib in a homily for the last day of Passover:

This is a midrash of the Song of Songs. For the words of this song are very obscure and puzzling, etc., and therefore it was declared to be Holy of Holies, for all its words are secrets of the Merkavah and the names of the Holy One, blessed be He, etc. But although its words are obscure and puzzling it also conveys an overt message, etc., and our Sages of blessed memory expounded overtly in the sense that the groom is the Holy One, blessed be He, and the bride is the community of Israel.[38]

---

[31] Lieberman, 'Mishnat shir hashirim' (see also n. 2 above).   [32] S. of S. 2: 14.
[33] BT *Shevu.* 35*b*; *Song of Songs Rabbah* 1: 2; *Song of Songs Zuta* 1: 33 (ed. Buber, p. 9): 'And the Sages say, it [the Song of Songs] was given from Mount Sinai.'   [34] *Song of Songs Rabbah* 1: 2.
[35] Mishnah *Yad.* 3: 5.   [36] Lieberman, 'Mishnat shir hashirim', 121.
[37] *Pesikta derav kahana*, 'Baḥodesh hashelishi', 107*b*.
[38] Lieberman, 'Mishnat shir hashirim', 125.

Lieberman summarizes his discussion of the Song of Songs, which tannaitic tradition declares was read out on Mount Sinai on Shavuot and was considered 'Holy
of Holies', as follows: 'The Midrash of the Song of Songs, *Ma'aseh merkavah* and
Shiur komah are one and the same.'[39] To this list of parallel textual esoteric traditions concerned with the mystical holy union or betrothal I would add *Heikhalot
zutarti*, a Merkavah work ascribed to Rabbi Akiva, as we shall see later, which, in
terms taken from the Song of Songs, describes God as a beloved and/or bridegroom:

> The great, mighty, awesome, strong, brave, magnificent, and noble God. My beloved is
> clear-skinned and ruddy, pre-eminent among ten thousand. His head is finest gold, his
> locks are curled and black as a raven. His eyes are like doves. . . . His hands are rods of
> gold, studded with beryl; his belly a tablet of ivory, adorned with sapphires. . . . Such is
> my beloved, the Holy One, blessed be He, my darling . . . strong and brave, great and
> mighty and awesome, magnificent and noble . . . Holy, holy, holy the Lord of Hosts . . .[40]

This text of Merkavah mysticism, with its unprecedented description of the Deity,
has reached us in such fragmented form that it is impossible to date it precisely and
thereby determine its historical context. One can nevertheless point to several
characteristic features: the combination of the tradition of seeing the invisible or
gazing at a mystical vision of the Merkavah, the tradition of Ezekiel's vision, the
tradition of the divine names and thereby of oaths, and the idea of 'entering the
Pardes', which may be linked with entering the Holy of Holies and seeing the
Merkavah. Also prominent are the metaphors for God's appearance, which, as I
have already noted, are borrowed from the Song of Songs.

Gazing upon the Merkavah in the priestly mystical tradition, or viewing the
sacred in the mythical ritual context, is perhaps reminiscent of the viewing of the
intertwined cherubim during the pilgrimage in the Temple tradition. In the same
spirit of association of ideas, the seven weeks elapsing from the sabbath after the
end of the Passover festival and the harvesting of the Omer (the 26th of the first
month) to Shavuot (the 15th of the third month), the time of the wheat harvest,
may parallel the seven days of purification prior to sexual union—or the seven
weeks of purification from the release from Egyptian bondage to the acceptance
of the Covenant of freedom at Sinai.[41] Shavuot, signifying the renewal of the
Covenant(s) in the ancient priestly tradition, is indeed described in later mystical
tradition—based on earlier priestly traditions—as celebrating a matrimonial
covenant, the heavenly nuptials of God and the Shekhinah, the hypostasized community of Israel, or of Moses and the Shekhinah. The night of the festival, known
in the *Zohar* as 'the night that the bride is united with her husband', and the special

---

[39] Lieberman, 'Mishnat shir hashirim', 126.

[40] Elior (ed.), *Heikhalot zutarti*, 34–5 (= Schäfer (ed.), *Synopse*, §419).

[41] None of these associations, however, is made explicit in the early traditions, only alluded to; see
Zohar III, 97*b*; Tishby, *Wisdom of the Zohar*, iii. 1242–3, 1256.

vigil (*tikun*, see below) held on that night, as prescribed by zoharic tradition,[42] establish a connection between the *Idra raba* ('Greater Assembly') of Rabbi Simeon b. Yohai and his companions and the theophany on Mount Sinai, as Yehudah Liebes has shown.[43] The purpose of the vigil on the night of Shavuot, known as the *hilula*, meaning 'wedding celebration', or *tikun*, meaning 'preparation, restoration', is to adorn and beautify the bride, namely, the Shekhinah, for her marriage on the morrow. But the idea of *tikun* is also applied in the *Zohar* to the restoration of the supernal worlds. This is accomplished by the companions, known as *benei ḥupata*, 'sons of the (wedding) canopy', who accompany the bride and read a long series of twenty-four texts—biblical, mystical, and liturgical—the same number as that of the priestly courses.

Gershom Scholem maintained that the author of the *Zohar* had drawn these ideas from the book of Enoch; but no such passage exists in Enoch as we have it today. Given the esoteric nature of the tradition of sacred matrimony associated with the Holy of Holies, the cherubim, Shavuot, and Merkavah tradition—all associated with images of love and fecundity from the love poems of the Song of Songs, with winged holy creatures, with angels, with the sacred Covenant, and with Temple traditions of appointed times and sacred conjugality—its sources and evolution are difficult to trace with any degree of confidence, and one should not, of course, project back in time. Nevertheless, several indisputable facts stand out. There is a striking linguistic relationship: certain terms—*berit*, 'covenant', *yiḥud* and *zivug*, both meaning '(sacred) union', *devekut*, 'cleaving, devotion', *kelulot*, 'matrimony', and the various terms related to *arayot*—seem to be common to the vocabularies of three distinct categories of union: the mystical union known as *yiḥud*, *zivuga kadisha*, and *kelulot*; the union of the cherubim intertwined in the Holy of Holies, which in turn is linked with the counting of seven weeks from the Omer to Shavuot and with Merkavah tradition; and the earthly pact of matrimony and sexual union between male and female, which according to priestly tradition may be consummated only after seven days of purification have been counted— this last category associated with 'covering' versus 'exposure' of hidden things in the most primary sense, hence also with procreation, fertility, creation, and the continuity of life.

The cherubim, also called 'holy creatures' or 'holy beings', are associated with life and ongoing creation, which depend on the sevenfold enumeration that calibrates the productive progress of time; but they are also associated with Shavuot, the festival of first fruits and fertility, with Merkavah tradition, with oaths, and with the Holy of Holies. This relationship, which, as I have repeatedly shown, is both conceptual and linguistic, between the heavenly and earthly variants of union and togetherness surely indicates some primeval level of language. Perhaps a faint memory of the connection has been preserved in the ancient mishnaic injunction,

---

[42] *Zohar* I, 8a–9a; III, 98a.   [43] Liebes, 'Messiah of the Zohar', 74–82.

'It is forbidden for three persons to discuss the secrets of sexual union [Heb. *arayot*], for two persons to discuss *ma'aseh bereshit*, and for a single person to discuss *ma'aseh merkavah*, unless [that person] is wise and insightful'.[44] These three injunctions, taken in reverse, precisely define the three categories of union just considered in the context of Merkavah tradition: (1) the intertwined (*me'urim zeh bazeh*) cherubim in the Holy of Holies (*arayot*), which left their imprint on the cherubim and sacred creatures in *ma'aseh merkavah*, that is, Ezekiel 1, and in the love poems of the Song of Songs, which speak of the lower worlds but allude to the upper; (2) *ma'aseh bereshit*, the act of creation, relating to heavenly cycles and signs and the order of time, to divisions of continuity and arrest, to the sacred number seven as the number of days in the week or days of purification, and thus to the calendar and the eternal cycles of nature, creation, and procreation described in brief in the first chapters of Genesis; and (3) *ma'aseh merkavah*, the cultic representation of cosmic order in Merkavah tradition, which establishes a link between visible and invisible cycles of time, or between visible and invisible patterns of fourfold and sevenfold numerical cycles and the Chariot Throne of the cherubim and is observed by priests and angels, as intimated in the first and last chapters of Ezekiel.

Origen, in the introduction to his commentary on the Song of Songs, written in Caesarea around the middle of the third century CE, points out that the Jews treat the Song of Songs with considerable circumspection:

It is a practice among the Hebrews that no one is permitted so much as to hold [the Song of Songs] in his hands, unless he has reached a full mature age.

He goes on to say that the Jews teach their youngsters all of the Bible, but keep four passages to the very end:

The beginning of Genesis, in which the creation of the world is described; the beginning of Ezekiel the prophet, which tells of the cherubim; the end [of Ezekiel], which deals with the building of the Temple; and this book of the Song of Songs.[45]

While the precise reasons for the restrictions on the reading of these texts[46] are disputed by contemporary scholars,[47] it seems obvious that they are precisely the esoteric texts associated with Merkavah tradition and parallel to the injunctions cited above from the Mishnah ('It is forbidden . . . to discuss . . .'). Indeed, the beginning of Genesis, with its account of Creation and the establishment of its natural order, clearly refers to *ma'aseh bereshit*, which took place in those seven days. The first chapter of Ezekiel, with its account of his Merkavah vision and the cherubim, refers to *ma'aseh merkavah* and thereby also to Shavuot and the fourfold and sevenfold enumerations underlying its cultic aspects. The last chapters (40–8) of Ezekiel are associated with the future Temple and the Zadokite priests, guardians

---

[44] Mishnah *Ḥag.* 2: 1.   [45] Origen, *Song of Songs*, 23.   [46] BT *Ḥag.* 13a.

[47] Scholem, *Jewish Gnosticism*, 38; Urbach, 'Traditions about Mysticism'; Halperin, *Faces of the Chariot*, 26; Elior, '*Merkabah* Mysticism'.

of the Merkavah tradition. Last, the Song of Songs has manifold connections with the upper worlds ('the Song of Songs is the Holy of Holies'), Shavuot (the festival of first fruits and procreation), Merkavah tradition, and the theophany at Sinai ('the Song of Songs was given at Sinai'); in addition, we have the obscure affinity with the concept of *hieros gamos*, the sacred union of heaven and earth, sexual aspects of the upper worlds ('*arayot* are the King's sceptre'), and the intertwined cherubim shown to the pilgrims coming up to the Temple with their first fruits, when the curtain covering the Holy of Holies was drawn aside.

Taken together, these diverse observations may point to ancient priestly-mystical traditions which claimed to sanctify the forces of nature that ensure the continuity of life and procreation or to place them in a theological or cultic frame-work. These forces figure in a positive sense in the Song of Songs and in the sacred nuptial union represented by the cherubim in the Holy of Holies. In a negative sense, in a power-oriented, chaotic, numberless, unrestrained, depraved dimen-sion, they appear in the story of the Watchers, who committed sins of forbidden union and incest, taking 'wives from among those that pleased them' without con-sideration of the boundaries between what is forbidden and what is permitted, the limitations imposed by taboo, religion and culture, Covenant and cycle, with dis-astrous consequences. In other words, the sacred union of members of the same species, as demonstrated by the intertwined cherubim; the permitted, sanctified coupling of two individuals, governed by sanctification, Covenant, counting, and agreement; or conjugal relations dependent on the sacred Covenant, on purity and sevenfold counting, aimed at fertility and the perpetuation of life—these are the antithesis of forbidden, licentious, chaotic sex, as represented by the sin of the Watchers, whose depravity violated the limits of taboo, profaned all bounds of sanctity and holy matrimony, and breached the boundaries between forbidden and permitted in heaven and earth. The cherubim, sacred beings associated with cre-ation and life, sanctity and holy matrimony, with appropriate covering and uncov-ering of what is properly hidden, with sacred union and connubiality, with fertility and procreation, with holiness, purity, and sevenfold enumeration, are the anti-thesis of the Watchers, who embody forbidden, unrestrained, monstrous sex, impurity devoid of enumeration, profanation of everything that is sacred, violation of boundaries and prohibitions, incest, idolatry and bloodshed, death and destruc-tion. These boundaries and prohibitions are the subject of the oath and the Covenant between heaven and earth, the very foundation stone of civilization; they are the very substance of the entire system of commands and precepts, of the whole complex of oaths and covenants associated with Shavuot, made with various generations from Noah and Abraham to the gathering at Sinai.

It is very probable that the mishnaic injunction against reciting the first chapter of Ezekiel as the prophetic reading on Shavuot[48] preserves an echo of these esoteric

---

[48] *Meg.* 4: 10.

traditions; this injunction, too, may be associated with the desire to restrict public discussion of Merkavah tradition, as illustrated by the Mishnah in tractate *Ḥagigah* ('It is forbidden . . . to discuss . . .'). Both injunctions reflect the struggle between, on the one hand, the priestly mystical tradition and its preoccupation with the Merkavah, the cherubim, Creation and the continuation of life in sanctity and purity, covenants and oaths, the festival of first fruits and fertility, and, on the other hand, the positions of the new ruling classes, who tried to curtail and even suppress these traditions because of their affinity with the former priests, the sacred calculations of the solar calendar, the controversial date of Shavuot, the mystical tradition of the Merkavah, and the reality of the Temple. These attempts were only partly successful, as it is still customary—and has been since antiquity, at the latest since the second century BCE—to recite Ezekiel's vision as the prophetic reading for Shavuot, and moreover, according to kabbalistic tradition, the Song of Songs is among the texts recited in the *tikun*. As Yehudah Liebes notes in this connection: 'Since it is unlikely that the custom (of reading the *merkavah* vision as the Shavuot *haftarah*) was instituted after and in opposition to the *Mishna*'s ruling, we would do better to assume that it predated the *Mishna* and that the *Tannaim* sought unsuccessfully to counter it. This is an indication both of the antiquity of the mystical understanding of *Shavuot* and of its power.'[49] Some of the mystical meanings of the festival, associated with Merkavah tradition, with nuptials in the supernal world, with heavenly beings and angelic creatures, with the Song of Songs and the 'marriage' of heaven and earth, were preserved in the vigil of the night of Shavuot in zoharic tradition, to be revived by Rabbi Joseph Karo in the kabbalah of Safed.

[49] Liebes, 'Messiah of the Zohar', 79.

EIGHT

Priests and Angels

And he turned to Levi first and began to bless him first, and he said to him . . . May the Lord, the God of all ages, bless you . . . May He draw you and your seed near to Him from all flesh to serve in His sanctuary as the angels of the Countenance and the holy ones.[1]

For He has established among the eternally holy the holiest of the holy ones, and they have become for Him priests of the inner sanctum, in His royal sanctuary, ministers of the Countenance in His glorious *devir* . . .[2]

MUCH of apocryphal, Heikhalot, and Qumran literature emphatically reflects the belief in celestial beings residing in heaven alongside the God of Israel, to a degree considerably beyond biblical and rabbinic understanding.[3] A characteristic feature of this literature, in all its ramifications, is the central position and presence of angels in the cosmos, in history, and in the cult. These celestial beings are variously referred to as 'holiest of the holy ones', 'congregation of *elim* [= god-like beings]', 'sons/children of *elim*', 'sons of heaven', 'holy angels', 'chief princes', 'priests of the inner sanctum' (*korev*), 'servants/angels of the Countenance', 'spirits of knowledge', 'lords', and 'host of angels'. They perform the sacred service in the supernal Heikhalot and are associated in many ways with the order of Creation, the cycles of the universe, the traditions of the priesthood, the sevenfold cycles of the Temple cult and their mythological origins.

The Creation story, as recounted by the Angel of the Countenance in Jubilees, describes the angels as the outcome of God's first act of creation, the foundation of cosmic order as embodied in seven acts:

[And the Angel of the Countenance told Moses at God's command: 'Write all the wo]rds of creation . . . [For on the first day He created the] upper [heaven]s, the ear[th], [the waters and all the spirits who serve before Him: the angels of] the Countenance, the angels of ho[liness,] the an[gels of the spirits of fire, the angels of the spirits of the current]s [and] the angels of the spirits of the [clouds], of dark[ness, ice, frost, dew, snow, hail and hoar]frost; and the angels of thunder[s] and the angels of the [storm-] winds [and the angels of the winds of cold and of] heat, of winter and of summer, [all]

---

[1] Jub. 31: 14.   [2] 4Q400, frg. 1 i, 3–4 (Newsom, *Songs*, 93).

[3] Urbach, *Sages*, 135–83; Rofé, *Belief in Angels*; Mach, 'Studies in Angelology'.

the spirits of His creatures [which He made in the heavens and which He made in the ear]th and in everything, the aby[sses], darkness, dawn, [light, the dusk which He prepared with] His [know]ledge. Then we saw His deeds and [blessed Him] on account of all His [d]eeds and [we praised Him in His presence because] He ma[de seven] great works on the first day.[4]

This tradition (preserved in another formulation in the Thanksgiving Hymns) is the basis for the collaboration of angels and priests, for the story of the angels begins with the sanctification of the sabbath and is woven around the sacred sevenfold pattern: '[On the sixth day the Lord God finished all His works and all that He had created] and rested on the [seventh] day [and made it holy for all eternity and placed it as a sign for all] His works.'[5] The Angel of the Countenance goes on to explain that the divine sign was given to the heavenly keepers of the sabbath—the angels: 'And He gave us a huge sign, the day of] the Sabbath on which He rested . . . that we observe the Sabbath on the sev[enth] day, [(refraining) from all work. For we, all the angels of the Countenance and all the angels of holiness—these] two kinds—He comman[ded us to observe the Sabbath with Him in the heavens and on the earth].'[6] The story of the angelic pattern of sabbath observance in the heavens, in a sevenfold cycle of cessation of labour, ends with the election of the people of Israel, which is unique by virtue of the fact that it, too, rests on the sabbath together with the angels:

[And He said to us: 'I am going to single out for Myself] a nation among all My nations. And [they will keep the Sabbath and I will consecrate them as My people and I will bless them. They will be My people and I will be their God].' And He chose the descendants of Jacob . . . The [seventh] day [I will teach them so that they keep the Sabbath on it above all. For I blessed them and consecrated them as an exceptional people] among all the peoples so that together [with us] they keep the Sabbath.[7]

In the literature of the secessionist priesthood and in Heikhalot literature, which continues the Merkavah tradition, the angels are the celestial counterparts of ideal priests, divinely elected from birth, who testify to the divine order of activity and rest, labour and freedom, and to the creative march of time and its sevenfold cessations. They safeguard the sacred sequence of the seventy days of rest—the sabbaths and the festivals—as determined by the seasons of the year and the sevenfold order, linking heaven and earth and bringing them closer together through their sacred service. The priests, for their part, are the earthly counterparts of the angels—witnesses to covenants and observers of oaths, adhering to the seasonal changes and the eternal cycle of the laws of nature, observing the sabbath and serving as 'priests of the inner sanctum', singing, chanting, and praising in the supernal

---

[4] 4Q216, col. V (*DJD* XIII, 13–14, ll. 1–11; cf. Charlesworth (ed.), *OT Pseudepigrapha*, ii. 55); cf. Jub. 2: 1–3.   [5] *DJD* XIII, 13–14, ll. 2–3.

[6] Ibid. 19–20, col. VII, ll. 5–9 (cf. García Martínez and Tigchelaar, *Study Edition*, i. 463).

[7] Ibid. 20, col. VII, ll. 9–11 (cf. García Martínez and Tigchelaar, *Study Edition*, i. 463–5).

sanctuaries, as they perform their part in upholding the same seventy days of rest. The prophet Malachi's formulation, 'for the lips of a priest guard knowledge, and men seek rulings from his mouth; for he is an angel of the Lord of Hosts',[8] and the dictum of Rav Huna in the Jerusalem Talmud,[9] 'Whoever sees the priests in the synagogue (reciting) the first benediction should say, "Bless the Lord, O His angels" ', hint at the existence of different traditions as to the relationship between the holy angels and the hallowed priests, the elect of God, acting with heavenly sanction and jointly responsible for maintaining the sacred service, based on the sacred calendar governing both heavenly temples and earthly shrine. Priests and angels serving in the sacred precincts are expressly identified in Jubilees, which cites the angels' account of patriarchal history: 'And the seed of Levi was chosen for the priesthood and the levitical (orders) to minister before the Lord always just as we (= the angels) do. And Levi and his sons will be blessed forever . . .'.[10] The angelic service is described in detail in the Songs of the Sabbath Sacrifice, where priests and angels are considered together: 'For He has established among the eternally holy the holiest of the holy ones, and they have become for Him priests of the inner sanctum, in His royal sanctuary, ministers of the Countenance in His glorious *devir* [Holy of Holies].'[11]

The affinity between angels and priests is considerably broadened and intensified in the secessionist priesthood's literature: both are referred to as guardians of the Covenant, observers of the sabbath, possessors of secret knowledge; both immerse and purify themselves, offer sacrifice, sing, play music, and recite the Kedushah, preserve the tradition of divine names and blessings, renew the Covenant, and attest to the sacred time observed in heaven and earth according to the solar calendar. Angels and priests are joint witnesses to divine order and to its realization in heaven and on earth; they share holiness and divine knowledge, give expression to that knowledge in cult and law, in book, number, and narrative, in benediction and song. In Songs of the Sabbath Sacrifice and the Blessings Scroll we find frequent descriptions of the angels ministering in the supernal sanctuaries. Sometimes the description is indirect, as in the verse already cited above, 'He has established among the eternally holy . . .'; and sometimes it figures in direct addresses to God: 'the c]ouncil of *elim* of purification with all those who have eternal knowledge, to prai[se and to bles]s Your glorious name in all [ever]la[sting ages]. Amen. Amen', or 'and all spirits of bearers of the sanctu[m] . . ., mighty *elim* in power . . . all [will bless toge]ther Your holy name'.[12] It may appear in invocative liturgical formulations, in which the priests address the angels and arouse them to participate in a sublime ceremony, extolling God in sacred song in the supernal

---

[8] Mal. 2: 7.   [9] *Ber.* 1: 1.   [10] Jub. 30: 18.

[11] 4Q400, frg. 1 i, 3–4; Newsom, *Songs*, 93; and see now *DJD* XI, 176, 178.

[12] 4Q286, frg. 7a, ii b, c, d, ll. 6–7 (*DJD* XI, 25–6); 4Q286, frg. 2 a, b, c (*DJD* XI, 17). Compare: 'To praise Your glory wondrously [with the *elim* of knowledge and praiseworthiness] of Your royal majesty together with the holiest of the holy ones' (4Q401, frg. 14: *DJD* XI, 207).

sanctuary and transforming the invisible heavenly sanctuaries into audible revelation or vocal, singing reality:

By the *Maskil*.
Song of the sacrifice of the seventh Sabbath on the sixteenth of the month.
Praise the God of the lofty heights, O you lofty ones among all the *elim* of knowledge.
Let the holiest of the godlike ones sanctify the King of glory
Who sanctifies by holiness all His holy ones.
O you chiefs of the praises of all the godlike beings,
praise the splendidly [pr]aiseworthy God.
For in the splendor of praise is the glory of His realm.
From it (come) the praises of all the godlike ones together with the splendor of all [His] maj[esty].
Exalt, exalt, to the heights, you most godlike ones of the lofty *elim*,
and (exalt) His glorious divinity above all the lofty heights.
For H[e is God of gods] of all the chiefs of the heights of heaven
and King of ki[ngs] of all the eternal councils.
{By the intention of} {His knowledge} at the words of His mouth come into being [all the lofty angels];
at the utterance of His lips all the eternal spirits;
[by the in]tention of His knowledge all His creatures in their undertakings.
Sing with joy, you who rejoice [in His knowledge with] rejoicing among the wondrous godlike beings.
Chant His glory with the tongue of all who chant with knowledge;
and (chant) His wonderful songs of joy with the mouth of all who chant [of Him.
For He is] God of all who rejoice {in knowledge} forever
and Judge in His power of all the spirits of understanding.
Thank, all you majestic *elim*, the K[in]g of majesty;
for His glory do all the *elim* of knowledge confess,
and all the spirits of righteousness admit His faithfulness.
And they make acceptable their knowledge according to the judgments of His mouth
and their thanks (do they make acceptable) at the return of His powerful hand for judgments of recompense.
Sing praises to the mighty God with the choicest spiritual portion,
that there may be [melod]y together with divine joy,
and (let there be) a celebration with all the holy ones, that there may be wondrous songs together with e[ternal] joy.
With these let all the f[oundations of the hol]y of holies praise
the uplifting pillars of the supremely lofty abode, and all the corners of its structure.
Sin[g praise] to Go[d who is dr]eadful in power, [all you spirits of knowledge and light] in order to [exa]lt together
the splendidly shining firmament of [His] holy sanctuary.
[Give praise to Hi]m, O you god[like] spirits, in order to pr[aise for ever and e]ver

the firmament of the uppermost heaven, all [its beams] and its walls, a[l]l its [for]m, the
    work of [its] struc[ture.
The spir]its of holie[st] holiness, the living godlike beings, [spir]its of [eter]nal holi[ness],
Above all the hol[y ones
Wonder, marvelous in majesty and splendor and wonder. And the God of gl]ory [is
    wondrous] with the most perfect light of
Kn[owledge] . . . [in all the wondrous sanctuaries;
The godlike spirits (*are*) round about the abode of the King
of truth and righteousness. All its walls . . .][13]

In this seventh sabbath song, which renews the divine Covenant with the angels and
with humanity, the earthly priests address seven calls to their heavenly counterparts, the angels, to praise God, and the Hebrew text uses seven different verbs.
Consecrating the sabbath in phrases that manifest sevenfold structure, it seems to
be renewing the ancient sevenfold covenant between the celestial observers of the
sabbath and their earthly counterparts. The song is written and chanted in rhyth-
mic language, which profoundly affects the worshipper and is in fact designed to
express the invisible in poetic and musical terms and thus transplant him to the
supernal worlds, to inspire in him a mystical ascent to the angelic world. This is
achieved through an associative liturgical shift, from the priestly service in the
earthly Temple—whose charge included observing the sacred service, tending for
the shewbread, and performing through their songs of praise and thanks a ritual of
knowledge, justice, and righteousness—to the service of the angels of the Countenance—godlike beings, bearers of celestial knowledge, who chant their songs of
praise in the heavenly sanctuary and bear names and designations relating directly
to the priestly and levitical service.

    There is considerable power and fascination in this heavenly liturgy, which, in
fixed patterns, using sublime language and strange, cyclic syntax—perhaps associated with the wondrous, secret language of the angels—repeats these priestly
formulations of praise and thanks, words expressive of cyclic song, of secret knowledge, of law and justice, revolving around the sacred service and its sevenfold
substrate and summoning up images of a wondrous, sacred realm. From time
immemorial, there was always a link between chant and enchantment, between
audible words, rhythm, and melody and the abstract, invisible mysteries they purported to portray, between poetic language and magic, miracle, and sorcery. This
ancient link rose to new heights in the world of the authors of the Songs of the
Sabbath Sacrifice—priests without a temple, barred from discharging their priestly
duties, from offering sacrifices or otherwise performing the actual sacred service.
As if to compensate for this situation, they sang and chanted together with the

---

[13] Newsom, *Songs*, 209–10, 211–13 (the layout of the poem as cited here is my own), and cf. discussion ibid. 213–25. Cf. *DJD* XI, 269, and discussion ibid. 270–8, where Newsom proposes corrections
and improvements to her earlier translation, some of which are incorporated in the present quotation.
For the seventh sabbath at Qumran see Maier, 'Shire Olat hash-Shabbat', 546.

angels, bent on bridging the gap between heaven and earth through their song and myth, books and numbers, divinely decreed tables and calendars revealed by angels and preserved by priests. The poetic language and ringing sounds of praise and thanksgiving create a celestial reality, and the cyclic order of the universe is reflected in the cycles of songs and their subdivisions, corresponding to the seven-fold divisions of time and to the sacrificial cycle. The language of the angelic priestly service thus becomes a kind of 'ladder set on the ground, its top reaching the sky'.

These poetic traditions may actually have accompanied the Temple service in First Temple times, perhaps also in the early phase of the Second Temple period; alternatively, the songs and their contents might have originated in mystical litur-gical traditions about an ideal, mythological past, visualized *a posteriori* after the priestly authors and their circles had seceded from the Temple service in Jeru-salem. Whatever the case, these liturgical traditions, dependent as they are on the seven-based solar calendar, had very little to do with the cultic reality of the late Second Temple period, which was anathema to the authors of the songs.

The secessionist priestly literature frequently gives prominence to traditions of a mutual relationship between the ministrations of the earthly and heavenly celeb-rants. Underlying the angelic service, described in such terms as 'priests of the inner sanctum who serve before the King of holiest holiness [{in the *devir*? of}] His glory',[14] is clearly the service of the priests with their thanksgiving and benediction in the earthly Temple: 'Give thanks to God, / bless His Holy Name always, / in the Heavens and their dominion, / all the angels of the holy firmament.'[15] Behind the depictions of the heavenly sanctuaries stands the earthly sanctuary, the Temple. The blurring of boundaries between priests and angels is clearly expressed in the songs of the *maskil*—a Qumranic term generally translated as 'master' or 'instruc-tor'; it seems, however, to have the connotation of an inspired poetic visionary who renders the traditions of the angelic priests. These songs apply the very same terminology to celestial and terrestrial priesthood, creating a linguistic reality that recognizes no barrier between esoteric and exoteric, between invisible sanctuaries and the poetic reality of cosmic calendars and Temple rituals:

> With those seven times refined and with the holy ones
> God will sanctify an everlasting sanctuary for Himself,
> And purity among the creatures.
> And they shall be priests, the people of His righteousness, His host,
> And servants, the angels of His glory,
> Shall praise Him with marvelous prodigies.[16]

---

[14] Newsom, *Songs*, 89, 93.

[15] Words of the Heavenly Lights (4Q 504, frgs. 1–2, VII, 4–6: *DJD* VII, 150; cf. García Martínez and Tigchelaar, *Study Edition*, ii. 1017).

[16] 4Q 511, frg. 35, 1–4 (*DJD* VII, 237; cf. Vermes, *CDSSIE*, 422; García Martínez and Tigchelaar, *Study Edition*, ii. 1033).

By the *Maskil*. A song. Praise the name of His holiness
And exalt Him all who know justice . . .
They who guard the way of God and the path of His holiness
For the saints of His people. By the discerning knowledge of God
He placed Israel in twelve camps . . .
[ ] the lot of God with the angels of the luminaries of His glory, in His name praises.
[ ] He established them for the set times of the year and a common government, to walk in the lot of God according to His glory and to serve Him in the lot of the people of His throne. For the God . . .[17]

The authors of this literature, as partners or counterparts of the angels, cognizant of that presence and assumed proximity, adopted the most stringent standards of purity. Angels, for them, were not merely a mythical, mystical reflection of the cult in the supernal worlds, or a shared poetic and liturgical reality that lent particular significance to their sacral duties—but also a divine representation of the relationship between surface appearances and underlying existence, preserved from time immemorial. This at once visible and invisible world was for them a divine source of authority, an eternal testimony, a cultic inspiration, a historical pledge; they sensed its presence as something palpable, a decisive mystical pattern endowed with divine meaning. Many of the works composed by the secessionist priests express this relationship between the Community (or Council) of 'togetherness' (Heb. *yahad*) and the holy creatures in heaven. This was in fact the source of the name by which, as frequently observed in previous chapters, the members of the Community referred to themselves—the *yahad*—reflecting the assumed 'togetherness' of priests and angels. This is the clear import of the following lines from the Thanksgiving Hymns:

To stand with the host of the Holy Ones, to enter into a community [Heb. *yahad*] with the congregation of the Sons of Heaven. You have allotted to man an everlasting destiny amidst the spirits of knowledge, that he may praise Your name with togetherness [*yahad*] of rejoicing and recount Your marvels before all Your works.[18]

to be sanctified to You . . . to be together [with] the sons of Your truth and partake of the lot of Your Holy Ones . . . to stand before You with the eternal host and with the spir[its of knowledge], to be renewed together with all the living and with them that know with togetherness of rejoicing [*yahad*].[19]

For You brought Your glorious mystery to all the men of Your Council, to those who share the lot of togetherness with the angels of the Countenance. And among them there shall be no mediator to their congregation.[20]

---

[17] 4Q511, frg. 2, 1–10 (*DJD* VII, 221; cf. Vermes, *CDSSIE*, 421).
[18] Thanksgiving Hymns XI, 22–3 (cf. Vermes, *CDSSIE*, 261). On the co-operation between the Community and the angels see Dimant, 'Men as Angels'.
[19] Thanksgiving Hymns XIX, 10–14 (cf. Vermes, *CDSSIE*, 288).
[20] Ibid. XIV, 12–13 (cf. Vermes, *CDSSIE*, 272).

The testimony of the Angel of the Countenance in Jubilees as to the angelic and human communities of observers of the sabbath—'to keep the sabbath together with us'—is echoed by the description in the Thanksgiving Hymns of the sacred service celebrated in tandem by the members of the Community and the sons of Heaven, jointly praising their Creator. We find similar exalted tones in the Community Rule, reminiscent of the verse in Ezekiel[21] concerning the portion of the priests and describing the divine gift conferred upon the elect who live, in spirit, together with the angels:

God has given them to His chosen ones as an everlasting possession, and has caused them to inherit the lot of the Holy Ones.
He has joined their assembly to the Sons of Heaven to be a Council of the Community [yaḥad],
A foundation of the Building of Holiness, an eternal Plantation throughout all ages to come.[22]

Elsewhere, too, we read of the presence of angels in the Community, participating in the sacred service:

And blessed are all the angels of His Holiness, May the Mo[st High] God [bless] you. [May he cause his face to shine upon you] . . . For God is wi[th you and the angels of his holiness are standing in your congregation, and the name of his holiness has been proclaimed ov[er you][23]

And we are gathered together, . . . and with those who know we shall sing to You and chant . . . With your mighty ones wondrously we shall recount together of the knowledge of God.[24]

The community of priests and angels, chanting its joint songs of praise and exaltation, is concerned to give perpetual cyclic testimony to the eternal divine order of the march of time, to bear witness through its liturgical order to this cosmic order in terrestrial and celestial existence:

We, Your people, will praise [You]r [name for] the deeds of Your truth.
[for] Your [migh]ty deeds we will extol [Your splendour
at every mom]ent and at the times indicated by Your eternal edicts,
at [the onset of day] and at night at the fall of ev[ening and at dawn.
For great is] the plan of Your glory,
and Your marvellous mysteries in [Your] h[eights] . . .[25]

The members of the Community were not content merely to experience life in the spiritual presence of the celestial host, as reflected by their insistence on extreme

[21] Ezek. 44: 28. [22] Community Rule XI, 7–8 (Vermes, *CDSSIE*, 115).
[23] 4Q285, frg. 8, 3–10 (*DJD* XXXVI, 241–3; cf. *DJD* XXIII, 246–9; see also Wacholder and Abegg, *Preliminary Edition*, ii. 223). [24] 4Q427, frg. 3 i, 4–5 (*DJD* XXIX, 110).
[25] 4Q491, frgs. 8–10, col. I, ll. 10–12 (*DJD* VII, 21).

purity, their liturgy, and the various rituals through which the proper sequence of sabbaths and festivals was maintained. In their view, the priesthood was of angelic origin; the collaboration of priests and angels in a cult based on sevens, sabbaths, oaths, signs, and Covenant, had its roots in heaven itself. These roots were described in a myth of priests and angels, woven from a variety of traditions concerning the beginnings of the priestly tradition and its heavenly origin. The beginnings of the priesthood were thus set back in time as far as possible, because of the relationship between cosmic order and ritual order, which was dependent on the relationship between priests and angels. The patriarchs of the world were thus portrayed as priests.

These origins were associated with Enoch son of Jared, the seventh patriarch of the world, who 'walked with God'. He was the first literate human being, the first to learn how to count and calculate, the first to offer incense, the first to acquire the secrets of the calendar of sabbaths and set times, and the divine knowledge and statutes associated with it, and the first person to guard, remember, and convey this angelic knowledge, both orally and in writing, to his sons the priests. The priesthood continued after the Flood, in which God, faced with a world that had rejected the proper order, obliterated it, purged it with water, and laid the arithmetical foundations of the solar calendar; this in turn was associated with Enoch's great-grandson Noah, 'a righteous and blameless man', who 'found favour with the Lord', began to offer sacrifices and incense on earth, renewed the Covenant with the angels, and understood to observe seven commandments, as against the sins of the Watchers.

Also mentioned in the priestly line is Melchizedek, 'priest of God Most High'; but the beginning of the dynastic continuum was associated with the name of Levi son of Jacob, who received the blessing of seven angels, as well as the blessing of his grandfather Isaac, who had been born on Shavuot, in keeping with the angelic promise given on that date. Levi, anointed as priest by the angels in a dream, was awarded this sacred, eternal status in recognition of his righteousness and loyalty, which were linked in his person with zeal and revenge. These privileges are in stark contrast to the attitude of biblical tradition, which does not confer such status on Levi but on the contrary links him with narratives that bespeak disgrace and sin.[26]

---

[26] 1 Enoch 81–2, 106–7 and 2 Enoch 68–73 recount the transmission of the priesthood from Enoch to Methuselah, Lamech, and Noah, Nir, and Melchizedek; and cf. Jub. 7: 38–9. 1 Enoch 68: 1 deals with the transmission to Noah of 'all the secret things'. For the consecration of Levi as priest cf. Jub. 30: 18–20; 31: 13–17; 32: 1–9. Cf. also the Aramaic Testament of Levi in *DJD* XXII (1996), 1–70 ('Parabiblical Texts'); on this text see Kugler, *From Patriarch to Priest*. For Levi as priest and angel see further 4Q213, frg. 2, 17–18 (*DJD* XXII, 30–1). For Levi's vision see *DJD* XXII, 40–1. Cf. Testament of Levi 1–19; see Hollander and de Jonge, *Testaments of the Twelve Patriarchs*; and cf. Kugel, 'Story of Dinah'; id., 'Levi's Elevation to the Priesthood'; Himmelfarb, *Ascent to Heaven*; Werman, 'Attitude to Gentiles', 223–40. For the history of the priesthood from Levi to Kohath, Amram, Aaron, and their descendants, down to the writers' own time, see 4Q245 (*DJD* XXII, 155–61), where mention is made, among others, of Levi, Kohath, Bukki, Uzzi, Zadok, Abiathar, Hilkiah, and Onias; cf. 1 Chr. 5: 27–41,

The literature of the secessionist priesthood, as opposed to the Bible, set out to lavish praise upon Levi, patriarch of the priestly tribe, highlighting his affinity with the supernal worlds and his special position in the angelic world. A striking example of this orientation is the treatment of the massacre that Levi (together with Simeon) perpetrated on the people of Shechem, earning him—in the Bible— Jacob's bitter curse: 'Simeon and Levi are a pair; their weapons are tools of lawlessness. Let not my person be included in their council, let not my being be counted in their assembly. For when angry they slay men, and when pleased they maim oxen. Cursed be their anger so fierce, and their wreath so relentless. I will divide them in Jacob, scatter them in Israel.'[27] Levi's actions are thus defined in the Bible as *ḥamas*, 'lawlessness', anger, and wrath (incidentally, the same term, *ḥamas*, is used to describe the sins of the Watchers which led to the Flood[28]). Contrast this with Isaac's blessing of Levi in Jubilees 31, following the retelling of the tribal ancestor's life in chapter 30. Instead of the curse, the angels bestow a special blessing on Levi for those very actions, which they deem praiseworthy in the extreme:

And the seed of Levi was chosen for the priesthood and levitical orders to minister before the Lord always just as we do. And Levi and his sons will be blessed forever because he was zealous to do righteousness and judgment and vengeance against all who rose up against Israel. And thus a blessing and righteousness will be written on high as a testimony for him in the heavenly tablets before the God of all. And we will remember for a thousand generations the righteousness which a man did during his life in all of the appointed times of the year . . . And he will be written down as a friend and a righteous one in the heavenly tablets.[29]

The Testament of Levi also links the priestly blessings with vengeance and zeal, not only expressing approval of Levi's action after the fact, but describing it as fulfilment of a divine command. Levi treated the Shechemites as he did in response to an explicit injunction, after having been promised priesthood:

which lists the priestly dynasty from Amram, father of Moses and Aaron, to the destruction of the First Temple. For Levi and the Levites at Qumran, as well as their association with angels, see further Kister, 'Levi who is Light'; Stallman, 'Levi and Levites'; Dimant, 'Children of Heaven'.

There are various traditions of 'a covenant of priesthood for all time' (Num. 25: 13) being awarded to zealous individuals who acted in the spirit of a 'vengeful God': Phinehas, grandson of Aaron (Num. 25: 7–14), for his willingness to kill transgressors of the divine will; Levi, following the slaughter of the Shechemites (Jub. 30: 17–18; Testament of Levi 5: 13); and the Levites, for their readiness to slay the worshippers of the golden calf, including even their own relations and friends (Exod. 32: 26–8). Moses' blessing of the tribe of Levi in Deut. 33: 8–11 makes of their uncompromising zeal a religious merit which entitles them to the priesthood, thus converting Jacob's curse into a benediction—whereas Simeon, also originally cursed by Jacob (Gen. 49: 3–7), receives no mention in Moses' blessing. The Temple Scroll, speaking in God's name, reiterates the election and blessing of Levi: 'And the priests, the sons of Levi, shall come forward, for I have chosen them to minister before me and bless My name' (col. LXIII, 3; cf. Vermes, *CDSSIE*, 216–17).

[27] Gen. 49: 5–7.   [28] Gen. 6: 11, 13.   [29] Jub. 30: 18–20.

At this moment the angel opened for me the gates of heaven and I saw the Holy Most High sitting on the throne. And he said to me: 'Levi, to you I have given the blessing of the priesthood until I shall come and dwell in the midst of Israel'. Then the angel led me back to the earth, and gave me a shield and a sword, and said to me, 'Perform vengeance on Shechem for the sake of Dinah, your sister, and I shall be with you, for the Lord sent me.'[30]

After receiving the heavenly blessing, as told in Jubilees, Levi receives the blessing of his grandfather Isaac at Bethel, in the seventh month—a blessing pronounced by one who was born on Shavuot in fulfilment of an angelic promise delivered to Abraham on that very festival,[31] thus rejecting the biblical account of his father Jacob's curse. In chapter 31, which is devoted to Levi—whose name is explained as meaning 'joined to the Lord'—he is associated in Isaac's blessing with the angels of the Countenance and the holy ones, referred to thus in the Thanksgiving Hymns,[32] 1 Enoch,[33] the Community Rule,[34] the Songs of the Sabbath Sacrifice,[35] the Blessings, Jubilees,[36] and the Testament of Levi,[37] as well as other Qumranic works:

And a spirit of prophecy came down upon his mouth. And he took Levi in his right hand. . . . And he turned to Levi first and he began to bless him first, and he said to him, 'May the God of all, the Lord of all ages, bless you and your sons in all ages. May the Lord give you and your seed very great honor. May he draw you and your seed near to him from all flesh to serve in his sanctuary as the angels of the Countenance and the holy ones. May your sons' seed be like them with respect to honor and greatness and sanctification. And may he make them great in every age. And they will become judges and rulers and leaders for all of the seed of the sons of Jacob. The word of the Lord they will speak righteously, and all of his judgments they will execute righteously. And they will tell my ways to Jacob, and my paths to Israel. The blessing of the Lord shall be placed in their mouth, so that they might bless all of the seed of the beloved.[38]

After the blessing at Bethel, reminiscent of the biblical story of Jacob's dream and the divine blessings associated with it (and with Moses' blessing of Levi in Deuteronomy 33: 8–11), Levi, too, has a dream, in which he envisions his accession to the priesthood: 'And he stayed that night in Bethel. And Levi dreamed that he had been appointed and ordained priest of the Most High God, he and his sons forever. And he woke from his sleep and blessed the Lord.'[39] The dream comes true when his father dresses him in the priestly vestments after he has been picked by lot to be a human tithe (Levi is the tenth son, reckoned from the youngest of Jacob's sons back to the eldest); he offers sacrifices halfway through the seventh month, on Sukkot, a seven-day festival whose sacrifices are counted in multiples of seven and

---

[30] Testament of Levi 5: 1–3 (Charlesworth (ed.), *OT Pseudepigrapha*, i. 789–90).
[31] Jub. 15: 1, 21; 16: 13.   [32] VI, 13; III, 23.   [33] 6: 2; 40; etc.
[34] IV, 25–6.   [35] Newsom, *Songs*, 89.   [36] 31: 14.
[37] Testament of Levi 3.   [38] Jub. 31: 12–15.   [39] Jub. 32: 1.

whose tithes are described in detail as the foundation for a ritual to be observed annually.[40] The story of Levi's elevation to the priesthood ends with a vision of an angel with seven tablets.[41] At the same time, God changes Jacob's name to 'Israel' and promises him the land, its fertility and its blessing, and dominion over all its inhabitants.[42] This change in Jacob's status is completed just before his death, when we are told how Levi inherited the written tradition: 'And (Jacob) gave all of his books and his fathers' books to Levi, so that he might preserve them and renew them for his sons until this day.'[43]

Such are the origins of the priestly myth of the sons of Levi, who was granted 'a covenant of priesthood for all time',[44] a blessing for his sons and their progeny 'for all posterity',[45] bringing blessing to the world in all ages from 'the God of all, the Lord of all ages',[46] ensuring abundance and fertility for all time[47]—the eternity of time and sanctity of place are here linked together in the celestial and terrestrial worlds. This myth, with the blessing thereby conferred upon sons of Levi giving them domination over all the other tribes,[48] in light of their sacred service in earthly and heavenly worlds, is thus linked irrevocably to the perpetual order of the universe, to the eternal law and march of time with its sevenfold divisions of appointed times and preordained sequence of days, months, and seasons, to the immortal angels, to perpetuation of the sacred service entrusted for ever to the priests—by virtue of the natural order. For priesthood is innate, hereditary, acquired only by being born into the tribe; it can be neither bought nor discarded. The priestly dynasty is eternal, as are its immutable privileges, but also its constant commitment to safeguard a sacred heritage; among the angels, however, it is each and every angel that is eternal, as is the angels' perpetual commitment to safeguard cosmic order.

The secessionist priests possessed several different, at times conflicting, traditions of the status of the priesthood, as is evident from a comparison of the Testament of Levi, the Aramaic Testament of Levi, and Jubilees, both with each other and with various chapters of biblical literature. The differences relate to the details of the traditional story of Levi's elevation to the priesthood, and also to the privileges of the priests and Levites that derive from the varying promises given to Levi. Most probably, these traditions reflect a complex historical picture of priestly and levitical status, duties, and privileges at different times, as is already evident in biblical tradition. This is not the place to discuss the issue of these traditions and their place in the Bible and in the literature of the Second Temple period; suffice it to point out that, despite the differences in substance and emphasis, the laws establishing the priestly and levitical privileges in Jubilees and the various traditions of Levi clearly differ from those in biblical tradition, in fact considerably expanding those privileges.

---

[40] Jub. 32: 1–10. [41] Jub. 32: 21. [42] Jub. 32: 17–20. [43] Jub. 45: 15.
[44] Num. 25: 13. [45] Testament of Levi 4: 4. [46] Jub. 31: 14. [47] Jub. 31: 18.
[48] Testaments of the Twelve Tribes; Testament of Judah 21: 1–2.

The particular emphasis on Levi's holiness and the circumstances of his consecration as priest should be considered not in isolation, but against the background
of opposing traditions which deny these claims (in the Bible, it is Levi's descendant Aaron, not Levi himself, who is considered the founder of the priesthood). The
priestly myth is associated, on the one hand, with merciless fanaticism, with
vengeance and the concept of a zealous, avenging God—a concept familiar from
biblical tradition. On the other hand, it is bound up with covenants and divine
promises, oaths and angels, sacrifices and tithes, festivals and appointed times,
heavenly tablets and sacred scriptures, none of which figures in the Bible in this
context; they are known solely from the literature of the secessionist priesthood,
where they are inextricably bound up with that same avenging deity.

The priests' capacity to kill without mercy, to treat their own kin as strangers, to
curse and anathematize, to take life in the name of the avenging God, is demonstrated in the Bible through three episodes in which priests reacted in that spirit to
violations of law and order or to personal alienation—the slaughter at Shechem,[49]
the slaughter after the worship of the golden calf,[50] and the assassination of Zimri,
chieftain of the tribe of Simeon, by Phinehas the priest.[51] This characteristic of the
priests is contrasted with their power to atone for sin and to grant life, to bless
in God's name and invoke divine favour and grace[52]—a beneficial power embodied
in the sevenfold rituals of sacrifice and incense entrusted to them, in oath and
Covenant, law and order, atonement and forgiveness, with their supernatural
association with God and his angels. An echo of this dualism may be discerned in
the blessing[53] pronounced by Moses, of the tribe of Levi, upon his Levite
brethren; a parallel version found at Qumran, in the work known as Testimonia,
has the singular instead of the Masoretic text's plural, so that the blessing is
addressed to Levi in person:

Masoretic version	Qumran version[54]
And of Levi he said:	And of Levi he said:
Let Your Thummim and Urim	Give to Levi Your Thummim
Be with Your faithful one,	And Your Urim to Your faithful one,
Whom You tested at Massah,	Whom I tested at Massah,
Challenged at the waters of Meribah;	Challenged at the waters of Meribah; He
Who said of his father and mother,	Who said to his father {not} . . .
'I know them not',	And to his mother, 'I know you not',
And did not acknowledge his brothers,	And did not acknowledge his brother(s)

---

[49] Gen. 23: 25–31.   [50] Exod. 32: 26–9.
[51] Num. 25: 7–13.   [52] Num. 6: 22–7.   [53] Deut. 33: 8–11.
[54] 4Q175, ll. 14–20 (translation here based on García Martínez and Tigchelaar, *Study Edition*, i.
357; cf. *DJD* V, 58; Vermes, *CDSSIE*, 496). The differences between this version and the Masoretic
one are striking. Besides the use of singular instead of plural, the text places special emphasis on Levi's
indifference towards his own relatives, for which he was rewarded with supernatural privileges, and
on God's presence between Moses, who delivered the benediction, and Levi, its recipient.

Masoretic version	Qumran version
Nor know his children.	Nor know his son(s).
They observed Your word	For he observed Your word
And kept Your covenant.	And kept Your covenant.
They shall teach Your judgments to Jacob,	They shall make Your precepts shine for Jacob,
Your law to Israel.	Your Law for Israel.
They shall put incense in Your nose	They shall put incense in Your nose
And a burnt-offering on Your altar.	And a burnt-offering on Your altar.
Bless, O Lord, his courage	Bless YHWH his courage
And accept the work of his hands.	And accept with pleasure the work of his hand
Smite the loins of his foes	Crush the loins of his adversaries
And let his enemies rise no more.	And those who hate him may they not rise.

Levi's misdeeds, his fanaticism and indifference, which enable him to kill his closest relatives and acquaintances, are present here as readiness to slay and be slain in God's name, as standing a divine test, proving his absolute loyalty to God and to God's laws and Covenant. It was these extreme positions *vis-à-vis* life and death, the utter devotion to God as against the ability to detach himself entirely from human emotions, that made Levi worthy of consecration, with the concomitant exclusive right to be close to the Holy of Holies, to receive the Urim and Thummim, symbols of the priesthood and its heavenly knowledge, to impart divine statutes to others and to serve before God, to pray and sing songs of praise, to offer sacrifices and burn incense as a memorialization and consecration of time, to atone for human frailty and invoke divine providence.

The priests possessed these life-giving powers by virtue of their observance of the sevenfold covenants and the associated laws of purity (counting of sabbaths, weeks, and appointed times; seven days of purification; calling God's name seven times; purification rituals and sacrifices counted in sevens; circumcision after seven days; the seven-branched lampstand); by virtue of their affinities with the angels, the witnesses to the Covenant, and their practice of a cult parallel to that observed in heaven (songs and blessings; angels of purity; angels of knowledge; priests of the inner sanctum); by virtue of their capacity to link upper and lower worlds (sacrifices); by virtue of their mythical, mystical, ritual links with the Garden of Eden and its denizens and their earthly representation through the Temple and its priests, associated with life and fertility, water and growth (Tree of Life, incense, gold, cherubim, the lampstand with its calyxes and petals, purity); and, finally, by virtue of their ability to promulgate divine law and order in an earthly environment. All these characteristics were dependent on meticulous observance in the sacred precinct of both holiness (the symbol of life, which had to be protected from defilement, the symbol of death) and purity (the numbered cycles that were a precondition for life). The priests, guardians of sanctity, watched over the creative march of *sacred time*, counted in sevens according to the solar calendar of sabbaths and the heavenly tablets; over the *sacred place*, associated with the seven Heikhalot or supernal sanctuaries where the angels minister, the heavenly Merkavah or Chariot Throne, the Garden of Eden and the Temple, fertility and the creation of life, Mount Sinai and Shavuot, the tablets of the Covenant, and the Holy of Holies; and over the *sacred ritual*, performed in multiples of seven and associated with sabbaths and covenants, angels and sacrifices, priestly courses, fire and incense, praise-song and blessings.

The sevenfold dimension, implicitly and explicitly present in the world of the priesthood, is reflected in law and myth, beginning with the seven days of Creation, Enoch the seventh patriarch, observance of the sabbath and the calendar, and culminating in Levi's vision of his consecration as priest by seven angels. The Testaments of the Twelve Tribes and its source, the Aramaic Testament of Levi, describe the vision of Levi son of Jacob, emphasizing the presence of white-clad angels[55] and the ceremonial representation of the seven-based tradition:

And we left there and came to Bethel. There I again saw the vision as formerly, after we had been there seventy days. And I saw seven men in white clothing, who were saying to me, 'Arise, put on the vestments of the priesthood, the crown of righteousness, the oracle of understanding, the garment of truth, the breastplate of faith, the headcover of honesty, and the apron for prophetic power'. Each carried one of these and put them on me and said, 'from now on be a priest, you and all your posterity'.[56]

The seven men mentioned in this vision as bringing Levi the seven priestly vestments recall the seven holy men who accompanied Enoch back to earth from heaven and instructed him to teach his sons, the founders of the priesthood, the knowledge of the cosmic order of heavenly time and space that he had learned from the angels in heaven.[57] They may also be associated with various traditions, common in the literature of the secessionist priesthood, concerning groups of seven ministering angels; or with the seven days of Creation and the seven branches of the lampstand, the seven firmaments, the groups of seven angels in the Songs of the Sabbath Sacrifice, the seven ingredients of the incense; and the figure of Enoch, the seventh patriarch of the world, serving as high priest in the supernal worlds. The Testament of Levi describes the association between the angelic service—'the archangels who serve and offer propitiatory sacrifices to the Lord . . . they present to the Lord a pleasing odor, a rational and bloodless oblation'[58]—and the priestly services as pictured in Levi's consecration vision—'The seventh (of the seven angels/men; cf. Ezek. 9: 2–3; 1 En. 20) placed the priestly diadem upon me and

---

[55] 1 En. 71: 2.
[56] Testament of Levi 7: 4–8: 3 (Charlesworth (ed.), *OT Pseudepigrapha*, i. 790–1).
[57] 1 En. 81: 5.
[58] Testament of Levi 3: 5–6 (Charlesworth (ed.), *OT Pseudepigrapha*, i. 789).

filled my hands with incense, in order that I might serve as priest for the Lord God.'[59]

The incense, made from seven ingredients, figures in the story of the two protagonists of the heavenly and earthly priestly myths: in the story of Enoch, who saw the incense trees in the Garden of Eden[60] and 'offered incense which was acceptable to God . . . (at) the holy place on the southern mount',[61] and in the actions of Noah,[62] who built an altar, offered sacrifices and fragrant incense after leaving the ark,[63] and received a divine undertaking that the natural order would thenceforth be maintained for ever. The incense, which as we have seen is associated with the trees of the Garden of Eden, with the fragrant odour, with the 365 days of the solar year and the solar calendar,[64] with the number seven,[65] with the Temple, with the gold altar—which is the incense altar[66]—with atonement and sacrifices, with the Day of Atonement and the coupling of the cherubim,[67] is the exclusive concern of priests and angels.

Throughout the literature of the secessionist priesthood, the angels, the immortal counterparts of the priests, provide a source of heavenly validity, a role model or reference group. It was the angels who communicated the solar calendar to Enoch and it was on their instructions that he taught it to his sons, committed it to writing, and testified to his experiences in the supernal worlds. The angels are the guardians of the heavenly tablets[68] and the keepers of the cosmic knowledge of the laws of heaven and earth. Jubilees, which relates the history of the world from Creation to the theophany at Sinai, was dictated to Moses by the Angel of the Countenance, who recounts the march of history and the proper sequence of the calendar, which is based on a sevenfold pattern. The details of the calendar, with its sabbaths and set times, the commandments, the particulars of the cult and the priestly tradition, the heavenly tablets, the oaths and covenants, the tradition of the Merkavah, the sacred song and the liturgical tradition—all are rooted in angelic revelation. The angels are the heavenly witnesses to the Covenant, in parallel to the priests, who fulfil that function on earth.

Angels and priests together also confirm the mythical, mystical conception of open passageways, as it were, between heaven and earth, through which angels and priests are constantly ascending and descending, in the past, the present, and the future. Angels and saints were frequently present in spirit in the time and place of

---

[59] Testament of Levi 8: 10 (Charlesworth (ed.), *OT Pseudepigrapha*, i. 791).   [60] 1 En. 28–32.

[61] Jub. 4: 25. There is some uncertainty as to the geographical name here translated as 'southern mount'. Wintermute, in the Charlesworth edn., renders it as 'Mount Qater', which might be associated with the Hebrew root *q-ṭ-r* of the word for 'incense' and perhaps translated as 'Mount of Incense' (cf. Wintermute's note n *ad loc.*: Charlesworth (ed.), *OT Pseudepigrapha*, ii. 63). Similarly, the name of Mount Moriah might be associated with the Hebrew word *mor*, meaning 'myrrh', one of the ingredients of the Temple incense.   [62] Jub. 65: 11–12; 106.

[63] Gen. 8: 20–2; Jub. 6; 3–4.   [64] BT *Ker.* 6a.

[65] Jub. 16: 21–34. Cf. Ben Sira 24: 15.   [66] 1 Kgs. 6: 23; cf. 1 Chr. 28: 18.

[67] See p. 162 above.   [68] 1 En. 93: 2.

the authors of the secessionist priestly literature, as in the Blessings Scroll: 'the holy angels in their whole congregation';[69] 'in them and all his hosts and angels . . . to serve man and to minister to him';[70] or in the account given in the War Scroll: 'For God is with you and His holy angels will be present in your congregation, and His holy name shall be invoked upon you';[71] 'For the multitude of the Holy Ones is with You in heaven, and the host of the angels in Your holy abode . . . For You are [   ], O God, in the glory of Your kingdom, and the congregation of Your Holy Ones is among us for everlasting succour . . . and the King of Glory is with us together with the Holy Ones.'[72]

Further indication of angelic presence is provided by the stringent laws of purity and impurity that the Community prescribed: 'None of these shall come to hold office among the congregation of the men of renown, for the Angels of Holiness are [with] their [congre]gation.'[73] A similar message is conveyed by the War Scroll, which describes the way in which the Sons of Light will take part in both heaven and earth, and forbids the participation of unclean persons, for the presence of angels is conditional upon the purity of the congregation: 'And no man shall go down with them on the day of battle who is not pure because of his "fount" [= bodily impurity], for the holy angels shall be with their hosts'; 'Whoever shall not be pure because of a nocturnal emission on that night shall not go with them to the battle, for the holy angels shall be with their formations together . . .'.[74]

Such particular attention to ritual purity and cleanliness in time of war is learned from Deuteronomy 23: 10–15, where we are told, 'Since the Lord God moves about in your camp . . . let your camp be holy.' It serves to stress the continuity between the biblical world and the world of the Community, but it also illustrates an important difference between the Qumranic and biblical understanding and usage of the Hebrew word *elohim*, generally translated as 'God' or 'gods'. In biblical tradition this word is indeed understood for the most part (but not always!) in that sense; whereas in the priestly tradition it is frequently understood as a plural designation for the angels. (Thus, for example, the biblical verse already

---

[69] 4Q289, frg. 1a, 5 (*DJD* XI, 68–9).   [70] 4Q381, frg. 1, 10–11 (*DJD* XI, 92, 94).

[71] 11Q14, frg. iii, 14–15 (*DJD* XXIII, 247–8; García Martínez and Tigchelaar, *Study Edition*, ii. 1211).   [72] War Scroll XII, 1, 6–7 (Vermes, *CDSSIE*, 175).

[73] 1Q28a, II, 8 (*DJD* I, 110; cf. Vermes, *CDSSIE*, 159); see also *DJD* XXIII, 247, 248. Cf. War Scroll XIII, 10: 'You appointed the Prince of Light from ancient times to come to our support' (Vermes, *CDSSIE*, 177).

[74] War Scroll VII, 5–6 (cf. Vermes, *CDSSIE*, 171); War Scroll fragments from Cave 4 (4Q491), l. 10 (Vermes, *CDSSIE*, 184). Compare: 'Who is like your people Israel which you have chosen for yourself from all the peoples of the lands; the people of the saints of the Covenant, instructed in the laws, and learned in wisdom . . . who have heard the voice of Majesty and have seen the Angels of Holiness' (War Scroll X, 8–10; Vermes, *CDSSIE*, 173). Similar passages abound throughout Qumran literature, for example in the Damascus Document (4Q266, frg. 8 i, 7–9: *DJD* XVIII, 63–4; cf. García Martínez and Tigchelaar, *Study Edition*, i. 593): 'And anyone feeble-minded and insane, those with eyes too weak to see, and the lame or one who stumbles, or a deaf person, or an under-age boy, none of these shall enter the Congregation, for the holy angels are amongst them.'

quoted several times here, 'And Enoch walked with *ha'elohim*', may also read either as 'with God' or 'with the angels'.) The holy angels who protect the righteous at the End of Days are described in Enoch's letter: 'He will set a guard of holy angels upon all the righteous and holy ones, and they shall guard them as the apple of the eye until all evil and all sin are brought to an end.'[75] Angels appointed to administer reward and punishment, or to ensure the eternity of the laws of nature and the march of history, are a constant feature of Enoch's heavenly journeys.

The affinity between the holy angels, the heavenly guardians of the Covenant, and the earthly guardians of the Covenant in the Community is conditional upon strict observance of the sabbath, as we learn from Jubilees, which lays emphasis on the sacred seven-based pattern; and on strict observance of the commandments and the festivals—appointed times—all of which are closely bound up with sanctity, purity, cessation of routine activity, and the maintenance of the sacred service as dictated by the calendar of weeks, that is, the solar calendar. These conditions are essential for the Community to be defined as *yaḥad*, a 'togetherness' or commonalty of priests and angels, joint guardians of the Covenant of sabbaths and appointed times, of sacred lore, and of a cultic and liturgical order common to heavenly and earthly beings, set out in an eternal sequence based on the weeks, sabbaths, and festivals of the solar calendar.

Somewhat generalizing, one might say that angels are not only the major subject of belief in the priestly literature, but also, as it were, an 'invention' or 'formation' of the priestly literature; they are the allies of the sons of Aaron, the members of the tribe of Levi, who minister in the holy precincts. This fact is the basis for their presence or absence in various bodies of literature, whether those that aim to confirm the priestly myth or those that wish to reject or weaken it. The angels are seen as a source of holiness and knowledge, testimony and revelation, authority and tradition, as witnesses to the Covenant and guardians of the cycles of cosmic time revealed in the seven-based calendar—in the mythological past, when there were no boundaries between heaven and earth. As such, they are a source of strength for those who have no power in earthly existence, a source of validity for the eternity of the cult that bridges the gap between heaven and earth. They also guarantee an eschatological future in which there will be no such boundaries, in which a new order will be established, a sacred order maintained by priests and angels, guardians of the Covenant and the testimony; and at the same time, evil will be obliterated on earth and light and perfection will reign over all. This reliance on heavenly entities as a source of validity and authority for the true order of things, beyond the borders of time and place, is reinforced simultaneously with heightened remonstration against a chaotic reality, against arbitrary usurpation of authority on earth; it is indeed further evidence of the fierce controversy over the traditions and authority of the cult, as control over these traditions was gradually expropriated by new forces, relying on other authority.

[75] 1 En. 100: 5.

The angels, expressing the eternal order dependent on the order of the universe and the laws of nature maintained through oaths and covenants, testify to an eternal metahistorical order founded on covenants between heaven and earth, a reality transcending arbitrary, earthly existence and its chaotic manifestations. They guarantee a deterministic link between beginning and end, negating a reality that the secessionist priests refused to recognize; they embody the continuity of the sacred service in the heavenly sanctuary—the very origin and fount of the priestly service, and therefore a re-creation of the real, true sacred service. While the books of Jubilees, Enoch, Aramaic Levi, and Testament of Levi describe the origins of the affinity between priests and angels, the oaths and covenants and the common mythological past, the Songs of the Sabbath Sacrifice and the Blessings Scroll celebrate the joint cultic world of priests and angels. The angels exemplify the continuity of the ritual shared by earthly priests, on the one hand, and 'sons of heaven' or 'priests of the inner sanctum', on the other; it is a ritual based on the solar calendar, beyond the boundaries of earthly time and place. The joint future is described in the War Scroll, where it is the angels that assure victory in the seventh eschatological battle and guarantee the eternal future of the Community.

The people of the Community, desirous of restoring traditional authority to its rightful place in the terrestrial world, in all its austerity, saw themselves as living in the heavenly world, relying on the supernatural authority of the angels who were actually present among them and joined them in worship. The members of the Community built an alternative mythical, mystical world, in which the ritual was performed in a strict, permanent order based on an angelic revelation and maintained together with the 'children of heaven' in a cyclic, sevenfold rhythm of weeks of days and weeks of years. The march of world history from beginning to end depends on the denizens of the supernal worlds and their priestly counterparts on earth, who regulate their lives by the solar calendar and the concomitant order of ritual and liturgy. The members of the Community experienced, through the sacred priestly ritual observed in accordance with the seven-based cyclic order, the actual presence of the angels among them; this visionary presence, celebrated in song and prayer, was bound up in their view with laws of sanctity and purity, through book, narrative, and counting. The angels were envisaged in a priestly guise; and the number seven—which for the members of the Community embodied both sacred time and sacred place, cult and calendar, oath, Covenant, and sacred service, indeed, the very essence of all manifestations of divine order—became the basic characteristic of the angelic and priestly participants in the sacred service in heaven and on earth.

The Songs of the Sabbath Sacrifice, which testify to the power of the sevenfold priestly ritual in angelic vision, offer numerous beautiful descriptions of the angelic priests discharging their duties in the seven heavenly sanctuaries, gathering in teams of seven to minister every sabbath: 'Every statute they confirm to the seven eternal councils/secrets; for He established them for Himself as the holiest of the holy ones who serve in the holy of holies.'[76] Those who perform the holy service in the 'lofty heavens' are 'priests of the inner sanctum who serve before the King of holiest holiness', the 'seven chief princes', 'seven deputy princes', and 'seven priests of the inner sanctum', who officiate in roles equivalent to those of the priests in the earthly Temple: 'The seventh among the chief princes will bless in the name of His holiness'; 'the seventh among the deputy princes' will bless 'seven times with seven words of wondrous exaltations'. Or 'with its seven wondrous blessings, and he will bless the King of all the eternal holy ones seven times with seven words of wondrous blessing'; 'seven times with seven words of wondrous rejoicing. Psalm of praise-song by the tongue of the seventh of the chief princes, a mighty praise-song to the God of holiness with its seven wondrous praise-songs'.[77]

The earthly priests, serving in seven-day courses, take part in oaths and invocations, uttering words of praise and exaltation together with the angels, who offer sacrifices and accompany them with the Songs of the Sabbath Sacrifice—paeans of praise in recurring patterns of seven psalms and songs chanted by seven 'chief princes'. The differences between terrestrial and celestial are blurred because of this cultic co-operation and the phraseology of worshippers in the lower and upper worlds. One frequently finds explicit descriptions of angels in terms appropriate to priests serving in the earthly sanctuary: 'priests of the lofty heavens who draw near', 'ministers of the Countenance in His glorious *devir*', 'priests of the inner sanctum who serve before the King of His holiest holiness', 'He established for Himself priests of the inner sanctum, the holiest of the holy ones.'[78] Conversely, there are descriptions of earthly priests that display obvious angelic inspiration, ranging from the same names to attribution of heavenly knowledge, or participation in heavenly song and service in sevenfold patterns of time, place, and cult. In a fragment of a long, detailed priestly blessing in the Blessings Scroll, referring to angels and humans as one, in words markedly different from the standard formulation, we find the high priest compared to the supreme archangel:

> . . . May you be as an Angel of the Countenance in the Abode of Holiness
> And may the glory of the God be before you
> And his magnificence upon you all around,
> As you serve in the Temple of the Kingdom
> And cast lots in company with the Angels of the Countenance,
> In common council [with the Holy Ones for] everlasting ages
> And time without end;
> For [you shall teach His st]atutes.
> May He make you hol[y among] His people,
> And a [great] light to the world with knowledge,
> And to enlighten the face of the Many [with Your teaching.

[76] Newsom, *Songs*, 89.
[77] Newsom, *Songs*, 187–9; see ibid., concordance; cf. *DJD* XI, 243–4, and ibid. 247, for a discussion of these various 'septuples'.   [78] Newsom, *Songs*, 89.

And may He place upon your head] a crown to the Holy of Holies.
For [you shall be] holy to Him and glorify His Name and His holiness. . . .[79]

The comparison of the high priest to the Angel of the Countenance and the reference to his service with the angels of the Countenance[80] recall the description of the Angel of the Countenance in Jubilees who, in the third month, after the giving of the Torah, dictates to Moses on Mount Sinai 'the divisions of the times of the Torah and of predestined time according to the weeks of their jubilees'.[81] The angel also tells Moses the story of the creation of the world and of the angels who observe sabbaths and festivals.[82] It is the Angel of the Countenance who relates what is written on 'the tablets which he placed in my hands so that I might write for you the law of each time and according to each division of its days'[83] and describes the history of the fifty jubilees that elapsed from the Creation to the theophany at Sinai, as set out in the fifty chapters of Jubilees.

The angel of Jubilees and of the Blessings Scroll is also associated with the founder of the priestly myth, Enoch son of Jared, the seventh patriarch, a figure signifying light and perfection, eternity and paradise, taken to heaven by the Angel of the Countenance, as hinted in the Wisdom of Ben Sira: 'Few have ever been created on earth like Enoch, for he was taken up to the Countenance';[84] 'Enoch was found perfect and walked with the Lord and was taken, a sign of knowledge, for all generations.'[85] This is made explicit in Jubilees: 'And he was taken from among the children of men, and we led him to the Garden of Eden.'[86] The angel–priest connection is mentioned in 2 Enoch 67: 2: 'And the angels hurried and grasped Enoch and carried him up to the highest heaven, where the Lord received him and made him stand before him for all eternity.' This account ultimately reappears as the mystical tradition of Enoch-Metatron, the Angel/Prince of the Countenance, serving as high priest in the seventh *heikhal* in the supernal worlds. The faint biblical tradition of the Angel of the Countenance, of whom God says, 'for My Name is in him',[87] is also related to this conception.

This account of Enoch, the seventh patriarch, who learned the solar calendar from the Angel of the Countenance and brought down to earth reading, writing, counting, calculation, and knowledge, and whose figure is associated with sign and number, with the 'great luminary' and the sabbath, may well be linked in some way with the description cited above of the high priest as responsible for divine justice, as the great luminary, crowned, perhaps in the likeness of the sun's rays—in the description of God in 1 Enoch 14: 21 we read: 'as for His gown, which was shining more brightly than the sun, it was whiter than any snow'.

---

[79] 1Q28b, IV, 25–31 (cf. Vermes, *CDSSIE*, 376). For earlier readings see *DJD* I, 126; Licht, *Rule Scroll*, 285–6; Habermann, *Judaean Desert Scrolls*, 63–8, 162. Cf. the descriptions in Ben Sira of Aaron (45: 6–24) and the high priest (50: 1–21). [80] Community Rule XI, 7–8.

[81] Jub. 1: 26, 29.   [82] Jub. 2: 1–3, 17–19.   [83] Jub. 50: 13.

[84] Ben Sira 49: 20.   [85] Ben Sira 44: 19.   [86] Jub. 4: 23.   [87] Exod. 23: 20; Isa. 63: 9.

The blessing bestowed in the Blessings Scroll on the sons of Zadok, the priests ministering in the sanctuary, also compares them to the congregation of holy ones, associated in Jubilees with 'the spirits which minister before Him, the angels of the Countenance, and the angels of holiness'.[88] No distinction is made in this blessing between the terrestrial sacred precinct and its celestial counterpart: 'May the Lord bless you from His holy abode; may He set you as a splendid jewel in the midst of the congregation of Holy Ones! May He renew for you the Covenant of His priesthood and make you a source of knowledge for the holy congregation.'[89]

The worship of the priests' celestial counterparts is described in similar terms in the Songs of the Sabbath Sacrifice: 'To praise Your glory wondrously with the *elim* [godlike beings] of knowledge and the praiseworthiness of Your royal power together with the holiest of the holy ones . . . Exalt His glory in all the heavens of His realm and in all the lofty heights wondrous psalms according to all [their insight do they sing, and all] the glory of the King of godlike beings do they declare in the habitations where they have their station.'[90] The most common designations of the angels in Songs of the Sabbath Sacrifice involve the word *da'at*, 'knowledge' ('godlike beings of knowledge', 'those who establish knowledge'); these are outnumbered only by the number seven.

The most characteristic link with holiness, wonder, glory, and the knowledge of the servants of God, guardians of the sanctuary, is common to angels and priests; it depends on the seven-based reckoning of the sabbath, the oath of the Covenant, and the calendar of the festivals or appointed times. Parallel to the angelic connection of the priesthood and its association with holy creatures and angels of the Countenance who observe the sabbaths and the appointed times; with the great luminary, the crown and the Holy of Holies; with the sacred liturgy; with the shining white holy vestments and the oil of anointing;[91] with fire, gold, and incense—parallel to that affinity we find the characteristic sevenfold pattern of the mystical priestly sacred song. This song is dedicated to describing the celestial priesthood referred to in the Bible in 'He makes the spirits His ministering angels, fiery flames His servants'[92] and to describing the praises uttered by those angels. This sevenfold pattern is found in the songs that refer to 'a burnt-offering for each and every Sabbath'[93] and are arranged around a liturgical calendar of weeks in cycles of thirteen sabbaths each. *Shevuah*, 'oath', is an appeal to the Divine Name; *shivah*, 'seven', is the basis of the cycle of divine time preserved by angels and priests; and *shabat*, 'sabbath', is the time appointed for the sacred service, conditioned by sevenfold counting and repetitive number. The phrase *shivah beshivah* recurs constantly in the Songs of the Sabbath Sacrifice, recalling the biblical phrase *shabat beshabato*, 'each and every Sabbath';[94] it signifies the liturgical link between the

---

[88] Jub. 2: 2.

[89] 1Q28b, III, 25–7 (cf. Vermes, *CDSSIE*, 375). For different readings see *DJD* I, 124; Licht, *Rule Scroll*, 281.   [90] Newsom, *Songs*, 111.   [91] 1 En. 14: 21; 2 En. 22: 8; 3 En. 1–20.

[92] Ps. 104: 4.   [93] Num. 28: 10.   [94] Ibid.

denizens of the upper worlds and those of the lower, founded on sequences each containing seven proclamations of God's praise or seven formulations of his blessing, chanted in a seven-based order, alternating by sabbaths, by seven praising angels/priests in seven supernal Heikhalot/sanctuaries that bind together *shivah*, 'seven', and *shevuah*, 'oath':

Psalm of exaltation by the tongue] of the third of the chief princes, an exaltation of his faithfulness to the king of lofty angels, with its seven wondrous exaltations, he will exalt the God of the lofty angels seven times with seven words of wondrous exaltations.

Psalm of exaltation by the tongue of the fourth to the Warrior who is above all [heavenly beings] with its seven wondrous powers; and he will praise the God of power seven times with seve[n] words of [wondrous] prais[e.

Psa]lm of thanksgiving by the tongue of the fif[th] to the [K]in[g] of Glory with its seven wondrous thanks[gi]vings; he will give thanks to the God of glory s[even times with seven wo]rds of wondrous thanksgivings.

. . . .

Psalms of [praise-song by the to]ngue of the seventh of the [chief] prin[ces], a mighty praise-song to [the Go]d of hol[iness] with i[ts] se[ven] wondrous [praise-songs. And] he will sing praise [to] the Kin[g of holi]ness seven times with [seven wo]rds of [wondrous] praise-[song.

Sev]en psa[lms of His blessings; seven psalm]s of the magnification [of his righteousness, seven psalms of the] exaltation of [His] kingdom; [seven] psalms of the praise of [His glory; sev]en ps[alms of thanksgiving for His wonders; seven psalms of re]joi[cing] in His strength; seven [psalms of] praise for His holiness, the generations of the exalted chiefs will bless seven times with seven wondrous words, words of exaltation. The first] of the chi[ef] princes [will bless] in the name of the g[lo]ry of God [all the . . . with seven] wondrous words . . .[95]

The song ends after some twenty more lines of such ceremonial declarations, in which various speakers, expressing themselves in seven wondrous words and seven words of holiness, pronounce blessings linking the septuples of time with septuples of cult:

[The sev]enth among the chief princes will bless in the name of His holiness all the holy ones who establish know[ledge] with sev[en] words of [His] wondrous holiness; [and he will bless] all who exalt His statutes with sev[en] wondrous [wor]ds, to be as strong shields; and he will bless all who are app[ointed for] righteous[ness, who pr]aise His glorious kingdom [. . .] forever, with seven [wondrous] wo[rds, to be for] eternal peace. And all the [chief] princes [will bless togethe]r the godlike hea[ven]ly [beings] in [His holy name with] all [their] sevenfold app[ointed testimonies; and] they will bless those appointed for righteousness; and the bles[sed . . . bles]sed for e[ve]r[. . .] to them . . .[96]

Oath, as an appeal in the name of the unseen God, is associated with creating barriers, with the passage from chaos and formlessness, without limit, measure, or

---

[95] Newsom, *Songs*, 187–8, 193. Cf. *DJD* XI, 256–7, 260–1.
[96] Newsom, *Songs*, 189, 194–5, and see Newsom's discussion ibid. 195–7; cf. *DJD* XI, 257, 260–1.

number, to Creation, which is founded upon boundaries, limits, and cycles. The
Divine Name is associated with invocation and oath, which impose limits upon the
order of Creation and the laws of nature, linking the eternity of time and place with
sign and number. It is the formal principle underlying existence, the antithesis of
chaos, which endows the world with its sacred image, signifying the world's connection with its divine roots, with an oath in God's name. God the Creator sets the
eternal limits of time and place, as expressed by the Psalmist: 'It was You who set in
place the orb of the sun; You fixed all the boundaries of the earth; summer and
winter—You made them';[97] 'He established the earth on its foundations, so that it
shall never totter . . . You set bounds they must not pass so that they never again
cover the earth.'[98] These boundaries are perpetuated by oath, bound up with the
divine names which constitute a perceptible, verbal representation of the hidden
divine essence of orderly existence. The pronunciation of these names by the
priests and the angels—what we call invocation in God's name—is associated with
the eternity of the natural order:

He spoke to Michael to disclose to him his secret name so that he would memorize this
secret name of his, so that he would call it up in an oath . . . the hidden things and this
power of this oath, for it is power and strength itself . . . These are the secrets of this oath
. . . The heaven was suspended . . . By it the earth is founded upon the water . . . from the
beginning of creation and forever! By that oath, the sea was created; and he put down for
it a foundation of sand which cannot be transgressed . . . By the same oath the sun and
the moon complete their courses of travel, and do not deviate from the laws (made) for
them, from the beginning (of creation): and forever![99]

Oath, *shevuah*, is related to the number seven, *shivah*, which has governed sacred
time since the seven days of Creation, through the cycle of sabbaths and appointed
times. It is also related thereby to the sanctified reckoning of seven days of purification, whereby one is transported from the realm of numberless, measureless defilement and death to the realm of sanctity and purity, which bear the eternal imprint
of number and counting, of knowledge and statute, of cycle, period, and season.
Oath is also related to the passage from a legendary, mythical world, not subject to
the laws of nature, to the earthly cultic world, where the laws of nature prevail.
This relationship is established by the 'seven wondrous words', through the seven-
based sacred service of the priestly courses in the Temple, each serving its appointed week, offering sacrifices counted in sevens and tending the lights of the
seven-branched lampstand.

　　The angels' language in Songs of the Sabbath Sacrifice, with its weave of ceremonial declarations, oaths, and sevenfold liturgical patterns, is replete with
phraseology interpreting the voices of celestial praise (figuring in the Bible in
Ezekiel 1: 24; 3: 12–13; and in Psalms). Such phrases, prominently featuring the
word *sheva*, or, more precisely, the root *sh-v'a*, in numerous derivatives and

---

[97] Ps. 74: 16–17.　　　[98] Ps. 104: 5, 9.　　　[99] 1 En. 69: 14–20.

combinations with the connotations of oath and Covenant, week and sabbath, name and number, sanctity and purity—these phrases create a numinous, all-pervading splendour, uniting the angelic world of the Merkavah and the priestly world of the Temple. The divine world of the Merkavah is perceived as if through a cyclic, sevenfold mirror, reflected in the liturgical cycles of the Songs of the Sabbath Sacrifice, which celebrate oath and Covenant every seven days: 'seven times with seven words of wondrous exaltations'; 'seven times with seven words of wondrous praise'; 'seven wondrous songs of joy'; 'seven psalms of praise for his holiness'; 'seven words of his marvellous glory'; 'seven words of lofty purity'; 'a mighty praise-song to the God of holiness with seven . . .'—and countless other, similar phrases. Such is the typical style of the 'praise-songs' chanted by the seven chiefs of the hosts of angels that minister in heaven, singing, praising, and blessing, every sabbath of the year, in seven supernal sanctuaries whose appearance and nature were inspired by the now ruined earthly Temple and *devir* (the Holy of Holies), and by the eternity of cosmic order with its sevenfold structure as represented in the heavenly sanctuaries. In the imagination of the secessionist priests, who linked the seventh part of sacred time with the seventh part of sacred place, these became seven sanctuaries, seven *devirim*, seven *merkavot* or Chariot Thrones, and seven angelic chief priests, charging the universe upon oath to continue its existence while they proclaim the Lord's name and proclaim his praises in the upper worlds:

And there is a voice of blessing from the chiefs of His *devir*. . . .

And the crafted furnishings of the *devir* hasten with wondrous psalms in the *devir* of wonder, *devir* to *devir* with the sound of holy multitudes.

And all their crafted furnishings . . . and the chariots of his *devir* give praise together, And their cherubim and their *ofanim* bless wondrously the chiefs of the divine structure. And they praise Him in His holy *devir*. . . .

Loftiness, seven wondrous territories according to the ordinances of His sanctuaries, the chiefs of the princes of the wondrous priesthoods. . . .[100]

The angelic ritual in the world of the Merkavah is the conceptual foundation for the priestly service in the Temple, just as the 'heavenly tablets'—whose laws, set out in Jubilees, are observed by the angels, witnesses to the Covenant in heaven—are the foundation for the tablets of the Covenant, the tablets of the Testimony, kept by the earthly priests. Such expressions as 'the seven *devirim* of the priesthoods', 'seven priesthoods in the wondrous sanctuary for the seven holy councils', 'his glorious chariots . . . which move continuously with the glory of the wondrous chariots' testify to the way the concepts of sacred space, divorced from the Temple and the Chariot Throne in the *devir*, incorporated in a personified sevenfold structure in heaven, have been combined with the sacred ritual of the seven chief princes of the angelic priesthood, who celebrate sacred time with the Songs of the Sabbath Sacrifice, likewise structured in sevenfold liturgical patterns revolving

---

[100] Newsom, *Songs*, 226, 229; and see ibid., concordance. Cf. 11Q17 (*DJD* XXIII, 269, 270).

around the solar calendar. This juxtaposition reflects a mystical chronotopy, imbued with the number seven, which fuses time, place, and ritual, perpetuating in a sevenfold pattern sacred place—represented by seven *merkavot* and Temples; sacred time—measured in sevens in relation to the weeks of the solar calendar and the ever-recurring sevenfold pattern of sabbaths; and sacred ritual—the angelic and priestly order of worship, celebrated by groups of seven reciting sevenfold liturgical formulas, binding together sign and number, solemnizing the oath that guarantees the eternity of heaven and earth, of time measured by the motion and cycles of the celestial bodies:

his secret name so that he would memorize this secret name of his, so that he would call it up in an oath . . . These are the secrets of this oath . . . The heaven was suspended . . . the earth is founded . . . By that oath, the sea was created; and he put down for it a foundation of sand which cannot be transgressed . . . And by that oath the depths are made firm; they stand still and do not move from their places from the beginning of creation; and forever! By the same oath the sun and the moon complete their courses of travel, and do not deviate from the laws (made) for them, from the beginning (of creation): and forever! And by the same oath the stars complete their courses of travel; he calls their names and they respond, from the beginning of creation; and forever! . . . This oath has become dominant over them; they are preserved by it and their paths are preserved by it so that their courses of travel do not perish.[101]

In sevens and sevens it completes all its light in the east, and in each seven parts it completes all its darkness in the west.[102]

The cosmic, heavenly order of the world of the Merkavah stands in a two-way relationship with its earthly reflection in time and space, not dissimilar to the relationship between myth and mysticism, on the one hand, and cult, on the other. Namely, the concealed is reflected in the revealed, through the unification of sacred time, space, and ritual; while, conversely, the revealed, being symbolic, ceremonial, and cyclic, is reflected in the hidden, as is clearly demonstrated by Merkavah tradition. The concept pairs sanctity and Temple, Shekhinah and sanctuary, rider on the cherubim and Merkavah and cherubim, angel and priest, sabbath/seven and oath, Name and invocation, secret and wonder—song and praise, divine appointed times and tablets of Testimony, or time and calendar— these pairs illustrate the relationship between the divine, the abstract, the infinite, and the eternal, on the one hand, and the tangible, humanly accessible representation, on the other; or the relationship between holy, hidden, eternal, cosmic infinity and its tangible, microcosmic representation in the sacred realm, embodying the conception of macrocosmic order. This two-way relationship between concealed and revealed bridges the chasm between macrocosmic infinity, as seen in the world of the heavenly Merkavah and its angels, and its microcosmic counterpart— the earthly Temple and its priests. It is a bridge consisting of tangible cultic and

---

[101] 1 En. 69: 14–25.   [102] 1 En. 74: 3.

liturgical concepts reflecting the divine, eternal, and cosmic with its laws and cycles, signs, infinite and finite numbers, both abstract and palpable.

The different stages of mystical priestly tradition present variegated pictures of the seven-based subdivision of time and space. Such are the representations of seven-based time and the descriptions of the seven firmaments and the heavenly entities described in sevenfold patterns and in a liturgical context, ranging from the seven-branched lampstand to 'seven phoenixes and seven cherubim and seven six-winged beings, having but one voice and singing in unison'.[103] Many other passages in the Enoch literature describe the angelic liturgy and the heavenly ritual in terms of sevens and holy song.[104] These motifs reach their peak in the Songs of the Sabbath Sacrifice, which combine septuples of time, place, and ritual, perpetuating the seven-based order of the universe, around images of the Merkavah.

Thus, we see that the angels, heavenly counterparts of the priests, were formed in the secessionist priestly literature in the image of the priesthood, the Temple, and the sacred service, while the priests themselves wove a complex myth linking those ministering in the earthly sanctuary to their heavenly counterparts in the supernal shrines. The angels' earthly counterparts, the Qumran priests, for their part, looked to the image of the high priesthood in the time of Moses and Aaron, as described in 1 Chronicles 5, where the Bible recounts the priestly generations from Levi, Kohath, Amram, and Aaron to the end of the First Temple period. This priesthood, associated with the tradition of the House of Zadok,[105] is described by the prophet-priest Ezekiel, who highlights the divine election of the Zadokites and their sacred world. In chapters 40–8 Ezekiel sets out the details of the future Temple and the priesthood, essentially drawing an ideal picture of the Temple and its cult. His account singles out the Zadokite priests—priests of the most distinguished ancestry, descended from Zadok the priest, who carried the Ark of God in David's time and anointed his son Solomon as king. Similarly, the priestly myth, as clearly emerges from many Qumran writings, considers the Zadokite priests, descendants of Aaron, as bearers of the tradition of the high priesthood in the past—from the time of the Davidic monarchy and of Solomon's Temple:

For, behold, a son is born to Jesse, son of Perez, son of Ju[dah] . . . to build the house for the Lord, God of Israel. . . . But his son, the younger, [will build it and Zadok the Priest] will officiate there first of [the sons of Ph]inehas [and Aaron,] and he will [propitiate] him [all the days of his life and will bless in ev]ery [a]bode from the heaven[s, because] the Beloved of the Lor[d] will dwell in safety for [all the] days, [and] his people will dwell for ever.[106]

---

[103] 2 En. 19: 6.

[104] For discussions of the various sources see Gruenwald, 'Angelic Song'; Bar-Ilan, *Mysteries of Jewish Prayer*.   [105] 1 Chr. 5: 34–41.

[106] 4Q522, frg. 9, ll. 6–7 (*DJD* XXV, 55–6). This Qumranic text, known as the Joshua Apocryphon, is essentially a prophetic vision of the construction of the Temple by David, seventh in line from

But the Zadokite priests also embody the ideal priesthood of the future, who continue to walk the hallowed path of the high-priestly dynasty descended from Eleazar and Phinehas, the sons of Aaron, protectors of law and order, of Torah and calendar, divinely elected, ever mindful of the requirements of absolute sanctity and purity, overseeing the sacred service from time immemorial. This priestly myth was of prime importance in the world of the secessionist priests, who in fact claimed descent from the House of Zadok. The position of the prophet Ezekiel in this context raises interesting questions in regard to the relationship between the historical past of the First Temple period and the invocation of that past in the Hasmonaean period.

There are four passages in Ezekiel where the divine choice of the Zadokite priests is made explicit, as well as their consequent exclusive right to perform the sacred service and their responsibility for the altar. These passages may indicate a latent controversy with other pretenders to the priesthood; whatever the case, the prophet-priest undoubtedly reserves a special, divinely appointed, place for the House of Zadok, descendants of Aaron and his sons, who were 'set apart . . . to be consecrated as most holy':[107]

the priests who perform the duties of the altar—they are the descendants of Zadok, who alone of the descendants of Levi may approach the Lord to minister to Him.[108]

You shall give to the levitical priests who are of the stock of Zadok, and so eligible to minister to Me—declares the Lord God . . .[109]

Abraham (Abraham, Isaac, Jacob, Judah, Perez, Jesse, David), and relates to the beginnings of the Zadokite priesthood. This sevenfold order does not agree with biblical historiography, and may be a consequence of the poor condition of the text in the manuscript. According to biblical historiography, David and Zadok are the fourteenth generation of the patrilinear dynasties of Judah and Levi. The privilege of performing the sacred service was entrusted to the sons of Aaron, as told in Exodus, but the priestly line of Abiathar and Eli was discredited even before the construction of Solomon's Temple (1 Sam. 2: 34; 2 Sam. 8: 17; 1 Kgs. 2: 26–7; according to 1 Chr. 24: 3, Ahimelech 'son of Abiathar' was descended from Ithamar, whereas Zadok was descended from Aaron's other son, Eleazar); only Zadokite priests served as high priests in the First Temple (1 Kgs. 2: 35; 4: 2; 1 Chr. 5: 29–41). The genealogical list in 1 Chr. presents the lineage of Joshua son of Jehozadak, who served as high priest at the beginning of the Second Temple period; this source associates him with the House of Zadok. Cf. the parallel list, which continues from Jeshua (= Joshua) to Jaddua son of Jonathan (Ezra 7: 1–5; Neh. 11: 11; 12: 10–11, 26). See Japhet, *I and II Chronicles*, 150–2. For the place of these priests in biblical tradition see 2 Sam. 15: 24–8; 1 Kgs. 1: 34–45; Ezek. 40–8; Ezra 7: 1–5; Neh. 11: 11; 12: 12; 1 Chr. 9: 11. The account of Hezekiah's reign in 2 Chr. 31: 10 refers to the high priest as descended from the Zadokite line: 'The High Priest Azariah, of the house of Zadok, replied to him . . .'. Japhet (*I and II Chronicles*, 966) suggests that this tradition represents a projection of historical reality from 1 Kgs. 4: 2 to the literary context of Chronicles. Josephus continues the line to Onias son of Jaddua (Onias I; *Antiquities*, XI. viii. 7), whose family held the post throughout the Ptolemaic period, up to the Hasmonaean revolt. Similarly Ben Sira 51: 29. For various traditions of the House of Zadok see Licht, *Rule Scroll*, 112–15; 246–7; Liver, 'Sons of Zadok'; id., *Bible Studies*; Cross, 'Early History'; North, 'Qumran Sadducees'; Schwartz, 'Two Aspects'; A. Baumgarten, *Flourishing of Jewish Sects*. For the sons of Zadok in Ezekiel's vision of the future Temple (Ezek. 40–8) see Zimmerli, *Ezekiel*, ii. 446, 456–64.

[107] 1 Chr. 23: 13.　　　　[108] Ezek. 40: 46.　　　　[109] Ezek. 43: 19.

But the levitical priests descended from Zadok, who maintained the service of My Sanctuary when the people of Israel went astray from Me—they shall approach Me to minister to Me; they shall stand before Me to offer Me fat and blood—declares the Lord God. They alone may enter My Sanctuary and they alone shall approach My table to minister to Me; and they shall keep My charge. And when they enter the gates of the inner court, they shall wear linen vestments. . . . They shall declare to My people what is sacred and what is profane, and inform them what is clean and what is unclean. In lawsuits, too, it is they who shall act as judges. . . . They shall preserve My teachings and My laws regarding all My appointed times; and they shall maintain the sanctity of My Sabbaths. . . . This shall be their portion, for I am their portion; and no holding shall be given them in Israel, for I am their holding.[110]

This consecrated area shall be for the priests of the line of Zadok, who kept My charge and did not go astray, as the Levites did when the people of Israel went astray. It shall be a special reserve for them out of the [total] reserve from the land, most holy, adjoining the territory of the Levites.[111]

This select status of the Zadokite priests, with their claimed lineage from Aaron, Eleazar, and Phinehas, charged in Ezekiel's vision with preservation of the covenants and commandments, of the sabbaths and 'appointed times' (festivals), their name associated with justice and righteousness, light and integrity, was an archetypal ideal which left its imprint on the Qumranites, who subordinated themselves to the leadership of the Zadokites in the spirit of Ezekiel's prophecy. They were convinced that their leadership was descended from the historical House of Zadok, and hence from Eleazar son of Aaron and his son Phinehas, through the line set out in detail in the genealogies of 1 Chronicles 1, Ezra 5, and Nehemiah 11 (in fact, in even earlier sources—2 Samuel and 2 Kings—though fragmentarily). The distinguished line was believed to culminate in the anonymous *moreh tsedek*, 'Teacher of Righteousness', the renewer of the Covenant, who is in fact designated in the Commentary on Psalms as 'the priest, the Teacher of Righteousness'.[112]

The people of Qumran called themselves 'House of Zadok', thus claiming to bear the hallowed tradition of the priesthood in the First Temple and the tradition of the House of David—the priesthood that had ministered in the Temple until the Hasmonaean period and that would minister, according to Ezekiel's vision, in the eschatological future.[113] The Qumran writings include detailed genealogies of

---

[110] Ezek. 44: 15–28.   [111] Ezek. 48: 11–12.

[112] 4Q171, III, ll. 15–16 (Vermes, *CDSSIE*, 489). The reader will recall the common root in Hebrew of the name *tsadok*, 'Zadok', and the noun *tsedek*, 'justice', 'righteousness' (see Ch. 1, n. 24, and p. 127 above).

[113] The sons of Zadok are mentioned, *inter alia*, in the Blessings Scroll (*DJD* I, 124; see n. 126 below); 'sons of Zadok the priests and the people of their Covenant' (1Q28a (Messianic Rule), I, 2; Vermes, *CDSSIE*, 157); 'under the authority of the sons of Zadok, the priests' (ibid. I, 24; Vermes, *CDSSIE*, 158; cf. Community Rule V, 2; Vermes, *CDSSIE*, 103); 'before the sons of Zadok, the priests' (Messianic Rule II, 3; Vermes, *CDSSIE*, 159); 'sons of Zadok, the priests, keepers of his Covenant and Seekers of his Will' (Community Rule V, 9; Vermes, *CDSSIE*, 104); 'The sons of Zadok are the elect of Israel, the men called by name, who shall stand at the end of days' (Damascus

the priesthood from the time of Moses and Aaron till the writers' times,[114] partly recalling the genealogies of 1 Chronicles 5: 27–41, which go up to the destruction of the First Temple.

The priestly dynasty of the House of Zadok came to a tragic end in the seventies and sixties of the second century BCE. The high priest Simeon II, known as Simeon the Just, had two sons: the high priest Onias III, who succeeded him, and the latter's brother Joshua–Jason, who aspired to usurp the post. When Antiochus IV Epiphanes came to power in 175 BCE, Jason, an advocate of Hellenization, bribed the Seleucid ruler to appoint him high priest, ousted his brother Onias, and officiated in that capacity from 175 to 172 BCE. Jason, in turn, was displaced by Menelaus, a member of the Tobiad family and one of the extremists among the Hellenizers. Menelaus, as high priest, co–operated with the desecration and Hellenization of the Temple. In 171 BCE an assassin acting on his behalf murdered Onias III in Antioch, as he feared the influence afforded to Onias by his legitimate claim to the high priesthood.

In sum, historical evidence places the fall of the Zadokite priests in the reign of Antiochus Epiphanes, in the wake of the struggles between the priestly brothers and between various factions supported either by the Ptolemies in Egypt or by the Seleucids in Syria; subsequently, the high priesthood was taken over by the Hasmonaeans. The process envisioned in the traditions of the sons of Zadok is in accord with this account. According to those traditions they served in the Temple in complete harmony up to the time of Ben Sira[115] in the eighties of the second

Document IV, 3–4 (Vermes, *CDSSIE*, 130), commenting on the verse Ezek. 44: 15, which refers to the sons of Zadok); 'until the coming of Zadok' (ibid. V, 5; Vermes, *CDSSIE*, 130). In the so–called Florilegium (4Q174, I, 16–18: *DJD* V, 53; García Martínez and Tigchelaar, *Study Edition*, i. 355), we read: 'This refers to those about whom it is written in the book of Ezekiel the Prophet [44: 10] that "They should no[t defile themselves any more with al]l their idols." This (refers to) the sons of Zadok and to the men of their Council, those who seek justice eagerly, who have come after them to the Council of the Community.'

An interesting variation is the occurrence of the term *benei tsedek*, 'Sons of Righteousness', in place of *benei tsadok*, 'sons of Zadok', as, for example, in a variant version (4QS MS E) of the Community Rule (IX, 14): '[He shall separate and we]igh the Sons of Righteousness according to their spirits'; see Charlesworth *et al.* (eds.), *Dead Sea Scrolls*, i. 89. There is probably some connection between the portrayal of the Community in eschatological times as a congregation of 'Sons of Righteousness' and their identification as the 'sons of Zadok'; see e.g. 11Q13, ll. 22–7 (*DJD* XXIII, 226, 230): '[And the congregation of all the Sons of Righteousness, those who] uphold the Covenant, who turn from walking [in] the way of the people. And your God is Melchizedek, who will save [them from the ha]nd of Belial . . .'. Surely it is no accident that the 'Teacher of Righteousness' is a scion of the House of Zadok; cf.: 'Interpreted, this concerns the Priest, the Teacher of [Righteousness, whom] God chose to stand before Him, for He established him to build for Himself the congregation of his true elect' (Commentary on Psalms (37: 22–3) = 4Q171, III, 14–17; cf. Vermes, *CDSSIE*, 489); '[Interpreted, this concerns] the Teacher of Righteousness, who [expounded the law to] his [Council] and to all who freely pledged themselves to join the elect of [God to keep the Law] in the Council of the *yahad*' (Commentary on Micah = 1Q14; cf. Vermes, *CDSSIE*, 472; García Martínez and Tigchelaar, *Study Edition*, i. 9). For the question of when the 'sons of Zadok' assumed leadership at Qumran see n. 122 below.

[114] *DJD* XXII, 155.　　　　　　　　　　　　　　　　　　[115] See Ben Sira 51: 29.

century BCE, but during the seventies their legitimacy was questioned and the position was taken over by the Hasmonaean dynasty in the sixties and fifties.

Josephus lists the priests of the House of Zadok who served as high priests before the Hasmonaeans,[116] as well as their objections to Hasmonaean aspirations and to the appointment of Mattathias' son Jonathan as high priest by the Seleucid ruler Alexander Balas in 152 BCE. At that time, Onias IV, the last Zadokite high priest, son of Onias III who had been assassinated in 171 BCE, established a rival temple in Egypt, which was in operation from 170 BCE to 74 CE, to protest the usurpation of the high priesthood by Menelaus and Alcimus, the Hellenizing priests who were appointed after bribing Antiochus Epiphanes,[117] and then by Jonathan the Hasmonaean. In addition, Onias claimed that the Temple in Jerusalem had lost its sanctity.[118] The Hasmonaeans had appropriated not only the high priesthood but the monarchy, and the combination of these two positions, both illegally usurped, aroused objections on the grounds of the privileged status of the House of Zadok regarding the priesthood[119] and biblical tradition, which reserved the monarchy for the tribe of Judah and the House of David.

An echo of these events may be discerned in the Qumranic work *Miktsat ma'asei hatorah* (MMT), written by priests who had seceded from the Temple in the wake of the Hasmonaean usurpation of the high priesthood. This work, dated by Qimron and Strugnell to the beginning of the Hasmonaean period, is concerned with controversies over laws relating to the Temple. Historians of halakhah have pointed out that the positions presented in the text reflect Sadducean halakhah, which predates the Hasmonaean period. This date also explains the parallels, in several areas of halakhah, between Jubilees, composed around 168 BCE, and Qumranic halakhah as represented by, for example, the Temple Scroll and MMT. All the laws treated in MMT are concerned with the Temple rituals, with purity and the sacrifices. Their basic premiss is that the Temple in Jerusalem is impure, defiled.

While in the real world the Zadokites had to contend with the loss of their rights in the Temple, they passionately justified those rights in a visionary world, vindicating their sacred sources, ritual manifestations, and super-temporal origin. Traces of this internal and external struggle may be found in Qumran literature, which we have seen to be associated with the Zadokites. There are various explanations of the term 'sons of Zadok' or 'Zadokites': a group of persons who identified with the biblical priesthood tradition, the sanctity and eternal authority of the

---

[116] *Antiquities*, x. viii. 6.

[117] 2 Macc. 3–4. On Onias IV, son of the murdered Onias III, who escaped to Leontopolis (to be equated with Heliopolis in Egypt, following Isa. 19: 18–19) and built a temple there, see Josephus, *War*, I. i. 1; VII. x. 2–4. However, Josephus dates this to 166 BCE, after Antiochus' desecration of the Temple, and erroneously ascribes the flight to Onias III. In *Antiquities* (XII. ix. 7; XX. x. 3) Onias IV is correctly identified, but with an incorrect date of 162 BCE, prompted by the appointment of Alcimus (Iakimos) as high priest in that year (officiated 162–160 BCE). See Bohak, *Joseph and Aseneth*, 19–40, 83–93.   [118] Josephus, *Antiquities*, XIII. iii. 1; *War*, VII. x. 2–3.

[119] 1 Chr. 5: 27–41 and the other traditions referred to above.

scriptures, who traced their lineage to the high priests who had ministered in the Temple from Solomon's day till Simeon the Just; or the designation of members of a priestly family which arrogated to itself the exclusive privilege to serve as high priests, together with their households and other supporters; or a generic term for opponents of the Hasmonaean priesthood, based on Ezekiel 40–8.

Whatever the true connotation of the term, the central position of the Zadokite priests as embodiments of the ideal priestly ethos in the Qumran community is unquestionable. The prominent priestly orientation of what I have called the literature of the secessionist priesthood, the intensity with which its authors rejected the defiled Temple and its desecrators, the controversy over the calendar and over matters of purity, the wide scope of the priestly traditions reflected in works found at Qumran and relating to the Temple, and the blessings showered on the sons of Zadok in some of the scrolls—all these corroborate the thesis that the authors of this literature were the ousted priests of the House of Zadok and their allies, heirs and creators of a rich priestly tradition.

Perhaps the prophetic future became a present reality for the members of the Community, who applied the eschatological elements of Ezekiel's vision to their own time, just as the authors of the *pesher* literature applied the prophecies of Micah, Nahum, and Habakkuk to the period of the Community. In the world picture of Qumran literature, the priests of the future in Ezekiel's vision of the Temple are associated with the future Temple service, to be performed after the Temple has been purged of all impure and wicked priests, when only the real guardians of the sacred charge, the priests of the House of Zadok, will remain. The sharp polemical tone of Ezekiel's prophecy about the sins of the priests who desecrated the Temple towards the end of the First Temple period—'Her priests have violated My Teaching: they have profaned what is sacred to Me, they have not distinguished between the sacred and the profane, they have not taught the difference between the clean and the unclean, and they have closed their eyes to My Sabbaths. I am profaned in their midst'[120]—aroused strong feelings among the secessionist priests, who claimed descent from the House of Zadok and considered themselves deprived by force of the priesthood by the Hasmonaean usurpers and desecrators of the Temple.[121] Their derogatory descriptions of their opponents, whom they accuse of following their own wilful desires and defiling the Temple, recall the language of Ezekiel, just as their priestly self-image and claim to Zadokite ancestry were clearly inspired by his prophecies.

In contrast to the 'Sons of Evil', the desecrators and defilers of the Temple, the secessionist priests established, in vision and in reality, a 'human temple', a

---

[120] Ezek. 22: 26.

[121] For the stormy political and religious history of the Hasmonaean period, see Schürer, *History*; Hengel, *Judaism and Hellenism*; Bar Kochva, *Judas Maccabaeus*; Levin, 'Political Struggle'; Stern, 'Judaism and Hellenism'; id., *Studies in Jewish History*; Schwartz, 'Priesthood, Temple, Sacrifices'; id., 'Desert and Temple'. From a Qumranic standpoint, cf. Cross, 'Early History'.

community of saints living a communal life, upholding the heritage of the Teacher of Righteousness and submitting to Zadokite leadership:

And this is the Rule for the men of the Community, who have freely pledged themselves to be converted from all evil and to cling to all His commandments according to His will. They shall separate from the congregation of the men of injustice and shall unite, with respect to the Law and possessions, under the authority of the sons of Zadok, the Priests who keep the Covenant, and of the multitude of the men of the Community who hold fast to the Covenant.[122]

The opening section of the Community Rule requires any person wishing to join the Community to take an oath of allegiance to the Law of Moses as revealed to the priests of the Community, that is, the priests of the House of Zadok:

Whoever approaches the Council of the Community shall enter the Covenant of God in the presence of all who have freely pledged themselves. He shall undertake by a binding oath to return with all his heart and soul to every commandment of the Law of Moses in accordance with all that has been revealed of it to the sons of Zadok, the Priests, Keepers of the Covenant and Seekers of His will, and to the multitude of the men of their Covenant who together have freely pledged themselves to His truth and to walking in the way of His delight.[123]

[122] Community Rule V, 1–3 (Vermes, *CDSSIE*, 103). Parallel texts from the Community Rule, omitting the reference to the 'sons of Zadok', were found in Qumran Cave 4 (4QS^b, 4QS^d). See Vermes, 'Preliminary Remarks'; A. Baumgarten, *Flourishing of Jewish Sects*. Where 1QS reads 'under the authority of the sons of Zadok, the priests who keep the Covenant, and of the multitude of the men of the Community who hold fast to the Covenant' (V, 2–3), 4QS MS D, thought to be an earlier version, reads 'under the authority of the Many'. Where the later version reads 'in accordance with all that has been revealed of it to the sons of Zadok, the priests, keepers of the Covenant and seekers of His will . . .' (V, 8–10), the supposedly earlier version reads 'in accordance with all that has been revealed of [the Torah] to [the multitude] of the Council of the men of the Community [and to separate from all the men of] injustice' (according to Charlesworth *et al.* (eds.), *Dead Sea Scrolls*, i. 73). This discrepancy has prompted numerous hypotheses in regard to the changing leadership of the Qumran Community. A. Baumgarten (*Flourishing of Jewish Sects*) infers from the appearance of the Zadokites in later copies of the Community Rule that the sect, originally a democratic society, evolved into a community led by an elite group of Zadokite priests. At the same time, however, he notes that from the start the Community was clearly headed by Aaronide priests; to my mind, there is no real difference—the Zadokite priests were of Aaronide patrilineal descent. I believe that the presence of the Zadokite priests at Qumran was not a late stage, but the core feature around which the Community was established, as may be deduced from the fragmentary literary corpus that has come down to us. The members of the Community called themselves 'sons of Zadok', 'sons of Aaron', and 'priests, sons of Levi' (Temple Scroll LXIII); their most basic identity was founded on the claim to a continuous priestly tradition, passed down the generations from Levi and Aaron, through Eleazar and Zadok, to the time of the books of Chronicles, Ezra, and Nehemiah, where the genealogy of the high priests is set out. Closely associated with this claim were their special attitude to the book of Ezekiel, which lavishes praise on the Zadokite priests, guardians of the altar and the sacred service (Ezek. 40: 46), and their support of the House of Onias, which traced its lineage to the House of Zadok—the family of the high priests from the early First Temple period to the rise of the Hasmonaean dynasty. The benediction cited in Ben Sira 51: 29 (see below) attests to the existence of this tradition around the beginning of the 2nd century BCE.   [123] Community Rule V, 8–11 (Vermes, *CDSSIE*, 104); cf. previous note.

The 'Law of Moses' referred to here may well be the law dictated to Moses, according to Jubilees, by the Angel of the Countenance and kept by the Zadokite priests, who clearly associated themselves with the Angel of the Countenance, as is clear from the blessing to the high priest quoted previously. The Community's future was also bound up with Zadokite leadership, as may be seen from the beginning of the Messianic Rule:

This is the Rule for all the congregation of Israel in the last days, when they shall join the Community to walk according to the law of the sons of Zadok the Priests and of the men of their Covenant who have turned aside from the way of the people, the men of His Council who keep His Covenant . . .[124]

The link with Ezekiel is explicitly mentioned in the Damascus Document:

As God ordained for them by the hand of the Prophet Ezekiel, saying, 'The priests, the Levites, and the sons of Zadok who kept the charge of my sanctuary when the children of Israel strayed from me' . . . The sons of Zadok are the elect of Israel, the men called by name who shall stand at the end of days.[125]

The Blessings Scroll presents a special blessing for the sons of Zadok, opening as follows:

Words of blessing. The M[aster shall bless] the sons of Zadok the Priests, whom God has chosen to confirm His Covenant for [ever, and to inquire] into all His precepts in the midst of His people, and to instruct them as He commanded; who have established [His Covenant] on truth and watched over all His laws with righteousness and walked according to the way of His choice.

May the Lord bless you from His holy [Abode]; may He set you a splendid jewel in the midst of the congregation of the saints!

May He [renew] for you the Covenant of the [everlasting] priesthood; may He sanctify you [for the House] of Holiness! . . .[126]

It is quite clear from the Qumran literature at our disposal that the leadership of the Community consisted of priests who traced their lineage to the House of Zadok and thereby to the high priesthood, beginning in the time of Moses and Aaron, through the reigns of David and Solomon, right up to the eschatological priesthood of the End of Days; in addition, they spoke of the angelic priesthood as their counterpart and the source of their authority.

The priestly and angelic identity of the House of Zadok is probably also indicated by the expression 'those appointed for righteousness', *no'adei tsedek*, appearing in the Songs of the Sabbath Sacrifice in reference to the heavenly priests

---

[124] Messianic Rule I, 1–2 (Vermes, *CDSSIE*, 157); cf. *DJD* I, 109.

[125] Damascus Document III, 21–IV, 4 (Vermes, *CDSSIE*, 129–30).

[126] 1Q28b, III, 22–7 (Vermes, *CDSSIE*, 375); Licht, *Rule Scroll*, 281, and discussion ibid. 275. For a different reading, see *DJD* I, 124; cf. J. M. Baumgarten, 'Heavenly Tribunal', 234–5.

ministering in the supernal worlds, as against the 'sons/children of righteousness' or 'sons of Zadok' officiating in the lower worlds; a similar connection is alluded to by other expressions in Qumran literature associated with righteousness (Heb. *tsedek*) or with Zadok (Heb. *tsadok*)—such as 'Teacher of Righteousness', 'priest of righteousness', 'righteous plantation', 'paths of righteousness', 'words of righteousness', and 'sons of Zadok, the elect of Israel'.[127] Children of righteousness or sons of Zadok are also mentioned, *inter alia*, in the Community Rule—'all the children of righteousness are ruled by the Prince of Light';[128] in the War Scroll— 'From of old You appointed the Prince of Light to assist us, and in [his] ha[nd are all the angels of just]ice, and all the spirits of truth are under His dominion';[129] and the expression 'elect of righteousness' appears in the Thanksgiving Hymns.[130]

It is intriguing that the biblical term 'sons of Zadok', endowed with special meaning by Ezekiel, and the term 'visions of the Merkabah', meaning visions of the heavenly Chariot Throne and referring to Ezekiel's Merkavah, appear in the Hebrew book of Ben Sira discovered at Qumran, where the Temple service and the high priesthood are explicitly associated with the House of Zadok. The book, written around 180 BCE, concludes with an 'appendix' consisting, *inter alia*, of a psalm of thanksgiving, presumably recited in the Temple at the time; one verse of this psalm reads, 'Give thanks to Him Who has chosen the Sons of Zadok to be priests, for His lovingkindness endures forever.'[131]

The historical identity of the authors of Qumran literature has been a bone of contention ever since the Dead Sea Scrolls were discovered, as is evident from even the most cursory glance at the relevant scholarly literature. It can hardly be denied, however, that the priests occupied a central role in the hierarchic structure of the Community. This clearly emerges from the Community Rule, from the halakhic writings found at Qumran, and from the Community's eschatological vision. The identity of the Community and its priestly affinity are defined in the following declaration: 'When these are in Israel, the Council of the Community shall be established in truth. It shall be an Everlasting Plantation, a House of Holiness for Israel, an Assembly of Supreme Holiness for Aaron. They shall be witnesses to the truth at the Judgement, and shall be the elect of Goodwill who shall atone for the Land . . .'.[132] The expression 'Holy of Holies', common in biblical literature in relation to the Temple and the sons of Aaron, is used in the

---

[127] Damascus Document IV, 3–4.

[128] III, 20 (Vermes, *CDSSIE*, 101).

[129] XIII, 10 (Vermes, *CDSSIE*, 177).

[130] II, 13.

[131] Ben Sira 51: 29. See M. Z. Segal's remark in his Hebrew edition of Ben Sira (*Complete Book of Ben-Sira*, 356), and in his introduction (ibid. 3–5). The chapter is also included in the Psalms Scroll 11QPs^a. The fact that the same passage occurs in two different texts indicates that it was a 'floating' unit, whose source is difficult to trace; nevertheless, Segal's suggestion (ibid.) that it was part of a psalm that was omitted from the sacred service in the Hasmonaean period, because of its praise for the House of Zadok, is quite plausible. For 'visions of the Merkavah' see Ben Sira 49: 11 [8]; for Ben Sira's praise of Enoch see ibid. 44: 19 [16]; 49: 20 [14].

[132] Community Rule VIII, 5–6 (Vermes, *CDSSIE*, 109).

literature of the secessionist priesthood in relation to priests, angels, and the supernal sanctuaries, as well as to the sons of Aaron as in biblical tradition. Verses stressing the superior rank of the priests may be found in the Damascus Document: 'The rule for the assembly of all the camps. They shall all be enrolled by name: first the Priests, second the Levites, third the Israelites, and fourth the proselytes. And they shall be inscribed by name, one after the other: the Priests first, the Levites second . . .'.[133] While in the Commentary on Isaiah we find the following metaphors in relation to the stones of the priestly breastplate:

I will make your foundations of sapphires [Isa. 54: 11]: Interpreted, this concerns the Priests and the people who laid the foundations of the Council of the Community . . . the congregation of the elect (shall sparkle) like a sapphire among stones.[134]

All this rich literary evidence tells us little about the general historical realities of the time. It is indeed difficult to gauge whether the various priestly traditions possessed any reality, or whether they were perhaps mythological reconstructions of the past in light of present needs. Neither can we determine the relationship between the different priestly houses from the standpoint of those involved, insofar as the voice of only one side has reached us. The relationship between priests and Levites in the Second Temple period or in Qumran circles are also shrouded in darkness, as the different traditions provide conflicting evidence: some identify priests with Levites; others separate the two groups and assign them different roles and ranks in the hierarchy; and still others ignore the Levites entirely. There is conflicting evidence and the questions involved are complex: biblical tradition itself reflects different voices, as do the priestly literature found in Qumran and the literature of the Second Temple period. Nevertheless, there is no doubt that the priestly literature lays particular emphasis on the divine election of the priests and their unique, heavenly sanctioned, sanctity, in a variety of ways. Their lifestyle, laws of conduct, and ritual were shaped in light of their claimed affinity with the ministering angels, in a constant effort to establish and justify their unique, exclusive position, both inwardly, within their own society, and outwardly, towards the environment from which they had been barred.

[133] D^a, frg. 2 (Vermes, *CDSSIE*, 143).
[134] Commentary on Isaiah (4Q164) V, 48–50 (cf. Vermes, *CDSSIE*, 469).

NINE

The Secessionist Priesthood and Rabbinic Tradition

And he shall undertake by the Covenant to separate from all the men of injustice who walk in the way of wickedness.[1]

And you know that we have segregated ourselves from the rest of the people and from mingling in these affairs, and from associating with them in these things.[2]

THE priests who held these separatist views, relying on a supernatural source of authority and linking their fate with that of the angels of the Countenance, the Prince of Light, cherubim, holy angels, and godlike beings of knowledge, defined themselves and their allies as 'chosen ones/knowers/Sons of Righteousness', 'righteous plantation', 'those appointed for righteousness', 'Sons of Light', 'those who enter into the Covenant', or 'those called by name', who walked 'in faith and with a whole heart', observed the sabbaths, the festivals, and the tablets of the Covenant, and walked in the ways of justice, righteousness, and perfection illuminated by the sun itself.

Enoch, the mythological hero called by God himself 'righteous man and scribe of righteousness',[3] embodied the values hallowed by the secessionist priests relating to knowledge, testimony and appointed time, calculation and number, righteousness, light, book and law, sabbath and oath. He defined his heritage through his exhortation to his sons: 'Now, my children, I say to you: Love righteousness and walk therein! For the ways of righteousness are worthy of being embraced.... But seek for yourselves and choose righteousness and the elect life!'[4]

The secessionists' opponents, in contrast, were associated with angels of Belial, the Prince of Darkness, the Watchers, angels of destruction, spirits of injustice, Azazel and *mastemah* (lit. 'malevolence', i.e. the forces of evil), the pit and the shadow of death. Members of their circles were defined as a 'congregation of wayward traitors', 'those who have turned aside from your Covenant', and treacherous men who walk 'in the stubbornness of their heart'.[5] They are described as 'Sons of Darkness', associated with unjust ways; they rely upon sensory perception, upon

---

[1] Community Rule V, 10–11 (Vermes, *CDSSIE*, 104).
[2] 4Q 397, frgs. 14–21 (= MMT: *DJD* X, 27, 59; cf. Vermes, *CDSSIE*, 227).
[3] 1 En. 15: 1.　　　　[4] 1 En. 94: 1–4.　　　　[5] Thanksgiving Hymns IV, 19, 15.

observation of the moon, upon error and distortion. These Sons of Darkness defined themselves in terms relating to sin and lawlessness, promiscuity and corruption;[6] and their hero Azazel, associated with proscription, wilderness, and darkness, is defined as having 'taught all forms of lawlessness upon the earth' and revealed 'every kind of sin'.[7]

The secessionist priestly writers perceived the 'Sons/lot of Light' and the 'Sons/lot of Darkness' as being poles apart. The contrast between the two camps in their writings could not have been sharper. On the one hand:

[You,] God, have created us for Yourself, an eternal people, and You have chosen us for the lot of light in Your truth; You have commanded the Prince of Light from of old to assist us, and in his lot are the angels of righteousness, and all spirits of truth are in his dominion . . .

while on the other:

And You created Belial for the pit, the angel Mastemah; in darkness is his dominion, and all the spirits of his lot are angels of destruction, they follow statutes of darkness and their urge is toward it.[8]

They identified all those who shared their convictions in terms derived from the Hebrew root *ts-d-k*, meaning 'righteous(ness)', as already listed above. Thus, they were the priests of the House of Zadok (*tsadok*); their leader was the Chief Priest or Teacher of Righteousness (*moreh tsedek*), likened to the 'sun of righteousness' or the great luminary; he guided his flock in the 'lot of righteousness', in the paths of truth and justice. Their opponents, however, were defined in terms denoting wickedness, lawlessness, evil, destruction, arbitrariness, and Belial; they were the 'dominion of the children of injustice', governed by the 'Wicked Priest', living by laws of darkness, walking in paths of sin and iniquity.[9] They described themselves, explicitly and implicitly, as 'Sons of Light', who conducted their lives in accordance with the solar calendar of sabbaths, fixed and predetermined; they walked in paths of light and innocence, faithfully observing the Lord's commandments and appointed times, upholding the sanctity which was a precondition for blessing, purity, and life itself. Their opponents, in contrast, were 'Sons of Darkness'; they held fast to the

---

[6] 1 En. 6: 3; 7: 1–6.   [7] 1 En. 9: 6, 8.

[8] 4Q495, frg. 2, xiii, 9–12 (*DJD* VII, 55; cf. García Martínez and Tigchelaar, *Study Edition*, ii. 987); War Scroll XIII, 9–12. Cf. Community Rule III, 13 ff.; IV, 9–14, and see Licht's discussion in his *Rule Scroll*, 88–98.

[9] The Hebrew title *kohen haresha*, meaning literally 'priest of evil', is a wordplay on *kohen harosh*, i.e. the 'chief priest', a title used in the Bible but completely superseded in the Hasmonaean period and later by the more familiar *kohen gadol*, 'high priest', which indeed appears on Hasmonaean coins; see Yadin (ed.), *Scroll of the War*, 207–8. For the Qumran title see Commentary on Habakkuk I, 13; VIII, 8; XII, 2, 8. For the 'dominion of the children of injustice' see Community Rule III, 20–1; cf. ibid. IV, 24. Other significant expressions are: 'those born of injustice [who] spring from a source of darkness' (ibid. III, 19); 'congregation/habitation of the men of injustice' (ibid. V, 1–2; VIII, 13).

changeable lunar calendar, distorted the sequence of sabbaths and festivals, dese-crated the sacred, and walked in the stubbornness of their hearts, in paths of licen-tiousness and abomination which led inevitably to curse, corruption, and death.

The Sons of Light gave expression, in a variety of ways—in the language of law and of myth, in their biblical interpretations, in poetic and visionary language—to their struggle over a hallowed tradition of oaths and covenants associated with the Temple rites and festivals, with the solar calendar, with calculation and number, purity and holiness, with an angelic tradition, with righteous precepts and prac-tices founded on letters and numbers, divine, infinite, cyclic, and eternal, which were the guarantee of blessing and life. Opposing them was a blasphemous tradi-tion, practised in a desecrated Temple, founded on the corrupt lunar calendar and hence on fallible, unstable human observation; it violated the Covenant, generated impurity, and distorted hallowed traditions, leading inevitably—so the Sons of Light believed—to curse and death.

The literature of those Sons of Light may be divided into two main literary cor-puses. The first was concerned with the foundation of a community of separatists who preserved these traditions and lived by them; subordinating themselves to priestly leadership, they looked, on the one hand, back to their past and, on the other, forward to the imminent End of Days, striving to transform their halakhic, cultic, and spiritual conceptions into reality. This corpus includes the following works: Community Rule, Messianic Rule, Damascus Document, the *pesharim*, War of the Sons of Light against the Sons of Darkness, *Miktsat ma'asei hatorah* (MMT), Thanksgiving Hymns. The roots of the second corpus, however, lay far back in antiquity; its works preserved the priestly and angelic Temple traditions of eternal divine order, Covenant and oath, blessing and life, as reflected in the seven-based ritual sequence of sabbaths and festivals based on the solar calendar: the Enoch literature, Jubilees, Testament of Levi, Second Ezekiel, Songs of the Sabbath Sacrifice, Psalms Scroll, Blessings, Calendars of Priestly Courses, and the Temple Scroll.

The two corpuses are intertwined; they share a common conception of the calendar and its appointed times, the Temple and its cult, the primacy of the priesthood, and the election of Levi and his descendants; and both are pervaded with a sensation of affinity with the angelic world. Some of the traditions to which they give expression touch, in a general sense, on matters of terrestrial significance, relating to the law and the commandments, the everyday life of the Community past, present, and future, with a marked polemical thrust. Others are preoccupied with the celestial world, revealing a mythical, mystical orientation that speaks of angels, priestly myth, and Covenant, of the order of nature and Creation, of the tradition of the Merkavah, the divine Chariot Throne, of the sanctity of the sab-bath and the solar calendar of weeks as the principle behind the seven-based Temple service and the seven holy festivals—all reflecting identification with the age-old sources of the tradition of the angelic priests.

Such are the positions that find rich, colourful literary expression in the works found at Qumran. These include legal (halakhic) works which endeavour to prescribe the proper rites of the Temple, to establish a community whose members—comparing themselves in their mind's eye to priests and angels testifying to the Covenant—would keep the Covenant and live their lives according to divinely ordained paths, set times, and commandments. Related to these are various polemical works devoted to different aspects of the struggle between the Sons of Light and the Sons of Darkness. In another category are mythical and mystical works, some displaying an affinity with the biblical book of Ezekiel in their treatment of the sacred place, the cult, and the Covenant tradition (Merkavah; cherubim and angels; Zadokite priests; tradition of covenants and oaths; sanctified realm and Temple; Holy of Holies and the holy bond between God and his chosen; fertility; the mystical Pardes and the Garden of Eden). Other works of this category uphold the tradition of Enoch literature and Jubilees concerning sacred time and appointed times (calendar; sabbaths; Shavuot; seven days of purification; seven Temple festivals; the seven ingredients of the incense; Covenant and oath).

These works—struggling, on the one hand, in the name of a myth of angelic priests against contemporary desecrators of holy time and holy place; and, on the other, concerned with the celestial Temple, the Merkavah, sacred song together with the angels, and ascent to heaven, the solar calendar, angelic priesthood and Zadokite priesthood, entering into the Covenant on Shavuot and observing ritual laws—were almost completely suppressed in rabbinic tradition, sinking into the depths of oblivion.

Scattered here and there in rabbinic literature are reports of halakhic disputes between Sadducees and Pharisees, which essentially echo the struggle between the secessionist priests of the House of Zadok and their allies, on the one hand, and their opponents in the ruling circles—the Hasmonaeans and their Pharisee supporters. Through these disputes, which all concern the Temple rites—the place where incense should be burned on the Day of Atonement, the libation of water on the altar, the burning of the red heifer, the time for harvesting the Omer, the counting of the Omer, and the date of Shavuot—one can perhaps discern traces, albeit seen through polemical spectacles, of the mystical metamorphosis of various cultic traditions relating to the Merkavah, the solar calendar, the angelic priesthood, and Shavuot, in their mythological and liturgical manifestations. These priestly traditions—and their literary expressions, resting on angelic authority—were most probably censored and silenced by the ruling leadership; this is not surprising, because that very leadership, branded by the secessionist priests as 'government of Belial', 'lot of darkness', 'children of destruction', 'government of *mastemah*', was the target of the vitriolic attacks, driven by hatred and loathing, in the works written by or under the inspiration of the Zadokite priests.

The stages in the consolidation of the new leadership, the transition from the priesthood of the Hasmonaean dynasty to the Pharisees and rabbinic tradition as we know it today, are shrouded in mystery, for lack of written evidence pertaining to the second and first centuries BCE. What is clear is that these circles, in their diverse historical phases (echoes of which are discernible in works written in the second and first centuries BCE—the books of the Maccabees—and in the first century CE—the works of Josephus Flavius and the New Testament), objected to the priestly predominance of the House of Zadok, denied the cultic authority which these priestly circles claimed, rejected their literature with its reliance on angelic origins and their solar calendar, and firmly opposed Sadducee halakhah.[10] The Sages' complex attitude to the various branches of the priesthood is evident, *inter alia*, in their omission of the priestly dynasty as a link in the chain of transmission of the Torah in the mishnaic tractate *Avot*.

Small wonder that early rabbinic tradition—which rejected the solar calendar of the Zadokite priests and its alleged angelic and mystical authority, its fixed calculation and celestial patterning of time, and instead adopted a lunar calendar based on changeable human judgement, opposing and suppressing any mention of angelic authority—also deprived Enoch of his central role, disregarding or actively repudiating Enoch literature, Jubilees, and Qumran literature, which were based on the divine secrets revealed by angels. In the same spirit, rabbinic tradition gave prominence to narratives that presented Levi in an unfavourable light, ignored his priestly privileges, and denied the exclusive right of the House of Zadok to the high priesthood and the kingly rights of the tribe of Judah and the House of David. The mainstream tradition denied that a person's worth or right of hegemony could depend on that person's birth and lineage (the tribe of Levi; priesthood exclusive to descendants of Aaron), insisting that all Jews had a part in the 'crown of Torah'. 'All Israel have a part in the World to Come'[11]—not only the Sons of Light, the elect, the righteous, or the priestly elite, who derived their authority from angelic revelation or 'heavenly tablets', and were assured of their position from birth as descendants of Aaron or of the tribe of Levi. Rabbinic tradition, which held that

---

[10] For discussions of the undoubted affinity between Sadducean halakhah as portrayed in rabbinic tradition and the halakhah as manifested in the works of the Zadokite priests discovered at Qumran (which do not use the word *halakhah* at all but rather *torah, mishpat/ mishpatim*, 'law(s)', *ḥok*, 'law'), see J. M. Baumgarten, *Studies in Qumran Law*; id., 'Pharisaic–Sadducean Controversies'; Sussmann, 'History of Halakhah'; Schiffman, 'New Halakhic Letter'; Schwartz, 'Law and Truth'; Kister, 'Some Aspects'; Schiffman, 'Temple Scroll'; Qimron and Strugnell in *DJD* X; eid., 'Unpublished Halakhic Letter'; Strugnell, 'MMT: Second Thoughts'. For the earliest treatments of the Damascus Document as a Sadducee document see Schechter, *Documents of Jewish Sectaries*; Rabin, *Zadokite Documents*. J. M. Baumgarten has warned against overly general conclusions that identify Qumranite and Sadducean halakhah; see Baumgarten, 'Disqualifications of Priests'. Some scholars have criticized the use of the term 'halakhah' in relation to Qumran writings; see Strugnell in *DJD* X; Talmon, 'Community of the Renewed Covenant'. For the distinction between a realistic conception of natural laws and eternal predeterminism as typifying the 'Sadducean halakhah' of MMT, the Temple Scroll, and the Damascus Document, in contrast to the nominalistic, anti-deterministic outlook of Pharisee halakhah, see Schwartz, 'Law and Truth'; Strugnell, 'MMT: Second Thoughts'.

[11] Mishnah *San.* 10: 1.

direct divine communication with man had ceased, that Haggai, Zechariah, and Malachi were the last prophets, took sharp exception to people who claimed to be privy to the Holy Spirit, to have contact with heavenly voices or with any other kind of continuous divine revelation after the destruction of the Temple. In addition, it suppressed the notion of joint prayer of angels and humans, minimized the role of angels in general, and marginalized the prophetic, priestly, and angelic traditions of the Merkavah.

The Torah, according to the Sages, had achieved its final formulation, and not one letter of the canonized text could be altered—contrary to the position of the Zadokite priests, who, denying that the wellsprings of divine revelation had dried up, continued well into the last centuries BCE to write books supposedly dictated by the angels and thus never canonized one single text. But that same canonical text was open, according to the mainstream, to autonomous, human interpretation; any student of the law could expound the law in this way, on the basis of human, earthly reason. There was strict separation between the heavenly and the earthly realms: 'It is not in the heavens.'[12]

The profound difference between the two ways of thinking comes to light in the controversy over the source of authority for calendrical calculations: a fixed, divine, source, based on calculations and numerical structures that predetermine the course of time from beginning to end—according to the Zadokite priests; and a variable, human source, based on human observation and decisions taken anew month after month.

Yet another manifestation of that difference is the idea of the Oral Law—a seminal concept in rabbinic tradition, implying the legitimacy of open discussion and pluralism (halakhah was not officially committed to writing or to final oral editing until the completion of the Mishnah by Rabbi Judah the Prince around 200 CE). This idea was anathema to the tradition of the House of Zadok, which recognized only sacred writings and 'heavenly tablets'; it was absolutely forbidden, they believed, to add anything to or subtract anything from these writings, in their sacred written versions, which were the special charge of the priests, representatives of angelic authority who had received them by dictation. Unlike rabbinic tradition, which considered the sacred writings permanent and final but on the other hand open to discussion and interpretation based on human reason and imagination, in the spirit of 'there are seventy aspects to the Torah', Qumran literature allowed no free interpretation or plurality of ideas; it was built on hallowed traditions that were copied and studied but could not be freely interpreted. The right to add or illuminate, as in biblical times, was the exclusive province of recipients of divine revelation, prophets or visionaries, guardians of hallowed ritual traditions who could convey the apocalyptic meanings of the prophetic text; it was not granted to savants and scholars drawing on their human intelligence in the effort to adapt the divine law to changing human experience.

[12] Deut. 30: 12.

While Qumran literature envisaged no end to the biblical world view, rabbinic tradition was based on the idea that the biblical period, characterized by divine authority and direct contact between heaven and earth, had come to an end. A new mode of thought, based on human authority to explicate the world order, on human partnership in the work of Creation, had emerged. The independent perception underlying rabbinic thought denied the legitimacy of all contrary traditions relying on continued divine revelation, on angelic authority, or on 'heavenly tablets' and sacred writings. It rejected the authority of the priestly circles whose members, claiming access to renewed prophetic vision or mythological priestly authority, continued to write books allegedly inspired by the Holy Spirit or by angels. All such deviant traditions and their bearers were therefore marginalized or totally suppressed. Moreover, it would appear that biblical tradition, in its recognized canonical guise, was re-edited by the new hegemony, which aimed to obscure various references to controversial issues, first and foremost to all dates originally associated with the seven-based priestly myth, the solar calendar, and the tradition of covenants concluded on Shavuot, halfway through the third month. This tendency is clearly reflected in differences concerning the dates of the Flood, which constitute the basis for calendrical calculations, as well as the dates of the Omer and Shavuot, between the Masoretic text and other versions. While these two 'appointed times' do not fall on a fixed day of the week or date in biblical tradition, Qumran writings place the elevation of the Omer on the 26th of the first month and Shavuot exactly seven weeks later, invariably on Sunday, the 15th of the third month.

Attempts to exclude the book of Ezekiel from the canon, because of its different priestly and sacrificial laws (chs. 40–8), which seem to contradict the Torah,[13] because of the danger inherent in studying Ezekiel's Merkavah vision,[14] or because of the centrality of the Zadokite priests in his prophecies, may also be associated, directly or indirectly, with that prophet's central position in the world of the secessionist priesthood, which considered itself descended from the Zadokite priests and consecrated by Merkavah tradition:

That man should be remembered with favour, his name being Ḥananiah son of Hezekiah, for were it not for him, the book of Ezekiel would have been suppressed and withdrawn, as its teachings contradict those of the Torah. What did he do? They brought him 300 jugs of oil, and he sat in the attic and expounded upon the texts [through the night].[15]

---

[13] Ezekiel generally adheres to the pentateuchal books of Leviticus and Numbers in matters of religious precepts and the Temple service (44: 15–31), but his vision of the laws of the Temple and the priesthood are pervaded by innovative elements, distinct from any of the ancient sources or differently formulated from the pentateuchal Priestly Code, sometimes in direct contradiction to its laws. See Zimmerli, *Ezekiel*, ii. 327–8, 456–64; Eichrodt, *Ezekiel*, 559–74; Haran, 'Topics in Bible'; Brooke, 'Ezekiel in Some Qumran and NT Texts'.　　　[14] BT *Ḥag.* 13a.　　　[15] BT *Shab.* 13b.

There is most probably a connection between this tradition of the attempted suppression of the book of Ezekiel in the time of Hananiah son of Hezekiah, a sage of the end of the Second Temple period, and the fact that detailed priestly teachings, conflicting with the contemporary cultic arrangements in the Temple and based on the sanctity of the solar calendar—such as the Temple Scroll, Damascus Document, and MMT—were based on the priestly laws outlined in Ezekiel and clearly favour the House of Zadok and Ezekiel's vision of the Temple. The present Masoretic text of Ezekiel apparently represents a heavily edited version. First, it would appear that the relationship between the time of the vision of the Merkavah and Shavuot has been heavily obscured—though this relationship clearly emerges from a comparison of the festival's date with its date as calculated in the solar calendar. Second, perhaps it is no accident that the word *merkavah*, prominent in all the parallel Qumranic accounts of Ezekiel's vision (e.g. 4Q 385) and other priestly references (as in Ben Sira and the Septuagint), does not appear at all in the Masoretic text.

Other biblical works of significance for priestly tradition were also most probably edited and abbreviated, or their chronological aspects modified. The story of the Watchers, for example, appears in a rather obscure biblical version; and—just as the dates in Ezekiel's vision were presumably modified in order to conceal their significance in relation to the solar calendar—the dates in the account of the Flood were clearly adapted to the lunar calendar, in contrast to the solar framework evident in Qumran literature. As already pointed out,[16] Origen, writing in 245 CE, observed that important chapters in priestly tradition, such as the story of the seven days of Creation, the story of the Watchers, and the story of the Flood in Genesis, the description of the Merkavah and the Temple in Ezekiel, and the Song of Songs, were neither read in public nor freely available, but reserved for a few elect individuals upon completion of their standard studies. This esoteric list, concerned as it is with *ma'aseh bereshit* (Creation), *ma'aseh merkavah* (the Chariot Throne), and *arayot* (the act of sacred union), shows a striking affinity with the well-known prohibition in the Mishnah, 'It is forbidden for three persons to discuss the secrets of sexual union, for two persons to discuss *ma'aseh bereshit*, and for a single person to discuss *ma'aseh merkavah*.'[17] The testimony of Origen and that of the Mishnah, to the effect that these traditions were confined to esoteric circles, point to the special regard in which they were held; they may also represent in part the efforts of the competing new hegemony of the Sages to suppress the priestly hegemony's world view by forcing it onto the periphery of public discourse.

Rabbinic tradition, however, does not represent a uniform opinion but is a composite of many voices. Thus, alongside voices that favoured suppression of the Merkavah tradition, others still viewed it as possessing special sanctity and significance, as is evident from allusions in rabbinic writings and later from Heikhalot literature. The ambivalent attitude to this tradition in the first centuries CE may be

---

[16] See p. 162 above.   [17] *Ḥag.* 2: 1.

associated with the ambivalent attitude to the priesthood, its ties with Merkavah tradition, and its struggle for hegemony in the last decades BCE.

The indications that biblical works relating to the world of the secessionist priesthood may have been edited to conceal their affinity with the solar calendar may be summarized as follows: (1) the differences between the story of the Flood (which refers to a year of 354 plus ten days) and its Qumranic parallels (a year of 364 days); (2) differences between the tradition of Enoch's birth in Genesis 4 and 5 and the parallel account in Jubilees; (3) analysis of the ambiguous dates in Ezekiel 1 based on the Metonic calculation, which associates them with Shavuot; (4) the fact that biblical tradition never explicitly specifies the number of days or weeks in the year; (5) the lack of a date for the theophany at Sinai; (6) discrepancies between the text of certain Psalms and the versions found at Qumran, which seem to allude to a different order of liturgy; (7) the rejection of psalms in praise of the sons of Zadok, of Ben Sira 51, and of other psalms found at Qumran; (8) the highly abbreviated version of the story of the Watchers in Genesis, in comparison with the much fuller accounts in Enoch and Jubilees.

In view of these probable modifications in what ultimately became the canonized version, it is not surprising that literature explicitly based on the solar calendar was excluded from the canon, and that priestly liturgy, such as the Songs of the Sabbath Sacrifice, which revolved around Ezekiel's Merkavah and performance of the sacred service in concert with angels, and was based on an alternative sacral year whose dates were derived from the solar calendar, met with a similar fate. This is all the more true with regard to emphatically polemical works, in which the rival priesthood were denounced as 'Sons of Darkness' and 'government of Belial'; these were banished both from the canon and from the traditions of study established by the accused circles and their successors.

It is most probable that these controversies were responsible, whether directly or indirectly, for the rabbinic interdict on exposition of *ma'aseh merkavah*—referring to the Chariot Throne of the cherubim in the Temple, and thus to the perception of cosmic time and the concept of sacred place, linking heaven and earth; referring also to the visionary metamorphosis of the Chariot Throne in Ezekiel's Merkavah. At stake was the basic conception of sacred place, sacred time, and sacred liturgical ritual, as represented in the literature of the secessionist priests, in fundamental conflict with contemporary conceptions concerning sabbaths and festivals, the Temple and its sacrificial rites, as represented by the Hasmonaean priesthood and its successors.

As already noted, Merkavah tradition was also associated with the tradition of covenants concluded on Shavuot according to the solar calendar—a basic motif in Jubilees; with the renewal of the Covenant in Ezekiel's vision, also on Shavuot; and with the covenant ceremony of the 'Sons of Light' on that same festival, as described in the Community Rule and the Damascus Document. It is most probably no accident that the Torah as we now have it does not specify the date of that festival. In fact, early rabbinic traditions, as represented by the Mishnah, the Tosefta, and the halakhic midrashim, *does not mention Shavuot at all*, and its date is a major bone of contention with the Sadducees in connection with the counting of seven weeks from the harvest of the Omer and the festival of first fruits. Moreover, the tradition of renewing the oath and the Covenant in a public, ceremonial recitation of blessings and curses, repeated annually on Shavuot, disappeared entirely and has been forgotten. Tannaitic literature[18] refers to this festival as *atseret*, namely 'assembly, gathering' (the exact meaning of the term is not clear), with no further qualification. There is no tractate of the Mishnah (or, consequently, of the Talmud) devoted to the festival, as there is for other festivals. The connotation of oath and Covenant, or festival of covenantal renewal, correlated with the weeks of the solar calendar and occupying a central position in the writings of the secessionist priesthood, was completely obliterated.[19]

Given this openly polemical position and the controversy over various precepts concerning sabbaths, festivals, and cultic matters, as well as the fierce conflict represented by the dualistic perception of Sons of Light versus Sons of Darkness, it was perhaps inevitable that the Sages and the Pharisees who shaped mainstream tradition after the destruction of the Second Temple should reject the literature that had been written and sanctified by the secessionist priesthood or, at the very least, suppress or ignore it.[20] The polemical sections of that literature were mostly composed during the Hasmonaean period, in the last two centuries BCE, though it is very probable that some of the cultic disputes reflected therein had roots far back in the time of the First Temple and the Restoration; this follows from the conflicting traditions of seven weeks and seven sabbaths in the biblical treatment of Shavuot, and from Ezekiel's championing of the House of Zadok, which presumably also implies rejection of other priestly circles.

---

[18] Mishnah *Shevi.* 1: 1.

[19] See Tabori, *Jewish Festivals*, 146–7. Only in amoraic literature does the name 'Shavuot' appear frequently. The formulation of the Community Rule II, 19, referring to the covenantal ceremony in the words 'Thus shall they do, year by year, for as long as the dominion of the sons of Belial endures', surely did not contribute to conserving Shavuot as a regular annual festival, marking the acceptance of the Covenant, among circles outside those of the secessionist priesthood. The notion of *berit*, 'covenant', in its communal sense, requiring the regular, annual renewal of the sacred undertaking on Shavuot, after seven weeks had been counted, in a priestly ceremony of blessings and curses, was completely forgotten (or suppressed) in rabbinic literature. The only remaining covenantal association was with circumcision, which is not insignificantly observed on the eighth day of an infant's life, that is, after seven days have been counted.

[20] The suppression was not absolute, for the Sages continue to dispute Sadducean halakhah in both Mishnah and Talmud, and traces of these works may be found in various late midrashic compilations (*Pirkei derabi eli'ezer*, *Midrash tadshe*, *Midrash vayisa'u*). Even before that, some elements of Sadducean writings found their way into Heikhalot literature and the prayer book, and eventually also into Karaite literature. See A. Kahana (ed.), *Apocrypha*, introduction, vol. i, pp. xii–xiv. The scholarly world is divided with respect to possible ties between Karaite literature and the Judaean Desert Scrolls; for a review of the various positions see Erder, 'When did the Encounter . . . Begin?'; Ben-Shammai, 'Methodological Remarks'.

The literature of the secessionist priesthood was written and edited over a lengthy period by a variety of groups and developed in different directions. It included older traditions, such as the Songs of the Sabbath Sacrifice, the Psalms Scroll, the Blessings Scroll and the Temple Scroll, the Book of the Watchers, the Book of Heavenly Luminaries, and the book of Jubilees. It also included frankly polemical works, written in a spirit of opposition and challenge to the contemporary Temple ritual and the priests of the Hasmonaean dynasty, who performed their false rites in the Temple, such as the Community Rule, the *pesharim*, the War of the Sons of Light against the Sons of Darkness, and MMT. I have already mentioned the division of this literature into an 'earthly corpus', which defines the authors' separatist identity and polemical stand, and a 'heavenly corpus', which claims supernatural authority and angelic tradition. Despite this diversity, there are several basic, typical, identifying features, recurring in all its works, which might be seen as opposed to rabbinic tradition. This opposition was quite clearly no accident, for even if we do not know whether—and if so, to what degree—the Sages were acquainted with the secessionist literature, they must have been aware of its separatist, polemical nature, and of the basic position of disagreement with the contemporary Temple priesthood in relation to the sanctity of time, place, and cult, a disagreement rooted in the shift of priestly hegemony centuries before.

I have already pointed out that the unexplained prohibitions imposed by the Sages in tractate *Ḥagigah* on the discussion of certain subjects are precisely mirrored, in a striking fashion, by certain major obligations in the literature of the secessionist priesthood: the Merkavah as the cosmic prototype of the celestial Temple, referring to the four points of the compass, the seven supernal sanctuaries, the twelve gates and the twenty-four passages associated with the world of the angels, the servants of the Chariot Throne, and the cherubim; *ma'aseh bereshit* as representing the totality of cosmological phenomena linking the sanctity of time and the solar calendar (four seasons, twelve months, seven days of the week, twenty-four hours of the day) with the sanctity of place and cult in a seven-based sequence guaranteeing the cyclic nature of life with its correlated fourfold and twelvefold divisions; and *arayot*, sexual union, representing the body of traditions relating to holy union, the Temple and holy matrimony, seven days of purification, oath and Covenant, pilgrimage, the intertwined cherubim in the Holy of Holies, sacred time correlated with sacred place, as against the sins of the Watchers (*irim*; the roots of the Hebrew words *irim* and *arayot* share two consonants), who sought to set aside the barriers between the upper and lower realms, corrupted the proper order of things, consummated forbidden sexual unions, and committed other cardinal sins, thus creating the sinful roots of the lunar calendar and prefiguring the government of Belial.

There may have been other reasons for the suppression of this apocryphal literature. We do not know whether the process was fortuitous, due to the formation of new institutions in the wake of the destruction, or to a split in the ranks of the

Zadokite priests themselves, at the time Josephus and the authors of the New Testament describe some of them as Sadducees in the first century CE. It is no less likely that the process was deliberate, aimed at reinforcing the biblical canon, buttressing the position of halakhah and the predominance of rabbinic over priestly authority. One also discerns in the rabbinic positions a clear preference for permitting wider access to study of the Torah and other sacred texts based on revealed knowledge, as against positions that prefer limited accessibility and exclusively inherited privilege and religious standing, based on esoteric knowledge shared by angels and priests.

Whatever the case, there is no denying the sharply polar relationship between that literature and rabbinic positions—an antithetical correlation, with one corpus negating what was advocated by the other. The Sages strove to establish clear-cut barriers between heaven and earth; between works written with divine inspiration and those written after the termination of prophecy; between a canonized, sanctified Torah, to which nothing could be added, and the ongoing composition of Torah under the influence of the Holy Spirit; between fixed heavenly time and fluctuating human time; between angels and humans; between heavenly voices and wondrous secrets as a source of authority, on the one hand, and human intelligence and earthly responsibility as the decisive factors, on the other; between the pre-determinism and predestination inherent in metahistorical myth and the cyclic eternity of the laws of nature, on one hand, and national history shaped by singular events and capricious human determination, on the other; or between a pre-determined divine eternity, preserved by angels and priests, on the one hand, and a variable time concept in whose measurement, definition, and subdivision human beings played a significant part, on the other.

In all these areas, the secessionist priestly literature represented a view diametrically opposed to that of the Sages. According to the priestly point of departure, numerical continuity and cyclic order were evidence of the divine order inherent in the laws governing heaven and earth, the basis for the relationship between visible and invisible. Time and nature went forward in fixed divisions, repeating cyclically in a permanent schematic relationship to one another, continuously testifying to the eternity of the divine order of Creation insofar as they were out of the reach of human understanding or action. Man could at most witness the laws of nature and its cycles, which were based on a fixed, numerical sequence; it was absolutely forbidden to tamper with the precise correlation between these two entities, as preserved in the solar calendar and manifested in the sequence of sabbaths, festivals ('appointed times'), seasons, and jubilees. There were fixed, cyclic, numerical relationships between the number of days in the solar cycle and the number of seasons; between the number of seasons and the number of sabbaths; between the number of sabbaths and the number of days in the year; between the number of days in the year, the number of hours in the day, and the number of months; between the number of hours in the day, the number of priestly courses, and the lengths of their service. All

these numbers, in turn, stood in fixed proportions to the number of supernal sanctuaries, the number of sides of the Merkavah, and the number of angelic divisions. The
existence of these numbers and relationships was considered a 'wondrous secret',
esoteric knowledge of angelic origin. This mathematization of the universe and its
manifestations in the cycles of nature and the cycles of the sacred service were fundamental to an understanding of the divine order; expressive of God's infinity and the
ongoing regularity of Creation, they were beyond human argument and determination, and as such were the crux of the controversy between the priests, who consecrated them as a framework unifying the visible and the invisible through number
and calendar, and those who refused to subjugate time and its divisions to an eternal,
unchanging divine order.

These oppositional texts, some of which preserved ancient traditions, while
others were written beginning in the first third of the second century BCE and
possibly later, up to the early decades of the first century CE, at different times and
in different places, represent the work of circles of clearly priestly affiliation, whose
social identity was forged and shaped in constant struggle and conflict. There are
about a dozen characteristics that set them apart as a single literary body from the
standpoint of self-definition, fields of interest, polemical thrust, and identification.
The almost symmetric opposites of these characteristics can be traced in rabbinic
tradition. These characteristics will now be discussed one by one.

Wondrous mysteries

Many of these works prominently feature a belief in ongoing divine revelation to
the elect, with an emphasis on angelic revelation of the traditions of priesthood and
prophecy at different times. Such revelation was granted Enoch and his sons the
priests, from Methuselah to Noah, Nir (Noah's brother according to 2 Enoch 70),
and Melchizedek; it was granted to Jacob's son Levi and to Moses, of the tribe of
Levi. After the biblical period and the prophets, divine, angelic revelation was
renewed in the time of the Teacher of Righteousness (presumably the author of the
Thanksgiving Hymns) and his followers, who considered themselves to be the
divinely inspired bearers of the biblical tradition. This idea is clearly expressed in
the description of the leader of the Community: 'Interpreted, this concerns the
Teacher of Righteousness, to whom God made known all the mysteries of the
words of His servants the prophets.'[21] It appears repeatedly in various references
to the revelation of secrets and mysteries in the Thanksgiving Hymns, the Rule
Scroll, the Damascus Document, and the War of the Sons of Light against the
Sons of Darkness: 'For You have given me knowledge through Your marvellous
mysteries and have shown Yourself mighty within me in the midst of Your marvellous Council';[22] 'Your wonderful mysteries on high . . .';[23] 'These things I know by

---

[21] Commentary on Habakkuk VII, 4–5 (cf. Vermes, *CDSSIE*, 481); cf. ibid. II, 8–10.
[22] Thanksgiving Hymns XII, 27 (cf. Vermes, *CDSSIE*, 265).   [23] War Scroll XIV, 14.

the wisdom which comes from You, for You have unstopped my ears to marvellous mysteries.'[24]

Analysis of the relevant texts from the Thanksgiving Hymns, Enoch literature, and Jubilees reveals the content of these 'mysteries': testimony and appointed times; the correlation between the manifestations of divine order in the cyclic sequence of nature, on the one hand, and in the liturgy and daily sacrificial rites in the Temple, on the other, both expressing fixed numerical relationships among the seasons, weeks, months, and days of the year; a fixed mathematical continuum of sacred, creative time and secrets of its quantification in cyclic numerical units, dependent on the celestial bodies, on numerical schemes reflecting the fixed relationships among its parts. The determinism of divine order as revealed in the cyclicity of nature and of the number sequence is described in exquisite language, interweaving the revealed with the concealed and creating a unity of time and space preserved by an ongoing ritual order.

The Sages, for their part, refused to tie time down to such 'wondrous mysteries', revealed in prophecy or by the Holy Spirit. Prophecy, they claimed, had ceased after the construction of the Second Temple: 'After the later prophets Haggai, Zechariah, and Malachi had died, the Holy Spirit abandoned Israel.'[25] Direct communication between God and humanity, common in biblical times, was no more: 'Hitherto [before the advent of Alexander the Great], prophets would prophesy in the Holy Spirit; from now on—"Incline your ear and listen to the words of the sages" (Prov. 22: 17).'[26] Another rabbinic tradition puts the disappearance of prophecy even earlier, dating it to the destruction of the First Temple;[27] it was stated that the Holy Spirit was one of five things that had been present in the First Temple but not in the Second[28]—and without the Holy Spirit there could of course be no prophecy.

The priestly circles, however, maintained the position expressed by the prophet Malachi concerning the relationship between themselves and the Holy Spirit: 'For the lips of a priest guard knowledge, and men seek rulings from his mouth; for he is an angel of the Lord of Hosts.'[29] The Sages reinterpreted this verse, which explicitly associates priests with angels: '[This means that] if the rabbi is like an angel of the Lord of hosts, people should seek the Law from his mouth.'[30] In addition, recounting the chain of transmission of the authority of the Torah and the Holy Spirit in tractate *Avot*, the Sages omitted the priestly stages. Instead of prophetic and priestly inspiration, derived from the angels and transmitted in sacred *written* books, which could therefore be neither freely learned nor disputed, they relied on acquired human wisdom and knowledge, on rationality, interpretation,

[24] Thanksgiving Hymns IX, 22 (cf. Vermes, *CDSSIE*, 254).

[25] BT *Yoma* 9b; Tosefta *Sot.* 13: 2.   [26] *Seder olam rabah* 30.   [27] BT *BB* 12a–b.

[28] BT *Yoma* 21b, *Hor.* 3b. For different views in regard to the end of prophecy and the removal of the Holy Spirit see Urbach, 'When did Prophecy Come to an End?'; Haran, *Biblical Anthology*, 74–8.

[29] Mal. 2: 7.   [30] BT *Ḥag.* 15b.

and exegesis based on accepted hermeneutical principles, on their own *oral* traditions, and on the concept of majority decision, open to question and discussion.

Ongoing composition of sacred works

Divine revelations confer the authority to extend the biblical corpus by adding further works under the influence of the Holy Spirit, by prophetic inspiration or angelic dictation, and justify the sanctification of such works on a par with the Bible. For the secessionist priesthood, the Bible was never finalized, but was continually developing, being built up into what was considered a sacred corpus but not a closed canon. Rabbinic circles, however, considered the divinely revealed and canonized text of the Scriptures a closed body, to which nothing could be added and from which nothing could be removed (although the controversy over Ecclesiastes, the Song of Songs, and Ezekiel continued well into the mid second century CE).[31]

The secessionist priests recognized only the Written Law, which was still being written on the basis of divine or angelic revelation, or further books written with such authority and mentioned in its literature. Their writings continue all the genres of biblical literature, such as historiography, prophecy, and psalms, which have no sequels in rabbinic tradition. The secessionist priesthood rejected the very idea of an Oral Law, in the sense of autonomous, human exegesis, unfettered by sacred origins or inborn privilege, and therefore would not countenance any authoritative works other than those sanctified by its own traditions. Rabbinic tradition, on the other hand, saw the biblical period as a thing of the past; they believed in an Oral Law, based on human sovereignty and open to study and interpretation by the entire Jewish people. Upon the canonized, inviolable, Written Law, therefore, they superimposed new layers and sources of authority, which were initially not committed to writing. Only later, as a result of historical necessity created by the destruction of the Temple and not by choice, did the written texts of the Oral Law (such as the Mishnah) come into being.

Freedom to retell and rewrite the biblical text

Characteristically, these works freely retell and rewrite the biblical text, invoking an alternative principle based on angelic revelation or primeval authority—as in Jubilees, which sets out a historical account differing from that of Genesis and Exodus, reckoned in jubilees and weeks of years; or in Enoch, which retells a considerable part of Genesis according to the priestly myth of the solar calendar; or in the Temple Scroll, which presents a stringent version of the priestly laws in the

---

[31] Mishnah *Yad.* 3: 5. The redaction and finalization of the canon was a protracted process, beginning around 200 BCE and ending around 100 CE. The differences between the Masoretic text of various biblical works, the Septuagint, and their Qumran versions attest to the complexity of this process. For different views regarding this process see Talmon, 'Old Testament Text'; Beckwith, *Old Testament Canon*; Haran, *Biblical Anthology*.

name of a divine voice; or in further works relying on divinely inspired exegesis. Such inspiration draws on revelation of 'hidden things', inscribed on the 'heavenly tablets' and pertaining to the perception of sacred time past and present;[32] or to the perception of sacred place in the future, as in the Temple Scroll, in which God speaks in the first person and dictates a new version of the biblical text.[33] Among the finds at Qumran are versions of biblical texts differing from the familiar traditional editions; it is clear that their authors felt free to emend and rework the text on the basis of principles other than those governing the Masoretic text. The priests, teachers, and scribes of the Community, seeing themselves as heirs to a hallowed tradition, or as having been granted divine revelation, believed that their laws were divinely ordained and not derived by exposition or exegesis of a text; hence, they believed, they possessed divine authority.

The priestly authors also took the liberty to intervene in prophetic writings, in the sense that they would convert a prophetic text pertaining to the future into a message for the present; they would thus interpret a prophecy referring to the End of Days as if it concerned the realities facing the Community in the present and the near future, as done, for example, in the *pesharim*.[34]

As against these liberties, permitting intervention in the text itself, with consequent changes in wording, content, and meaning, addition of laws, and structural and editorial emendation, as reflected in the many works discovered at Qumran which are based on the Bible, but in non-standard order and interpretations, the rabbinic position prohibited the slightest tampering with the sacred text, permitting only episodic interpretations and aggadic–midrashic exposition of isolated words and verses, expanding their content and meaning on the basis of authority derived from the Oral Law or human logic. Only in this way was extension of the law allowed, never through divine revelation or on heavenly authority. The Sages would not tolerate intervention in the canonized biblical text, such as altering the identity of prophets and their prospective audiences, augmenting or suppressing elements of the biblical plot; even more intolerable in their view were alternative versions of entire biblical books in the name of heavenly authority, divinely inspired exegesis, or angelic revelation.

Angels

Much of the literature of the secessionist priesthood treats the angels as the heavenly counterparts of the priests, also giving expression to many myths linking the two groups—those ministering in the heavenly and terrestrial sanctuaries. One

---

[32] See 1 En. 81; 89: 16; 'revealing to them the hidden things in which all Israel had gone astray' (Damascus Document III, 13–15; Vermes, *CDSSIE*, 129); and cf. 'how [Azazel] has taught all (forms of) oppression upon the earth. And they revealed eternal secrets which are performed in heaven . . .' (1 En. 9: 6); 'all the secrets of the angels . . .' (1 En. 65: 6).

[33] See Yadin (ed.), *Temple Scroll*; Brooke (ed.), *Temple Scroll Studies*; Qimron, *Temple Scroll*.

[34] See Horgan, *Pesharim*.

detects here a particular interest in the mythical, mystical elevation of human beings to supernal realms, whether in a waking or a dreaming state, in association with the myths of the priesthood and the calendar (Enoch; Melchizedek; Noah, Levi). Conversely, angels are portrayed as descending to earth in the past (it was they who initiated and witnessed the Covenant: see Jubilees and the Testament of Levi); in the present (as members of the Community, partners in the liturgical order as described in the Community Rule and the Songs of the Sabbath Sacrifice; as responsible for the cosmic order of things—see the story of their creation in Jubilees and the accounts in 1 and 2 Enoch and the Thanksgiving Hymns); and in the future (as protectors of the Sons of Light in their battle with the Sons of Darkness, and as guarantors of reward and punishment in eschatological times, in heaven and on earth). Throughout the pages of this literature one finds angels in a central position, playing a participatory role in ritual, ranging from the angels who raised Enoch to the Garden of Eden, showed him the laws of nature and the forces of the universe, and taught him reading, writing, and arithmetic, as well as the secrets of the calendar and the 'heavenly tablets'; through the angels in Jubilees, who observe the sabbath, celebrate Shavuot, and enter into covenants with the keepers of the Covenant, the keepers of the sabbath and the festivals; to the 'priests of the inner sanctum' in the Songs of the Sabbath Sacrifice and the angels who anointed Levi as priest and promised him and his progeny eternal blessing.[35] Contrary to such reliance on angelic authority and celestial allies, typical of the secessionist priestly literature, one has the down-to-earth view of the Sages, who limit the role of angels and frown on discussing them; witness the glaring absence of angels in the Mishnah, as well as rabbinic criticism of people associated with them.[36]

This point is even more striking if one compares parallel treatments in biblical and priestly tradition. Whereas angels are very prominent in the priestly tradition, references to them are either omitted entirely or severely curtailed in biblical literature (as in the story of the 'sons of God', the Flood, various episodes associated with Noah, Levi, and Enoch, the accounts of the various covenants, the giving of the Torah and the calendar of festivals in the third month). Nowhere in rabbinic tradition is there any reference to a central role of angels as guardians of time and its cycles, whose song links the visible cycles of divine order with the hidden mysteries of nature, who together with the priests observe the liturgical calendar in the cycles of the sacred service. While biblical tradition emphasizes the misdeeds of Levi himself (bloodshed, lawlessness, excessive zeal) and Jacob's curse upon

---

[35] Cf. Josephus on the secret names of the angels as believed by the Essenes (*War*, II. viii. 7). For the importance of angels at Qumran see Yadin (ed.), *Scroll of the War*, 229–42; Newsom, *Songs*, 23–38; Mach, 'Studies in Angelology'; Noll, 'Angelology in the Qumran Texts'.

[36] For biblical attitudes to angels see Rofé, *Belief in Angels*. For some of the post-biblical evidence relating to the Hellenistic Jewish world, see Mach, 'Saints–Angels'. For rabbinic views of angels see Urbach, *Sages*, 135–83.

him, as well as the murderous fanaticism of his descendants (after the sin of the golden calf, the episode of Phinehas and Zimri), priestly tradition associates Levi's actions with angelic command; the sinful and accursed acts linked with his name in the Bible become meritorious and righteous deeds, by virtue of which Levi and his descendants are granted eternal priesthood and blessing, as well a special relationship with the angelic world (Jubilees; Testament of Levi). The angels missing in the Mishnah nevertheless reappear as ministering angels and liturgical partners, in the Kedushah, in connection with mystical traditions in the three books of Enoch and in Heikhalot literature, and in synagogue tradition; they play a renewed role in later magical literature, which preserves various traditions involving sevens, angels, and priests; finally, they are frequently featured in liturgical poetry (*piyut*) and, of course, in all phases of kabbalistic literature.

Heavenly knowledge

Secret knowledge or lore is a characteristic feature of accounts of angels, who are referred to as 'godlike beings of knowledge', 'angels of knowledge', 'those who know', 'those who know wondrous mysteries', 'singers of knowledge', 'those who establish knowledge', and the like. God himself is designated 'the God of knowledge', as we read in the Songs of the Sabbath Sacrifice:

For from the God of knowledge came into being everything which exists forever. And from His knowledge and His purposes have come into existence all things which were eternally appointed. He makes the former things in their seasons and the latter things in their due time.[37]

This knowledge is associated with numbers and books, with testimony and set times, with cycles, counting, calculation, and thought, with reading and writing, with memory, knowledge of the past and the future; it is the hallmark of angels and priests. Knowledge is the characteristic quality of Enoch, as he himself declares to the archangel Michael upon ascending to heaven: 'I answered, saying, "I am desirous of knowing everything . . ." '.[38]

In *Sefer yetsirah*, the knowledge extolled in Qumran literature as 'your wondrous mysteries' becomes the mystery of Creation: the universe was created in thirty-two wondrous paths of wisdom, in twenty-two letters, and in ten numbers, whose combinations, interpreted as verbal and numerical patterns, make humans partners in divine Creation. The secessionist priestly writers (or the protagonists of their works) constantly invoke heavenly knowledge and angelic authority, revealed to people considered worthy of mystical access to the heavenly Heikhalot, or to people who have received traditions based on such knowledge, that is, the priests. This conception is aptly expressed in the angel Uriel's address to Enoch before his return to earth:

---

[37] Newsom, *Songs*, 170.   [38] 1 En. 25: 2.

In those days, the angel Uriel responded and said to me, 'Behold I have shown you everything, Enoch, and I have revealed everything to you . . .'. Then he said to me, 'Enoch, look at the tablets of heaven; read what is written upon them and understand (each element on them) one by one . . .'. Then the seven holy ones brought me . . . and said to me, 'Make everything known to your son, Methuselah, and show to all your children . . .'[39]

All this knowledge and lore concerning the laws governing heaven and earth, their numbers, cycles, and calculations, is recounted in the books of Enoch and Jubilees.

The Sages rejected these books and their underlying arithmetical traditions of cyclic time anchored in angelic knowledge. They refused to recognize angelic lore, heavenly tablets, and divine arithmetical cyclicity as being of any significance in earthly affairs. They would not even allow divine authority a part in halakhic debate on earth, as manifested in the famous story of the oven of Achnai and in its final message: 'It is not in the heavens.'[40]

In the first centuries CE, the religious ecstatics who claimed angelic and priestly knowledge and looked up to the figure of Enoch as their mentor were known as 'descenders to the Merkavah'; their writings form that part of mystical lore known as Heikhalot and Merkavah literature. The Sages, who recognized the sanctity of their tradition and referred to it as *ma'aseh merkavah*,[41] forbade teaching it in public and confined its study to the 'wise and insightful'.[42] Remnants of the position that assigned knowledge and mystical lore to the angels, associated with cosmic order and the progress of heavenly time, may indeed be found in Heikhalot and Merkavah literature, which frequently refers to the concept of *razim*, 'mysteries',[43] and in various magical works, such as *Sefer harazim*.

Hidden world order and its affinity with cosmic order

These bodies of literature are much concerned with the divine visions revealed to certain people who ascend to heaven, visions which reflect the eternal cosmic order and its sevenfold structure, or the unity of time and place as manifested in the seven days of Creation and in the cyclic regularity of nature as dependent on calculation and counting; it is regularity that guarantees the continuity of Creation and life (Book of Heavenly Luminaries; 1 and 2 Enoch; Jubilees). Here, too, there is a powerful affinity with the world of the angels and the Merkavah. The angels whose task it is to maintain cosmic order and its cyclic eternity, as reflected in number and calculation, in cyclic divisions of day, week, season, year, month, and set time— these angels raise their voices in song in the celestial sanctuary and perpetuate the eternal march of sabbaths and appointed times through their sacred service (Second Ezekiel; Blessings; Songs of the Sabbath Sacrifice; 1 and 2 Enoch). Also treated in

---

[39] 1 En. 80–1.
[40] BT *BM* 59*b*; cf. S. J. D. Cohen, 'Significance of Yavneh'.
[41] BT *Suk.* 28*a*.
[42] Mishnah *Ḥag.* 2: 1.
[43] Schäfer (ed.), *Synopse*, §§73, 326, 512, 544, 675.

these traditions is the fate of those who violate the eternal laws, corrupt the proper order of time, and breach the limits of law and order, cycle and appointed time, causing death and destruction; they are doomed to eternal punishment, condemned to perpetual life in the desolate wilderness of oblivion (the tradition of the Watchers and the angels of destruction; Azazel, Belial, spirits and demons in Enoch, Jubilees, and the Testaments of the Twelve Tribes; the traditions of the scapegoat and the sacred union associated with the Day of Atonement).

The Sages, however, forbade inquiry into 'what is above and what is beneath, what is before and what is after',[44] shunned attempts to decipher the arithmetical secrets of cosmic order allegedly in angelic keeping, and, as already noted, disapproved of public study of *ma'aseh bereshit* and *ma'aseh merkavah*. Any reference to such matters was alluded to indirectly in such evasive terms as 'entering into the Pardes'; and the angelic world with the associated calendar calculations was entirely ignored.[45] As to the third prohibition in that passage of the Mishnah, concerning public study of the mysteries of sacred sexual union, if one links it, on the one hand, to the sexual meaning of the cherubim in the Holy of Holies[46] and their association with the cycles of seasons and appointed times, with fertility and plentiful produce (pilgrimage), and, on the other, to the sins of forbidden marital bonds reflected in the story of the Watchers and their disruption of calendrical regularity (descent from heaven to earth), as treated at length in Enoch and Jubilees, it seems very likely that the prohibition—which is surely not to be taken at face value—should be understood in that context.

Enoch and the solar calendar

As we have repeatedly observed, much prominence is given in the secessionist priestly literature to the seventh patriarch of the universe, Enoch son of Jared, to whom were revealed, in a mystical trance, the secrets of the solar calendar and the cycles of seven-based cosmic time, the deterministic progressions of metahistory, advancing in jubilees and ages as engraved on the heavenly tablets, from beginning to end. This figure, representing the proper distance from the incestuous ties inevitably associated with the emergence of mankind—a distance of seven generations—also personifies the origins of civilization; the beginnings of literacy and numeracy; books and tablets; arithmetic and cyclic counting; memorialization and predestination through books, tablets, numbers, and letters; all originating in heaven. These were, as we have seen, heavenly secrets or mysteries revealed to Enoch by the angels for him to impart to his sons the priests.[47]

Associated with Enoch is the special, sacred status of the solar calendar as based on permanent calculation, cyclic counting, the mathematization of nature, and

[44] Mishnah *Ḥag.* 2: 1.
[45] This is the subject of the second chapter of tractate *Ḥagigah* in the Mishnah, whose opening passage I have already had occasion to discuss (see p. 162 above).
[46] BT *Yoma* 54a.   [47] 1 and 2 En.; Jub. 4: 16–26.

heavenly testimony. The lunar calendar, however, was rejected, as being based on variable counting and reliance on sensory perception and human testimony. Pervading the literature of the secessionist priests is this struggle between the two calendars, between abstract mathematization, a system of permanent numerical relationships and eternal numerical divisions of the cycles of nature, with the visible and the invisible interwoven through the power of numerical regularity and cyclic computation, on the one hand; and counting based on fluctuating human observation, prone to error, relying exclusively on the senses, on the other. The literary expression of this struggle was the myth of the solar calendar, associated with Enoch, who 'walked with God', and the myth of the lunar calendar, linked with the Watchers, who 'walked in the stubbornness of their hearts' and transgressed the laws of heaven and earth. The implacable struggle between the secessionist priesthood and the ruling priests was symbolized by the contrast. On one side are the Sons of Light, walking in God's paths, adhering to the solar calendar and its ways, in a world of eternity, regularity and cyclicity, synchronization between the cosmic order and the cultic order of the calendar of sabbaths and festivals, priestly courses and seasons. On the other side are the Sons of Darkness, walking in the stubbornness of their hearts, holding fast to the lunar calendar with its connotations of change and inconstancy based on human observation, disruption of the proper order of the sacred service, and violation of the synchronization between nature and ritual.

Contrast this with the rabbinic attitude, which belittled Enoch and portrayed him in a negative light.[48] The Sages suppressed the literature that was concerned with knowledge of heavenly lore relating to calendrical calculations, or with the fate of violators of the heavenly order. They rejected theories of the solar calendar based on angelic knowledge and testimony, perpetuating the eternity of Creation according to a fixed, preassigned, divine order. Rabbinic tradition chose the lunar calendar, which was based on human observation, decision, and knowledge here on earth, and established a changeable, human order. This calendar recognizes no fixed number of days per year, no fixed number of sabbaths or weeks, no fixed time intervals between festivals; festivals or first days of seasons do not always fall on the same day of the week. Lacking a stable numerical foundation, a firmly imprinted and permanent basic unit of time, the entire calendar is based on subjective estimate, on the fluctuating times of the moon's rising, on human discretion and decision, open to change and error.

In order to distance themselves from the position of the priestly champions of the solar calendar, the Sages took care that the festivals should not fall on those days prescribed in the solar calendar. Whereas, in the solar calendar, the first day of the first month and the first day of the seventh month always fell on a Wednesday, the Day of Atonement on a Friday, the Festival of Unleavened Bread and Sukkot on

---

[48] *Genesis Rabbah* 25: 1; see Urbach, *Sages*, 335.

a Wednesday, the elevation of the Omer and Shavuot on a Sunday, and no festival could ever fall on a sabbath, the lunar calendar was arranged so that none of the festivals named would ever fall on those specific days, while festivals in general *could* fall on the sabbath. Rabbinic law rules that the New Year can never fall on Sunday, Wednesday, or Friday (the only days on which a month can begin in the priestly calendar), the Day of Atonement can never fall on Sunday, Tuesday, or Friday, the Festival of Unleavened Bread can never fall on Monday, Wednesday, or Friday, and the Omer can never be harvested on Tuesday, Thursday, or the sabbath: these are precisely the days reserved for these festivals in the priestly calendar or the days that will determine the priestly dates.[49]

Interestingly enough, as against the tradition counting Enoch as the seventh patriarch, singling him out in life and death[50] and linking him with purity and sanctity, wisdom and knowledge, God and the angels, and with the origins of priestly tradition,[51] biblical sources also preserve a contrary tradition, associating Enoch's name with sin and impurity. In this alternative tradition, Enoch is linked with a forbidden union and bloodshed as the son of Cain, murderer of his brother and son of his mother Eve. The name of Enoch's mother is not given in the Bible; but since the only woman in existence was Cain's mother Eve, we may have here an allusion to an incestuous relationship of Cain with his mother, she being the mother of his son Enoch. Jubilees, retelling the story of Cain's line, states that Cain's wife was his sister 'Awan, daughter of Adam and Eve, who bore him his son Enoch'.[52] Admittedly, the text is seemingly concerned here with two Enochs and with two diverging traditions of Adam's progeny in chapters 4 and 5 of Genesis: the tradition in Genesis 4 places Lamech and his father Methusael in the line of Cain and Enoch (bloodshed, incest). However, Jubilees opens the tradition with the marriage of Seth and his sister Azura, who give birth to Enosh, and continues with his son Kenan, who weds his sister Mahaleleit and begets Mahalalel; Mahalalel then weds his cousin and begets Jared. Only then, with these incestuous bonds sufficiently far back in time,[53] does the text arrive at Enoch son of Jared, founder of the priestly dynasty, and his descendants Methuselah, Lamech, and Noah, who are associated with the solar calendar, the priesthood, and the sacrificial rite.[54] The tradition of Genesis 4 lists Lamech as the seventh in the incestuous dynasty of Cain and his son Enoch, whereas that of Genesis 5 lists Enoch as the seventh in a line that had avoided incest since the time of Mahalalel and Jared, as recounted in Jubilees. No doubt the portrayal of the same person as sanctified and pure in one tradition, but as associated in another tradition with the gravest sins in the Bible, is no accident; it surely reflects an ancient controversy over the very origins of sanctity and authority, of sacred book, sacred number, and sacred narrative.

---

[49] *Maḥzor vitri* 378.   [50] Gen. 5: 18, 21–4.   [51] 1 En. 1, 2; Jub. 4: 16–20.
[52] Gen. 4: 18; Jub. 4: 9.   [53] Jub. 4: 7–16.   [54] Jub. 4: 17–28.

Preordination

The predeterministic schematization of divine time implies that the present is preordained and confined between fixed durations of time, measured in numerical terms. This predeterminism links Creation and its eternal laws and cultic representation, all measured and counted in sevens, with the march and preordained course of metahistory, which is measured and counted in years, sabbaticals, and jubilees. Time, thus structured and predetermined, strives to eliminate the arbitrary, chaotic, meaningless, and hopeless nature of existence, anchoring it instead in a pattern of order and meaning, destiny and mission. This deterministic perception of reality links the earthly and the heavenly through eternal testimony and prescribed liturgical order, faithfully observed by priests and angels. Divine justice is thus ensured for those who keep the Covenant, and an apparently fluctuating existence is tied down to a fixed, cyclic, numerical fulcrum.

Such was the world of the secessionist priests, based as they saw it on the divine origin of time, on its symmetrical division into predetermined sequences of days, sabbaths, seasons, festivals, months, years, sabbaticals, and jubilees, observed and demarcated in terms of the sequence of priestly courses and sacred festive occasions. The laws governing heaven and earth were fixed and known in advance, founded on a fixed, constant, mathematical, astronomical calculation of the relationships among the parts of time—cycles of years, sabbaticals, jubilees, and ages—the charge of the angels. The Sages, in contrast, advocated human control of the march of time, denying any role to angelic testimony in that context. Each month was consecrated anew by eyewitnesses to the re-emerging moon; while prescribed, fixed calculations of time, based on the fixed orbit of the sun, were opposed. The Sages, rejecting the fixed solar calendar, consequently objected to any predeterministic perception of history, that is, to reliance on an angelic and priestly concept of cultic time, in which the Temple servants were entrusted with the demarcation of time. They favoured human sovereignty, dependent on the changing needs of time and place, rather than a preordained, divine system relating to cosmic cycles beyond the confines of time and place.

Seven

The literature of the secessionist priests attaches paramount importance to the number seven and all its derivatives: the seven days of the week, sabbath, sabbatical year, jubilee, seven weeks of years, and Shavuot, the Festival of Weeks/Oaths, celebrated seven full weeks after the elevation of the Omer in commemoration of the seven weeks that elapsed from the Exodus to the giving of the Torah on Mount Sinai—all predetermined, seven-based derivatives of number, counting, and time. These sevenfold divisions mark times of cessation of routine activity, resignation of human sovereignty, 'appointed times of freedom'—a pattern of time in which the natural, continuous course of events, actions, and enslavement is interrupted and brought to a halt. The resulting sevenfold units establish an eternal, liturgical, cosmic order, a preordained course of history, imprinted upon nature since the seven days of Creation: days of the week, sabbaths, seven predetermined festivals. The sacred service is predetermined in terms of priestly courses, each performing its ministry in turn for seven days, and in terms of the liturgical calendar of Songs of the Sabbath Sacrifice, sung in seven-day cycles by priests and angels in a prescribed sequence. They establish what we might call 'Jewish' time, a unique line of reference or identification founded on testimony and appointed times, on counting and calculation, independent of external, changing circumstances or unexpected human shortcomings. This permanent schematization of time, according to a divine, sevenfold pattern shared by angels and priests, shapes both the annual ritual calendar, measured in sabbaths, and the course of history, measured and counted in sabbaticals and jubilees. The predeterministic historical outlook makes the future foreordained in conformity with past regularities. The seven-based structure brings together septuples of time, place, and ritual, suspending the natural course of time and replacing days of labour with days of cessation and rest. Reflected in this structure is the priestly mythical goal of uniting heaven and earth, uniting the super-temporal and the temporal, the angelic and the priestly, and basing such unity on calculation of number and cycle, combining abstract and tangible.

In the secessionist priestly literature the calendar, like the law, the sanctity of the priesthood, and the order of liturgy and ritual, was seen as associated with cyclic numerical patterns, as derived from a sacred, divine source, from angelic testimony. Like them, it reflected an eternal order, unchangeable by human agency, an order strictly maintained in seven-based patterns and correlated with a system of divine covenants, perpetuated in the heavenly tablets and celebrated at set times in heaven and on earth, observed by angels and priests.

In Jubilees, festivals are associated with covenants between angels and human beings from the times of Noah, the patriarchs, and the twelve tribes, until the theophany at Mount Sinai. Not so in rabbinic tradition, which aims both to erect a barrier between celestial and terrestrial and to enhance human participation in the application and interpretation of divine law. The basis for this outlook is that time is subordinated to human reason; the dates of the festivals are dependent on a changing calculation relating to certain historical events in the nation's history, from the time of the Exodus from Egypt and the theophany and later. Determination of the calendar, interpretation of the law, and the dating of festivals and other 'appointed times' are entrusted to human beings and subject to human discretion and earthly interpretation. The choice of the lunar calendar, which is based on human observation and dependent on changing decisions by human beings, expresses this position. Out of the whole priestly system of sevens, in which the number seven was a crucial factor in distinguishing between impurity and purity, chaos and order, death and life, enslavement and freedom, human labour and

divine rest—all bound by covenant and oath, memory, counting, and observance—rabbinic tradition retained only its non-deterministic aspects, that is, the
seven days of purification, which depend on autonomous human counting; the
seven days of the week and the sabbath as a basis for the religious calendar;
the seven days of mourning practised after life has come into contact with death,
and their antithesis, the seven days before circumcision, during which the
newborn child is transported from the realm of chaos to that of Creation, from
impurity to purity. It is very probable that the seven days of the wedding feast, as
well as the 'seven benedictions' of the betrothal ceremony and perhaps also the
seven times the phylactery straps are wound around the arm, were also originally
associated with the sanctity of the number seven in its multiple meanings—oath
and covenant, the sanctity and continuity of life, counting and number, heavenly
sign and divine promise of blessing.

Festivals / appointed times

The secessionist priestly literature offers various links, unknown in other sources,
between the solar calendar and the underlying reasons for the commandments and
the festivals. These links tend to minimize the historical character of the festivals
and their dependence on single, unique, national events, associating them as far as
possible with the primeval past—the days of Creation, angelic testimony, the
cyclic laws of nature, the rhythms of fertility and first fruits, and the cultic agricultural year, recurring in permanent cyclic sequence since the beginning of time:

> You have allotted to them judgement in their appointed times according to their rule, for
> You have established their ways for ever and ever . . . All things are graven before You
> on a written reminder for everlasting ages, and for the numbered cycles of the eternal
> years in all their appointed times.[55]

One of the major goals of Jubilees is to trace the roots of the festivals to primeval
times and the time of the patriarchs; to link them with the angels; to associate them
with significant seasons of the agricultural year occurring at intervals of seven
weeks—and thus to weaken the association of the festivals with the Exodus from
Egypt. The festival calendar in the seven months from the first month to the
seventh, with the first fruits of barley, wheat, wine, oil, and the ingathering, following one after another in a continuous series at intervals of seven weeks, is set out in
the Temple Scroll and alluded to in biblical tradition.

The Sages, for their part, made every effort to stress the reverse elements:
the novelty inherent in the festivals, in the sense of their dependence on singular,
historical events associated with the Exodus from Egypt and the years in the
wilderness. They marginalized the schematic, cosmic, numerical, cyclic element,
relating to the seasons of the year and the cycles of agricultural produce, obscuring

---

[55] Thanksgiving Hymns IX, 17, 24 (cf. Vermes, *CDSSIE*, 254).

allusions to mythical, angelic, priestly, agricultural, fertility-related, and cultic elements.

Jubilees links Shavuot (the Festival of Weeks and/or Oaths: I remind the reader that the Hebrew root of the festival's name, *sh-b-ʿ*, has the multiple connotation of oath, testimony, covenant, and week) with the Covenant with Noah and the angels, the Covenant between the Pieces, and the Sinai Covenant, with the annual renewal of the Covenant in the third month, and with the first fruits of the wheat harvest. The name of the festival, with these associations, was forgotten in the Mishnah and the Tosefta, and the mystical traditions associated with it and its public ceremonial aspects faded into the mists of time.[56] In consequence, the time for harvesting the Omer (Sunday, the 26th day of the first month, according to the secessionist priests) and hence also the date of Shavuot, which falls exactly seven weeks later on the 15th day of the third month (also a Sunday), were a major bone of contention between the secessionist priesthood, on the one hand, and the Hasmonaean Temple priests and rabbinic tradition, on the other. It is striking that the mystical character of the festival, associated with the theophany on Mount Sinai and the revelation of the Merkavah, and its pentecostal nature were preserved in New Testament tradition, which refers to it as Pentecost, that is, the fiftieth day, celebrated after the counting of seven weeks, and describes the descent of the Holy Spirit in connection with the revelation of Ezekiel's Merkavah or the theophany at Sinai.[57]

Merkavah

The literature of the secessionist priests evinces repeated interest in the tradition of the Merkavah—the Chariot Throne—and the Temple ritual, the idea of a heavenly Temple aligned with the four cardinal directions and containing twelve gates, seven firmaments and seven *heikhalot*, seven *merkavot* and seven *devirim*, contrary to the rabbinic view, which, as we have seen, frowned on the study of the Merkavah. Merkavah tradition was associated, on the other hand, with the four dimensions of the universe and the four seasons of the year, with the twelve months and the cycle of years; with Shavuot, first fruits, and fertility; with the chariot throne of the cherubim in the *devir* as seen by the pilgrims to the Temple; with mystical traditions of communion with the Godhead; with the perception of the heavens as possessing a sevenfold structure; with the idea of angelic participation in the ritual, in the chanting of the Kedushah together with the priests, and in sevenfold harmonies of 'seven wondrous words' sung by 'seven chief princes' in the Songs of the Sabbath Sacrifice.

But Merkavah tradition was associated above all with the book of Ezekiel, the scriptural work that the Sages had at one time intended to exclude from the

---

[56] See p. 204 above.

[57] Acts 2: 1–4. Similar traditions of the pentecostal nature of Shavuot figure in Tobit (see Ch. 6, n. 22); in the Samaritan calendar, which to this day celebrates the festival after fifty days; and in Philo's account of the festival (see Ch. 1, n. 59).

canon.[58] Through its intimate relationship with Shavuot—the Sages had actually tried to abolish the recitation of the first chapter of Ezekiel, with its detailed account of the Merkavah vision, as the prophetic reading (*haftarah*) for that festival[59]—it represented the ancient perception of the festival as celebrating the acceptance or renewal of the Covenant, an idea that the Sages wished to suppress. In the present text of Ezekiel, representing the traditional redaction, the word *merkavah* is not mentioned anywhere in the vision, though it occurs as expected in the Septuagint and in Qumran parallels.

The fact that the vision occurred on Shavuot was also suppressed in the opening passage of the book, so as to conceal the significance of the vision in relation to the time of pilgrimage and the priestly tradition of the Temple. As I have pointed out, the name 'Shavuot' does not occur in the Mishnah or the Tosefta; the public, ceremonial meaning of the festival was forgotten and its very date was disputed by the Sages and the secessionist priests, whom the Mishnah calls 'Sadducees' (Heb. *tsedukim*); while the latter called themselves the 'House of Zadok' (Heb. *beit tsadok*), stressing the association with the connotation of the root *ts-d-k*, 'righteousness', at the same time branding their opponents as 'walking in the stubbornness of their hearts' and disrupting the proper order of the festivals.

Heavenly ordained priesthood

Secessionist priestly literature repeatedly celebrates the divine origin of the priesthood and its connection with the angelic ritual, the heavenly Chariot Throne, and the seven-based traditions involving the figure of the seventh patriarch of the world, Enoch, the scribe of righteousness. This tradition continues with the guardians of the priestly covenant—Levi son of Jacob and the tribe of Levi; the Sons of Aaron, referred to in MMT as 'most holy of the holy', a designation applied to their successors, the Zadokite priests, descended from Eleazar son of Aaron the priest, his son Phinehas, and his descendants, guardians of the patrilineal tradition going back to Levi, Kohath, Amram, Aaron, and later. Special interest is evinced in the Zadokite priests, 'appointed by the Lord', from whose ranks the position of the high priest was filled from the foundation of the First Temple to the middle of the Second Temple period (up to the time of Onias III, son of Simeon), and in the Teacher of Righteousness of Qumran and his followers, keepers of the traditions of sabbaths and appointed times, covenants and oaths. This priestly pre-eminence was founded on a claim to hereditary sanctity, passed down from consecrated father to son and rooted in divine election, in natural law; it was an innate privilege of the descendants of Aaron, qualified by divine law to enter the Holy of Holies.

Such inborn primacy was contrary to rabbinic perception. While the Sages recognized the unique position of the Aaronide priests as commanded in the Torah, they set limits to the hegemony that ensued from the priestly privileges,

---

[58] See p. 207 above.   [59] See p. 154 above.

restricting the priests' authority and their claims to exclusive knowledge. Determination of the proper sequence of the calendar and interpretation of the law—these were not the exclusive prerogative of the priests; any person participating in the study of the law could share that burden and don 'the crown of Torah', regardless of descent.

Another topic of central importance in the literature of the secessionist priests was the figure of Levi. In contrast to biblical tradition, which does not link Levi with the priesthood but, on the contrary, refers to him disapprovingly (the massacre of the Shechemites, Jacob's curse), Qumran literature describes him as having received angelic revelation and as having been consecrated on various occasions to serve in the holy precincts; moreover, he receives his grandfather Isaac's blessing, nullifying his father Jacob's curse. This approach is central to the Testament of Levi, which is concerned above all to glorify Levi and recount his pre-eminence and eternal sanctity.[60]

Qumran literature also concerns itself intensively with the mythological origins of the priesthood prior to the tribe of Levi. Thus, it recounts priestly traditions relating to Enoch, father of the antediluvian high priesthood, and to his descendants, founders of the sacrificial ritual: Methuselah, Nir, Noah, and Melchizedek, who create the link between angelic myth, divine Covenant, and the eternity of the laws of nature, between the heavenly tablets and the tablets of the Covenant. Rabbinic tradition, however, viewed some of these figures in a negative light, obscured the Enochide associations of the priesthood, and disparaged, or rejected outright, the literature that relied on the heavenly tablets and angelic revelation; neither did it devote attention to the myths of priestly origins. I have already pointed out that the chain of tradition in the mishnaic tractate *Avot* omits the priestly link in the transmission.

Sadducean halakhah

Alongside such mythical and mystical ideas, envisaging channels of free access between heaven and earth, with the celestial realms as sacred sanctuaries where the angels officiate and study and teach the fundamentals of the holy ritual, one also finds in these works legal material: stringent priestly laws pertaining to cultic matters, as clearly represented in MMT, Jubilees, the Temple Scroll, and the Damascus Document. Such material is represented by precepts relating to the Temple and its ritual, observance of the sabbath and the sacrificial rites. The striking

---

[60] Cf. Jub. 31: 13–17 for Isaac's blessing of Levi and the link between priests and angels; Jub. 32: 1–12 for the choice of Levi as priest; Testament of Levi 5: 1–2; 8; Hollander and de Jonge, *Testaments of the Twelve Patriarchs*, 461; Aramaic Testament of Levi (Levi Apocryphon), in *DJD* XXII, 1–70; 5Q13, frg. 2, in Licht, *Rule Scroll*, 306; *Joseph and Aseneth*, in Charlesworth (ed.), *OT Pseudepigrapha*, ii. 239. See also Kister, 'Levi who is Light'; Stone, 'Enoch, Aramaic Levi and Sectarian Origins'; Stallman, 'Levi and Levites'; Kugel, 'Levi's Elevation to the Priesthood'; Kugler, *From Patriarch to Priest*. In the Testaments of the Twelve Tribes, the patriarch of each tribe instructs his descendants to obey the members of the tribe of Levi, to whom God granted priesthood and leadership.

similarity between certain aspects of the law, opposed by the Sages as representing 'Sadducean' tendencies, and the legal material in these works has not gone unnoticed by modern scholars (witness the generally accepted but anachronistic designation 'Sadducean (or Zadokite) halakhah').

Sons of Light and Sons of Darkness

Much of this polemical literature represents a dualistic perception, a confrontation between eternal, sacred truths of divine origin, the legacy of the Sons of Light, the righteous members of the Community, on the one hand; and twisted, false truths, associated with the Watchers and the Sons of Darkness, the 'government of Belial', who 'walk in the stubbornness of their hearts', on the other. This extreme approach, whose mythological expression in the stories of Enoch and of the fallen angels I have already reviewed, and whose detailed apocalyptic expression is the Qumranic War of the Sons of Light against the Sons of Darkness, probably emerged against the backdrop of the perceived usurpation of priestly supremacy and desecration of the sacred service. The Qumran priests' sensation of unjust deprivation, usurpation, and persecution (as in the Commentaries on Isaiah and Habakkuk) left no neutral ground, promoting instead an impenetrable barrier between brotherhood, loyalty, love, and blessing, on the one hand, and secession, hate, and curse, on the other. The Community Rule demanded that the faithful 'love all the Sons of Light, each according to his lot in God's design, and hate all the Sons of Darkness, each according to his guilt in God's vengeance'.[61] The schism affected both celestial and terrestrial matters—an uncompromising dualism in heaven as on earth.

Rabbinic literature, however, conceives of man as an individual; it does not consider the question of group identity, nor does it discuss such basic confrontations between groups avowing distinct and mutually exclusive spiritual and social identities, struggling for legitimacy; it does not present dualistic positions that result in the rejection of whole groups. Nevertheless, there are clear and consistent traces of the polemic against positions attributed to the Sadducees, heirs to the Zadokite tradition, in relation to the proper order of ritual in the Temple. At the same time, the Sages were repeatedly at pains to express the view that 'all Israel have a part in the World to Come'.[62]

*

The common denominator of all works in the secessionist priestly literature is the challenge to the authority of the ruling priesthood and to the prevalent world view of their time and place in everything connected with the communication of divine authority, Temple and cult, calendar and appointed times, sabbaths and festivals, sanctity and purity. This challenge was based on biblical tradition and on the associated tradition of the House of Zadok. Presenting a typically priestly orientation

---

[61] Community Rule I, 10 (cf. Vermes, *CDSSIE*, 99).   [62] Mishnah *San.* 10: 1.

and an extreme oppositional position to the ruling priesthood, these works expound a sweeping alternative deriving from a different source of authority—associated with the tradition of the angelic priests and relying on a different cultic tradition, as represented in such works as Ezekiel, Jubilees, Enoch, the Temple Scroll, and the Scroll of Priestly Courses. Superimposed on these views were a comprehensive dualist position, unique socio-religious views, and exceptionally stringent legal arguments relating both to the schism of the present and to the hegemony of the future.

Emerging from this literature is an alternative to the views held by the secessionists' foes concerning sacred time, sacred place, and sacred ritual; an alternative arising from angelic revelation, a distinctly different account of primeval events; unique perceptions expressed in song, law, and myth displaying a mystical conception of God and his heavenly company; positions whose claim to legitimacy lay in divine revelation, in a continuous mutual relationship with the angelic world, in the heavenly tablets, and in covenants of priests and angels. Basic to these ideas, in addition, was a conception of divine time as a creative continuum underlying all understanding of reality; human testimony to this conception established a priestly ethos founded on this evolution of time, a mythology concerning the beginning and the end, governing all related calculations and measurements. History, too, was written from an idiosyncratic point of departure, dividing time into weeks of years and jubilees, dictating the course of events from the beginning to the end of time (as in the War Scroll), and shaping the isolated existence of the Community along the lines of the prophecies of Ezekiel, priest and prophet, who—on an earthly level—advocated the supremacy of the Zadokite priests and—on a heavenly level—offered his vision of Temple and Chariot Throne.

The ritual envisaged in the literature of the secessionist priesthood was founded on a fixed, cyclic calculation pertaining to the solar calendar: fifty-two weeks/sabbaths, adding up to a year of 364 days and divided into four seasons correlated with the major agricultural landmarks of the year and with four liturgical cycles of thirteen sabbaths each. The calendar thus prescribed a sequence of sabbaths, recurring every seven days; of appointed time and seven Temple festivals, occurring at intervals of seven weeks in the first seven months of the year; and of sabbaticals and jubilees, also dependent on seven-unit intervals. The fifty-two sabbaths and eighteen festivals amounted to a total of seventy days every year on which all work and everyday activities ceased. The annual calendar of sabbaths and the multi-annual calendar of sabbaticals and jubilees were both maintained by twenty-four priestly courses, which relieved each other at weekly intervals in thirteen cycles of recurring poems; both calendars, the exclusive province of the guardians of this sacred heritage, were based on the Enoch myth in relation to the basic cycles of cosmic order, and on the myth of angels and priests who share a joint liturgical sequence as found in the Psalms Scroll and the Songs of the Sabbath Sacrifice. On the other hand, this cosmic liturgical calendar, with its sevenfold and fourfold cycles, was associated with the tradition of the Chariot Throne, Ezekiel's Merkavah, the Covenant at Sinai and Shavuot, the heavenly tablets and the tradition of covenants renewed periodically in the third month, and with angelic participation in the ritual.

On the basis of this calendar, the authors of these works provide a detailed account of the seven-based rules governing the Temple ritual and sacred space in general; also based on sevens are the rules relating to purity and impurity, betrothal and fertility; and the association of all these elements with the Chariot Throne and the cherubim creates a rich literary space, closely related to the celestial Temple and the angelic priesthood, on the one hand, and to the sacred Community with its priestly leadership, on the other—a creative space of almost unmatched variety and compass.

Until the discovery of the Dead Sea Scrolls in 1947, this entire literature had almost completely disappeared from Jewish history. The literature of the priestly opposition was doomed to 'concealment', to oblivion and suppression, not only because of questions relating to the source of authority and the legitimacy of one tradition or another—such questions could be debated; not only because of the alternative myth and law that it advocated and its emphatically polemical tone; but primarily because it adopted an exclusive position, claiming to be based on divine election, angelic and priestly authority, and eternal heavenly truths and defining the absolute truth to be the sole legacy of a select group of 'Sons of Light'. Any other world view was rejected out of hand and its believers condemned as 'Sons of Darkness', doomed to destruction in this world and the next. By contrast, the opposing, rabbinic, tradition, the butt of its polemics, championed the overriding pre-eminence of accumulated human knowledge and reason, leaving room in its gradual historical development for different positions; it defined itself from the start by the all-inclusive declaration: 'All Israel have a part in the World to Come.'

TEN

Heikhalot Literature

THE third stage of mystical tradition in antiquity took shape in the wake of the destruction of the Second Temple, around the time of the Mishnah and the Talmud, when certain priestly circles, deprived of their focus of earthly ritual and unable to perform the sacred service, created Heikhalot and Merkavah litera-ture.[1] It is not known precisely when this literature was composed, and the identity of the authors and editors of the Heikhalot tradition is anonymous, pseudepi-graphic, or disputed, although the works concerned were written in the first per-son, as if by eyewitnesses to the supernal worlds, and attributed by the authors to the high priest Rabbi Ishmael b. Elisha[2] and Rabbi Akiva, who entered the Pardes (i.e. engaged in esoteric speculation pertaining to the heavenly sanctuaries; see BT *Ḥagigah* 14*b*).[3] Anonymous or pseudepigraphic as they are, these works display a distinct affinity with many of the mystical priestly traditions which envis-aged humans and angels moving freely between the terrestrial and celestial realms. The authors of Heikhalot literature, however, were concerned solely with the

---

[1] See references listed above in the Introduction, n. 43; and see further M. Smith, 'Some Observa-tions'; Elior (ed.), *Heikhalot zutarti*; Chernus, 'Visions of God'; id., 'Pilgrimage to the Merkavah'.

[2] BT *Ber.* 7*a*.

[3] Some scholars date Heikhalot literature to the tannaitic period (2nd–3rd centuries CE) and con-sider it against the background of the world of the Mishnah and the Talmud; this is the view of Scholem, *Jewish Gnosticism*; id., *Major Trends*, 40 ff.; Green, *Keter*. Supporters of this view rely on the priestly character of this literature and its ties with the destruction of the Temple and with traditions of angelic priests from the last centuries BCE; see Maier, *Vom Kultus zur Gnosis*; Gruenwald, 'Place of Priestly Traditions'; Elior, 'From Earthly Temple to Heavenly Shrines'. Others cite the antiquity of prayer formulae (Bar-Ilan, *Mysteries of Jewish Prayer*). Other aspects of this school of thought are the partial links of Heikhalot literature with the earlier apocalyptic literature (Odeberg, *3 Enoch*; Gruen-wald, *Apocalyptic and Merkavah Mysticism*), or the connection between its mythological nature and the indirect influence of Mesopotamian civilization (Arbel, 'Mythical Elements'). Another group of scholars places the origins of Heikhalot literature further forward, towards the end of the amoraic period (5th–6th centuries); see Urbach, *Sages*, 122–3, 212–13; Dan, 'Hidden Chambers'; id., *Ancient Jewish Mysticism*; Halperin, *Merkabah in Rabbinic Literature*; Alexander, 'Hebrew Apocalypse of Enoch'; Schäfer, *Hidden and Manifest God*. Even the geonic period (9th–10th centuries) has been pro-posed; see M. S. Cohen, *Shi'ur Qomah: Liturgy*; id., *Shi'ur Qomah: Texts*. It has been suggested that the authors of this literature were giving expression to social opposition within the rabbinic world; thus Halperin, *Faces of the Chariot* (for a critique of this view see Elior, '*Merkabah* Mysticism'). For rabbinic attitudes to esoteric tradition and to other priestly traditions see Urbach, 'Traditions about Mysticism'; Lieberman, 'Mishnat shir hashirim'; Schwartz, 'Priesthood, Temple, Sacrifices'; S. J. D. Cohen, 'Significance of Yavneh'.

'heavenly corpus' of the secessionist priestly tradition—that dealing with the mystical metamorphoses of the Temple and the priesthood: Merkavah, angels, Enoch and sevenfold configurations, sacred song and Song of Songs, holy names and oaths. They disregarded the 'earthly corpus' and its preoccupation with the reclusive Community, its polemics revolving around the priesthood and the Temple, the halakhic controversies and dualistic conceptions reflecting the fierce struggle over supernatural authority, sacred tradition, and ritual pathways. The Heikhalot authors neutralized the oppositional disposition of the priestly trad- itions, for the terrestrial polemic had lost its import with the destruction of the Temple, the abolition of the high priesthood, and the cessation of the sacred service. What they preserved was the mystical nature of the Temple traditions pertaining to the heavenly world; their object was to perpetuate the traditions of the Temple (Heb. *heikhal*) and the priestly ritual, beyond the boundaries of time and place.

Much of Heikhalot literature consists of mystical poetry describing the service of the angels in the supernal sanctuaries—the *heikhalot*—according to the percep- tion of the priestly service in the earthly sanctuary: the preponderance of the figure seven, song and music, the Kedushah, purification and sanctification, trumpets blowing, the priestly benediction, pronunciation of the Ineffable Name, burning of incense, eternal fire, use of holy names, and benedictions of praise and exaltation. These elements, and others, were transferred from the ritual, mystical, and litur- gical traditions pertaining to the service of priests and Levites in the terrestrial Temple to ritual, mystical, and liturgical traditions of princes, angels, and arch- angels ministering in seven celestial sanctuaries. Qumran literature, which had preserved and created a rich liturgical and mystical tradition of a celestial sanctuary and angelic ritual, provided a wealth of material and a conceptual context for Heikhalot literature. The mystical world of the secessionist priesthood lay at the foundations of this literature, although, as noted above, the latter concentrated only on the affinity between the earthly and the heavenly as reflected in Merkavah tradition, and on the affinity between the priests and the angels, as expressed in the Enoch tradition, the Songs of the Sabbath Sacrifice, and the diverse traditions of sevenfold configurations, avoiding any earthbound conflict, dualistic position, cultic polemic, or social withdrawal.

We cannot pinpoint any historical contact between the various priestly circles who committed chapters of Merkavah tradition to writing, both because we have no idea what happened to the Qumran priests and because of the mists that shroud the circumstances and locations in which the authors of Heikhalot literature wrote. In addition, we have no independent documentation of the historical identities and real existence of those authors. Nevertheless, there is no denying their common spiritual horizon and their distinct spiritual identity, the continuity of their con- ceptual tradition, their shared linguistic propensities and recurrent patterns of reference, as I shall illustrate below.

The mystical and priestly essence of Heikhalot literature is clearly related to Qumran Merkavah tradition. This was aptly stated by Gershom Scholem in 1965, when he noted the affinity between the Songs of the Sabbath Sacrifice, fragments of which had just been published for the first time, and Heikhalot poetry: 'These fragments [of Songs of the Sabbath Sacrifice] leave no doubt that there is a connection between the oldest Hebrew Merkabah texts preserved in Qumran and subsequent development of Merkabah mysticism as preserved in the *Heikhalot* texts.'[4] The connection is clearly evident in the many motifs shared by the two traditions: seven heavenly sanctuaries and seven-based patterns of angelic service;[5] preoccupation with Temple traditions and angelic priesthood, featuring the ministering angels in Heikhalot literature and the priests of the inner sanctum in Qumran literature; the tradition of groups of seven angels associated with Ezekiel's Merkavah; the joint participation of angels and human beings in the sacred service; angelic songs of praise and glorification in heaven, which is seen as a Temple with seven sanctuaries or *heikhalot*. They clearly share an affinity with the tradition of Enoch, the 'seventh',[6] the ceremonial recitation of the Kedushah and its exaltation of the Ineffable Name in an angelic ritual of song and benediction, the concept of the holy names by which the world is adjured and bound, of ceremonial oaths and the centrality of the priesthood.[7] Both corpuses are concerned with Merkavah tradition and cherubim, with the fourfold and sevenfold relationships of cosmic order, with the traditions alluding to the mystical Pardes and the sacred plantation, with the Holy of Holies and the Song of Songs. The authors of Heikhalot literature took over these concepts, which originated in the tradition of Ezekiel's vision of sacred place and sacred service, in the Enoch traditions of the sevenfold configuration of sacred, cyclic time and the link between priests and angels, and in various traditions of the Covenant oath and Shavuot, the Festival of Weeks/Oaths; they further combined these old traditions with the concept of blessing and imprecation,

[4] Scholem, *Jewish Gnosticism*, 128. For the relationship between the Songs and Heikhalot poetry see also Strugnell, 'Angelic Liturgy'; Schiffman, *'Merkavah* Speculation'; J. M. Baumgarten, 'Qumran Sabbath *Shirot*'; Halperin, *Faces of the Chariot*, 49–55; Elior, 'Merkavah Tradition'.

[5] For the Merkavah tradition in Qumran and Heikhalot literature see n. 3 above. Further concerning angelic priesthood and seven *heikhalot* in Qumran and Heikhalot literature see M. Smith, 'Dead Sea Sect'; Schiffman, *'Merkavah* Speculation'; id., 'Heikhalot Literature'; Newsom, 'Merkabah Exegesis'; M. Smith, 'Ascent to the Heavens'; Elior, 'From Earthly Temple to Heavenly Shrines'. For examples of Merkavah descriptions in Heikhalot literature see 3 Enoch in Odeberg, *3 Enoch*, 146–79; Schäfer (ed.), *Synopse*, §§30–4, 39–44; Elior (ed.), *Heikhalot zutarti*.

[6] For the relation between Enoch traditions in Qumran and Heikhalot literature see Odeberg, *3 Enoch*; Milik, *Books of Enoch*; Gruenwald, *Apocalyptic and Merkavah Mysticism*; Alexander, 'Historical Setting'; id., Introduction to 3 Enoch in Charlesworth (ed.), *OT Pseudepigrapha*; Stone, 'Enoch, Aramaic Levi and Sectarian Origins'.

[7] For the Kedushah in relation to celebration of the Ineffable Name in angelic ceremonies in Heikhalot literature see Gruenwald, 'Angelic Song'; Bar-Ilan, *Mysteries of Jewish Prayer*; Elior, 'From Earthly Temple to Heavenly Shrines'. For these elements at Qumran see Nitzan, *Qumran Prayer*, 237–78. For the priesthood and the tradition of holy names see Elior, 'Mysticism, Magic and Angelology'; ead., 'From Earthly Temple to Heavenly Shrines'; Mach, 'Saints–Angels'.

the conflict between life and death on the Day of Atonement; all these ingredients were reworked in what is now known as Heikhalot and Merkavah literature.

This literature, transforming the ruined Temple into seven heavenly sanctuaries revealed to those who 'observed the Merkavah' or 'descended to the Merkavah', centred attention on the world of the Merkavah, with its angels ministering as priests and Levites, counterparts of the mystics who ascended to those supernal worlds. It represents a mystical metamorphosis of the Temple and the sacred ritual of the priesthood in a new language, based on the previous concepts of the priestly Merkavah tradition.[8] Throughout the works of Heikhalot literature one finds such Qumranic words as *raz*, 'mystery', *pele*, 'wonder', *ranen*, 'to sing', *ofanei or*, '*ofanim* of light', *gilah*, 'joy', *degel*, 'banner' or 'camp', *da'at*, 'knowledge', *kelil*, 'crown'; or such concepts as *merkavot*, 'Chariot Thrones', *ofanim*, 'wheels (of the Merkavah)', *heikhalot*, '(celestial) sanctuaries', *heikhalei melekh*, 'royal palaces', *kise kevod malkhuto*, 'royal throne of glory', *kise pele*, 'wondrous throne', *te'udah*, 'pre-ordination', *tushbaḥa*, 'praise'. The texts are replete with verbs and nouns relating to angelic song, blessing and praise, trumpet flourishes—as well as numerous other expressions connected with the priestly service in heaven. There are references to Enoch 'the seventh' and to the sevenfold configurations of the celestial rites performed in the heavenly sanctuaries; there are descriptions of princes, cherubim, ministering angels and angels of the Countenance, and *ḥayot*—holy creatures of the Chariot Throne. All these expressions, and many others, are reminiscent of Qumran literature in general and of the Songs of the Sabbath Sacrifice in particular.[9] Other points of similarity are the profound relationship of both bodies of literature with Ezekiel's vision and the central role given to the figure of Enoch son of Jared, the Angel of the Countenance.

All these similarities testify to the influence of Qumranic Merkavah literature on Merkavah tradition in Heikhalot literature. They constitute ritual, mystical, mythical, and liturgical representations of a perception that strove to transcend the limits of the senses, to portray a comprehensive, divine reality revealed in number, book, and narrative of heavenly origin. An interest in abstract numbers and arithmetical patterns which explain the concealed cosmic order, in invisible angels who explain the harmonic order of the universe in terms of numerical concepts and both macrocosmic and microcosmic reflections of the world of the Merkavah, is common to both these priestly mystical traditions. Both are concerned with the laws governing the universe and its cyclic motions, which can be predicted and calculated with the utmost precision. Both rely on angelic testimony and heavenly voices, on cyclic, arithmetical symmetry and harmonic schematization of the

---

[8] Elior, 'Concept of God'; and my articles cited in the previous note.

[9] A comparison of the vocabularies of the Songs of the Sabbath Sacrifice and the Heikhalot, based on Newsom's and Schäfer's respective concordances for their editions of these works, reveals a high degree of similarity. Out of 150 words from the former that I have checked, only eight do not occur at all in Heikhalot literature.

eternal divine beauty reflected in the infinite numbers of the unseen world of the Merkavah; that world itself reflects the structure of cosmic order and is expounded in angels' voices and in the testimony of their counterparts the priests, who 'descend to the Merkavah'. Priestly mystical Merkavah tradition transcends the limits of human apprehension; it seeks to attain infinity as represented by numbers and cycles relating to one another in eternal, fixed proportions, in mutually reflecting symmetrical patterns.

The wealth of individual works and variety of texts and genres that comprise Heikhalot literature possess three basic characteristics:

1. The bulk of this literature is preoccupied with supernal worlds whose hidden essence, measured in cosmic numbers and figures amounting to thousands of myriads of parasangs between the different parts of the Merkavah, became known to humanity through both angelic and human testimony, the latter conveyed by the 'descenders to the Merkavah'.

2. Much of Heikhalot literature is written in the sublime language of poems, hymns, and sacred prayers of angels, who preserve the numerical ceremonial traditions of the Temple and the priesthood in their mystical guise, in the supernal sanctuaries where the angels minister.

3. The authors of this literature describe the heavenly Temple in visionary language—the heavenly Merkavah, with its four sides, myriads of parasangs, seven *heikhalot*, twelve gates, and twenty-four regiments of angels, all combining time and place in cosmic proportions; they make these the direct object of mystical experience, of active speculation. Hence they use such active verbs as 'observe', 'descend', 'ascend', 'enter', 'exit', in relation to calculations and measurements, prayer, song, and blessing.

All this activity takes place in the imagination of those who refer to themselves as 'descending to the Merkavah' or 'observing the Merkavah', who 'measure the *shiur komah* [stature] of our Creator' and 'know the size of the Creator'. In their vision, they convert the ruined Temple into seven heavenly sanctuaries, participating in the sacred service performed by the ministering angels, which ranges over the cosmic extent of the universe, over the cycles of nature that unify time and space. They paint the whole in a typically priestly colour, linking the passage and fluctuations of time with the diversity and variation of nature. The mystical phraseology of *shiur*, that is, measurement, and calculations relating to the size of the universe, is preserved in the *Shiur komah* texts, where poetic language becomes the storehouse for numinous traditions associated with Temple and priesthood, *heikhal* and *merkavah*, and mystical hymns become a poetic memorialization, through song and ceremony, of the ruined focus of sanctity and ritual, no longer existent but represented by a heavenly model in the celestial world of the Merkavah.

In the various traditions of Heikhalot literature, all parts of the heavenly Merkavah proclaim the holiness of God, in the words of the seraphim who uttered their threefold 'Holy'—the Kedushah formula—in Isaiah's vision,[10] in the sounds of the creatures' wings and the rush of wheels in Ezekiel's vision,[11] and with the music sung and played by priests and Levites in the Temple.[12] All components of the Merkavah, arranged in cosmic numerical patterns based on four and twelve, measured in parasangs or in the seven-based units that delineate time and space, participate in the heavenly ceremony in the supernal sanctuaries, in the language reserved for the sacred service: the song and instrumental music of the Levites accompanying the sacrificial rites; the enigmatic enunciation of the Ineffable Name as in the priestly benediction—pronounced by the priests in the Temple at the close of the sacrificial rites and by the high priest on the Day of Atonement. The language of the biblical priestly sources is expanded through patterns and concepts evolved in the literature of the secessionist priesthood, with its sevenfold configurations extending to the structure of time and place, as well as the prominent role of Enoch 'the seventh patriarch'.

A central protagonist in the traditions assembled in Heikhalot literature, as expressed in several of its works, is Enoch son of Jared, who serves as high priest in the celestial sanctuary. We have already seen how Enoch, initiator of the calendar and founder of the priestly myth, figures prominently in the five parts of 1 Enoch, in Jubilees, in 2 Enoch, and in the Genesis Apocryphon and other Qumran fragments, all written long before Heikhalot and Merkavah literature, which postdates the destruction of the Temple. Alongside Enoch, the mystical hero of Heikhalot literature and a source of heavenly inspiration to many of its writers, a good many of its works are attributed to two second-generation *tana'im*, who were thought to possess mystical ties with the priesthood and the Temple: Rabbi Ishmael, the high priest, who was said in the Babylonian Talmud[13] to have 'entered the innermost sanctum', where he offered incense, and Rabbi Akiva, who 'entered the Pardes'—a mystical heavenly counterpart of the Holy of Holies, associated with Paradise, the supernal Temple, and the Heikhalot.[14] These two sages teach and write down what was revealed to them from on high during their 'descent to the Merkavah'.

Heikhalot and Merkavah traditions were committed to writing in a series of works: *Sefer heikhalot*, also known as the Third Book of Enoch; *Heikhalot zutarti* and *Heikhalot rabati*; *Shivḥei ḥanokh-metatron* and *Shiur komah*; *Merkavah rabah* and *Ma'aseh merkavah*. The goal of this literature was to preserve and perpetuate the numinous essence of the ruined Temple and the sacred service of old, by mystically transforming them into the heavenly Heikhalot and angelic service. This new goal was incorporated into, or combined with, the mystical and liturgical conceptions of 'descending to the Merkavah', 'entering the Pardes', 'ascending to the Heikhalot', and 'entering the innermost sanctum' (Heb. *lifnai velifnim*—a phrase literally meaning 'in the innermost part', designating the Holy of Holies in

[10] Isa. 6: 3.   [11] Ezek, 1: 24; 3: 12–13; 10: 5.
[12] 2 Chr. 5: 12–13; Pss. 98: 4–6; 149: 3; Neh. 12: 27–47.   [13] *Ber. 7a.*   [14] *Ḥag. 14a.*

the Temple: 'he shall purge the Temple of Holiness (Lev. 16: 33)—that is *lifnai velifnim*[15]). All these expressions imply freedom of access between heaven and earth, a mutual mystical and liturgical relationship between angels and human beings.

The Heikhalot poems were influenced by earlier priestly mystical traditions associated with the perception of the Temple as representing cosmic order and its cycles as reflected in Merkavah tradition; with the twenty-four priestly courses; with Ezekiel's vision; with the heavenly Temple—the seven *heikhalot* and seven merkavot; with the participation of angelic priests in the ritual; with the angelic liturgical tradition of Kedushah; with the various phases of the Enoch tradition; and with the ritual and liturgical visionary traditions of oaths and sevenfold numbers, fourfold and twelvefold divisions of the Merkavah, divine names, the divine 'dimensions', and visible and hidden manifestations of God as portrayed in *Shiur komah* and learned from the angels.

As already noted, some of the authors of Heikhalot literature placed the hero of the ancient mystical priestly tradition, Enoch son of Jared, at the centre of their heavenly picture. They gave him the additional name of 'Metatron, Angel of the Countenance (or the Presence)',[16] and described him as heavenly high priest, ministering in the supernal Heikhalot. This image is associated with the above-mentioned priestly dimension: in Qumran literature, the expression 'Angel of the Countenance' refers on occasion to the high priest serving in the Temple. In the benediction dedicated to the high priest in the Blessings Scroll we read:

May you be as an Angel of the Countenance in the Abode of Holiness, and may the glory of God be upon you and His magnificence all around. May you attend upon the service in the Temple of the Kingdom and cast a lot with the Angels of the Countenance and the Congregation of the *yaḥad* with Holy Ones, for everlasting ages and time without end.[17]

Similarly, the communion of priests and angels is described in the Thanksgiving Hymns[18] by the expression 'For You have brought Your glory to all the men of Your Community, to those who share the lot of the *yaḥad* with the Angels of the Countenance'. This connection reappears in Jubilees, where the angel who dictates the tablets of the Covenant and the divisions of time to Moses is called the 'Angel of the Countenance'. Moreover, in the blessing of Levi we read: 'May He draw you and your seed near to Him from all flesh to service in His sanctuary as the Angels of the Countenance and the Holy Ones.'[19]

---

[15] BT *Yoma* 61a.

[16] It has been suggested (Milik, *Books of Enoch*, 125–35) that the name 'Metatron' refers to the four faces of the Merkavah (Greek *tetra* = four). Alternatively, it may be a combination of the two Greek words *meta* and *thronos*, meaning 'one who serves behind (or beyond) the throne', alluding to his high heavenly position (Lieberman, in Gruenwald, *Apocalyptic and Merkavah Mysticism*, 235–41).

[17] 1Q28b, IV, 25–6 (cf. Vermes, *CDSSIE*, 376). Cf. García Martínez and Tigchelaar, *Study Edition*, i. 106–7.

[18] XIV, 13 (cf. Vermes, *CDSSIE*, 271).   [19] Jub. 31: 14.

The designation 'Angel of the Countenance' (Heb. *malakh (ha)panim*), or sometimes 'Angel/Prince of the Countenance' (Heb. *malakh sar hapanim* or simply *sar hapanim*), refers in Heikhalot literature to Enoch-Metatron, who becomes the source of testimony to the unseen celestial reality, with its measurements and numbers, its ceremony of angelic priests on high, and its tradition of angelic song.[20] The relationship between 'the God of Israel and His Angel of Truth',[21] or between God and the Angel of the Countenance, is not entirely clear. It is associated with an expression in Isaiah 63: 9, 'The Angel of His Countenance delivered them',[22] and with God's promise to Israel, 'I am sending an angel before you . . . Do not defy him . . . for My Name is in him.'[23] Moreover, it is this relationship that caused the sin attributed to Elisha b. Avuyah, who mistook Metatron, the Angel of the Countenance, for God (see below).

The super-temporal figure of Enoch-Metatron is a unique combination of a threefold existence: divine, angelic, and human-priestly. Indeed, he appears in Heikhalot literature as 'Little YHWH, whose name is like that of his Master', 'Metatron YHWH the God of Israel, God of the heavens, and God of the earth',[24] or, as already noted, 'the Angel/Prince of the Countenance', the archangel appointed over all angels, high priest of the supernal sanctuary, one of whose tasks is to teach the cosmic Merkavah tradition. He is Enoch son of Jared, who in mythological times was a mortal, born of woman, before being taken up to the heavens as an eternal witness and righteous scribe. One of the Aramaic translations of the Torah describes Enoch-Metatron as a heavenly scribe:

And Enoch served in truth before the Lord, and he is no longer with the denizens of the earth, because he was withdrawn and ascended to heaven by an utterance before the Lord, and [God] called him Metatron, the great scribe.[25]

He is similarly described in the Babylonian Talmud, which however obscures his role as the intermediary who brought literacy from heaven to earth and founded the priestly myth: 'He [Elisha b. Avuyah] saw that permission was granted to Metatron to sit and write down the merits of Israel.'[26]

---

[20] On Metatron, the Angel of the Countenance, see Schäfer, *Konkordanz*, s.v. *Metatron*; Odeberg, *3 Enoch*, 79–146; Scholem, *Jewish Gnosticism*, 43–55; A. Segal, *Two Powers in Heaven*; Gruenwald, *Apocalyptic and Merkavah Mysticism*; Alexander, 'Hebrew Apocalypse of Enoch'; Halperin, *Faces of the Chariot*; Himmelfarb, *Ascent to Heaven*; Elior, 'From Earthly Temple to Heavenly Shrines', 228–9, 248–9; Liebes, *Sin of Elisha*.   [21] Community Rule III, 24.

[22] The wider context, as given in the New Jewish Publication Society Translation, is 'In all their troubles He [God] was troubled, and the angel of His Presence delivered them.' However, emendation of the vocalization (supported by the Septuagint version) yields: 'In all their troubles. No angel or messenger, [but] His own Presence delivered them.' See Licht, *Rule Scroll*, 284 n. 25.

[23] Exod. 23: 20–1.

[24] Schäfer (ed.), *Synopse*, §678; and cf. ibid., §279: 'That is Metatron YYY the God of Israel, God of the heavens, and God of the earth'; or §678 (MS New York): 'Metatron YHWH God of the heavens and the earth, God of the sea, and God of the land'.

[25] *Targum yerushalmi* to Gen. 5: 24.   [26] BT *Ḥag.* 15a.

The choice of Enoch—founder of the priesthood and initiator of the calendar; the first human being who learned to read and write, to count and calculate, to bear witness and to teach; the scribe whom the angels taught to write and who then brought written testimony from heaven regarding the solar calendar and its set times; the mythical hero of the secessionist priestly tradition and its association of priests with angels—as the mystical protagonist of Heikhalot literature cannot possibly be accidental, given the cultural environment of the times, namely, the Sages' disapproval of Enoch and the suppression of the literature associated with his name. Neither is it any accident that in the central moral tale in rabbinic literature relating to the prohibition of inquiry into Merkavah tradition, the story of the four sages who entered the Pardes,[27] it is Enoch-Metatron who is punished, humiliated, and flayed with sixty fiery lashes for the mistake of Elisha who, upon seeing his stature and magnificence, marvels aloud, 'Truly, there are two Divinities in heaven!'[28] It is not inconceivable that rabbinic tradition, which could not tolerate the infinite glorification of Enoch-Metatron in Heikhalot literature—where there is no end to his beauty, his cosmic magnitude, to the extent that he is almost indistinguishable from the Creator—reacted with this tale of humiliation, punishment, and banishment. The ambivalent attitude to Enoch in the first centuries CE, of which there are no signs in the hallowed figure of the angelic priest reflected in earlier literature (except in Genesis 4), finds its expression in Heikhalot literature, which on the one hand describes his greatness and immeasurable glorification, and on the other reports his punishment and his subordination to his Creator.

Alongside Enoch, the celestial protagonist of Heikhalot literature, the authors placed two mortal figures, Rabbi Ishmael the high priest, doubling for Aaron the priest, and Rabbi Akiva, who 'entered the Pardes' and is seen in this literature as a counterpart of Moses, who ascended to heaven.

Rabbi Ishmael the high priest is said in the Babylonian Talmud[29] to have 'entered the innermost sanctum' (on the Day of Atonement), where he offered incense, saw Akatriel Yah the Lord of Hosts, and blessed him—this at a time when the Temple no longer existed—and he is referred to similarly in *Heikhalot rabati*, where he 'offers up a burnt offering on the altar', observes, and blesses.[30] In the mystical, ahistorical thought of the authors of Heikhalot literature, it was as if Rabbi Ishmael were the last representative of the dynasty of earthly high priests, a continuous line from Enoch, Methuselah, Noah, Nir, Melchizedek, Levi, Kohath, Amram, Aaron, Eliezer, Phinehas, and Zadok; through the sons of Zadok as described in Chronicles, up to the destruction of the First Temple; and up until the time of the authors themselves—but omitting the priests of the Hasmonaean dynasty.

Rabbi Ishmael, who was born in the first century CE, continues the mystical priestly conception shaped in the Merkavah tradition of the last centuries BCE; but he is also the first representative of the mystical priestly dynasty of 'descenders to

---

[27] Tosefta *Ḥag.* 2: 3; BT *Ḥag.* 14*b* ff. [28] BT *Ḥag.* 14*b* ff.; Schäfer (ed.), *Synopse*, §20.
[29] *Ber.* 7a. [30] *Heikhalot rabati* (Schäfer (ed.), *Synopse*, §151).

the Merkavah' after the destruction of the Second Temple. When he enters 'the innermost sanctum', the mystical Holy of Holies, which is equivalent to 'descent to the Merkavah', 'ascent to the seven supernal Heikhalot', or 'entering the Pardes', Rabbi Ishmael meets Enoch son of Jared, the heavenly high priest, who greets him and shows him the world of the Merkavah, teaches him angelic song, and allows him to participate in the sacred service perpetuated in those upper realms. The opening section of *Sefer heikhalot*—also known as the Third Book of Enoch and thought to be the latest work of this literature, though it also preserves early elements[31]—attests to the conceptual continuity between the Merkavah tradition created after the destruction of the First Temple, the supposed (in the minds of the secessionist priesthood) desecration of the Second Temple, and the Merkavah tradition that emerged after the destruction of the Second Temple among the circles of the mystical priesthood, which probably bore some relationship to the concept of the synagogue as a 'miniature Temple' and to synagogal liturgy:

'Enoch walked with God; then he was no more, for God took him.' Said Rabbi Ishmael: When I ascended on high to look upon and observe the Merkavah, I would enter six *heikhalot*, chamber within chamber, and upon reaching the portal of the seventh *heikhal* I stood in prayer. . . . And I said: Sovereign of the Universe, I beg of you to grant me at this time the merit of Aaron son of Amram . . . who received the crown of priesthood before your glory on Mount Sinai. . . . Forthwith he brought me [Enoch] Metatron his servant, the Angel/Prince of the Countenance. . . . And he said to me: Come in peace, for you have been found worthy before the most lofty King to gaze upon the pattern of the Merkavah. Thereupon I entered the seventh *heikhal*.[32]

The super-temporal figure of Enoch, the Angel of the Countenance, the ascent to heaven as the source and origin of all priestly lore, the heavenly world of the Merkavah reflecting cosmic order and the recollection of its earthly pattern, the crown of priesthood of the Aaronide priests handed down from Sinai, generation to generation, and the seven sanctuaries/Heikhalot—all these may also be encountered in the literature of the secessionist priests found at Qumran and extensively discussed in previous chapters. The concept of 'observing' the Merkavah is unknown, however, as is the idea of gazing upon the pattern of the Merkavah, which had not been seen directly by mortal eyes since the times of Enoch, Moses, David, and Ezekiel. But contemplation of cosmic order and comprehension of its cyclic nature are the concern of the Enoch literature and the tradition of the calendar, as well as the traditions of the priestly courses and the consequent liturgical traditions. The hallowed essence of the Merkavah, its infinite numbers and cosmic dimensions, its mythical representations and ritual pattern as perpetuated in the Songs of the Sabbath Sacrifice, and its elements, which shaped the

---

[31] See the survey of Enoch literature at the beginning of Ch. 4.

[32] *Sefer heikhalot* (Schäfer (ed.), *Synopse*, §1). Cf. Odeberg, *3 Enoch*; Alexander, 'Hebrew Apocalypse of Enoch', for analyses of the influence of earlier Enoch traditions on this passage. For the expression 'gaze upon the pattern of the Merkavah' see Schäfer (ed.), *Synopse*, §856.

world of the Qumran community, came down in some unknown process to the authors of Heikhalot literature.

The direct dialogue in heaven between the awestruck human being (Rabbi Ishmael) who is gazing and listening, and God who is speaking, counting and recounting the numerical aspects of the Merkavah, has a detailed precedent in the Merkavah tradition of Enoch literature.[33] The angelic mediation between the divine infinite presence expressed in speech and in the vision of the Chariot, and the awestruck human being addressed by God, also has a precedent in the former Enoch literature. Even where the language is different and a new world of concepts emerges, the imprint of the earlier Merkavah tradition, with its priestly associations, cosmic view, numerical proportions, and seven-based patterns, is clearly visible through the veil of the new version.

Rabbi Ishmael's partner, Rabbi Akiva, is associated in Heikhalot literature with the figure of Moses, who ascended to the heavens.[34] He, too, is referred to in the context of a mystical ascent to the supernal worlds or of entry into the Pardes,[35] and also in Merkavah traditions associated with heavenly song, with the Song of Songs, and with *Shiur komah*. But Rabbi Akiva is also associated with the Qumranic concept of 'wondrous mystery/mysteries' (Heb. *raz/razei pele*) in the prologue to *Heikhalot zutarti*, which is attributed to him: 'If you wish to become One with the world, to discover for yourself eternal mysteries and secrets of the Merkavah . . .'.[36] He thus continues the prophetic mystical archetype of ascent to heaven, listening to the angels, and returning to earth with celestial knowledge of the secrets of the universe—or with the Torah.

Thus, Heikhalot tradition sees Rabbi Akiva and Rabbi Ishmael as mystical counterparts of Moses and Aaron. The first plays the role of the prophet, the man of God transcending the limits of time and space, who 'descends to the Merkavah', achieves direct contact with God and the angels, learns the secrets of the Merkavah, its dimensions and cosmic order, hears and sees heavenly mysteries and celestial song. Upon returning to earth, he transforms the invisible knowledge into an audible, verbal and therefore communicable, sacred textual tradition. The second is the priest, who 'ascends' to the heavenly Holy of Holies and perpetuates the dynasty of Enoch, Levi, Aaron, and his sons the priests. It is his task to create a ritual representation and translation of the heavenly tablets and the tablets of the Covenant, of the celestial laws and mysteries, to remember and protect them and to impart them to man.[37]

---

[33] See e.g. 1 En. 14: 8–25; 2 En. 20–38.

[34] Elior (ed.), *Heikhalot zutarti*, 22. Compare BT *Shab.* 88b–89a.

[35] BT *Ḥag.* 14a; *Heikhalot zutarti*, 23.   [36] Schäfer (ed.), *Synopse*, §335, MS Munich.

[37] While Heikhalot tradition associates the descent to the Merkavah with Rabbi Akiva, Rabbi Ishmael is generally given the role of an intermediary to Enoch-Metatron. The expression 'to descend to the Merkavah' is used exclusively of Rabbi Akiva: 'All these songs did Rabbi Akiva hear when he descended to the Merkavah' (Schäfer (ed.), *Synopse*, §106). Rabbi Ishmael frequently notes that he learned from Rabbi Akiva, whose knowledge was revealed to him from heaven. The relationship between the two sages is similar to that between Moses and Aaron.

The divine revelation and mystical exultation associated with the theophany are linked with the figures of Moses, Ezekiel, and Akiva (Sinai; the Merkavah vision and Shavuot; the Pardes); while the priestly sacred service is associated with the priests Enoch, Aaron, and Ishmael (sanctuary and Temple; Holy of Holies and *devir*/inner sanctum; Day of Atonement; incense; the Chariot Throne of the cherubim).

The authors of Heikhalot literature attach much importance to the mystical apotheosis or transformation involved in ascent to the heavens, which they call 'descent to the Merkavah' and associate with the figure of Rabbi Akiva and thereby with Moses' ascent to Mount Sinai and Shavuot, the mystical, prophetic, and priestly festival of covenants and divine revelation, of testimony and entry into the Covenant, of oaths and septuples, of the heavenly Merkavah/Chariot Throne. No less important in their spiritual world is the ascent to the supernal sanctuaries, the Heikhalot, associated with the figure of Rabbi Ishmael the high priest and the Day of Atonement—the priestly festival of atonement and purification, on which incense was burned and the Ineffable Name was pronounced in the Holy of Holies, symbolizing the very fount of life. All these images are linked in their minds with purification, sanctification, and a holy mission relating to the earthly Merkavah. Shavuot is associated with Ezekiel's Merkavah, with cherubim and angels, with divine revelation, with the Covenant at Sinai, with sevens and oaths, with the union of heaven and earth, with renewal of the oath and the Covenant and preservation of the continuity of life. The Day of Atonement symbolizes, on the one hand, the struggle between life and death as epitomized in the high priest's venturing into the Holy of Holies, the life-source, the abode of the entwined cherubim; on the other, through the sprinkling of blood and other elements of the sacred service it symbolizes atonement for the sin of the Watchers—the paradigm of all sins that disrupt and endanger life—through the dispatch of the scapegoat to the desert, to Azazel.

If the heavenly festival is the counterpart of Shavuot observed in heaven, as related in Jubilees, associated with Ezekiel's vision of the Merkavah and the sequence of covenants concluded between heaven and earth, the earthly priestly festival is the parallel of the heavenly angelic festival and thereby associated with Enoch-Metatron, who ministers, sealed with seals, in the supernal sanctuary and utters the Ineffable Name in a ceremony similar to that performed by his earthly counterpart on the Day of Atonement, wearing the seven holy vestments, carrying the Urim and Thummim with the names of the twelve tribes, attired in the frontlet upon which the Tetragrammaton was inscribed. Enoch, performing his duties in the supernal Heikhalot before the celestial Merkavah, is referred to as 'Metatron, the holy, beloved attendant, the great prince', who has seventy names but is called briefly a servitor or 'youth' (Heb. *na'ar*):

And this youth Metatron, Angel-Prince of the Countenance . . . stands on high in the heavens and ministers before him, fire eating fire, that is Metatron, the Prince of the

Countenance, written in one letter in which were created heaven and earth, and sealed with a ring, I am that I am . . . And it was written in seven signs and in twenty-two letters and in seventy names and with seven *kedushot* . . . And it is inscribed on twelve stones and written in seven voices in six by six and given in the greatest magnificence and the greatest wonders. And the angels that were with him come and surround the Throne of Glory, they on the one side and the *ḥayot* on the other side, and the Shekhinah upon the Throne of Glory in the middle. And one creature [and one spirit] rises up above the seraphs and descends to the abode of the youth whose name is Metatron, and says in a pure, still voice, Pure is the Throne of Glory. Thereupon the angels fall silent and the Watchers are mute and the Holy Ones hasten and rush to the river Dinur and the *ḥayot* prostrate themselves upon the ground. And that youth whose name is Metatron brings deafening fire and places it in the ears of the *ḥayot*, so that they should not hear the voice of the Holy One, blessed be he, speaking, and the Ineffable Name that the youth whose name is Metatron pronounces at that time in seven voices in the name of the Living, Pure, Venerated, Awesome, Holy, and Magnificent. . . . YHWH, I am that I am . . .[38]

Of crucial significance in the view of Heikhalot tradition are the Kedushah formulas recited in the supernal Heikhalot by the angels, as described in the traditions of the secessionist priesthood,[39] and the prayers recited on earth in parallel, as well as the various sevenfold elements relating to the priesthood and the Temple, to the Heikhalot and the angels, to the sacred songs and the divine names—all bound up inherently with the mystical metamorphosis of the Temple rites and together offering an eternal, heavenly alternative to the ruined earthly Temple. The liturgical tradition of this literature, describing rites performed jointly with the angels, Kedushah, and Merkavah song, is intimately connected with the priestly traditions of angelic ritual and with the ancient Merkavah traditions as reflected in the literature of the secessionist priesthood. The figure of the high priest and that of Metatron, the Prince of the Countenance, the holy names, the twelve stones of the high priest's breastplate, the angels prostrating themselves, the Ineffable Name (Tetragrammaton) and its ceremonial enunciation, the high priest entering the Holy of Holies—all these elements appear in the service of the Day of Atonement in the earthly Temple as portrayed in rabbinic tradition (Mishnah *Yoma*) and in the rites performed in the heavenly sanctuary as portrayed in esoteric traditions.

I have already referred to the mishnaic tradition of Rabbi Ishmael the high priest, who entered *lifnai velifnim*—into the inner sanctum, the Holy of Holies—and saw Akatriel Yah the Lord of Hosts.[40] It emerges clearly from various parallels to this tradition in Heikhalot writings that 'entry into the Pardes' and *lifnai*

---

[38] Schäfer (ed.), *Synopse*, §§389–90 (MS New York 8128; MS Munich 40); §488. The vision of divine fire is associated with Exod. 24: 17; Lev. 6: 6; Deut. 4: 12, 24; 9: 3; Ps. 29: 7; and Ezek. 10: 7. The expression 'the abode of the youth' is reminiscent of Paul's description of the high priest on the Day of Atonement (Heb. 9: 7, and cf. Schäfer (ed.), *Synopse*, §597). The river Dinur (which means 'river of fire' in Aramaic) is from Dan. 7: 10, and 'deafening fire' is based on Jonah 4: 8.

[39] 1 En. 39: 12–13; 2 En. 21: 1.   [40] BT *Ber. 7a*.

velifnim' are one and the same thing: entry into the sphere of sanctity, representing the source of life, *after* the destruction of the Temple. Indeed, both Rabbi Ishmael and Rabbi Akiva were third-generation *tana'im*, active in the second century CE, when the Temple was no longer standing. The action of 'entering' or 'ascending'—the two verbs are interchangeable in the different versions of the tale of the four who 'entered into the Pardes'—entails in both cases a transformation from the terrestrial plane of priestly service, in the Holy of Holies in the Temple, to the celestial plane of sacred service in the inner sanctum of the supernal sanctuaries— the Heikhalot. The terrestrial Holy of Holies is a representation of the Garden of Eden or Paradise—that is to say, of the Pardes (see below)—and the location of the Chariot Throne of the cherubim, which represents the world of the heavenly Merkavah, as explained previously. Hence the Holy of Holies, *lifnai velifnim*, Merkavah, Pardes, or the Garden of Eden are equivalent concepts in the priestly tradition of earthly representation of the heavenly; similarly equivalent are the actions designated as entering them or going out to them, of ascending to them or descending into them. These traditions, concerning representation of the invisible by the audible, the liturgical, the mystical, and the textual, bringing together heaven and earth, also relate to Shavuot, the tradition of the Merkavah and its visionary heavenly revelation, on the one hand, and to the Day of Atonement and the priestly traditions of sacrifice and incense, benediction and song, holy names and sacred service performed in purity, on the other.

The Heikhalot tradition I have been referring to in *Berakhot* 7*a* reads as follows:

It was taught: R. Ishmael b. Elisha said: I once entered into the inner sanctum [Heb. *lifnai velifnim*] to offer incense and saw Akatriel Yah, the Lord of Hosts, seated upon a high and exalted throne. He said to me: Ishmael, My son, bless Me!

While the reference here is explicitly to service in the Temple on the Day of Atonement, the parallel text in *Heikhalot rabati* obscures the link with time and place:

Rabbi Ishmael said: I was once offering a burnt offering on the altar and I saw Akatriel Yah, the Lord of Hosts, seated upon a high and exalted throne . . .[41]

Yet another version figures in a Heikhalot tradition known as the Mystery of Sandalfon:

Said Elisha b. Avuyah: When I ascended to the Pardes I saw Akatriel Yah, the Lord of Hosts, seated at the entrance to the Pardes, surrounded by one hundred and twenty times ten thousand ministering angels . . .[42]

In this version, the account of Elisha's sin is associated with Akatriel, who in turn is identified with Metatron, recalling the version of *Heikhalot zutarti*, which expands at length on the story of the four who entered the Pardes, where we read, 'it was said: When Elisha descended to the Merkavah, he saw Metatron, who had been

---

[41] *Heikhalot rabati* (Schäfer (ed.), *Synopse*, §151).   [42] Schäfer (ed.), *Synopse*, §597.

given permission to sit one hour a day and write . . .'.[43] The different versions which present 'ascent to the Pardes' and 'descent to the Merkavah' as parallels split into different accounts (perhaps Elisha, like Akiva, saw himself as the counterpart of such visionaries as Moses and Ezekiel).

It should be noted that the tradition relating to entry into the sacred realm and observing the figure of Akatriel or Metatron concerns locations clearly associated with the Temple: Holy of Holies, *lifnai velifnim*, the incense altar, the sacrificial altar, Merkavah and Chariot Throne, *heikhal* or Pardes; and all these locations are involved in the realm of contact with sanctity in earthly and heavenly dimensions. Rabbi Akiva describes his entry into the Pardes in terms appropriate to the high priest, who 'entered [the Holy of Holies] safely and came out safely' on the Day of Atonement: 'We were four who entered the Pardes . . . I entered safely and came out safely.'[44] As already stated, the account cited above of Rabbi Ishmael entering *lifnai velifnim* and burning incense recalls the rite performed by the high priest in the earthly Temple on the Day of Atonement—only then was he permitted to enter the sacred precinct. If the Pardes or the Garden of Eden is a celestial model of the terrestrial Holy of Holies, as we shall see below, or a representation of the Temple in part forbidden to human beings in general, it is clearly dangerous to attempt entry, as is evident from the story of the four who entered the Pardes:

These are those who entered Pardes: Simeon b. Azai, Simeon b. Zoma, Elisha b. Avuyah and Rabbi Akiva b. Joseph. Rabbi Akiva said to them: Beware, when you reach stones of pure marble, do not say, 'Water, water' . . . Ben Azai [stole a look at the sixth *heikhal* and saw the brilliance of marble stones with which the *heikhal* was paved. His body could not endure, and he opened his mouth and asked them, 'What is the nature of this water?'— and he died] stole a look and died . . . Ben Zoma stole a look [at the brilliance of the marble stones and thought it was water and his body endured, for he did not ask them, but his mind could not endure] and he became demented . . . Elisha b. Avuyah [descended and] mutilated the shoots . . . It was said: When Elisha descended to the Merkavah he saw Metatron, who had been given permission to sit and write down the merits of Israel one hour per day. Said he: The Sages taught: On high there is no standing and no sitting. He thought, Perhaps there are two divinities in heaven. Whereupon they led Metatron forth from behind the curtain and struck him with sixty fiery lashes . . . Rabbi Akiva ascended and descended safely, and of him Scripture says: 'Draw me after you, let us run! the king has brought me to his chambers' [S. of S. 1: 4].[45]

Enoch is described in the Genesis Apocryphon and in the earlier Enoch literature as a righteous scribe in the Garden of Eden; and Elisha, who descends to the Merkavah and observes Enoch-Metatron writing down 'the merits of Israel' is

---

[43] *Heikhalot zutarti* (Schäfer (ed.), *Synopse*, §§345, 672).

[44] Ibid., §314. See also Mishnah *Yoma* 7: 4; JT *Hag.* 2: 1 [77*b*]. Cf. the Musaf (Additional Service) for Yom Kippur. In later mystical tradition describing the entrance of the high priest into the inner sanctum we are told that *lifnai velifnim* is a pattern of paradise (*Zohar hadash* 19*a*); see n. 58 below.

[45] Schäfer (ed.), *Synopse*, §672, bracketed passages from §345.

none other than Elisha entering the Garden of Eden, or the Pardes, and reviving an ancient tradition.

Descent to the Merkavah or ascent to heaven is also parallel, at least in part, to entering the Pardes or entering *lifnai velifnim*, for the earthly Holy of Holies, where stands, as we have seen, 'the pattern of the chariot—the cherubim—those with outspread wings screening the Ark of the Covenant of the Lord',[46] is the parallel ('pattern') of the heavenly Merkavah. The interchange of verbs in the various traditions, 'enter' versus 'ascend', 'come out' versus 'descend', also implies a close relationship between the Pardes, the Merkavah, the seventh *heikhal*, and the heavenly Holy of Holies, which in turn are associated with priestly tradition and with the visionary tradition of the Chariot Throne and thereby with the Day of Atonement and Shavuot. The word *pardes* occurs in the second century BCE in the Aramaic text of Enoch discovered at Qumran, in the expression '*pardes* of truth',[47] and several centuries later in the New Testament in the words of Paul, who, like Enoch, hears the song of the angels in the third firmament, the location of the Garden of Eden,[48] also known as Paradise/*pardes*: 'I know a man . . . who was taken up to the third heaven . . . [he] was taken up into the Garden of Eden . . . and he heard things that cannot be told, which man may not utter.'[49]

Another possible link with the concept of *pardes*/Paradise/Garden of Eden may be found in the Genesis Apocryphon discovered at Qumran.[50] The text of this highly fragmentary scroll describes Methuselah's journey to his father Enoch, seated in the supernal worlds in a place called Parvayin, Parvayim, or perhaps Peruyim: '. . . to Enoch his father to learn everything from him truthfully, his will, and he went to (the ends of the earth?) to Parvayin and there found him'. The parallel version of Methuselah's journey, as told by Lamech and Enoch in 1 Enoch 106: 7–8, reads: 'So I am beseeching you now, my father . . . that you may go to Enoch, our father, and learn from him the truth, for his dwelling place is among the angels. When Methuselah heard the words of his son, he came to me at the ends of the earth.' The phrase 'ends of the earth' also occurs in the account of Noah's journey to his grandfather Enoch, who is described as dwelling at the 'ends of the earth', in heaven[51] or in the Garden of Eden.[52]

Milik and Grelot are both of the opinion that the word they read as *parvayin*/ *parvayim* means 'Paradise' or the Garden of Eden.[53] The word is indeed used as a

---

[46] 1 Chr. 28: 18.

[47] 4Q209, frg. 23, 9 (*DJD* XXXVI, 159–60, which, however, translates 'paradise of righteousness'). [48] 2 En. 8.

[49] 2 Cor. 12: 2–4 (cf. ibid., vv. 2–10). Paul's evidence pertains to the middle of the 1st century CE. For discussion of the similarity between Paul's allusions and the story of Rabbi Akiva and the Pardes see Scholem, *Jewish Gnosticism*, 14–19; Schäfer, *Hidden and Manifest God*; Morray-Jones, 'Paradise Revisited'; and cf. A. Segal, 'Heavenly Ascent'.

[50] 1QapGen II, 22–3 (García Martínez and Tigchelaar, *Study Edition*, i. 30–1; cf. Avigad and Yadin, *Genesis Apocryphon*). [51] 1 En. 65: 2–5. [52] Jub. 4: 23.

[53] Milik, *Ten Years of Discovery*, 569; Grelot, 'Parwain des Chroniques', 35–7.

synonym for the Garden of Eden in a document found in an ancient synagogue in Beirut.[54] It may also be associated, via a change in vocalization (*peruyin*), with the root *p-r-y*, meaning 'fertility', and in addition with a certain type of gold mentioned in connection with the Temple: 'He overlaid the House with precious stones for decoration; the gold was from Parvayim/Peruyim [cf. 'He overlaid the cherubim with gold', 1 Kgs. 6: 28]. He overlaid the House with gold—the beams, the thresholds, its walls and doors; he carved cherubim on the walls. He made the Holy of Holies . . . He overlaid it with fine gold.'[55] The expression 'gold of Parvayim' is thus associated with the pure gold with which the Holy of Holies was overlaid, and of which all seven sacred appurtenances were made: the cover and the Chariot Throne of the cherubim, the Ark of the Covenant, the incense altar, the seven-branched lampstand, the shewbread table, the tongs, and the fire pans.[56]

That same 'fine' (lit. 'good') gold originated in the Garden of Eden: 'the land of Havilah, where the gold is. The gold of that land is good'.[57] The Garden of Eden, in turn, is associated with the beginning of Creation, hence with the continuity of life and the cyclic order of nature (the Hebrew root of the word 'Eden' also yields words with the connotation of eternity and fertility: *eden/ad/idan/ednah*). And I have already alluded to the link with the Hebrew *pardes*, which is derived from a Persian word meaning 'garden', which originally possessed no religious connotation. However, the Septuagint to Genesis 2: 3 translates 'Garden of Eden' into Greek as *paradeisos*, giving the word its mythical and mystical meaning, as it has today in many European languages (such as the English 'Paradise'). The equivalence of the Garden of Eden and the Temple may already be found in Jubilees: 'And he knew that the Garden of Eden was the Holy of Holies and the dwelling of the Lord.'[58] Similar associations among these concepts—gold, the fragrance of spices and incense, cherubim and angels, the Tree of Life (described in 2 Enoch 8: 4 as having the appearance of gold), and the golden lampstand—may be found in the priestly literature. (The associative, if not grammatical, relationship between that first garden, the fount of life and fertility, on the one hand, and the term *genesis*, as relating to creation, birth, reproduction, and generation, is surely striking.)

Gold is the metal most frequently mentioned in the Bible. Referring to various modifiers accompanying 'gold' in the Bible, and Babylonian Talmud counts 'seven[!] kinds of gold: gold; good gold; gold of Ophir;[59] refined (*mufaz*) gold;[60] beaten (*shahut*) gold;[61] pure or solid (*sagur*) gold;[62] gold of Parvayim',[63] but there are even more expressions; the meaning of some of them cannot be determined

---

[54] See Grelot, 'Parwain des Chroniques', 35–7.   [55] 2 Chr. 3: 6–8.
[56] Exod. 25–6; 30: 1–3; 2 Chr. 3: 5–13; 4: 19–22.   [57] Gen. 2: 11.
[58] Jub. 8: 19. Cf. *Midrash hane'elam, Zohar hadash* 19a: '*Lifnai velifnim* is a model of the Garden of Eden, and when the priest went in there he did so in soul but not in body . . . If the priest so merited, he went in safely and came out safely.'   [59] 1 Kgs. 10: 11.   [60] 1 Kgs. 10: 18.
[61] 1 Kgs. 10: 16.   [62] 1 Kgs. 10: 21.   [63] BT *Yoma* 44b.

today.[64] Whatever the case, gold, associated with the light of the sun and the Tree of Life (i.e. the mystery of fertility; 2 Enoch 8), and incense, associated with fragrance, spice trees, garden, and Pardes (the mystery of growth)—thus both originating in the Garden of Eden—are characteristic of the sacred place and the sacred service.

It is surely no accident that the ritual representations associated with the Holy of Holies and the vestments of the high priest involve fertility symbols and were all made of gold:[65] calyxes (*tsitsim*);[66] pomegranates (a fruit symbolizing fertility);[67] palms (*timorot*, perhaps symbolizing the Tree of Life);[68] cherubim;[69] Merkavah[70] (in later Hebrew the root *r-k-b* also has the connotation of grafting one species onto another); the seven-branched lampstand[71] (perhaps yet another symbol for the Tree of Life?). These tangible but symbolic objects, which gave the Holy of Holies the semblance of a fragrant garden of gold, with 'carvings of gourds and calyxes', 'reliefs of cherubim, palms, and calyxes', and winged cherubim,[72] may have been associated with fertility in the Garden of Eden and with the heavenly Pardes, just as the word *parvayim/peruyim* seems to be synonymous with the Garden of Eden, the source of life, or the realm of fertility connected with the heavenly sanctuary. Besides their shared association with the Garden of Eden and the Holy of Holies, it is also striking that these various objects, or similar ones, also figure prominently in the Song of Songs, which may be seen on one level as epitomizing earthly love and conjugal union; and here, again, the mystics portray the cherubim in the Temple, entwined like male and female, as revealed in the Temple on the pilgrimage festivals.[73]

The common denominator of all the traditions concerned with entry into the inner sanctum, the Pardes, the Holy of Holies and the Merkavah, the Garden of Eden and the Heikhalot, the firmament and the sacred abode, is that all relate to supernatural, divine, and angelic entities; to cosmic patterns and hidden realities; and to people who imagined themselves as crossing the borders between visible and invisible, the boundaries of time and place, of heaven and earth. These people, already familiar to us as 'descenders to the Merkavah' or 'observers of the Merkavah', entered the Pardes, ascended to the Heikhalot, or entered the inner sanctum (*lifnai velifnim*), rising up to a mythical and mystical space (the Garden of Eden, Pardes, Merkavah, the Holy of Holies, the seventh *heikhal*). There they were granted a glimpse of the cosmic pattern of the universe, through its cultic representations in the heavenly sanctuary, through contact and conversation with the denizens of those supernal realms, or through participation as observers in the

---

[64] The translations of these biblical terms as given here are of course speculative; I have used the New Jewish Publication Society Translation of the Bible. [65] 1 Kgs. 6: 20–35; 2 Chr. 3: 4–10.

[66] 1 Kgs. 6: 29. [67] 2 Chr. 3: 16; 4: 13.

[68] 1 Kgs. 6: 29; 2 Chr. 3: 5. It is perhaps not insignificant that the Greek and Latin term for the palm tree is *phoenix*; and moreover that male and female flowers are borne on separate plants.

[69] 1 Kgs. 6: 23–8; 2 Chr. 3: 10–13. [70] 1 Chr. 28: 18. [71] 2 Chr. 4: 20–1.

[72] 1 Kgs. 6: 18–29, 32, 35. Cf. BT *Yoma* 21b. [73] See Ch. 2, n. 39.

heavenly ceremony involving these patterns. Upon returning to terrestrial reality, they testified to this ongoing divine revelation in the heavenly sanctuary, to the continuous cultic ceremony of praise and song observed by the angelic priests in the supernal sanctuaries, linking heaven and earth.

The heavenly rites are portrayed in a typically priestly colour, and such expressions as 'the sacred *ḥayot* sanctify themselves and purify themselves'[74] abound in numerous versions. But there is a significant difference. Whereas access to the Holy of Holies in the earthly Temple was permitted exclusively to the high priest, and access to the Temple's other inner parts was reserved for priests and Levites, access to the celestial Holy of Holies was not, apparently, conditional on priestly descent. Rabbi Ishmael is indeed described in Heikhalot tradition as a high priest, as is Enoch–Metatron, the Angel/Prince of the Countenance. But Rabbi Akiva, who appears in this tradition as a counterpart of Moses, the Levite and supreme prophet, was not of priestly stock, although he is described as privy to the secrets of the Merkavah, as having entered the Pardes safely and come out safely, just like the high priest in the Holy of Holies on the Day of Atonement.[75]

A 'descender to the Merkavah' desirous of approaching the holy realm was required to fulfil three obligations, stemming from the priestly tradition of the sacred service, which were a prerequisite for crossing over from the mortal to the celestial realm: (1) ritual immersion, purification, and self-abnegation, removing oneself from the physical world for at least seven days and thus achieving the spiritual level necessary for contact with the supernal worlds; (2) a knowledge of the names of God and of the angels, the concomitant oaths, seals, and invocations, a knowledge of the names of the components of the Merkavah and the seven-based pattern of the supernal Heikhalot; (3) a knowledge of the poems and songs describing ascent to the celestial world and the essence of that world—for the whole celestial world sings, and song is the visible and audible cultic representation of that invisible world. These three elements were also part of the world of the secessionist priests and the Qumran community: all the sources describing the Community evince the most stringent attitude to ritual purification, as is also evident in the large number of ritual baths found at Qumran.[76] Josephus mentions a knowledge of angelic names, kept in sacred esoteric books, as one of the Essenes' characteristics;[77] and a knowledge of the songs describing the celestial world and the mutual proportions of its different parts is clearly expressed in the Songs of the Sabbath Sacrifice and in other poetic works discovered at Qumran. A late version of this ancient tradition may be found in Heikhalot literature:

Whosoever is merited to descend to the Merkavah, when he stands before the Throne of Glory, begins by uttering song, for the Throne of Glory is engaged in song each and

---

[74] Schäfer (ed.), *Synopse*, §184; cf. §§188, 555.   [75] Mishnah *Yoma* 5: 1.
[76] See Reich, 'Ritual Baths at Qumran'; but see also Magness, *Archaeology of Qumran*, 137–42, 151–8.   [77] *War*, II. viii. 7.

every day, praise, song and music, blessing, praise and exaltation and adoration, thanks-giving . . . joy, bliss, elation, pleasant song, brilliant beauty . . . truth, righteousness, hon-esty . . . Magnificent King, adorned in magnificence, glorified in embroidery of song.[78]

Among the many traditions of poetry and song in the supernal worlds, as recounted in Heikhalot literature, the opening poem of *Heikhalot rabati*, which is concerned with God's seat or Chariot Throne and with his servants' song, is of particular interest:

> SAID RABBI ISHMAEL:
> What are the songs that a person sings and descends to the Merkavah?
> He begins and recites the beginnings of the songs:
> Beginning of praise and genesis of song
> Beginning of rejoicing and genesis of music
> Sung by the singers who daily minister
> To YHWH, God of Israel, and his Throne of Glory.
> They raise up the wheel of the Throne of Glory,
> Sing, O sing, Supreme Seat,
> Shout, O shout, delightful object,
> made in the most wondrous way.
> You surely delight the King who is upon you
> as a bridegroom delights in his nuptial chamber.
> All the seed of Jacob delights and rejoices . . .
> As Scripture says, Holy, Holy, Holy,
> YHWH of Hosts, his Glory fills all the earth.
> Of praise and song of each and every day,
> Of rejoicing and music of each and every season,
> And of *higayon* [melody? recitation?] issuing from the mouths of holy ones
> And of *nigayon* [singing?] gushing from the mouths of servants,
> Mountains of fire and hills of flame, heaped up and concealed,
> Paths each and every day, as Scripture says,
> Holy, Holy, Holy, YHWH of Hosts.[79]

This glorification of the Throne of Glory draws on a variety of biblical sources, among others: 'The Lord of Hosts enthroned on the cherubim';[80] 'He mounted a cherub and flew';[81] 'God is seated on His holy Throne';[82] Ezekiel's Merkavah vision, which ends with the scene, 'the semblance of a throne, in appearance like sapphire; and on top, upon this semblance of a throne, there was the semblance of a human form';[83] Isaiah's vision of 'YHWH seated on a high and lofty Throne'[84] and his allusion to the cosmic nature of the divine seat: 'The heaven is My throne and the earth is My footstool.'[85] Similar images may be found in Enoch literature as well.[86]

---

[78] *Heikhalot rabati* (Schäfer (ed.), *Synopse*, §260).
[79] Ibid., §§94–5. Cf. Scholem, *Jewish Gnosticism*, 20–6.   [80] 1 Sam. 4: 4; Isa. 37: 16.
[81] Ps. 18: 11.   [82] Ps. 47: 9.   [83] Ezek. 1: 26.   [84] Isa. 6: 1.
[85] Isa. 66: 1.   [86] Cf. 1 En. 9: 4; 14: 21; 2 En. 20: 3; 25: 4.

It is clear from this passage that the Throne, God's seat, and the Merkavah are one and the same. The expression 'delightful object' (Heb. *keli ḥemdah*) is associated with the Throne of Glory in other Merkavah traditions,[87] and the terms *higayon* and *nigayon* create a link with the book of Psalms and the Temple singers, praising the magnificence of the unseen God. We may also recall various phrases from the Songs of the Sabbath Sacrifice, some already cited in previous chapters, such as:

The cherubim fall before Him and bless. As they rise, the sound of divine stillness [is heard], and there is a tumult of jubilation as their wings lift up . . . The pattern of the Chariot-throne do they bless (which is) above the firmament of the cherubim. [And the splendo]r of the luminous firmament do they sing (which is) beneath His glorious seat. And when the wheels move, the holy angels return. They go out from between its glorious [h]ubs. Like the appearance of fire (are) the spirits of the Holy of Holies.[88]

Another striking poetic passage referring explicitly to the Temple, the Ark, the cover, the cherubim, and the Holy of Holies, and implicitly to the Merkavah, may be found in a tradition attributed to the amora Rabbi Isaac Napaha (mid-third century CE), as pointed out by Gershom Scholem.[89] The song he cites, whose opening, 'Sing, O sing, acacia tree' recalls the Heikhalot phrase 'Sing, O sing, Supreme Seat', is addressed to the acacia tree—the desert tree from which significant furnishings of the sanctuary were made and then overlaid with gold: the incense altar and the sacrificial altar, the tabernacle, the Ark, the table, and the posts.[90] Rabbi Isaac's song reads as follows:

> Sing, O sing, acacia tree,
> Ascend in all thy gracefulness.
> With golden weave they cover thee,
> The *devir* palace hears thy eulogy,
> With diverse jewels art thou adorned.[91]

In structure and language, this poem recalls the above passage from *Heikhalot rabati*: 'Magnificent King, adorned in magnificence, / glorified in embroidery of song, / adorned in glory and magnificence, / pride diadem and awesome crown', which in turn recalls the Songs of the Sabbath Sacrifice: 'a radiant substance of glorious weave, wondrously hued, purely blended'.[92] Another version of the call 'Sing, O sing' in Rabbi Isaac Napaha's song is 'Rise up, O rise up . . .', which also recalls a phrase from Qumran: 'Rise up, rise up, O God of gods, raise Yourself in might, O King of Kings . . . May the light of Your greatness shine forth.'[93]

---

[87] Schäfer (ed.), *Synopse*, §§634, 686, 876. The origin of the expression *keli ḥemdah* in relation to the Temple is 2 Chr. 36: 10; cf. BT *Yoma* 53*b*–54*a*.   [88] Newsom, *Songs*, 303, 306.
[89] Scholem, *Jewish Gnosticism*, 25.   [90] See Exod. 25–7 etc.
[91] BT *AZ* 24*b*; *Genesis Rabbah* 54.   [92] Newsom, *Songs*, 306.
[93] War Scroll XIV, 15–16 (cf. Vermes, *CDSSIE*, 179).

As I have noted, various traditions link the Ark of the Covenant, shielded by the cherubim, with the Throne of Glory—the seat of 'the Lord of Hosts enthroned on the cherubim', as observed in *Midrash tanḥuma* ('Vayakhel' 7): 'He who sits on the cherubim is the same as he who sits between the two cherubim on the Ark.' Similarly, the earthly and heavenly Chariot Throne of the cherubim is clearly echoed in the passages quoted above (and elsewhere) from the Songs of the Sabbath Sacrifice, in such phrases as 'the pattern of the Chariot Throne do they bless', or 'as [the cherubim] rise, the sound of divine stillness is heard'.

The transition from the cultic system of Temple and Holy of Holies, Merkavah and cherubim, Throne and *devir*, *galgalim* and *ofanim*, woven song and incense, priestly song and sacred service, mirrored in its heavenly counterpart in the world of the Merkavah, to a mystical system, all of whose parts sing like the cherubim, angels, and creatures of the Merkavah, is the major characteristic of the traditions of Heikhalot and Merkavah literature. At the end of the long poetic passage cited above, Rabbi Ishmael specifies its source: 'Said Rabbi Ishmael: All these songs were heard by Rabbi Akiva when he descended to the Merkavah and grasped and learned them before the Throne of Glory, where his servants were singing before him.'[94] These heavenly servants are described as godlike creatures (*benei elohim*, lit. 'sons of God'), similar to those mentioned in the book of Psalms—'He makes the winds His angels, fiery flames His servants.'[95] The angelic, priestly archetype of sacred song as represented at Qumran and in Heikhalot poetry is clearly discernible in the song that accompanies the sacred service in the Bible,[96] as exemplified in Psalm 103: 19–22:

> The Lord has established His throne in heaven,
> and His sovereign rule is over all.
> Bless the Lord, O His angels,
> mighty creatures who do His bidding,
> ever obedient to His bidding;
> bless the Lord, all His hosts,
> His servants who do His will;
> bless the Lord, all His works,
> through the length and breadth of His realm;
> bless the Lord, O my soul.

I have dealt elsewhere in detail with the mystical nature of Heikhalot literature and its close relationship with priesthood, Temple, sacred song, and the angelic world, with ministering priests and angels; I also considered there various questions concerning the relationship between the priestly and angelic elements of this literature and earlier mystical priestly genres.[97] Suffice it to note here that there is a highly complex relationship between the different stages of the Merkavah tradition in its

---

[94] Schäfer (ed.), *Synopse*, §106.   [95] Ps. 104: 4.   [96] 1 Chr. 23: 30; 25: 1; 2 Chr. 29: 25.
[97] Elior, 'From Earthly Temple to Heavenly Shrines'.

diverse historical manifestations. Common to all those stages is the priestly perception of an invisible reality, dependent on the infinite dimensions and measurements deriving from the various accounts of the Merkavah world and transmitted through poetry, melody, and narrative, transforming the invisible into audible and visual. This priestly tradition is concerned with both abstract and tangible representations, with the numerical and poetic features of the Merkavah that dictate the sequence of the sacred service and the cycles of sabbath song, in perceived emulation of the angelic world. The various stages of the Merkavah tradition share a common conceptual world of priests and angels, a common liturgical framework treating the Temple and the sacred service as representations of the eternal, cyclic, cosmic order of the universe, the guarantee of life and blessing.

This common world is evidence of the conception of a common source of authority, despite the different historical, cultural, and social circumstances. The common point of departure was severance from the centre of earthly ritual, voluntarily or by duress (Ezekiel the priest in exile after the destruction of the First Temple; the Zadokite priests barred from service in the Second Temple; the authors of Heikhalot literature, writing after the destruction of the Second Temple), along with a resumption of mythical and mystical patterns underlying the primeval origins of the cult, based on angelic tradition and prophetic testimony establishing a relationship between the order of the universe and the earthly ritual. Similarly, all stages of the tradition were imbued with a desire to perpetuate the sacred essence of the numinous cult in an ideal, heavenly guise (Merkavah and heavenly throne, angels, sevens, songs, Kedushah, heavenly priesthood). In addition, they share a linguistic affinity with the conceptual world of the Temple and the priesthood—but in an ideal, mystical, liturgical, and visionary frame that brings together visible and invisible (Holy of Holies, *lifnai velifnim*, Pardes, Garden of Eden, *devir*, Merkavah, gold, incense, the Temple furnishings, angels of the Countenance, priests of the inner sanctum, cherubim, *ofanim*, and so on).

All these stages had a common objective: to create a mystical alternative to the tangible cultic reality of the terrestrial Temple, with its covenants and appointed times—a mystical liturgical tradition of Merkavah and angels establishing a link, through eternal, fixed patterns, between celestial and terrestrial. They addressed a common source of authority: the angelic and priestly traditions relating to the laws of heaven and earth, observed by an eternal priesthood charged with preserving and protecting a sacred heritage. As against the earthly components of the Holy of Holies and their association with the Garden of Eden, Heikhalot literature pictures the Merkavah in association with the Pardes. The earthly Ark and its *kaporet* (cover) were replaced by the divine seat, the Chariot Throne of the cherubim; the fixed ritual order of the seven 'chief princes' and the twenty-four priestly courses were replaced by a detailed description of the seven princes of the seven firmaments and twenty-four angelic princes; the days of the solar calendar and the portions of incense, divided among the 365 days of the solar year, became 365 thousand myriad ministering angels, all participating in singing and chanting the Kedushah. Heikhalot traditions attach great importance to knowing the most detailed names of the angelic camps and the proper order of sacred song and chant; there is a marked similarity between the service in the earthly sanctuary and that in the heavenly *heikhal*, in the details of the priestly blessings, in the course of which God's Ineffable Name is enunciated, and in the rite of the Day of Atonement, in the course of which the congregation proclaims seven times, 'The Lord is God', and Enoch—the seventh patriarch—'that youth whose name is Metatron brings deafening fire and places it in the ears of the *hayot*', and he too proclaims God's name seven times.[98]

One example, using the notion of *ofan* (*galgal*, 'wheel'), will demonstrate the basic continuity between the three stages of mystical priestly tradition and its derivation from Merkavah tradition, as well as the conceptual transformation that took place in the course of the transition from the historical, tangible, earthly cult, inspired by heavenly patterns, to the eternal, heavenly tradition of a mystical liturgy memorializing the lost cult. The first stage in the metamorphosis of the notion of *ofan* reflects the transition from the cultic reality of First Temple times to a heavenly, visionary existence in the priest and prophet Ezekiel's Merkavah vision; the second stage is the transition in Qumran literature from Ezekiel's Merkavah to the visionary, liturgical, angelic Merkavah; and the third marks the transition from Qumranic Merkavah literature to the mystical, visionary Merkavah of Heikhalot literature.

1. The description of Solomon's Temple in 1 Kings (and in Chronicles) includes a huge, four-sided cult bowl ('sea') supported by four threesomes of animals (twelve oxen) facing all four points of the compass[99] and symbolizing various twelvefold divisions of the physical world (months, constellations of the zodiac, tribes, gates, stones of the breastplate, diagonal boundaries). Nearby stood the laver stands, whose frames were engraved with cherubim, lions, and palms,[100] similar to those adorning the Holy of Holies. These stands, in which parts of the burnt offerings were rinsed, were supported by four bronze wheels, probably representing the four points of the compass and the four seasons of the year:

Each laver stand had four bronze wheels [*ofanim*] . . . And below the insets were the four wheels . . . and the height of each wheel was a cubit and a half. The structure of the wheels was like the structure of chariot wheels; and their axletrees, their rims, their spokes and their hubs were all of cast metal.[101]

2. In Ezekiels' vision, the four bronze 'wheels' undergo a mythical, visionary metamorphosis, from an inanimate cultic representation of a cosmic pattern in the sacred precinct, subject to the confines of time and place, to a living, heavenly

---

[98] Schäfer (ed.), *Synopse*, §§390, 476 (for the whole passage see pp. 243–4 above).
[99] 1 Kgs. 7: 25; 2 Chr. 4: 4.   [100] 1 Kgs. 7: 36; 2 Chr. 4; 6, 14.   [101] 1 Kgs. 7: 30–3.

entity and mystical representation, representing both masculine and feminine elements, beyond the limits of time and place. The fourfold structure of the cult object and the brilliance of the bronze material, manifested in the movement of its wheels, are retained in the mystical metamorphosis:

the figures of four living creatures [*hayot*] . . . like the lustre of burnished bronze. . . . As I gazed on the creatures, I saw one wheel [*ofan*] on the ground next to each of the four-faced creatures. As for the appearance and structure of the wheels, they gleamed like beryl. All four had the same form; the appearance and structure of each was as of two wheels cutting through each other. . . . Their rims were tall . . . for the rims of all four were covered all over with eyes. And when the creatures moved forward, the wheels moved at their sides. . . . And when those (the creatures) were borne above the earth, the wheels were borne alongside them—for the spirit of the creatures was in the wheels.[102]

I could see that there were four wheels beside the cherubim, one wheel beside each of the cherubim; as for the appearance of the wheels, they gleamed like the beryl stone. . . . And the wheels, the wheels of the four of them, were covered all over with eyes. It was these wheels that I had heard called 'the wheelwork' [*galgal*].[103]

3. Ezekiels' vision, in which the cherubim from the Holy of Holies were depicted as living creatures, now undergoes a mystical, liturgical metamorphosis in the Songs of the Sabbath Sacrifice: all the components of the Merkavah become luminous, personified celestial beings that sing, praise, utter thanks and blessings inspired by the sacred service of the priests and the Levites. The fourfold pattern so emphasized in Ezekiel's vision is somewhat obscured in this fragmentary liturgical corpus, though we read in one place of 'four foundations of the wondrous firmament'; but the Merkavah/Chariot Throne, cherubim, *devir*, Seat of Glory, *ofanim* and *galgalim*, and Holy of Holies come together in a sublime liturgical sequence:

His glorious chariots . . . holy cherubim, luminous ofanim in the *devir* . . . [And the splendo]r of the luminous firmament do they sing (which is) beneath His glorious seat. And when the wheels move, the holy angels return. They go out from between its glorious [h]ubs.[104]

And the chariots of his *devir* give praise together, and their cherubim and their ofanim bless wondrously.[105]

4. Finally, Heikhalot literature subjects the sacred service of the *ofanim* to a mystical, ritual metamorphosis, describing them alternately in masculine and feminine gender; their service is described in terms appropriate to the sacred service of the priests in the Temple, as reported in the testimony of those who descend to the Merkavah, rise up in their vision to stand before the Throne of Glory, and recount their experience in terms of an erotic union:

---

[102] Ezek. 1: 5–8, 15–22.   [103] Ezek. 10: 9–13.
[104] Newsom, *Songs*, 303, 306.   [105] Ibid. 226.

And in the seventh *heikhal* there were luminous *ofanim*, sprinkling pure unguent and balsam, and a twofold *ofan* blowing [on the ram's horn] a *tekiah* [long drawn-out blast], a *teruah* [tremulous note], and again a *tekiah*, proclaiming: Let everyone worthy of seeing the King in his beauty enter and see. Whereupon powerful *ofanim* embrace him and glorious cherubim kiss him, the *ḥayot* lift him up and the brilliance dances before him and the *ḥashmal* sings before him . . . until they lift him up and seat him before the throne of his glory.[106]

And when the time comes to sing, a tumult of *galgalim* clamouring. . . . All the angels and *degalim* [camps] dance and utter sounds, *galgal* to *galgal*, cherub to cherub, *ḥayah* to *ḥayah*, *ofan* to *ofan*, *saraf* [seraph] to *saraf*.[107]

For in six voices they sing before him the dimensions of the bearers of his Throne, the cherubim and *ofanim* and holy *ḥayot*.[108]

And the *ofanim* are all full of eyes, and all full of wings, seven wings and as many eyes as wings.[109]

Beginning of praise and genesis of song . . . Sung by the singers who daily minister to YHWH, God of Israel, and his Throne of Glory. They raise up the *galgal* of the Throne of Glory . . .[110]

These quotations—but a few of many similar passages—clearly demonstrate how the physical objects of Solomon's Temple, the bronze wheels/*ofanim*, also called *galgalim*, become, in the first stage—Ezekiel's vision—moving visionary entities: 'for the spirit of the creatures was in the wheels'. In the next stage, Qumran, these same entities acquire the power of speech, blessing, ministering, and singing in the priestly ritual: 'their cherubim and their *ofanim* bless wondrously'. In the third, final stage, they play an even more active role, becoming part of the mystical experience of descent to the Merkavah: 'a twofold *ofan* blowing a *tekiah*, a *teruah*, and again a *tekiah* . . . and . . . powerful *ofanim* embrace him'. This twofold *ofan* blowing the ram's horn is simply a visionary metamorphosis of the two priests doing so in the context of the Temple service, as described in the Mishnah:

When the high priest desired to burn the offerings, he used to go up the ascent . . . Two priests stood on the table of the fat with two silver trumpets in their hands. They blew a *tekiah*, a *teruah* and a *tekiah* . . .[111]

---

[106] *Heikhalot zutarti* (Schäfer (ed.), *Synopse*, §411). Cf. *Heikhalot rabati* (ibid., §192): 'Horns issue from beneath the throne of his glory, company by company, and blow *tekiot* and *teruot* and bless.' After the destruction of the Temple, such ritual appurtenances as trumpets and horns, or other musical instruments, fell into disuse, since once the priestly service had been discontinued, the Levites no longer sang and the priests themselves no longer blew the trumpets (cf. Mishnah *Tam.* 7: 3). It therefore became necessary to memorialize them in mystical poetry.

[107] *Sefer heikhalot* (Schäfer (ed.), *Synopse*, §30).

[108] *Heikhalot rabati* (ibid., §103).   [109] *Sefer heikhalot* (ibid., §40).

[110] *Heikhalot rabati* (ibid., §94). For more examples and a discussion of the affinities between the Temple service and the rituals performed in the supernal Heikhalot see Elior, 'From Earthly Temple to Heavenly Shrines', 239–45.   [111] Mishnah *Tam.* 7: 3.

Two priests stood by the upper gate which leads down from the court of the Israelites to the court of the women, with two trumpets in their hands. When the cock crowed they blew a *tekiah*, a *teruah* and again a *tekiah*.[112]

These *ofanim* and similar entities, creating a visionary and ritual representation of the Temple, the sacrificial rite, and the priesthood, found their place in the tradition of *piyut* (liturgical poetry in sabbath and festival prayers) and the prayer book; they figure even in the present-day liturgy of Orthodox Jews, in the Kedushah of Yotser (a part of the daily morning service) and elsewhere, though their origin in mystical Temple tradition and priestly lore is not always realized. It is interesting to note that poetical liturgical sections known as *kedushtaot*, found among the manuscripts of the Cairo Genizah and serving as adornments to the Kedushah of the Amidah, are entitled *ofanim* or *ofanaya* in reference to the wheels of Ezekiel's Chariot.

All the elements of the Temple underwent a similar metamorphosis. The cherubim of the Holy of Holies, including those engraved on the laver stands and adorning the walls and doors of the Temple, became the cherubim of the Merkavah in Ezekiel's vision, the wondrous cherubim reciting blessings at Qumran, and the glorious cherubim kissing and embracing the 'descender to the Merkavah' and raising him to the Throne of Glory in the seventh *heikhal* in Heikhalot and Merkavah tradition. (The bisexual nature of these winged creatures, the protagonists of a mystical existence beyond the confines of time and place, alluded to in the text of Ezekiel's vision and in the phraseology of Heikhalot literature, was preserved in late mystical tradition, which speaks of the redeeming angel who switches from male to female, or of the metamorphic image of the Shekhinah, the divine Presence, which also seems to fluctuate from female to male and back.[113])

Merkavah tradition readily switched to and fro between an inanimate cultic object, reflecting a celestial pattern, and a living visionary entity, reflecting cosmic order as represented in cultic and numerical terms, a luminous reality of a mythical and metamorphic nature, a celestial liturgy performed ceremonially in the supernal sanctuaries. In so doing it essentially invoked creative imagination, the poetic power of memory embedded in language, to combine remembrance of song and sacred service in the earthly Temple, their immortalization in the visionary

---

[112] Mishnah *Suk.* 5: 4. Cf. also Mishnah *Suk.* 4: 9, *Pes.* 5: 5; Tosefta *Sot.* 7: 15, for further descriptions of the priestly service in the Temple blowing trumpet blasts. The terms *tekiah* and *teruah* and the verbs from which they are derived are used for blasts on both trumpet and ram's horn; see 2 Kgs. 11: 14; Hos. 5: 8; Ps. 98: 6. These instruments were used in the Temple by the priests, as we learn from Num. 10: 8: 'The trumpets shall be blown by Aaron's sons, the priests . . .'; cf. also Ben Sira 50: 16: 'Then the sons of Aaron blew the trumpets of hammered metal and shouted and sounded a mighty fanfare as a reminder before the Most High.' This verse is reminiscent of biblical references to the celestial retinue, the heavenly counterparts of the priests: 'When the morning stars sang together, and all the divine beings [Heb. *benei elohim*] sounded a fanfare'. For the trumpets in Qumran literature see Yadin (ed.), *Scroll of the War*, 87–113.   [113] *Zohar* I, 232*a*.

Temple, and the renewed experience of them in the mystical *heikhal*, the world of the ministering angels and the descenders to the Merkavah. All these are brought together by the remembrance of the cult recited by cherubim and angels, referred to briefly in the biblical account of the Garden of Eden, in greater detail in Jubilees,[114] in Enoch literature, and implicitly in the Thanksgiving Hymns. They reappear in the biblical account of the cherubim on the Ark in the desert sanctuary, whose wings touch one another,[115] and in the description of Solomon's Temple, 'the gold for the pattern of the chariot—the cherubim—those with outspread wings screening the Ark of the Covenant of the Lord'.[116] The four-winged cherubim are then immortalized through a mystical metamorphosis as the cherubim of the Merkavah in Ezekiel's vision, where all the parts of the Merkavah—cherubim, *hayot*, *ofanim*, and *galgalim*—are described in emphatic fourfold terms. The process continues in the Songs of the Sabbath Sacrifice, which emphasize the vertical, sevenfold dimensions of the Merkavah and its liturgical essence. Finally, we reach the picture of the sacred service in the heavenly Temple in Heikhalot tradition, which retains both the fourfold and sevenfold patterns of the liturgical calendar: 'and the cherubim and the *ofanim* over against the entrance of the seventh *heikhal*'; 'they utter sounds, *galgal* to *galgal*, cherub to cherub, *hayah* to *hayah*, *ofan* to *ofan*. . .'; '*galgalim* rejoice, cherubim glorify, *hayot* bless . . .'; 'holy cherubim sing a pleasant song, holy *hayot* utter song in the mystery of their mouths'.[117] Faced with the unbridgeable distance between the ruined Temple and the discontinued earthly cult, on the one hand, and the yearning to approach the sacred realm, the invisible cosmic reality of cyclic patterns and infinite, numerically measured harmonic relationships, on the other, mystical tradition created a bridge of verbal remembrance, built out of speech and song, measurement and number, mythical imagination and mystical vision. Through a visionary metamorphosis of the priestly Temple traditions, Merkavah tradition erected seven supernal sanctuaries, *heikhalot*, in which the descender to the Merkavah could observe the ongoing sacred service performed by twenty-four divisions of angels, and then return to testify to the continuity of the cult in heaven, as if rejecting the destruction witnessed on earth: 'Wherefore do the sacred *hayot* and glorious cherubim sanctify and purify themselves, and the glorious cherubim kiss him and the *hayot* raise him up . . . until they elevate him and seat him before his Throne of Glory.'[118]

Heikhalot literature, eschewing the struggle to prove the truth of the alternative cultic tradition after the destruction of the Temple, neutralizing its secessionist, oppositional dimension, became as it were a repository of diverse priestly traditions—mystical, liturgical, and cultic—concerning the Merkavah, the Heikhalot, and the angelic priesthood, preserving the divine pattern of sacred time. I am not implying here that there was any historical, chronological continuity linking the

---

[114] Jub. 2: 2–3.   [115] Exod. 25.   [116] I Chr. 28: 18.
[117] Schäfer (ed.), *Synopse*, §§245, 30, 188, 593; with all of these compare §815.
[118] Ibid., §411.

different stages of Merkavah tradition. Indeed, we have no reliable data as to the location, precise dates, and extra-textual identities of the authors, and the span of time involved is far too long to provide any fixed points of reference and continuity. My contention is that these diverse stages seem to share a common religious infrastructure, a distinct, priestly-oriented, cultural identity; that the authors of the various versions of Merkavah tradition shared a spiritual universe of discourse which seems to indicate a significant, continuous line linking the memory of the Temple and its rites, as well as the cosmic world view that it represented through eternal, fixed numerical proportions of the parts of the Merkavah, symbolizing the infinite dimensions and cycles of the universe, with the beginnings of Jewish mysticism.

Early Jewish mysticism is essentially a revival of the myth of the angelic priests and an immortalization of the earthly, tangible Temple and priesthood as reflections of the infinite, invisible dimensions of the Merkavah and the angels. Joint cycles of song and sacred ceremonies represent the cyclic order of the universe, its numerical proportions manifested in the fixed, eternal cyclic march of time and the transformations of nature. This cyclic principle, with its ceremonial manifestations in the world of the angels and the priests, is associated with mystical thought, which envisages open pathways between heaven and earth. These pathways enable angels and human beings, the protagonists of the priestly myth, to pass to and fro, bearing testimony to the numerical, cosmic reflections of the eternal, permanent, cyclic, divine, invisible interchange of the annual seasons (4); the passage of days, marked by sunrise and sunset (24); the sequence of months (12), of sabbaths (7), and of fertility and lunar renewal (13); all these relate to the number of days in the year (364) and its subdivisions, as preserved in the service of the twenty-four priestly courses, changing every seven days, counting thirteen sabbaths per quarter-year, four times a year, in what was virtually a living ritual calendar. The *sevenfold* cycles associated with the resignation of human sovereignty, rest, liberty, purity, and sanctity are founded on *audible* hidden divine-angelic sources and on calculations taught by the angels and kept by the priests, whereas the *fourfold* cycles are associated with the *visible* changes in nature founded on the fixed astronomical phenomena observed by the twenty-four priestly courses and translated into tables which they kept watch over, integrating the fourfold cycles with the sevenfold invisible cycles. The visionary testimony to the synchronization of sabbaths, seasons, cycles, and festivals, some visible and some dependent on abstract, divine numbers, creating a mystical, ritual chronotopic system of fours and sevens—four seasons, seven days in the week, cycles of twelve months and thirteen sabbaths, the four points of the compass; and on the other hand the four faces of the Merkavah, the seven Heikhalot—this visionary testimony was made possible by human beings ascending to heaven or angels descending to earth, in order to give tangible form and structure to the super-sensory, the numerical, the cyclic, and the eternal in the language of narrative, number, cycle, and song.

The narrative is concerned with the world of the angels and the creatures of the Merkavah, which transcend the limits of time and place, representing and observing the appointed times and epochs since the seven days of Creation, within the limits of time and place. Number relates to the fixed, infinite numerical relationships among the weekly, monthly, daily, annual, and seasonal cycles of time, reflecting the eternity of the laws of nature. Cycle relates to the continuous, recurrent cultic representation of cycles of divine time. Finally, song is the joint ritual expression of the guardians of the sacred realm, linking those who observe the cycles of sabbaths, set times, seasons, and days in heaven and on earth. In the context of that tangible form, the parts of the heavenly Merkavah, combining cosmic time and place with visible and unseen aspects of the cycles of nature and the cycles of ritual, are described. The fixed, eternal relationship between the numerical proportions of the Merkavah, reflecting changes on a cosmic scale, is represented in song and in cycles of sacred service, preserving the passage of earthly time in the joint worship of angels and priests; hence we have twenty-four priestly courses, thirteen Songs of the Sabbath Sacrifice, each recited every seven days, with the full cycle repeated four times a year; and the liturgical calendar of the Psalms Scroll discussed in Chapter 1, which sets out the details of the sacrificial rites and their liturgical expression in poems and songs of praise relating to sevenfold configurations and the fixed numerical subdivision of divine time:

David son of Jesse was wise and brilliant like the light of the sun; (he was) a scribe, intelligent and perfect in all his ways before God and men.

And YHWH gave him an intelligent and brilliant spirit, and he wrote 3,600 psalms [ten psalms each day, the number of days being the number of months in a year times the number of days in a month, $12 \times 30 = 360$] and 364 songs to sing before the altar for the daily perpetual sacrifice, for all the days of the [solar] year; and 52 songs for the Sabbath offerings [364 divided by 7 gives 52, the number of weeks or sabbaths in a year, which are divided into four seasons of thirteen sabbaths each, for which the Songs of the Sabbath Sacrifice were composed]; and 30 songs for the offerings for the beginnings of months, for all the festivals and for the Day of Atonement [12 first days of months plus 18 days of the seven festivals or appointed times, according to the list of festivals in Leviticus].

In all, the songs which he uttered were 446, and 4 songs to make music on the intercalary days [Heb. *peguim*, designating the four 'extra' days added to the 360 to mark the changes of season and to make up the full solar year].

In all, they were 4,050.

All these he uttered through prophecy which was given him from before the Most High.[119]

---

[119] 11QPs^a XXVII, 2–11 (= 11Q 5; see *DJD* IV, 91–3) (translation based on Vermes, *CDSSIE*, 307; my explanatory comments are added in square brackets). In the original document the numbers were written not as numerals but in full. Numerals were too mutable, especially when written on parchment, and were thought unsuitable for the expression of numbers considered to be holy.

There is an exact numerical relationship between the invisible division of divine time, which is dependent on number, counting, song, and priestly service (sabbath, year, month, songs and their appointed times, according to the order prescribed in Leviticus), and the visible rhythm of time, which is dependent on the sun and is measured in cycles of natural change (sunrise and sunset, day, seasons). The crucial importance of this relationship is clearly evident in the structure of the priestly calendar, which complies with the numerical synchronization between visible and invisible changes in relation to the Temple and the song accompanying the sacred service. After the destruction of the Temple, this tradition was observed through descent to the Merkavah, ascent to the Heikhalot, and entry into the Pardes, in all of which human beings witness the heavenly song of the angelic camps who follow this cosmic order in the seven supernal sanctuaries. Throughout all stages of Merkavah tradition, it is evident that the various priestly traditions upon which the cult was based, which expressed the ritual affinity between the heavenly macrocosmic and earthly microcosmic orders, assumed a new guise after the earthly cult had been discontinued. What emerged was a mystical tradition, concerned with the invisible cosmic realm. The ritual focus shifted to the heavenly Merkavah, to visionary Heikhalot and angelic liturgy.

Heikhalot literature is organized around numbers corresponding to the days of the week and the hours of the day, the sabbaths and the priestly courses; but these now take on an added, infinite, cosmic dimension, measured in myriads of parasangs. Basic to the various works of this literature is a visionary schematization of the sublime, in parallel to the components of the Merkavah, revolving around seven supernal sanctuaries—*heikhalot*—as proclaimed by Rabbi Akiva: 'Who can meditate on seven *heikhalot* and gaze upon the highest heavens and see the innermost chambers and say, I have seen the chambers of Yah?'[120] They are concerned with God's 'stature' (*shiur komah*), measured in infinite units of myriads of parasangs, divided into twenty-four ('Each and every parasang of the Holy One, blessed be he, amounts to twenty-four times ten thousand human parasangs'[121]); they count twenty-four wings to the sacred *ḥayot* and 'twenty-four times ten thousand fiery *galgalim*, twelve above and twelve below',[122] or 'twenty-four thousand fiery angels, each of them has the measure of the ocean'.[123]

The relative proportions of the components of the Merkavah are built on the same pattern: 'Between cherubim and *ofanim* there are twenty-four times ten thousand parasangs; between *ofanim* and chambers, twenty-four times ten thousand parasangs; between Merkavah and Merkavah, twenty-four times ten

---

[120] Schäfer (ed.), *Synopse*, §554. Compare Song of Songs 1: 4: 'The king has brought me to his chambers . . .'; cf. Scholem, *Jewish Gnosticism*, 101–17.

[121] Schäfer (ed.), *Synopse*, §703; cf. M. S. Cohen, *Shi'ur Qomah: Liturgy* for the significance of all these numbers.   [122] Schäfer (ed.), *Synopse*, §546.

[123] Schäfer (ed.), *Geniza-Fragmente*, §G21, 2b, 16–17. The Hebrew word here translated as 'ocean' is *tarshish*; see Mishor, 'Tarshish'.

thousand parasangs.'[124] Multiples of twenty-four also appear: 'Between Merkavah and cherubim are one hundred and sixty-eight times ten thousand parasangs' ($168 = 7 \times 24$).[125] They express the cyclic nature and pattern of cosmic order. As against this cosmic figure we have the cultic counterpart: they recite 'twenty-four Kedushahs', or perform 'twenty-four [ritual] immersions each day'.[126]

Heikhalot literature was written after the destruction of the Temple, when priestly tradition had lost its terrestrial fulcrum, and moreover when the controversy over the determination of the festivals had been settled: the festivals were based, once and for all, on the course of the moon, and their final determination was entrusted to a human agency, the *beit din* (rabbinical court), on the evidence of human witnesses who testified to seeing the crescent of the new moon. This is emphatically stated in the Mishnah:

'These are the appointed times of the Lord, holy convocations, which ye shall proclaim'—whether at their proper time or not at their proper time, I have no appointed times save these.[127]

A court composed of three men announced (the Hebrew word used means 'consecrated') the beginning of each month based on the sighting of the new moon; human authority had priority over cosmic evidence, on the sole basis of the court's discretion.

Thus, the struggle for the domination of heavenly time, fixed calculation, the predetermined, priestly and angelic solar calendar—and hence also the cyclic liturgical order associated with it and the concomitant priestly hegemony—had been lost. The losers abandoned the polemical thrust of their thought and returned to the fold on a terrestrial plane, recognizing that the physical Temple and priesthood were no more. But while they conceded defeat, accepted rabbinic authority, and co-operated with the established leadership on an earthly level, they did not renounce their vision in the spiritual sense. The creators of the myth of angelic priests and their successors in Heikhalot and Merkavah literature, whether defiantly, longingly, or hopefully, preserved the memory of the seventh priestly, angelic patriarch, Enoch-Metatron, the super-temporal witness to the solar calendar (who lived 365 years!). They also preserved the memory of the number of days in the solar year in relation to the cosmic pattern of the Merkavah world with its seven *heikhalot*: 'The Holy One, blessed be he, placed his hand upon me and blessed me with three hundred and sixty-five thousand blessings . . . And each and every wing was like the whole world, and there were fixed in me three hundred

---

[124] Schäfer (ed.), *Synopse*, §559.   [125] Ibid.   [126] Ibid., §§376, 728, 314.

[127] *RH* 2: 9. The biblical verse Lev. 23: 4 concerning the appointed time of the Lord is quoted in the Mishnah in a truncated and deformed way: the last word, *bemo'adam*, 'at their appointed time', is omitted, and the word preceding it is converted from *otam*, 'them [i.e. the appointed times]', to *atem*, 'you'. See BT *RH* 25a and JT *RH* 1: 3 [57b] on the passage from the biblical-priestly calendar of predetermined holy convocation to the rabbinic lunar calendar determined by the Sages.

and sixty-five thousand eyes.'[128] The angels are counted in multiples of 365 thousand or 365 times ten thousand, and they 'drive the sun's orb in the firmament,
three hundred and sixty-five thousand parasangs each day'.[129] Their description is
based on the numbers characteristic of the solar calendar: 'That is his height, the
height of seven firmaments; his wings are like the days of the year . . . The measure
of each and every letter that they write is three hundred and sixty-five parasangs.'[130]
In opposition to the Sages' declaration, 'whether they are proclaimed at their
proper time or not at their proper time', the guardians of the priestly heritage did
not relinquish their duty to perpetuate the concept of sacred time in relation to the
sacred service: 'Whenever the ministering angels utter song not at the correct time,
and not in the proper manner, and not in the legitimate manner, they are burned
and glow with the fire of their Creator . . . And a stormy wind . . . hurls them into
the river Dinur.'[131]

Heikhalot literature thus created a new metamorphosis of the very mystical
priestly traditions that had been rejected by the Hasmonaean priests in the Second
Temple period and were later blurred and repudiated by the Sages. Reading the
works of Heikhalot literature, one receives the impression that what had earlier
been excluded from the canon and had been, as it were, thrown out through the
front door, now crept back in through the window, perpetuated by the efforts of a
select elite. A considerable part of the secessionist priesthood's traditions, originally
suppressed, re-emerged in Heikhalot literature. Since the destruction of the
Second Temple, the earthly controversies over the validity of the legacy of sacred
time, place, and cult were no longer relevant, and the need to preserve the sacred
service was answered by assigning it to the angelic priesthood in the supernal
sanctuaries. The descenders to the Merkavah testified to the continuity of this
sacred service in the heavens, conserving the living memory of the priestly ritual in
its angelic version after the destruction of the Second Temple. As the no longer
existent terrestrial experience receded in time, these mystics invoked all their
poetic imagination and mystical inspiration, ascending in their minds' eye to the
highest heavens.

The Sages frowned upon these traditions, limiting their accessibility:

It is forbidden for three persons to discuss the secrets of sexual union, for two persons to
discuss *ma'aseh bereshit*, and for a single person to discuss *ma'aseh merkavah*, unless [that
person] is wise and insightful.[132]

---

[128] Schäfer (ed.), *Synopse*, §12.   [129] Ibid., §22.   [130] Ibid., §29.   [131] Ibid., §67.
[132] Mishnah *Ḥag.* 2: 1. The words 'wise and insightful' allude to the description of the divine
inspiration that was bestowed upon Bezalel ben Uri, the craftsman that built the tabernacle, the Ark,
and the chariot of the cherubim, transforming the heavenly vision granted to Moses into a ritual
precinct of the Holy of Holies (see Exod. 31: 3, 6–11). In mishnaic Hebrew the three words alluding to
the 'permitted' student of the chariot tradition—*ḥakham umevin mida'ato* (Mishnah *Ḥag.* 2: 1)—
correspond to the three biblical words describing the divine inspiration needed to constitute the
priestly holy precinct: *Va'amale oto ruaḥ elohim beḥokhmah uvitevunah uveda'at* (Exod. 31: 3).

These reservations are surely understandable, given the origins of Merkavah tradition and its later metamorphoses in the circles of the priestly opposition. Nevertheless, some talmudic authorities attached considerable sanctity to these mystical priestly traditions—concerned as they were with the supernal worlds; with the order of the universe and the laws of nature; with numerical relationships between visible and invisible in the divisions of time, deriving from divine command and from the cycles of nature and heavenly testimony to that effect; with the priestly guardians of the order of covenants and set times; with the angelic witnesses and their song in the celestial Merkavah and their counterparts in the terrestrial Temple; with immortalizing the memory of the ruined Temple and the discontinued sacred service through a mystical, liturgical metamorphosis. There are in fact indications that some considered the mystical tradition superior to halakhic tradition, which addressed earthly matters: ' "Great matters" means *ma'aseh merkavah*, "small matters"—the discussions of Abaye and Rava.'[133] The variety of traditions in Heikhalot and Merkavah literature proves that many studied and observed the Merkavah for the first centuries after the destruction of the Second Temple. The inclusion in the prayer book of the Kedushah, bringing together prayers uttered in heaven and on earth; the existence of lists of priestly courses in various places, hundreds of years after the destruction, and evidence that the order of the priestly courses was observed in synagogue worship in many locations; the various traditions of the 'miniature Temple', based on the sevenfold order of the cycle of sabbaths; and the persistence of the recitation of Ezekiel's vision as the prophetic reading for Shavuot—all these attest to the vigour of the liturgical memory, nurtured by the mystical derivatives of the Merkavah tradition and its Temple origins, through a thousand years from the destruction of the First Temple to the finalization of the Talmud, and to the complex transformations of the sacred service of priests and angels in the earthly Temple and the supernal sanctuaries.

[133] BT *Suk. 28a.*

Glossary

devir (pl. *devirim*) The sanctuary, inner sanctum, Holy of Holies, the innermost part of the Temple. Mentioned often in the description of the Temple in 1 Kings 6–8 and 2 Chronicles 3–5.

galgal (pl. *galgalim*) Literally 'wheel', as on a chariot; in Ezekiel's vision (Ezek. 10: 13) also a heavenly creature; part of the heavenly Chariot associated with ritual structures in the Temple.

hashmal A word unique to the account of Ezekiel's vision (Ezek. 1: 27), where it is used in the description of the visible glory. The meaning is obscure and disputed, but is connected with a luminous fiery vision or colour.

hayah (pl. *hayot*) A holy creature depicted as a living being in Ezekiel's vision, associated with the cherubim from the Temple (Ezek. 1, 10).

heikhal The biblical name for the Temple in Jerusalem; also a heavenly sanctuary or visionary sanctuary in biblical prophecy and poetry. The plural *heikhalot* refers to the seven heavenly sanctuaries in the priestly mystical writings. Heikhalot literature is mystical literature from the period of the Mishnah and the Talmud (2nd–5th centuries CE) which discusses the heavenly and angelic world as reflected in seven heavenly sanctuaries and in Ezekiel's vision of the Chariot.

kaporet The biblical word for the cover of the Ark of the Covenant on which the cherubim stand.

kedushah The triad *kadosh, kadosh, kadosh* ('holy, holy, holy'). Inspired by Isaiah 6, and a central part of prayer derived from Temple worship and associated with angelic worship. It is often mentioned in Heikhalot literature, but not in the rabbinic discussion of prayer.

ma'aseh bereshit 'Work of Creation', relating to the divine mysteries of Creation and to the laws of nature. In biblical priestly language the form *ma'aseh* is connected with ritual utensils and with the work of the tabernacle and the Temple.

ma'aseh merkavah 'Work of the Chariot', relating to mystical speculations concerning the divine Chariot (Ezek. 1, 10) and to the esoteric tradition pertaining to the mysteries of the divine world.

merkavah (pl. *merkavot*) The divine Chariot appearing in Ezekiel's vision; the name of the chariot of the cherubim in the Temple as described in 1 Chronicles 28: 18, 'and gold for the pattern of the chariot of the cherubim'; a concept associated with the mystical tradition of the priesthood concerning heavenly patterns of holy time and holy place.

ofan (pl. *ofanim*) 'Wheel(s)', as mentioned among the ritual fixtures of the Temple (1 Kgs. 7: 32–3), and depicted in Ezekiel's vision (Ezek. 1, 3, 10) as heavenly creatures and as part of the heavenly Chariot associated with ritual structures in the Temple.

pardes 'Orchard' or 'plantation'. Associated with Paradise, since the Septuagint translated 'Garden of Eden' from Hebrew into Greek as *paradeisos*. In Hebrew and Aramaic mystical literature from as early as 1 Enoch (3rd–2nd centuries BCE) the expression *pardes koshta* means 'paradise of justice and righteousness' and is known to signify a heavenly mystical enclave.

pesher A type of interpretation of biblical prophecies found at Qumran in which the prophetic texts describing the future are interpreted as applying to the present life of the Community and as describing its destiny.

shiur komah 'The stature of God'. A concept found in Heikhalot literature describing the measures of the divine body in transcendental numbers and visual images taken from the Song of Songs.

yaḥad 'Together'. The name by which the priestly community of Qumran refers to itself, signifying the togetherness of priests and angels, who (along with other followers) are the joint guardians of the Covenant, of righteousness and justice, and of the way of God. Possibly the name alludes to Isaiah 45: 8, 'let righteousness spring up together'.

Bibliography

I. DISCOVERIES IN THE JUDAEAN DESERT

Altogether thirty-nine volumes of *Discoveries in the Judaean Desert* [*DJD*] have appeared to date. The following are cited in this study:

DJD I: *Qumran Cave 1*, ed. D. Barthélemy and J. T. Milik (Oxford, 1955).

DJD IV: *The Psalms Scroll of Qumrân Cave 11 (11QPsᵃ)*, ed. J. A. Sanders (Oxford, 1965).

DJD V: *Qumrân Cave 4, I (4Q158–4Q186)*, ed. J. M. Allegro with A. A. Anderson (Oxford, 1968).

DJD VII: *Qumrân Grotte 4, III (4Q482–4Q520)*, ed. M. Baillet (Oxford, 1982).

DJD X: *Qumran Cave 4, V: Miqṣat Maʿaśe Ha-Torah*, ed. E. Qimron and J. Strugnell, with Y. Sussmann and A. Yardeni (Oxford, 1994).

DJD XI: *Qumran Cave 4, VI: Poetical and Liturgical Texts*, Part 1, ed. E. Eshel, H. Eshel, C. Newsom, B. Nitzan, E. Schuller, and A. Yardeni (Oxford, 1998).

DJD XIII: *Qumran Cave 4, VIII: Parabiblical Texts*, Part 1, ed. H. Attridge, T. Elgvin, J. T. Milik, S. Olyan, J. Strugnell, E. Tov, J. VanderKam, and S. White (Oxford, 1994).

DJD XV: *Qumran Cave 4, X: The Prophets*, ed. E. Ulrich *et al.* (Oxford, 1997).

DJD XVIII: *Qumran Cave 4, XIII: The Damascus Document (4Q266–273)*, ed. J. M. Baumgarten and J. T. Milik (Oxford, 1996).

DJD XXI: *Qumran Cave 4, XVI: Calendrical Texts*, ed. S. Talmon, J. Ben-Dov, and U. Glessmer (Oxford, 2001).

DJD XXII: *Qumran Cave 4, XVII: Parabiblical Texts*, Part 3, ed. G. Brooke *et al.* (Oxford, 1996).

DJD XXIII: *Qumran Cave 11, II (11Q2–18, 11Q20–31)*, ed. F. García Martínez, E. Tigchelaar, and A. van der Woude (Oxford, 1998).

DJD XXV: *Qumrân Grotte 4, XVIII: Textes hébreux (4Q521–4Q528, 4Q576–4Q579)*, ed. E. Puech (Oxford, 1998).

DJD XXVI: *Qumran Cave 4, XIX: Serekh Ha-Yaḥad and Two Related Texts*, ed. P. S. Alexander and G. Vermes (Oxford, 1998).

DJD XXVIII: *Wadi Daliyeh, II, and Qumran Miscellanea*, Part 2: *The Samaria Papyri from Wadi Daliyeh*, ed. D. M. Gropp, J. VanderKam, and M. Brady (Oxford, 2001).

DJD XXIX: *Qumran Cave 4, XX: Poetical and Liturgical Texts*, ed. E. Chazon, E. Schuller, *et al.* (Oxford, 1999).

DJD XXX: *Qumran Cave 4, XXI: Parabiblical Texts*, Part 4: *Pseudo-Prophetic Texts*, ed. D. Dimant and J. Strugnell (Oxford, 2001).

DJD XXXV: *Qumran Cave 4, XXV: Halakhic Texts*, ed. J. Baumgarten *et al.* (Oxford, 2000).

DJD XXXVI: *Qumran Cave 4, XXVI: Cryptic Texts and Miscellanea*, ed. S. J. Pfann, P. Alexander, *et al.* (Oxford, 2000).

2. OTHER SOURCES AND SCHOLARLY LITERATURE

ALEXANDER, P. S., 'The Historical Setting of the Hebrew Book of Enoch', *Journal of Jewish Studies*, 28 (1977), 156–80.

——'3 (The Hebrew Apocalypse of) Enoch', in J. H. Charlesworth (ed.), *The Old Testament Pseudepigrapha*, 2 vols. (Garden City, NY, 1983–5), i. 223–315.

ALLEGRO, J. M., 'Further on the History of the Qumran Sect', *Journal of Biblical Studies*, 75 (1956), 89–95.

APTOWITZER, A., 'The Heavenly Temple according to Aggadah' [Beit hamikdash shel malah al pi ha'agadah], *Tarbiz*, 2 (1931), 137–53, 257–87.

ARBEL, D., 'Mythical Elements in Heikhalot Literature' [Yesodot mitiyim besifrut haheikhalot] (diss., Hebrew University, Jerusalem, 1997).

ARTOM, E. S. (ed.), *The Apocrypha* [Hasefarim hahitsonim], 9 vols. in 8 (Tel Aviv, 1958–67).

AVIGAD, N., and Y. YADIN, *A Genesis Apocryphon* [Megilah hitsonit livereshit] (Jerusalem, 1957).

AVI-YONAH, M., 'An Inscription from Caesarea about the 24 Priestly Courses' [Ketovet mikeisariyah al 24 mishmerot hakohanim], *Eretz-Israel*, 7 (1964), 24–8.

BAKHTIN, M. M., *The Dialogic Imagination*, ed. M. Holquist (Austin, Tex., 1981).

BAR-ILAN, M., *The Mysteries of Jewish Prayer and Heikhalot* [Sitrei tefilah veheikhalot] (Ramat-Gan, 1987).

——'On the Interpretation of a *baraita* about the Reading of the Torah' [Leferushah shel baraita be'inyan keriat hatorah], *Sinai*, 112 (1993), 126–34.

BAR KOCHVA, B., *Judas Maccabaeus: The Jewish Struggle against the Seleucids* (Cambridge, 1989).

BARRERA, J. T., and L. V. MONTANER (eds.), *The Madrid Qumran Congress*, 2 vols., Studies on the Texts of the Desert of Judah, 11 (Leiden, 1992).

BAUMGARTEN, A., *The Flourishing of Jewish Sects in the Maccabean Era: An Interpretation* (Leiden, 1997).

BAUMGARTEN, J. M., 'The Beginning of the Day in the Calendar of Jubilees', *Journal of Biblical Literature*, 77 (1958), 355–60.

——'The Calendars of the Book of Jubilees and the Temple Scroll', *Vetus Testamentum*, 37 (1987), 45–70.

BAUMGARTEN, J. M., 'The Disqualifications of Priests in 4Q Fragments of the Damascus Document: A Specimen of the Recovery of Pre-Rabbinic Halakha', in J. T. Barrera and L. V. Montaner (eds.), *The Madrid Qumran Congress*, 2 vols., Studies on the Texts of the Desert of Judah, 11 (Leiden, 1992), ii. 503–13.

—— 'The Heavenly Tribunal and the Personification of Sedek in Jewish Apocalyptics', *Aufstieg und Niedergang der römischen Welt*, ser. ii, 19/1 (1979), 233–9.

—— 'The Pharisaic–Sadducean Controversies about Purity and the Qumran Texts', *Journal of Jewish Studies*, 31 (1980), 155–70.

—— 'The Qumran Sabbath *Shirot* and Rabbinic *Merkabah* Tradition', *Revue de Qumran*, 13 (1988), 199–213.

—— 'Qumran Studies', *Journal of Biblical Literature*, 77 (1958), 249–57.

—— *Studies in Qumran Law* (Leiden, 1977).

BECKWITH, R., *The Old Testament Canon of the New Testament Church and its Background in Early Judaism* (London, 1985), 63–80.

BEN-SHAHAR, Z., 'The Calendar of the Judaean Desert Sect' [Luah hashanah shel kat midbar yehudah] (diss., Tel Aviv University, 1975).

BEN-SHAMMAI, H., 'Methodological Remarks on the Study of the Relationship between the Karaites and Ancient Jewish Sects' [He'arot metodiyot leheker hayahas bein hakara'im uvein kitot yehudiyot kedumot], *Cathedra*, 42 (1987), 69–84.

BIETENHARD, H., *Die himmlische Welt im Urchristentum und Spätjudentum* (Tübingen, 1951).

BLACK, M. A., 'Bibliography on 1 Enoch in the Eighties', *Journal for the Study of the Pseudepigrapha*, 5 (1989), 3–16.

—— *The Book of Enoch or 1 Enoch*, Studia in Veteris Testamenti Pseudepigrapha, 7 (Leiden, 1985).

BOCCACCINI, G., *Beyond the Essene Hypothesis: The Parting of the Ways between Qumran and Enochic Judaism* (Grand Rapids, Mich., 1998).

BOHAK, G., *Joseph and Aseneth and the Jewish Temple in Heliopolis* (Atlanta, Ga., 1996).

BÖTTRICH, C., *Weltweisheit, Menschheitsethik, Urkult* (Tübingen, 1992).

BREUER, M., *Festival Chapters* [Pirkei mo'adot] (Jerusalem, 1993).

BRIN, G., and B. NITZAN (eds.), *Fifty Years of Dead Sea Scrolls Research: Studies in Memory of J. Licht* (Jerusalem, 2001).

BROOKE, G. J., 'Ezekiel in Some Qumran and New Testament Texts', in J. T. Barrera and L. V. Montaner (eds.), *The Madrid Qumran Congress*, 2 vols., Studies on the Texts of the Desert of Judah, 11 (Leiden, 1992), i. 317–37.

—— (ed.), *Temple Scroll Studies*, Journal for the Study of the Pseudepigrapha Supplement Series, 7 (Sheffield, 1989).

BROSHI, M. (ed.), *The Damascus Document Reconsidered* [text of the Cairo Genizah version of the Damascus Document edited by E. Qimron] (Jerusalem, 1992).

—— 'Visionary Architecture and Town Planning in the Dead Sea Scrolls', in D. Dimant and L. H. Schiffman (eds.), *Time to Prepare the Way in the Wilderness: Papers on Qumran Scrolls* (Leiden, 1995), 9–22.

—— *et al.* (eds.), *The Judaean Desert Scrolls: Forty Years of Research* [Megilot midbar yehudah: arba'im shenot mehkar] (Jerusalem, 1992).

BÜCHLER, A., *Die Priester und der Cultus im letzten Jahrzehnt des Jerusalemischen Tempels* (Wien, 1895).

BURROWS, M., *et al.*, *The Dead Sea Scrolls of St. Mark's Monastery*, i (New Haven, Conn., 1950).

CASSUTO, M. D., 'Ezekiel, Book of Ezekiel' [Yehezkel, Sefer yehezkel], in *Encyclopaedia Biblica*, 3 (1965), 636–55.

—— 'The Story of the Sons of God and the Daughters of Man' [Ma'aseh benei elohim uvenot ha'adam], in I. Epstein *et al.* (eds.), *Essays in Honour of J. H. Hertz on the Occasion of his 70th Birthday* (London, 1942), Hebrew section, 35–44.

CHARLES, R. H. (ed.), *The Apocrypha and Pseudepigrapha of the Old Testament in English*, 2 vols. (Oxford, 1913).

CHARLESWORTH, J. H. (ed.), *The Old Testament Pseudepigrapha*, 2 vols. (Garden City, NY, 1983–5).

—— with F. M. Cross *et al.* (eds.), *The Dead Sea Scrolls: Hebrew, Aramaic and Greek Texts with English Translation*, i: *Rule of the Community and Related Documents* (Tübingen, 1994).

CHERNUS, I., 'The Pilgrimage to the Merkavah', *Jerusalem Studies in Jewish Thought*, 6 (1987), 1–35.

—— 'Visions of God in Merkabah Mysticism', *Journal for the Study of Judaism*, 13 (1982), 123–46.

CHYUTIN, M., 'Numerical Mysticism in the Ancient World' [Mistikat hamisparim ba'olam ha'atik], *Beit Miqra*, 41 (1996), 14–30.

—— *The War of Calendars in the Period of the Second Temple* [Milhemet luhot hashanah bitekufat bayit sheni] (Tel Aviv, 1993).

CLEMENTS, R. E., *God and Temple* (Oxford, 1965).

COHEN, M. S., *The Shi'ur Qomah: Liturgy and Theurgy in Pre-Kabbalistic Jewish Mysticism* (Lanham, Md., 1983).

—— *The Shi'ur Qomah: Texts and Recensions* (Tübingen, 1985).

COHEN, S. J. D., 'The Significance of Yavneh: Pharisees, Rabbis, and the End of Jewish Sectarianism', *Hebrew Union College Annual*, 55 (1984), 27–53.

COLLINS, A. Y., 'The Seven Heavens in Jewish and Christian Apocalypse', in J. J. Collins and M. Fishbane (eds.), *Death, Ecstasy, and Other Worldly Journeys* (Albany, NY, 1995).

COLLINS, J. J. (ed.), *Apocalypse: The Morphology of a Genre*, Semia, 14 (Missoula, Mont., 1979).

COLLINS, J. J. (ed.), *The Apocalyptic Imagination* (New York, 1987).

CROSS, F. M., *The Ancient Library of Qumran* (Garden City, NY, 1961).

—— 'The Early History of the Qumran Community', in D. Freedman and J. Greenfield (eds.), *New Directions in Biblical Archeology* (Garden City, NY, 1971), 63–79.

CUMONT, F., *Astrology and Religion among the Greeks and Romans* (New York, 1960).

DAHOOD, M., *Psalms I*, Anchor Bible, 16 (Garden City, NY, 1960).

DAN, J., *The Ancient Jewish Mysticism* (Tel Aviv, 1993).

—— 'Chambers of the Merkavah' [Ḥadrei merkavah], *Tarbiz*, 47 (1978), 463–83.

—— 'The Concept of Pleroma in Heikhalot and Merkavah Literature' [Tefisat hapleroma besifrut haheikhalot vehamerkavah], in R. Elior and Y. Dan (eds.), *Many Voices* [Kolot rabim], Rivka Shatz-Uffenheimer Memorial Volume, Jerusalem Studies in Jewish Thought [Meḥkerei yerushalayim bemaḥashevet yisra'el], 12 (Jerusalem, 1996), 61–140.

—— 'Hidden Chambers' [Heikhalot genuzim], *Tarbiz*, 56 (1987), 433–7.

—— (ed.), *Proceedings of the First International Conference on the History of Jewish Mysticism: Early Jewish Mysticism* [Divrei hakenes letoldot hamistikah ha'ivrit hakedumah], Jerusalem Studies in Jewish Thought [Meḥkerei yerushalayim bemaḥashevet yisra'el], 6 (Jerusalem, 1987).

—— 'Revealing the Secret of the World: The Beginning of Early Jewish Mysticism' [Gilui sodo shel olam: reshitah shel hamistikah ha'ivrit hakedumah], in Y. Dan (ed.), *On Sanctity: Religion, Ethics and Mysticism in Judaism and Other Religions* [Al hakedushah: dat, musar umistikah bayahadut uvedatot aḥerot] (Jerusalem, 1997), 179–201.

DE JONGE, M., *The Testaments of the Twelve Patriarchs: A Study of their Text, Composition and Origin*, 2nd edn. (Assen, 1975).

DIMANT, D., 'Children of Heaven—Angelology in the Book of Jubilees in Light of the Writings of the Qumran Community' [Benei shamayim—torat hamalakhim besefer hayovelim le'or kitvei adat kumran], in D. Dimant, M. Idel, and S. Rosenberg (eds.), *Minḥah lesarah: Studies in Jewish Philosophy and Kabbalah Presented to Prof. Sarah Heller Wilensky* (Jerusalem, 1994), 97–118.

—— 'Men as Angels: The Self Image of the Qumran Community', in A. Berlin (ed.), *Religion and Politics in the Ancient Near East* (Bethesda, Md., 1996), 93–103.

—— 'The Qumran Manuscripts: Contents and Significance', in D. Dimant and L. H. Schiffman (eds.), *Time to Prepare the Way in the Wilderness: Papers on Qumran Scrolls* (Leiden, 1995), 23–58.

—— 'Qumran Sectarian Literature', in M. E. Stone (ed.), *Jewish Writings of the Second Temple Period*, Compendia Rerum Iudaicarum ad Novum Testamentum, 2/2 (Assen, 1984), 483–550.

—— 'Sinning Angels in the Judaean Desert Scrolls and in Related Non-Canonical Books' [Malakhim sheḥatu bimegilot midbar yehudah uvesefarim haḥitsonim hakerovim lahem] (diss., Hebrew University, Jerusalem, 1974).

——and U. RAPPAPORT (eds.), *The Dead Sea Scrolls—Forty Years of Research* (Leiden and Jerusalem, 1992).

——and J. STRUGNELL, 'The Merkabah Vision in Second Ezekiel (4Q 385 frg. 4)', *Revue de Qumran*, 14 (1990), 331–48.

DOERING, L., 'The Concept of the Sabbath in the Book of Jubilees', in M. Albany, J. Frey, and A. Lange (eds.), *Studies in the Book of Jubilees* (Tübingen, 1997), 179–205.

DRIVER, S. R., *An Introduction to the Literature of the Old Testament*, 9th edn. (Cleveland, Ohio, 1967).

EICHRODT, W., *Ezekiel: A Commentary* (Philadelphia, 1970).

EISENMAN, R. H., and J. M. ROBINSON, *A Facsimile Edition of the Dead Sea Scrolls* (Washington, DC, 1991).

ELIADE, M., *Images and Symbols* (New York, 1969).

—— *The Myth of the Eternal Return, or Cosmos and History* (New York, 1959).

ELIOR, R., 'The Concept of God in *Hekhalot* Literature', in J. Dan (ed.), *Binah*, ii (New York, 1989), 97–129.

——'From Earthly Temple to Heavenly Shrines: Prayer and Sacred Song in the Hekhalot Literature and its Relation to Temple Traditions', *Jewish Studies Quarterly*, 4 (1997), 217–67.

——*Heikhalot zutarti* [The Lesser Heikhalot], Jerusalem Studies in Jewish Thought [Mehkerei yerushalayim bemahashevet yisra'el], Suppl. 1 (Jerusalem, 1982).

——'The Jewish Calendar and Mystical Time' [Haluah hayehudi vehazeman hamisti], in *The Jewish Calendar: President's House Study-Group . . .* [Luah hashanah ha'ivri. Hug beit hanasi . . .] (Jerusalem, 1996), 22–42.

——'*Merkabah* Mysticism, A Critical Review (of D. J. Halperin's *The Faces of the Chariot*)', *NUMEN*, 37 (1990), 233–49.

——'The Merkavah Tradition and the Emergence of Jewish Mysticism', in A. Oppenheimer (ed.), *Sino-Judaica: Jews and Chinese in Historical Dialogue* (Tel Aviv, 1999), 101–58.

——'Mysticism, Magic and Angelology—The Perception of Angels in *Hekhalot* Literature', *Jewish Studies Quarterly*, 1 (1993), 3–53.

——'R. Joseph Karo and R. Israel Ba'al Shem Tov: Mystical Metamorphosis and Spiritual Transformation' [Rabi yosef karo verabi yisra'el ba'al shem tov: metamorfozah mistit utemurah ruhanit], *Tarbiz*, 65 (1996), 671–710.

——'Schäfer's *Synopse zur Hekhalot-Literatur*', *Jewish Quarterly Review*, 77 (1986–7), 213–17.

ENDRES, J. C., *Biblical Interpretation in the Book of Jubilees*, Catholic Biblical Quarterly, Monograph Series, 18 (Washington, DC, 1987).

ERDER, Y., 'When did the Encounter between Karaism and Apocryphal Literature Related to the Dead Sea Scrolls Begin?' [Eimatai hehel hamifgash shel hakara'ut im sifrut apokrifit hakerovah lesifrut hamegilot hagenuzot?], *Cathedra*, 42 (1987), 54–68.

FITZMYER, J. A., *The Dead Sea Scrolls: Major Publications and Tools for Study*, rev. edn. (Atlanta, Ga., 1990).

FLINT, P. W., *The Dead Sea Psalms Scrolls and the Book of Psalms*, Studies on the Texts of the Desert of Judah, 17 (Leiden, New York, and Cologne, 1997).

FLUSSER, D., 'The Judaean Desert Sect and its Views' [Kat midbar yehudah vehashkafoteiha], *Zion*, 19 (1954), 89–103.

——*Judaism and the Origins of Christianity* (Jerusalem, 1988).

FUJITA, S., 'The Temple Theology of the Qumran Sect and the Book of Ezekiel' (Ph.D. diss., Princeton Theological Seminary, Ann Arbor, Mich., 1970).

GARCÍA MARTÍNEZ, F., and D. W. PARRY, *A Bibliography of the Finds in the Desert of Judea 1970–95*, Studies on the Texts of the Desert of Judah, 19 (Leiden, New York, and Cologne, 1996).

——and E. J. C. TIGCHELAAR, *The Dead Sea Scrolls Study Edition*, 2 vols. (Leiden, 1997–8).

GARTNER, B., *The Temple and the Community in Qumran and the New Testament* (Cambridge, 1965).

GIL, M., 'Studies in the Book of Enoch' [Iyunim besefer hanokh], in A. Oppenheimer and A. Kasher (eds.), *From Generation to Generation* [Dor ledor], Collection of Studies in Honour of Y. Efron (Jerusalem, 1995), 155–95.

GOODENOUGH, E. R., *Jewish Symbols in the Greco-Roman Period*, 13 vols. (New York, 1953–68).

GOUDOEVER, J. VAN, *Biblical Calendars* (Leiden, 1961).

GREEN, A., *Keter: The Crown of God in Early Jewish Mysticism* (Princeton, NJ, 1997).

GREENBERG, M., *Ezekiel 1–20*, Anchor Bible (Garden City, NY, 1983).

GREENFIELD, J. C., and M. E. STONE, 'The Books of Enoch and the Traditions of Enoch', *NUMEN*, 26 (1979), 89–103.

————'The Enochic Pentateuch and the Date of the Similitudes', *Harvard Theological Review*, 70 (1977), 51–65.

GRELOT, P., 'Parwain des Chroniques à l'apocalypse de la Genèse', *Vetus Testamentum*, 11 (1961), 30–8.

GRINTZ, Y. M., 'The Scroll of Light and Darkness—its Date and its Creators' [Megilat or vahoshekh—zemanah veyotsreiha], in Y. Yadin and Ch. Rabin (eds.), *Studies in the Dead Sea Scrolls* [Mehkarim bamegilot hagenuzot], E. L. Sukenik Memorial Volume (Jerusalem, 1961), 19–30.

GRUENWALD, I., 'Angelic Song, the Kedushah, and the Problem of the Composition of Heikhalot Literature' [Shirat hamalakhim, hakedushah uva'ayat hiburah shel sifrut haheikhalot], in A. Oppenheimer, U. Rappaport, and M. Stern (eds.), *Chapters in the History of Jerusalem in Second Temple Times* [Perakim betoledot yerushalayim bimei bayit sheni], A. Schalit Memorial Volume (Jerusalem, 1981), 459–81.

——*Apocalyptic and Merkavah Mysticism* (Leiden and Cologne, 1980).

—— *From Apocalypticism to Mysticism* (Leiden and Frankfurt, 1988).

—— 'The Place of Priestly Traditions in Works of Mysticism, Merkavah, and *Shi'ur Komah*' [Mekoman shel masorot kohaniyot bayetsirah shel hamistikah shel hamerkavah veshel shiur komah], in J. Dan (ed.), *Proceedings of the First International Conference on the History of Jewish Mysticism: Early Jewish Mysticism* [Divrei hakenes letoldot hamistikah ha'ivrit hakedumah], Jerusalem Studies in Jewish Thought [Meḥkerei yerushalayim bemaḥashevet yisra'el], 6 (Jerusalem, 1987), 65–119.

—— (ed.), *Re'uyot yeḥezkel* [The Visions of Ezekiel] (= *Temirin*, 1 (Jerusalem, 1972), 101–39).

GUNKEL, H., *Introduction to Psalms: The Genres of Religious Lyric of Israel* (Macon, Ga., 1998).

HABERMANN, A. M., *The Judaean Desert Scrolls* [Megilot midbar yehudah] (Tel Aviv, 1959).

HALPERIN, D. J., 'The Exegetical Character of Ezek. X 9–17', *Vetus Testamentum*, 26 (1976), 129–41.

—— *The Faces of the Chariot: Early Jewish Responses to Ezekiel's Vision* (Tübingen, 1988).

—— *The Merkabah in Rabbinic Literature* (Leiden, 1980).

HANSON, P. D., *The Dawn of Apocalyptic* (Philadelphia, 1979).

—— 'Rebellion in Heaven: Azazel and Euhemeristic Heroes in 1 Enoch 6–11', *Journal of Biblical Literature*, 96 (1977), 195–234.

HARAN, M., *The Biblical Anthology: Its Gradual Crystallization up to the End of the Second Temple Period and Transformations up to the End of the Middle Ages* [Ha'asupah hamikra'it: tahalikhei hagibush ad sof yemei bayit sheni veshinuyei hatsurah ad motsa'ei yemei habeinayim] (Jerusalem, 1996).

—— *Temples and Temple Service in Ancient Israel* (Oxford, 1978).

—— 'Topics in Bible: The Legal Codex of Ezekiel 40–8 and its Relationship to the Priestly School' [Sugyot bamikra. Kovets haḥukim shel yeḥezkel 40–48 veyaḥaso la'eskolah hakohanit], *Tarbiz*, 44 (1975), 30–53.

HELLHOLM, D. (ed.), *Apocalypticism in the Mediterranean World and the Near East* (Tübingen, 1989).

HENGEL, M., *Judaism and Hellenism* (Philadelphia, 1974).

HERR, M. D., 'The Calendar', in S. Safrai and M. Stern (eds.), *The Jewish People in the First Century*, 2 vols., Compendia Rerum Iudaicarum ad Novum Testamentum, 1 (Assen/Amsterdam, 1974–6), ii. 834–64.

—— 'Jerusalem, the Temple, and the Temple Service in Reality and in Consciousness in Second Temple Times' [Yerushalayim, hamikdash veha'avodah bamtsiut uvatoda'ah bimei bayit sheni], in A. Oppenheimer, U. Rappaport, and M. Stern (eds.), *Chapters in the History of Jerusalem in Second Temple Times* [Perakim betoledot yerushalayim bimei bayit sheni], A. Schalit Memorial Volume (Jerusalem, 1981), 166–77.

HIMMELFARB, M., *Ascent to Heaven in Jewish and Christian Apocalypses* (New York, 1993).

HOLLANDER, H. W., and M. DE JONGE, *The Testaments of the Twelve Patriarchs: A Commentary* (Leiden, 1985).

HORGAN, M., *Pesharim: Qumran Interpretations of Biblical Books* (Washington, DC, 1979).

JANOWITZ, N., *The Poetics of Ascent: Theories of Language in a Rabbinic Ascent Text* (New York, 1989).

JAPHET, S., *I and II Chronicles: A Commentary*, Old Testament Library (London, 1993).

JAUBERT, A., 'The Calendar of Qumran and the Passion Narrative in John', in J. H. Charlesworth (ed.), *John and Qumran* (London, 1972), 62–76.

—— 'Le Calendrier des Jubilées et de la secte de Qumran: Ses origines bibliques', *Vetus Testamentum*, 3 (1953), 250–64.

—— 'Le Calendrier des Jubilées et les jours liturgiques de la semaine', *Vetus Testamentum*, 7 (1957), 35–61.

KAHANA, A. (ed.), *The Apocrypha* [Hasefarim haḥitsonim], 2 vols. (Tel Aviv, 1937).

KAHANA, T., 'The Priests according to their Courses and their Places of Residence' [Hakohanim lemishmeroteihem velimekomot hityashvutam], *Tarbiz*, 48 (1979), 9–29.

KAMPEN, J., and M. BERNSTEIN (eds.), *Reading 4Q MMT: New Perspectives on Qumran Law and History* (Atlanta, Ga., 1996).

KISTER, M., '5Q13 and the Avoda: A Historical Survey and its Significance', *Dead Sea Discoveries*, 8 (2001), 136–48.

—— 'Levi who is Light' [Levi shehu or], *Tarbiz*, 45 (1976), 327–30.

—— 'On the History of the Essene Sect: Studies of the Vision of the Beasts, the Book of Jubilees, and the Damascus Covenant' [Letoldot kat ha'isiyim: iyunim baḥazon haḥayot, sefer hayovelim uverit damesek], *Tarbiz*, 56 (1987), 1–15.

—— 'Some Aspects of Qumranic Halakhah', in J. T. Barrera and L. V. Montaner (eds.), *The Madrid Qumran Congress*, 2 vols., Studies on the Texts of the Desert of Judah, 11 (Leiden, 1992), ii. 571–88.

—— 'Studies in the Scroll of *Miktsat ma'asei hatorah* and its World: Halakhah, Theology, Language, and Calendar' [Iyunim bimegilat miktsat ma'asei hatorah ve'olamah: halakhah, te'ologiyah, lashon veluaḥ], *Tarbiz*, 68 (1999), 317–71.

KLEIN, S., 'The *baraita* of Twenty-Four *mishmarot*' [Baraita shel arba'ah ve'esrim mishmarot], in *Miscellaneous Articles relating to the Study of the Land of Israel* [Ma'amarim shonim laḥakirat erets yisra'el] (Vienna, 1924), 1–29.

—— *The Land of Galilee* [Erets hagalil] (Jerusalem, 1946).

KLINZING, G., *Die Umdeutung des Kultus in der Qumrangemeinde und im Neuen Testament* (Göttingen, 1971).

KNIBB, M. A., *The Ethiopic Book of Enoch: A New Edition* (Oxford, 1978).

KNOHL, Y., *The Sanctuary of Silence: The Priestly Torah and the Holiness School*, trans. J. Feldman and P. Rodman (Minneapolis, 1995).

KOCH, K., *The Rediscovery of Apocalyptic* (Naperville, Ill., 1972).

KUGEL, J., 'Levi's Elevation to the Priesthood in Second Temple Writings', *Harvard Theological Review*, 86 (1993), 1–64.

—— 'The Story of Dinah in the Testament of Levi', *Harvard Theological Review*, 85 (1992), 1–34.

KUGLER, R. A., *From Patriarch to Priest: The Levi-Priestly Tradition from Aramaic Levi to Testament of Levi* (Atlanta, Ga., 1996).

KVANVIG, H. S., *Roots of the Apocalyptic* (Neukirchen-Vluyn, 1988).

LAMBERT, W. G., 'Enmeduranki and Related Matters', *Journal of Cuneiform Studies*, 21 (1967), 127–37.

LAUTERBACH, J. Z., 'The Sadducees and Pharisees', in id., *Rabbinic Essays* (Cincinnati, 1951), 23–162.

LESSES, R. M., *Ritual Practices to Gain Power* (Harrisburg, Penn., 1998).

LEVIN, Y., 'The Political Struggle between the Pharisees and the Sadducees in the Hasmonean Period' [Hama'avak hapoliti bein haperushim latsedukim batekufah hahashmona'it], in A. Oppenheimer, U. Rappaport, and M. Stern (eds.), *Chapters in the History of Jerusalem in Second Temple Times* [Perakim betoldot yerushalayim bimei bayit sheni], A. Schalit Memorial Volume (Jerusalem, 1981), 61–83.

LICHT, J., 'The Judaean Desert Sect and its Writings' [Kat midbar yehudah ukhetaveiha], in M. Avi-Yonah and Z. Baras (eds.), *Society and Religion in the Second Temple Period* [Hevrah vadat bimei bayit sheni] (Jerusalem, 1983), 83–103.

—— *The Rule Scroll from the Judaean Desert Scrolls* [Megilat haserakhim mimegilot midbar yehudah] (Jerusalem, 1965).

—— *The Scroll of Thankgsviging Hymns* [Megilat hahodayot] (Jerusalem, 1957).

—— 'The Temporal Doctrine of the Judaean Desert Sect and of Other Eschatologists' [Torat ha'itim shel kat midbar yehudah veshel mehashvei kitsin aherim], *Eretz-Israel*, 8 (Jerusalem, 1967), 63–70.

LICHTENBERGER, J., 'Atonement and Sacrifice in the Qumran Community', in W. S. Green (ed.), *Approaches to Ancient Judaism* (Chico, Calif., 1980), 159–71.

LIEBERMAN, S., 'Mishnat shir hashirim', appendix to G. Scholem, *Jewish Gnosticism, Merkabah Mysticism and Talmudic Tradition* (New York, 1965), 118–26.

LIEBES, Y., *The Creation Doctrine of Sefer Yetsirah* [Torat hayetsirah shel sefer yetsirah] (Jerusalem and Tel Aviv, 2001).

—— 'The Messiah of the Zohar—On R. Simeon bar Yochai as a Messianic Figure', in id., *Studies in the Zohar* (New York, 1993), 1–84, 163–93.

—— *The Sin of Elisha: Four Who Entered the Pardes and the Nature of Talmudic Mysticism* [Heto shel elisha: arba'ah shenikhnesu lapardes vetivah shel hamistikah hatalmudit], 2nd edn. (Jerusalem, 1990).

LIVER, J., *Bible Studies and the Judaean Desert Scrolls* [Ḥikrei mikra umegilot midbar yehudah] (Jerusalem, 1972).

—— *Chapters in the History of the Priesthood and the Levites: Studies of the Lists in Chronicles and Ezra–Nehemiah* [Perakim betoldot hakehunah vehaleviyah: iyunim barshimot shebedivrei hayamim ve'ezra uneḥemiyah] (Jerusalem, 1987).

—— 'The Sons of Zadok in the Judaean Desert Sect' [Benei tsadok shebekhat midbar yehudah], *Eretz-Israel*, 8 (1967), 71–81.

—— (ed.), *Studies in the Judaean Desert Scrolls* [Iyunim bimegilot midbar yehudah] (Jerusalem, 1957).

LURKER, M., *The Gods and Symbols of Ancient Egypt* (London, 1988).

LUST, J. (ed.), *Ezekiel and his Book* (Leuven, 1986).

MACH, M., 'Saints–Angels: God and Heavenly Liturgy' [Kedoshim-malakhim: ha'el vehaliturgiyah hashemeimit], in M. Oron and A. Goldreich (eds.), *Masu'ot: Studies in Jewish Kabbalistic and Philosophical Literature in Memory of Ephraim Gottlieb* (Jerusalem, 1994), 298–310.

—— 'Studies in Angelology in the Hellenistic-Roman Period' [Meḥkarim betorat hamalakhim batekufah hahelenistit-romit] (Ph.D. diss., Tel Aviv University, 1996).

MAGNESS, J., *The Archaeology of Qumran and the Dead Sea Scrolls* (Grand Rapids, Mich., 2002).

MAIER, J., 'Shire Olat hash-Shabbat: Some Observations on their Calendric Implications and on their Style', in J. T. Barrera and L. V. Montaner (eds.), *The Madrid Qumran Congress*, 2 vols., Studies on the Texts of the Desert of Judah, 11 (Leiden, 1992), ii. 543–60.

—— *Vom Kultus zur Gnosis*, Religionswissenschaftliche Studien, 1 (Salzburg, 1964).

MARGALIOT, M. (ed.), *Sefer harazim* [Book of Secrets] (Tel Aviv, 1967).

MARGALIOT, R., *Heavenly Angels* [Malakhei elyon] (Jerusalem, 1945).

—— (ed.), *Zohar ḥadash* [New Zohar] (Jerusalem, 1978).

MENDELS, D., *The Land of Israel as a Political Concept in Hasmonean Literature* (Leiden, 1987).

MILGROM, J., 'Further Studies in the Temple Scroll', *Jewish Quarterly Review*, 71 (1980), 1–17, 89–106.

—— 'The Temple Scroll', *Biblical Archaeology Review*, 4 (1978), 105–20.

MILIK, J. T., *The Books of Enoch: Aramaic Fragments of Qumran Cave 4* (Oxford, 1976).

—— *Ten Years of Discovery in the Judean Desert* (Oxford, 1959).

MISHOR, M., 'Tarshish = Sea in Rabbinic Language' [Tarshish = yam bedivrei ḥazal], *Leshonenu*, 34 (1970), 318–19.

MOLENBERG, C., 'A Study of the Roles of Shemihaza and Asael in 1 Enoch 6–11', *Journal of Jewish Studies*, 35 (1984), 136–46.

MORAG, S., 'Style and Language in the *Miktsat ma'asei hatorah* Scroll: Did the Teacher of Righteousness Write this Letter?' [Signon velashon bimegilat miketsat ma'asei hatorah—ha'im katav moreh hatsedek igeret zot?], *Tarbiz*, 65 (1996), 209–23.

MORRAY-JONES, C. R. A., 'Paradise Revisited (2 Cor. 12: 1–12): The Jewish Mystical Background of Paul's Apostolate. I: The Jewish Sources', *Harvard Theological Review*, 86 (1993), 203–15.

—— 'Transformational Mysticism in the Apocalyptic-Merkavah Tradition', *Journal of Jewish Studies*, 48 (1992), 1–31.

NA'EH, S., 'Did the *tana'im* Interpret the Script of the Torah Differently from the Authorized Reading?' [Ein em lamasoret; o ha'im darshu hatana'im et ketiv hatorah shelo kikeriato hamekubelet?], *Tarbiz*, 61 (1992), 401–48.

NEWSOM, C., 'He has Established for Himself Priests: Human and Angelic Priesthood in the Qumran Shabbat Shirot', in L. H. Schiffman (ed.), *Archeology and History in the Dead Sea Scrolls* (Sheffield, 1990), 100–20.

—— 'Merkabah Exegesis in the Qumran Sabbath *Shirot*', *Journal of Jewish Studies*, 38 (1987), 11–30.

—— 'Sectually Explicit Literature from Qumran', in W. H. Propp *et al.* (eds.), *The Hebrew Bible and its Interpreters* (Winona Lake, Ind., 1990), 167–87.

—— *Songs of the Sabbath Sacrifice: A Critical Edition*, Harvard Semitic Studies, 27 (Atlanta, Ga., 1985).

NICKELSBURG, G. W. E., 'Apocalyptic and Myth in I Enoch 6–11', *Journal of Biblical Literature*, 96/3 (1977), 383–406.

NITZAN, B. (ed.), *The Pesher Habakkuk Scroll of the Judaean Desert Scrolls* [Megilat pesher havakuk mimegilot midbar yehudah] (Jerusalem and Tel Aviv, 1986).

—— *Qumran Prayer and Song* [Tefilat kumran veshiratah] (Jerusalem, 1997).

NOLL, S. F., 'Angelology in the Qumran Texts' (Ph.D. diss., Manchester, 1979).

NORTH, R., 'The Qumran Sadducees', *Catholic Biblical Quarterly*, 17 (1955), 164–88.

ODEBERG, H., *3 Enoch, or the Hebrew Book of Enoch* (Cambridge, 1928; repr. New York, 1973, with 'Prolegomenon' by J. C. Greenfield).

OPPENHEIMER, A., U. RAPPAPORT, and M. STERN (eds.), *Chapters in the History of Jerusalem in Second Temple Times* [Perakim betoldot yerushalayim bimei bayit sheni], A. Schalit Memorial Volume (Jerusalem, 1981).

ORIGEN, *The Song of Songs: Commentary and Homilies*, trans. R. P. Lawson (London, 1957).

Pesikta derav kahana, ed. D. Mandelbaum (New York, 1962).

Pesikta rabati, ed. M. Ish-Shalom (Tel Aviv, 1963).

PHILO OF ALEXANDRIA, *Collected Works*, 12 vols., Loeb Classical Library (London, 1929–62).

PINES, S., 'Eschatology and the Concept of Time in the Slavonic Book of Enoch', in R. J. Z. Werblowsky and C. J. Bleeker (eds.), *Types of Redemption* (Leiden, 1970), 72–87.

PUECH, E., 'Review of *Songs of the Sabbath Sacrifice: A Critical Edition*', *Revue Biblique*, 94 (1987), 604–13.

QIMRON, E., 'A Review Article of *Songs of the Sabbath Sacrifice: A Critical Edition*, by Carol Newsom', *Harvard Theological Review*, 79 (1986), 349–71.

—— *The Temple Scroll: A Critical Edition with Extensive Reconstructions* (Beersheba and Jerusalem, 1996).

—— and J. STRUGNELL, 'An Unpublished Halakhic Letter from Qumran', in J. Amitai (ed.), *Biblical Archeology Today* (Jerusalem, 1985), 400–7.

RABIN, CH., *Qumran Studies* (Oxford, 1957).

—— *The Zadokite Documents*, 2nd edn. (Oxford, 1958).

REICH, R., 'Ritual Baths at Qumran' [Mikve'ot tohorah bekumran], *Cathedra*, 30/2 (1997), 125–8.

ROFÉ, A., *The Belief in Angels in the Bible* (Jerusalem, 1979).

ROWLAND, C., *The Open Heaven: A Study in Apocalypticism in Judaism and Early Christianity* (London, 1982).

—— 'The Visions of God in Apocalyptic Literature', *Journal for the Study of Judaism*, 10 (1979–80), 137–54.

ROWLEY, H. H., *The Zadokite Fragments and the Dead Sea Scrolls* (Oxford, 1952).

RUBINSTEIN, A., 'Observations on the Slavonic Book of Enoch', *Journal of Jewish Studies*, 13 (1962), 1–21.

RUSSELL, D. S., *The Method and Message of Jewish Apocalyptic* (Philadelphia, 1964).

SACCHI, P., 'The Two Calendars of the Book of Enoch', in id., *Jewish Apocalyptic and its History*, trans. W. J. Short (Sheffield, 1990).

SAFRAI, Z., 'When did the Priests Relocate to Galilee? A Response to Dalyah Trifon's Article' [Matai avru hakohanim lagalil? Teguvah lema'amarah shel daliyah trifon], *Tarbiz*, 62 (1993), 287–92.

SANDERS, J. A., *The Dead Sea Psalms Scroll* (Ithaca, NY, 1967).

SCHÄFER, P. (ed.), *Geniza-Fragmente zur Hekhalot-Literatur*, Texte und Studien zum antiken Judentum, 6 (Tübingen, 1984).

—— *The Hidden and Manifest God: Some Major Themes in Early Jewish Mysticism* (Albany, NY, 1992).

—— *Konkordanz zur Hekhalot-Literatur* (Tübingen, 1986–8).

—— (ed.), *Synopse zur Hekhalot-Literatur*, Texte und Studien zum antiken Judentum, 2 (Tübingen, 1981).

SCHECHTER, S., *Documents of Jewish Sectaries*, with Prolegomenon by J. A. Fitzmyer (New York, 1970) (= *Fragments of a Zadokite Work* (Cambridge, 1910)).

SCHIFFMAN, L. H. [Y.], 'Heikhalot Literature and Qumran Writings' [Sifrut ha-heikhalot vekhitvei kumran], in J. Dan (ed.), *Proceedings of the First International Conference on the History of Jewish Mysticism: Early Jewish Mysticism* [Divrei ha-kenes letoldot hamistikah ha'ivrit hakedumah], Jerusalem Studies in Jewish Thought [Mehkerei yerushalayim bemahashevet yisra'el], 6 (Jerusalem, 1987), 121–38.

——'*Merkavah* Speculation at Qumran', in J. Reinharz *et al.* (eds.), *Mystics, Philosophers and Politicians: Essays in Jewish Intellectual History in Honor of Alexander Altmann* (Durham, NC, 1982), 15–47.

——'The New Halakhic Letter (4QMMT) and the Origins of the Dead Sea Sect', *The Biblical Archeologist*, 33 (1990), 64–73.

——'The Temple Scroll and the Nature of its Law', in E. Ulrich and J. VanderKam (eds.), *The Community of the Renewed Covenant*, The Notre Dame Symposium on the Dead Sea Scrolls (Notre Dame, Ind., 1994), 37–55.

——' "The War of the Scrolls"—Developments in the Study of the Dead Sea Scrolls' [Milḥemet hamegilot—hitpatḥuyot beḥeker hamegilot hagenuzot], *Cathedra*, 61 (1992), 3–23.

SCHIMMEL, A., *The Mystery of Numbers* (Oxford, 1993).

SCHOLEM, G., *Jewish Gnosticism, Merkabah Mysticism and Talmudic Tradition* (New York, 1965).

——*Major Trends in Jewish Mysticism* (New York, 1967).

SCHÜRER, E., *The History of the Jewish People in the Age of Jesus Christ (175 B.C.–135 A.D.)*, ed. G. Vermes, F. Millar, M. Black, and M. Goodman, rev. edn., 3 vols. (Edinburgh, 1973–86).

SCHWARTZ, D. R., 'Between Sages and Priests in Second Temple Times' [Bein ḥakhamim vekhohanim bimei bayit sheni], in D. Kerem (ed.), *Selected Views and Opinions in Jewish Culture* [Migvan de'ot vehashkafot betarbut yisra'el], ii (Tel Aviv, 1992), 63–79.

——'Desert and Temple: On Religion and State in Judaea in Second Temple Times' [Midbar umikdash: al dat umedinah bihudah bimei bayit sheni], in Y. Gafni and G. Motzkin (eds.), *Priesthood and Kingship* [Kehunah umelukhah: yaḥasei dat umedinah beyisra'el uva'amim] (Jerusalem, 1987), 61–78.

——'Law and Truth: On Qumran-Sadducean and Rabbinic Views of Law,' in D. Dimant and U. Rappaport (eds.), *The Dead Sea Scrolls—Forty Years of Research* (Leiden and Jerusalem, 1992), 229–40.

——'On Two Aspects of a Priestly View of Descent at Qumran', in L. H. Schiffman (ed.), *Archeology and History in the Dead Sea Scrolls* (Sheffield, 1990), 157–79.

——'Priesthood, Temple, Sacrifices: Opposition and Spiritualization in the Late Second Temple Period' (Ph.D. diss., Hebrew University, Jerusalem, 1981).

——'Qumran between Priesthood and Christianity' [Kumran bein kohaniyut venatsrut], in M. Broshi *et al.* (eds.), *The Judaean Desert Scrolls: Forty Years of Research* [Megilot midbar yehudah: arba'im shenot meḥkar] (Jerusalem, 1992), 176–81.

——(ed.), *Studies in Jewish History in the Second Temple Period: Selected Articles* [Meḥkarim betoldot yisra'el bitekufat habayit hasheni: ma'amarim nivḥarim] (Jerusalem, 1996).

SEGAL, A. F., 'Heavenly Ascent in Hellenistic Judaism, Early Christianity and their Environment', *Aufstieg und Niedergang der römischen Welt*, ser. ii, 23/2 (Berlin, 1980), 1333–94.

SEGAL, A. F., *Two Powers in Heaven: Early Christianity and Gnosticism* (Leiden, 1977).

SEGAL, M. Z. (ed.), *The Complete Book of Ben-Sira* [Sefer ben-sira hashalem] (Jerusalem, 1972).

SMITH, J., *Imagining Religion: From Babylon to Jonestown* (Chicago, 1982).

SMITH, M., 'Ascent to the Heavens and Deification in 4Qmᵃ', in L. H. Schiffman (ed.), *Archeology and History in the Dead Sea Scrolls*, Journal for the Study of the Pseudepigrapha Supplement Series, 8 (Sheffield, 1990), 181–8.

—— 'The Dead Sea Sect in Relation to Ancient Judaism', *New Testament Studies*, 61 (1960), 347–60.

—— 'Some Observations on Hekhalot Rabbati', in A. Altmann (ed.), *Biblical and Other Studies* (Cambridge, 1963), 142–60.

STALLMAN, R. C., 'Levi and Levites in the Dead Sea Scrolls', *Journal for the Study of the Pseudepigrapha*, 10 (1992), 163–89.

STEGEMANN, H., 'The Qumran Essenes—Local Members of the Main Jewish Union in Late Second Temple Times', in J. T. Barrera and L. V. Montaner (eds.), *The Madrid Qumran Congress*, 2 vols., Studies on the Texts of the Desert of Judah, 11 (Leiden, 1992), i. 83–166.

STERN, M., *Greek and Latin Authors on Jews and Judaism*, 3 vols. (Jerusalem, 1974–84).

—— 'Judaism and Hellenism in Palestine in the 3rd and 2nd Centuries BCE' [Yahadut veyavnut be'erets yisra'el bame'ot hashelishit vehasheniyah lifnei hasefirah], in M. Stern and Y. Kaplan (eds.), *Assimilation* [Hitbolelut utemiah] (Jerusalem, 1989), 41–60.

—— *Studies in Jewish History in Second Temple Times* [Mehkarim betoldot yisra'el bimei habayit hasheni], ed. Y. Gafni *et al.* (Jerusalem, 1991).

STONE, M. E., 'The Books of Enoch and Judaism in the Third Century B.C.E.', *Catholic Biblical Quarterly*, 40 (1978), 479–92.

—— 'Enoch, Aramaic Levi and Sectarian Origins', in *Selected Studies in Pseudepigrapha and Apocrypha with Special Reference to the Armenian Tradition*, Vetus Testamentum Supplements, P 9 (Leiden, 1991).

—— (ed.), *Jewish Writings of the Second Temple Period*, Compendia Rerum Iudaicarum ad Novum Testamentum, 2/2 (Assen, 1984).

—— *Scriptures, Sects and Visions* (Philadelphia, 1980).

STRUGNELL, J., 'The Angelic Liturgy at Qumran—4Q Serek Širot Olat haššabat', in *Congress Volume* (Oxford, 1959) (= *Vetus Testamentum* Supplements, 7; Leiden 1959–60), 318–45.

—— 'MMT: Second Thoughts on a Forthcoming Edition', in E. Ulrich and J. Vander-Kam (eds.), *The Community of the Renewed Covenant*, The Notre Dame Symposium on the Dead Sea Scrolls (Notre Dame, Ind., 1994), 57–73.

—— and D. DIMANT, '4Q Second Ezekiel', *Revue de Qumran*, 13 (1988), 45–58.

SUKENIK, E. L., *The Dead Sea Scrolls of the Hebrew University* (Jerusalem, 1955).

SUSSMANN, Y., 'The History of Halakhah and the Judaean Desert Scrolls: First Talmudic Thoughts in Light of the *Miktsat ma'asei hatorah* Scroll' [Ḥeker toldot hahalakhah umegilot midbar yehudah: hirhurim talmudiyim rishonim le'or megilat 'miketsat ma'asei hatorah'], *Tarbiz*, 59 (1990), 11–64.

SUTER, D., 'Fallen Angel, Fallen Priest: The Problem of Family Purity in 1 Enoch 6–16', *Hebrew Union College Annual*, 50 (1979), 115–36.

SWARTZ, M. D., *Mystical Prayer in Ancient Judaism: An Analysis of Maaseh Merkavah* (Tübingen, 1992).

TABORI, Y., *The Jewish Festivals in the Period of the Mishnah and the Talmud* [Mo'adei yisra'el bitekufat hamishnah vehatalmud] (Jerusalem, 1997).

TALMON, S., 'Apocryphal Psalms in the Hebrew Language from Qumran' [Mizmorim hitsonim balashon ha'ivrit mikumran], *Tarbiz*, 35 (1966), 214–34.

—— 'The Calendar of the Covenanters of the Judean Desert', in Ch. Rabin and Y. Yadin (eds.), *Aspects of the Dead Sea Scrolls*, Scripta Hierosolymitana, 4 (Jerusalem, 1958), 162–99 (reprinted in S. Talmon, *The World of Qumran from Within: Collected Studies* (Jerusalem, 1989), 147–50, 273–300).

—— 'The Calendar of the *yahad* Community' [Luaḥ hashanah shel benei adat hayaḥad], *Qadmoniyot*, 30/2 (114) (1998), 105–14.

—— 'The Calendrical Calculation of the Judaean Desert Sect' [Ḥeshbon haluaḥ shel kat midbar yehudah], in Y. Yadin and Ch. Rabin (eds.), *Studies in the Dead Sea Scrolls* [Meḥkarim bamgilot hagnuzot], E. L. Sukenik Memorial Volume (Jerusalem, 1961), 77–105.

—— 'The Community of the Renewed Covenant: Between Judaism and Christianity', in E. Ulrich and J. VanderKam (eds.), *The Community of the Renewed Covenant*, The Notre Dame Symposium on the Dead Sea Scrolls (Notre Dame, Ind., 1994), 3–24.

—— 'The Covenanters' Calendar of Holy Seasons according to the List of King David's Compositions in the Psalms Scroll from Cave 11' [Luaḥ hamo'adim bishenat hahamah shel adat hayahad al pi reshimat shirei david bimegilat hamizmorim mime'arah 11], in G. Brin and B. Nitzan (eds.), *Fifty Years of Dead Sea Scrolls Research: Studies in Memory of J. Licht* (Jerusalem, 2001), 204–19.

—— 'The Cycle of Benedictions of the Judaean Desert Sect' [Mahazor haberakhot shel kat midbar yehudah], *Tarbiz*, 29 (1960), 1–20.

—— 'The Old Testament Text', *Cambridge History of the Bible*, i (Cambridge, 1970), 164–70.

—— *The World of Qumran from Within: Collected Studies* (Jerusalem, 1989).

—— and I. KNOHL, 'A Calendrical Scroll from a Qumran Cave: Mishmarot Bª, 4Q 321', in D. P. Wright *et al.* (eds.), *Pomegranates and Golden Bells: Studies in Biblical, Jewish, and Near Eastern Ritual, Law, and Literature in Honor of Jacob Milgrom* (Winona Lake, Ind., 1995), 267–302.

TISHBY, I., *The Wisdom of the Zohar: An Anthology of Texts*, trans. D. Goldstein, 3 vols. (Oxford, 1989).

TOV, I., 'The Qumran Scrolls in Light of Latest Scholarship' [Megilot kumran le'or hamehkar hehadash], *Mada'ei hayahadut*, 34 (1994), 37–67.

—— 'The Unpublished Qumran Texts from Caves 4 and 11', *Biblical Archeologist*, 55 (1992), 94–104.

—— 'The Unpublished Qumran Texts from Caves 4 and 11', *Journal of Jewish Studies*, 43 (1992), 101–36.

TRIFON, D., 'Did the Priestly Courses Relocate from Judaea to Galilee after the Bar-Kokhba Revolt?' [Ha'im avru mishmerot hakohanim mihudah lagalil aharei mered bar-kokhva?], *Tarbiz*, 59 (1990), 77–93.

TUR-SINAI, N. H., 'The Problem of the Ark' [Ba'ayat ha'aron], in id., *The Language and the Book*, iii: *Beliefs and Doctrines* [Halashon vehasefer, iii: Kerekh ha'emunot vehade'ot] (Jerusalem, 1955), 3–7.

URBACH, E. E., *The Sages: Their Concepts and Beliefs*, trans. I. Abrahams (Cambridge, Mass., 1979).

—— 'The Traditions about Mysticism in the Period of the *tana'im*' [Hamasorot al torat hasod bitekufat hatana'im], in E. E. Urbach *et al.* (eds.), *Studies in Kabbalah and the History of Religions, Presented to Gershom Scholem* [Mehkarim bakabalah uvetoldot hadatot mugashim legershom sholem] (Jerusalem, 1968), 1–28.

—— 'When did Prophecy Come to an End?' [Matai paskah hanevuah?], *Tarbiz*, 17 (1946), 1–11.

VANDERKAM, J. C., *The Book of Jubilees: A Critical Text*, Corpus Scriptorum Christianorum Orientalium 510–11, Scriptores Aethiopici 87–8, 2 vols. (Louvain, 1989).

—— *Calendars in the Dead Sea Scrolls: Measuring Time* (London and New York, 1998).

—— *Enoch—A Man for All Generations* (Columbia, SC, 1995).

—— *Enoch and the Growth of an Apocalyptic Tradition*, Catholic Biblical Quarterly, Monograph Series, 16 (Washington, 1984).

—— 'The Jubilees Fragments from Qumran Cave 4', in J. T. Barrera and L. V. Montaner (eds.), *The Madrid Qumran Congress*, 2 vols., Studies on the Texts of the Desert of Judah, 11 (Leiden, 1992), ii. 635–48.

—— 'The Origin, Character and History of the 364 Day Calendar: A Reassessment of Jaubert's Hypotheses', *Catholic Biblical Quarterly*, 41 (1979), 390–411.

—— 'The Temple Scroll and the Book of Jubilees', in G. J. Brooke (ed.), *Temple Scroll Studies*, Journal for the Study of the Pseudepigrapha Supplement Series, 7 (Sheffield, 1989), 211–36.

—— *Textual and Historical Studies in the Book of Jubilees*, Harvard Semitic Monographs, 14 (Missoula, Mont., 1977).

—— and J. T. MILIK, '4Q Jub c(4Q218) and 4Q Jub e(4Q220): A Preliminary Edition', *Textus*, 17 (1994), 43–56.

VERMES, G., *The Complete Dead Sea Scrolls in English* [*CDSSIE*] (London, 1997).

—— *The Dead Sea Scrolls: Qumran in Perspective* (London, 1994).

—— 'Preliminary Remarks on Unpublished Fragments of the Community Rule from Qumran Cave 4', *Journal of Jewish Studies*, 42 (1991), 250–5.

—— and M. D. GOODMAN, *The Essenes according to the Classical Sources* (Sheffield, 1989).

WACHOLDER, B. Z., and M. G. ABEGG, *A Preliminary Edition of the Unpublished Dead Sea Scrolls: The Hebrew and Aramaic Texts from Cave Four*, fascs. i–ii (Washington, DC, 1991–2).

WAGNER, A. M., 'Zwischen Engeln und Menschen: Die Rolle Henochs im slavischen Henochbuch' (diss., Evangelisch-Theologische Fakultät zu Tübingen, 2000).

WEINFELD, M., 'Pentecost as Festival of the Giving of the Law', *Immanuel*, 8 (1978), 7–18.

—— ' "Temple Scroll" or Pericope of the King' [Megilat hamikdash o parashat hamelekh], *Shenaton lemikra ule̠heker hamizra̠h hakadum*, 3 (Jerusalem, 1979), 214–37.

WERMAN, C., 'The Attitude to Gentiles in the Book of Jubilees and in Qumran Literature, Compared with Early Tannaitic Halakhah and Contemporaneous Non-Canonical Literature' [Hayaḥas lagoyim besefer hayovelim uvesifrut kumran behashva'ah lahalakhah hatana'it hakedumah velasifrut haḥitsonit bat hatekufah] (Ph.D. diss., Hebrew University, Jerusalem, 1995).

—— 'The Structure of the Events of the Flood Generation in the Book of Jubilees' [Itsuv me'oraot dor hamabul besefer hayovelim], *Tarbiz*, 64 (1995), 183–202.

YADIN, Y. (ed.), *The Dead Sea Scrolls* [Hamegilot hagenuzot mimidbar yehudah] (Jerusalem, 1957).

—— (ed.), *The Scroll of the War of the Sons of Light against the Sons of Darkness*, trans. B. and Ch. Rabin (London, 1962).

—— (ed.), *The Temple Scroll*, 3 vols. (Jerusalem, 1983).

ZIMMERLI, W., *Ezekiel: A Commentary on the Book of the Prophet Ezekiel*, trans. R. E. Clements and J. D. Martin, 2 vols. (Philadelphia, 1979–83).

ZIPOR, M., 'The Flood Chronology: Too Many an Accident', *Dead Sea Discoveries*, 4/2 (1997), 207–10.

Index

in Enoch literature 93, 102, 124–5
and heavenly Temple 77, 187
in Heikhalot literature 60, 233–4, 237,
254–5, 259–60
in Merkavah tradition 32, 34–62, 231
and secessionist priests 60, 61, 191, 223–5,
237
and Shavuot 147, 151
see also lampstand; place, sacred; time
sexuality, forbidden unions 111–13, 114–17,
119–21, 122–4, 158, 163, 211, 220
Shavuot (Festival of Weeks):
and Covenant 60, 68, 129, 132, 135–52,
153–8, 163, 204, 209–10, 226–7, 231,
243
and Ezekiel's vision 60, 153–63, 208, 209,
227, 243, 265
in Heikhalot literature 243, 247
and Merkavah tradition 154, 161–2, 226,
245, 247
in rabbinic tradition 151, 204, 207–8,
209–10, 222, 227
and sacred union 68, 157–64
and secessionist priests 36, 151
and solar calendar 41, 50, 52–3, 85, 104,
109, 132, 150–1, 153, 164, 204, 207–10,
222
vigil 154, 161, 164
Shekhinah 68 n. 39, 159, 160–1, 244, 258
shiur komah (measurement) 13, 21, 236, 262
Shiur komah texts 21, 160, 236–7, 242
Shivhei metatron 21, 35 n. 23, 237
signs, see *otot*
Simeon b. Azai 246
Simeon b. Mattathias the Hasmonean 9, 38 n.
30
Simeon b. Yohai 161
Simeon b. Zoma 246
Simeon II 'the Just' (high priest) 8, 194, 196
Similitudes of Enoch 89, 91, 147–8
sin:
cardinal 115, 118, 120–3, 211
origin 112–13, 122, 130, 202
of the Watchers 111–22, 129, 132, 140, 211,
243
Sinai:
and Covenant 136–7, 143, 148–50, 154–6,
163, 226, 231
theophany 100, 136–7, 154–61, 209, 226,
243
Smith, Jonathan 37
Sokolov, M. 90

Solomon's Temple, *see* First Temple
solstices 104, 108, 139
song, sacred 2–3, 167–70, 186–7, 191, 204
in Heikhalot literature 35, 234–5, 239,
250–3, 255–7, 259, 261, 264
in Merkavah tradition 70–5, 79–80
Song of Songs:
as canonical 215
and Heikhalot tradition 234, 249
and priestly tradition 13, 69
and Shavuot 162–4
and Sinai theophany 159–61, 163, 242
Songs of the Sabbath Sacrifice 4, 11, 15–16,
34 n. 22, 211
and angelic service 32–3, 167–70, 179,
183–4, 186–7, 188–91, 198–9, 209, 217
and cherubim 76, 162, 253, 256
and heavenly Temple 36, 39, 41–2, 57,
58–9, 72, 75, 79–81, 183
and Heikhalot literature 233, 234–5, 241,
250, 252
and knowledge 218
and Levi 175
and Merkavah tradition 226, 256, 259
and sacred space 44, 81
and solar calendar 45, 51, 61, 75, 85, 88,
100–1, 104–6, 203, 209, 224, 230
Sons of Darkness:
and Covenant 146–7, 150
Hasmonean priests as 39, 122
and lunar calendar 87, 125–7, 130, 143,
150–1, 203, 221
and Sons of Light 201–3, 204, 209–10, 229,
231
sons of God:
descent to earth, *see* Watchers
as heavenly servants 253
Sons of Light:
and Covenant renewal 146–7, 150–1, 209
and Qumran community 25, 97, 181, 231
and secessionist priests 35, 39, 86, 126–7,
130, 143, 201–2
and solar calendar 125, 221
and Sons of Darkness 201–3, 204, 209–10,
229
and Uriel 119, 127
space, sacred, *see* place, sacred
Stegemann, H. 38 n. 30
Strugnell, J. 195
Sukenik, Eliezer 25–6
Sukkot (Festival of Booths) 52, 74 n. 69, 104,
175–6, 221–2

Printed and bound by CPI Group (UK) Ltd, Croydon, CR0 4YY

13/04/2025

14656583-0003